Unraveling HTML5, CSS3, and JavaScript

The Ultimate Beginners Guide with over 170 Samples

2nd Edition

By István Novák

ISBN: 153351738X

ISBN 13: 978-1533517388

To Henriett, Eszter and Réka, who supported me in writing this book with their love and appreciation

Table of Contents

About the Author

Istvan Novak is an associate and the chief technology consultant of SoftwArt, a small Hungarian IT consulting company. He works as a software architect and community evangelist. In the last 20 years, he participated in more than 50 enterprise software development projects. In 2002, he co-authored the first Hungarian book about .NET development. In 2007, he was awarded with the Microsoft Most Valuable Professional (MVP) title, and in 2011 he became a Microsoft Regional Director. As the main author, he contributed in writing the Visual Studio 2010 and .NET 4 Six-In-One book (Wiley, 2010), and in Beginning Windows 8 Application Development (Wiley, 2012). He is the main author of Beginning Visual Studio LightSwitch Development (Wiley, 2011). István holds a master's degree from the Technical University of Budapest, Hungary, and also has a doctoral degree in software technology. He lives in Dunakeszi, Hungary, with his wife and two teenage daughters. He is a passionate scuba diver. You may have a good chance of meeting him underwater at the Red Sea in any season of the year.

Introduction

Two years ago, when I published the first edition of this book, I wrote these sentences in the introduction:

"As an experienced C# programmer and enterprise architect, I found myself in a strange situation after 20 years of experience. Even if I worked on project teams that implemented big systems including satellite web sites, I was dropped behind those team members who started their professional life pretty close to new generation—neat, asynchronous, dynamic, etc.—web page development. It took months to find the right way to be able to communicate with them, and find the common language with them. During these months I read many books, blog posts, articles, and went through many small programming exercises to get into the picture.

Well, I decided to create a series of booklets using my experiences—to help you cope with similar situations."

That time I would not have thought that so many readers would buy this book. I decided to review it, change it to the current state of HTML, CSS and JavaScript—and make it even simpler to work with the code samples.

Whom This Book Is For

I wrote this book for those developers who are—or might be—in a situation I was years ago. If you worked on the server side for a long time, or you used only desktop UI technologies, this is the book you should read to get acquainted with HTML, CSS, and JavaScript—in order to understand them quickly, and keep up the race with youngsters.

If you're already a web developer who is familiar with these technologies, this book may help you to pass this knowledge to your team's new members who are novices in web UI.

What This Book Covers

As its title states, this book teaches you the basic web UI technologies including HTML, CSS, and JavaScript. Instead of just giving only an overview of them, or being a reference material, this book explains how these technologies work together, and lets you get acquainted with all the fundamentals, so that you'll be able to create your own web pages with HTML5 markup, CSS3-based design, and interactions built with and JavaScript (and jQuery).

This book focuses only on the UI, so you must apply these technologies in the context of other server side technologies—such as PHP, ASP.NET Web Forms, ASP.NET MVC, or others—to create full-fledged web sites and web applications.

How This Book Is Structured

This book is divided into ten chapters that will help you understand the concepts and technologies behind web UI. These chapters are built on each other, so you'd better read them sequentially from the first to the last one.

Chapter1: A Short Tour of HTML, CSS, and JavaScript

This chapter provides an overview of the fundamental technologies—through a number of short examples that explains to you the role and behavior of them.

Chapter 2: Getting to Know HTML5

In this chapter you will learn the basics of HTML5, and you will create a few simple HTML pages using the concepts learned here.

Chapter 3: Achieving Richer User Experience with HTML

HTML5 provides you rich structure and semantics that help you design and render web pages with images, tables, and multimedia. In this chapter you will learn these elements and utilize them.

Chapter 4: Forms and Controls

This chapter will teach you creating and using HTML web forms.

Chapter 5: A Few More Things about HTML

To provide additional knowledge on HTML5, in this chapter you will learn about special HTML elements and techniques, such as painting the new HTML5 canvas, and using HTML compatibility and validation tools.

Chapter 6: Exploring the Document Object Model

To provide interactive and dynamic web pages, getting familiar with the Document Object Model (DOM) is a key element. In this chapter you will learn all the basics that let you understand and manipulate the DOM.

Chapter 7: Getting to Know JavaScript

JavaScript is often mentioned as the assembly of the web. In this chapter you will learn the basics of this simple programming language that vivifies your web pages with only a few lines of code.

Chapter 8: Advanced JavaScript Programming

JavaScript is very easy to use, and it also can be used for very advanced web programming tasks in the browser. This chapter teaches you these advanced programming topics.

Chapter 9: Getting to Know Cascading Style Sheets

In this chapter you will learn the concepts of the Cascading Style Sheets technology that provides the power of great-looking web pages.

Chapter 10: Basic Style Patterns

In this chapter you will learn the most important CSS patterns that add great appearance to your web pages.

Downloading the Source Code

This book provides many examples. You can download the source code from this link: `http://tinyurl.com/UnravelingHtml5-2nd`.

Chapter 1:
A Short Tour of HTML, CSS, and JavaScript

WHAT YOU WILL LEARN IN THIS CHAPTER

Creating a simple HTML page and styling it
Understanding how CSS works together with HTML
Adding JavaScript code to your web page to make it interactive
Using jQuery to write concise and powerful code

In today's modern web sites, the fundamental markup technology, HTML, is rarely used alone to create web pages, it is practically always used together with its companions, CSS and JavaScript. In this chapter you will learn about how these technologies work together to provide the essential user experience:

As a developer, you must have met many HTML pages and viewed their source codes. You probably know most of the HTML markup elements, and you can even create simple pages. If you already know the basics of HTML, CSS, and JavaScript, this chapter will provide a recap for you. Should you be a novice in this field, here you will obtain the fundamentals to master your knowledge on these topics.

Preparing Your Study Environment

You need three software components to be able to follow the examples treated in this book. These components are: a code editor, a web server and a browser, respectively.

My aim was to use a set of tools that run on any of the Linux, Mac, or Windows platforms, so I decided to use Visual Studio Code as the editor and Node.js as the web server. I tested all examples on three different browsers on Windows: Chrome 49, Microsoft Edge, and Internet Explorer 11.

To edit the code, you can use an integrated development environment such as Webstorm, Visual Studio, Eclipse, or even utilize a simple code editor such as Sublime Text, TextMate, Notepad++, or whatever you prefer.

HINT: Use an editor that supports syntax highlighting for HTML, CSS, and JavaScript, because this feature definitely makes your life easier.

You need a web server to host sample pages. If you have great experience with any web servers, keep using it for hosting the sample pages. You can also choose from a broad range of web servers, including Apache, Node.js, and IIS. Apache and Node.js are supported on all major platforms, while IIS (and its little brother, IIS Express) runs only on Windows.

In this book I use Node.js, because it is very easy to install, configure and use—and this is the best feature I like—, with a very simple preparation step it allows live coding: as you modify the source files, the changes are immediately reflected in the browser.

HINT: Even if this is the first time you've read about Node.js, consider using it.

In this section, you will prepare the study environment to create and run the accompanying code samples of the book.

The Samples Working Folder

While you are learning HTML and related web technologies, you will examine code samples. To save your time, I established a folder (directory) structure. The root of this structure is a folder—hereinafter I will call it `Samples`. `Samples` contains subfolders for each chapter, named as `ChapterNN`, where `NN` is a two-digit chapter number, such as `Chapter01`, `Chapter02`, and so on. Within the chapter folders you can find exercise folders. For example, the third exercise of Chapter 4 can be found in the `Samples/Chapter04/Exercise-04-03` folder. Each exercise has its own source files.

Each exercise folder contains two important files. The `package.json` defines the `start` command that—as its name suggests—launches the web server and displays your page in the browser. The `index.html` file is the page that is rendered in the browser.

All exercises use a copy of the very same `package.json` file. In the root folder, you can find a `package.json` file to copy and use in your own exercise projects.

NOTE: Download the sample code of this book, and extract the content of the downloaded `.zip` file into your preferred working folder. The structure of the extracted code will be exactly the same as described earlier.

Installing and Node.js

As I mentioned, I will use Node.js as web server. Evidently, you need to download Node.js to carry out the exercises. You can obtain the appropriate setup kit for your platform from `http://nodejs.org/download`. Installing Node.js is very easy, it takes only a few minutes.

A Concise Overview of Node Package Manager

HINT: If you have already experiences with Node.js and `npm`, you can skip this short section.

Node.js installs its own package management tool, nmp (Node Package Manager). The main role of this utility is to manage those Node.js packages and components your app or development process depend on.

The npm tool can install packages from a repository to your machine. These packages can be installed globally—all Node app can access them—, or locally to your project. You can save the references to the installed packages into a package.json file that can be used by npm later to update or install missing components.

Preparing for Live Coding

As I mentioned before, you will be able to edit the sample code and observe the changes in the browser immediately without restarting the web server or manually refreshing the browser page.

This magic is brought to you by the live-server package. Open the command prompt on your machine, and run this command line:

```
npm install live-server -g
```

This instruction starts the Node Package Manager that downloads the live-server package from the web—with all of its dependencies—, and installs it globally.

Working with the Sample Code

If you are patient enough, I suggest you typing the sample code manually—and using copy from the downloaded sample code sparingly. Create your own samples folder, and mirror the structure of the code—use separate folders for chapters and subfolders for exercises. Whenever you create a new exercise, do not forget to put the package.json file into the exercise folder.

Most exercises build on the previous ones, so copying an exercise folder to create a new one is the fastest option carry on. In this book, I notify you when you'd better copy an existing exercise instead of creating a new one from scratch.

Now, you're ready to start learning HTML.

Creating a Basic HTML Page

An HTML page is a simple file with .htm or .html extension and can easily be displayed in a web browser. You do not need any development tools to create it, the most unadorned text editor—such as vi or nano in Linux on Mac, Notepad in Windows—is enough. For example, you can type the following text into a file:

```
<html>
<head>
  <title>HTML page written in Notepad</title>
</head>
<body>
```

```
  <p>I would not have thought it is easy!</p>
</body>
</html>
```

After you save it to the `easy.html` file—or in any other file with `.htm` or `.html` extension, you can open it with your default browser—or with any other browsers installed on your computer. Most web page development could be done with such simple text editors, but as you turn from web pages to web sites with multiple pages and other related files, you immediately recognize that you need a code editor tool that makes you more productive.

In this book, I use Visual Studio Code (hereinafter I refer it as *Code*) that is available on Linux, Mac and Windows for free (`http://code.visualstudio.com`). The "Visual Studio" prefix in its name is rather for marketing purposes, technically it is a totally new—and very lightweight— product, nothing to do with the heaviness of the old Visual Studio IDE.

Instead of Code, you can use your own favorite code editor such as TextMate, Sublime, Brackets or whatever you like.

EXERCISE 1-1: Creating a Simple HTML Page

Follow these steps to create and display a very simple HTML page:

1. Create a working folder for this exercise—I suggest you to name it `Exercise-01-01`—and copy the `package.json` file from the `Samples` root. Start your editor, and take care that its working folder is `Exercise-01-01`.

2. Create a new file, `index.html`. Now, you have two files in your exercise folder, as Figure 1-1 illustrates.

Figure 1-1: There are two files, `index.html` *and* `package.json` *in the exercise folder*

3. Depending on the type of the code editor you use, you might get an empty file, or one with in initial HTML markup. Type the following code into `index.html` to display some content:

```
<!DOCTYPE html>
<html>
<head>
  <title>Table of Contents</title>
</head>
```

```
<body>
  <h1>Introduction</h1>
  <p>We'll create more content later...</p>
</body>
</html>
```

4. Go to the command line prompt, select the `Exercise-01-01` folder, and display the page with the `npm start` command. The content of the `index.html` file is displayed in your default browser, as shown in Figure 1-2.

Figure 1-2: The page rendered in Chrome

5. Keep your browser open, and go back to your code editor. Add this line right before the closing `</body>` tag:

```
<p>Live coding works!</p>
```

6. Save `index.html`, and turn back to the browser. Thanks to `live-server`, the modified markup is immediately displayed in the browser (Figure 1-3).

7. In the command line, terminate the running `npm start` process (with Ctrl+C).

HOW IT WORKS

The `package.json` file defined what the `npm start` command should do:

```
{
  "name": "unraveling-html5-2nd-edition",
  "version": "1.0.0",
  "description": "Code samples for the Unraveling HTML5, CSS...",
  "scripts": {
    "start": "live-server --port=8080"
  },
  "keywords": [],
  "author": "Istvan Novak (dotneteer@hotmail.com)",
  "license": "ISC"
}
```

Figure 1-3: The modifications go alive immediately

As you typed `npm start` in the command line, `live-server` started a mini web server listening for requests on port 8080, launched the web browser and navigated to the 127.0.0.1:8080 address. As a result for the browser's request, the web server retrieved the `index.html` file (the default file for the specified URL). The browser displayed the content of that file.

Let's see, how the browser processes `index.html`! The file starts with the following line:

```
<!DOCTYPE html>
```

When reading it, the browser understands that this file will use HTML5 markup (HTML5 is the newest version of the Hypertext Markup Language). The file follows the standard structure of the markup that embeds a *head* and a *body* section enclosed between `<head>` and `</head>`, and between `<body>` and `</body>` elements, respectively. The content of the whole markup is put within `<html>` and `</html>` elements, so the skeleton of the page looks like this:

```
<!DOCTYPE html>
<html>
  <head></head>
  <body></body>
</html>
```

The markup you typed in in step 3 adds three HTML markup elements to the originally empty page, `<title>`, `<h1>`, and `<p>`, respectively. The text within the `<title>` tag is a metadata element, which won't be rendered in the page. It defines the title of the page to be displayed outside of the page in the web browser—in most cases as the caption of the tab holding the page.

The `<h1>` element defines a first level heading; `<p>` describes a simple paragraph. These are nested into the `<body>` section, and so they are rendered as the content of the page, as shown in Figure 1-2.

In step 5, you added a new `<p>` element to the markup. When the mini web server sent back the `index.html` file to the browser, it added a short JavaScript code that synchronizes the web page with the server. The server detected that the `index.html` file had been changed, and notified the browser about this fact. The client-side JavaScript received this notification, re-queried index.html, and refreshed the screen.

Formatting the HTML Page

The HTML elements you have used in the previous exercise added only content to your web page. The page was rendered by the default style settings of your browser. As a result—I set Chrome as the default browser—all text was displayed using the Times New Roman font, and as it can be expected, the first level heading used a larger font size than the ordinary paragraph following it. The default style—except from a very few cases—does not suit webpages, because it lacks appropriate typography, coloring, and layout.

Since its early days, the HTML specification allows setting up the outlook of markup elements. In the following exercise you are going to set up a neater rendering of the `index.html` page.

EXERCISE 1-2: Setting font type and color

To change the typography of the `index.html` page, follow these steps:

1. Create a copy the `Exercise-01-01` folder and its contents, and name the new folder `Exercise-01-02`.

2. In the code editor, open the index.html file from within this new folder. Add a `style` attribute to each of the `<body>`, `<h1>`, and `<p>` HTML elements:

```
<!DOCTYPE html>
<html>
<head>
  <title>Table of Contents</title>
</head>
<body style="font-family: Verdana, Arial, sans-serif">
  <h1 style="color: white; background-color:navy">
    Introduction
  </h1>
  <p style="margin-left: 40px; margin-top: 80px;">
    We'll create more content later...
  </p>
  <p style="margin-left: 40px;">
    Live coding works!
  </p>
</body>
</html>
```

2. In the command line prompt, select the `Exercise-01-02` folder as the current working folder, and display the web page with the `npm start` command. Now, the page appears with new layout and style, as shown in Figure 1-4.

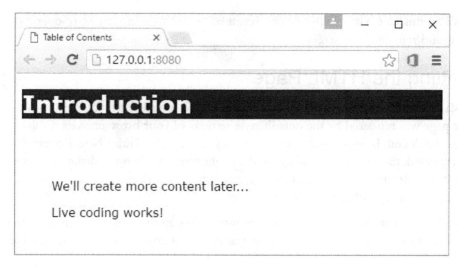

Figure 1-4: The `index.html` file with style applied on HTML elements

7. In the command line, terminate the running `npm start` process (with Ctrl+C).

NOTE: Let's stop repeating obvious things. Thereinafter, when I ask you to display the page, you should run `npm start` in the command line. Unless I tell you explicitly otherwise, please terminate the live server process after the last step of a particular exercise.

HOW IT WORKS

The `style` attribute in `<body>` defines the font type to be used with the `font-family` property. The property value is set to `Verdana, Arial, sans-serif`, and as a result the browser tries using the Verdana font first. If that is not found, it falls back to Arial, and in the worst case—assuming that even Arial cannot be found—it falls back to a sans-serif font of the browser's choice. The `font-family` is a property that inherits in all nested elements, so setting it in `<body>` instructs the browser that this font type should be used in all elements within `<body>`, unless it is overridden. That is why all the text elements in Figure 1-4 use the same font.

The `<h1>` tag uses a `style` attribute that sets the background color to navy blue, and the color of the font to white. This attribute is assigned to the `<h1>` tag, so it affects only this tag's appearance. As the sample code shows, the first `<p>` uses a style attribute that sets a margin around the `<p>` element. The left margin is set to 40 pixels, while the top margin to 80 pixels. The second `<p>` sets only the left margin.

Using Inline Styles

Using the `style` attribute is quite simple—assuming you are acquainted at least with the most basic properties (from the few hundred) you can use within `style`.

However, formatting an HTML page in this way is not a welcomed practice. If you need to apply the same style on many elements, maintaining changes may easily become a nightmare. In the following exercise you will learn why you should avoid using the style attribute.

EXERCISE 1-3: Using the Style Attribute to Adorn a Web Page

To apply style attributes to index.html, follow these steps:

1. Create a copy of the Exercise-01-02 folder, and name it Exercise-01-03. In the next steps, use the files within this new folder.

2. Open the index.html file, remove the `<p>` element from the `<body>` section, and add more content, as the highlighted markup shows:

```
<!DOCTYPE html>
<html>
<head>
  <title>Table of Contents</title>
</head>
<body style="font-family: Verdana, Arial, sans-serif">
  <h1 style="color: white; background-color:navy">
    Introduction
  </h1>
  <h2>Whom this book is for?</h2>
  <h2>Errata</h2>
  <h1>Chapter 1</h1>
  <h2>What you will learn in this chapter</h2>
  <h2>Summary</h2>
  <h1>Chapter 2</h1>
  <h2>Recap</h2>
  <h2>Conclusion</h2>
</body>
</html>
```

2. Display the page in the browser (use npm start as you did in the previous exercises). As you expect, all content uses the font set in the `<body>` tag, except the first `<h1>` tag, all others are rendered with the default appearance, as shown in Figure 1-5.

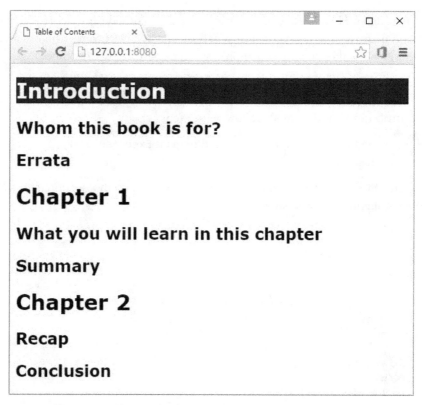

Figure 1-5: Adding some more content to the web page—without specifying style

3. Copy the style attribute from the `<h1>` tag, and copy it to each of the other `<h1>` tags. Type the `style="color: red; margin-left: 40px"` attribute to the first `<h2>` tag, then copy it and paste it to each other `<h2>` tags. After this change your markup should look like this:

```
<!DOCTYPE html>
<html>
<head>
  <title>Table of Contents</title>
</head>
<body style="font-family: Verdana, Arial, sans-serif">
  <h1 style="color: white; background-color:navy">
    Introduction
  </h1>
  <h2 style="color: red; margin-left: 40px">
    Whom this book is for?
  </h2>
  <h2 style="color: red; margin-left: 40px">
    Errata
  </h2>
  <h1 style="color: white; background-color:navy">
    Chapter 1
  </h1>
  <h2 style="color: red; margin-left: 40px">
```

```
   What you will learn in this chapter
  </h2>
  <h2 style="color: red; margin-left: 40px">
   Summary
  </h2>
  <h1 style="color: white; background-color:navy">
   Chapter 2
  </h1>
  <h2 style="color: red; margin-left: 40px">
   Recap
  </h2>
  <h2 style="color: red; margin-left: 40px">
   Conclusion
  </h2>
</body>
</html>
```

4. Turn back to the browser, and take a look at the page now. This time all the headings look like as shown in Figure 1-6.

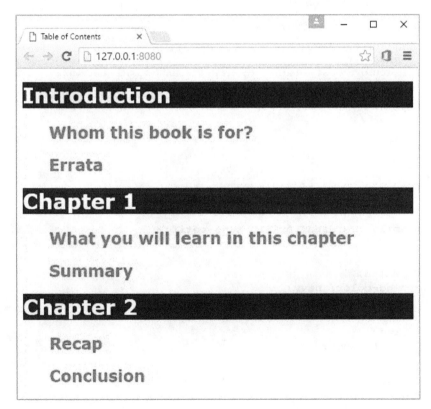

Figure 1-6: Now all headings are rendered with the correct style settings

Styles in this sample work exactly on the same way as in the previous exercise, and this is why all `<h2>` elements became red and indented.

Using an Embedded Style Sheet

In the last exercise you applied exactly the same `style` attribute to three occurrences of `<h1>` and six occurrences of `<h2>`. Just think it over: what happens, if your customer does not like the red color used in `<h2>`? What if she insists to change red to green? You need to update each `style` attribute belonging to `<h2>` elements one-by-one. Well, you can imagine how much effort it would take with long HTML pages, moreover with websites built from several hundred pages.

A sibling technology, CSS (*Cascading Style Sheets*) that works in tandem with HTML offers solution for this issue. At the moment, just take CSS into account as something that describes styles; later you will learn more nitty-gritty details about it.

With CSS you can transform the HTML page describing the book's table of contents into a more maintainable—and even more easily readable—form, as you will learn it from the next exercise.

EXERCISE 1-4: Embedding a Style Sheet into the Web Page

To convert the `style` attributes into a style sheet, follow these steps:

1. Create a copy of the `Exercise-01-03` folder, and name it `Exercise-01-04`. In the next steps, use the files within this new folder.

2. In `index.html`, remove all `style` attributes from the `<body>`, `<h1>` and `<h2>` tags.

3. Add a style sheet to the `<head>` section of the HTML page, as highlighted in the following code:

```
<!DOCTYPE html>
<html>
<head>
  <title>Table of Contents</title>
  <style>
    body {
      font-family: Verdana, Arial, sans-serif;
    }
    h1 {
      color: white;
      background-color: navy;
    }
    h2 {
      color: red;
      margin-left: 40px;
    }
  </style>
</head>
<body >
  <h1>Introduction</h1>
  <h2>Whom this book is for?</h2>
  <h2>Errata</h2>
  <h1>Chapter 1</h1>
  <h2>What you will learn in this chapter</h2>
```

```
  <h2>Summary</h2>
  <h1>Chapter 2</h1>
  <h2>Recap</h2>
  <h2>Conclusion</h2>
</body>
</html>
```

4. Display the page. As you can see, it is exactly the same at the end of the previous exercise (Figure 1-6).

5. Change the style of <h2> by turning the color into green and adding a border at the top:

```
h2 {
  color: green;
  margin-left: 40px;
  border-bottom: 4px dotted black;
}
```

6. Now, as you can see in the browser (Figure 1-7), the style of the second level headings has changed according to the modified style definition.

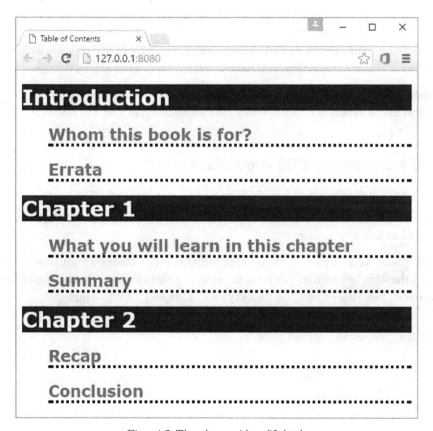

Figure 1-7: The web page with modified styles

HOW IT WORKS

In step 3, you moved the content of style attributes into a *style sheet*. This is a series of rules within the `<style>` element in the `<head>` section. The `body`, `h1` and `h2` are so-called *selector*s that associate the style rules—described between braces—with the corresponding HTML tags, just like if you had written them into the style attribute of the corresponding tags.

When you modified the appearance of all `<h2>` elements in step 5, you only changed the definition of the `h2` selector in the style sheet, instead of rewriting the style attribute of each `<h2>` tag, as you had done in the previous exercise.

The main virtue of this type of description is that is separates the *content* of the page from its *style*. While the HTML elements within `<body>` define the content to render, the style sheet described within `<style>` assigns visual properties to the content.

Moving Styles into a Separate File

It is a great thing that you can build up an HTML page to separate style from the content. But wait a minute! If you have many styles, and dozens of pages (or even more), you still may suffer from maintainability issues if you embed the `<style>` into each HTML pages. Just imagine what it means to update a single style setting: you have to change it in each affected page.

Evidently, there is a simple technique to resolve this issue. You can move the content of the `<style>` section into a separate CSS file (with `.css` extension), as you will learn from the next exercise.

EXERCISE 1-5: Adding a CSS File to the Project

To move the style information into a separate `.css` file, follow these steps:

1. Create a copy of the `Exercise-01-04` folder, and name it `Exercise-01-05`. In the next steps, use the files within this new folder.

2. In the code editor, add a new file, `style.css`, to the exercise folder. From `index.html`, copy the content of the `<style>` section (without the opening and closing `<style>` tags) into the newly created `style.css` file. After this operation `style.css` should look like this:

```
body {
  font-family: Verdana, Arial, sans-serif;
}
h1 {
  color: white;
  background-color: navy;
}
h2 {
  color: green;
  margin-left: 40px;
  border-bottom: 4px dotted black;
```

}

3. In `index.html`, replace the whole `<style>` section with this markup:

```
<link href="style.css" rel="stylesheet" />
```

4. Now, the `<head>` section of `index.html` should look like this:

```
<head>
  <title>Table of Contents</title>
  <link href="style.css" rel="stylesheet" />
</head>
```

5. When you display the page, it has the same appearance as at the end of the previous exercise.

HOW IT WORKS

The `<link href="style.css" rel="stylesheet" />` markup in the `<head>` section tells the browsers that style definitions can be found in the `style.css` file (within the same folder as the page). The browser reads this file, and uses the style definitions there to render the web page.

Because in this exercise you did not change any style definitions, the page was shown exactly the same as earlier, however, this time those definitions were applied from the `style.css` file.

When creating web pages, not only one, but multiple CSS files can be referenced by the `<link>` markup. Moreover, you can combine CSS files with nested `<style>` declarations and even with the `style` attribute.

NOTE: Sometimes it may happen that you change style definitions in your web page, but the browser does not reflect it. This is because the browser may cache the `.css` file, and even if you change it, it uses the one in the cache. Refreshing the page in the browser will resolve this issue.

Defining Visual Behavior with CSS

If you take CSS into account as the visual appearance of the content described by the HTML, you're on the right track. Nonetheless, CSS provides more than just simply defining the static outlook of a web page, it can be used to define visual behavior including transitions and animations, as you will learn from the next exercise.

EXERCISE 1-6: Changing the Visual Behavior of the Page through CSS

Here you will change the `style.css` file created in the previous exercise, so that it reverses the colors of the first level headings when you move the mouse over them. To implement this simple feature, follow these steps:

1. Create a copy of the `Exercise-01-05` folder, and name it `Exercise-01-06`. In the next steps, use the files within this new folder.

2. In `style.css`, add the following new style definition after the `h1`:

```
h1:hover {
  color: navy;
  background-color: lightgray;
}
```

Now, the **style.css** file looks like this:

```
body {
  font-family: Verdana, Arial, sans-serif;
}
h1 {
  color: white;
  background-color: navy;
}
h1:hover {
  color: navy;
  background-color: lightgray;
}
h2 {
  color: green;
  margin-left: 40px;
  border-bottom: 4px dotted black;
}
```

3. Display the page in the browser. When you move the mouse over a first level heading, the originally blue background and white text changes to light gray background and navy blue text, as shown in Figure 1-8. As you move out the mouse from the heading, its style changes back to the original.

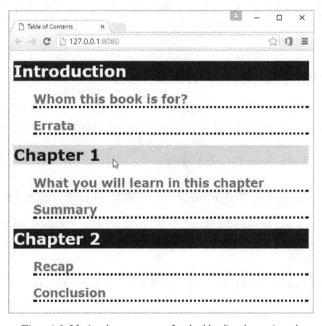

Figure 1-8: Moving the mouse over a first level heading changes its style.

4. In `style.css`, add the following line to the `h1:hover` definition:

```
transition: all 500ms ease-in-out;
```

This style definition now looks like this:

```
h1:hover {
  color: navy;
  background-color: lightgray;
  transition: all 500ms ease-in-out;
}
```

5. Check the page again. Now, when you move the mouse over a first level heading, colors change just like in step 3—but wait a minute!—it transitions smoothly in a half second instead of an instant change. As you move the mouse from the heading, the style returns back to the original one.

NOTE: The `transition` CSS property is a part of the CSS3 standard. Newest browser versions (like Chrome 28 and above, IE 10 and above, etc.) support this attribute, but older browsers may not recognize it. Extend the style definition with vendor specific attributes (you'll learn them later in this book), to make it work with other browsers as well:

```
h1:hover
{
  color: navy;
  background-color: lightgray;
  -webkit-transition: all 500ms ease-in-out;
  -moz-transition: all 500ms ease-in-out;
  -o-transition: all 500ms ease-in-out;
  -ms-transition: all 500ms ease-in-out;
  transition: all 500ms ease-in-out;
}
```

HOW IT WORKS

The `hover` is a so-called pseudo-class in CSS. The `h1:hover` style represents the visual settings that should be applied when the mouse is over a first level heading. As soon as the mouse leaves the heading, the original style is restored. That is how the colors changed when you displayed the web page in step 3.

In step 4, you added the `transition` property to the style definition. This property causes `all` style settings in `h1:hover` to be altered from the original values to the target values in 500 milliseconds (`500ms`) so that the animation has a slow start and a slow end (`ease-in-out`). During the transition, property values are calculated from the original and target values according to the time elapsed from the start. This is how you see a smooth transition of colors.

When you moved the mouse out of the heading, the colors changed back to their original values—without transition.

By now, during the exercises you saw a number of examples that helped you understand that HTML defines the content of the web page, while CSS adds style and appearance to it. These samples only scratched the surface of possibilities that you can be done with HTML and CSS. With these technologies you can build spectacular pages—using only declarative elements like page structure and type definitions.

In a real-world web page, to provide rich user experience, you need another great technology. This is JavaScript.

Adding Actions to the Web Page with JavaScript

JavaScript—its career started in 1996—is a scripting language that browsers can execute while a web page is being loaded or displayed in the browser. Even its developer, *Brendan Eich* would not have thought that it was such a powerful language that would become the de-facto assembly of the web. Today there is virtually no powerful web page that works without any JavaScript code snippet.

In this section, you will understand the importance of this programming language—without learning its nitty-gritty features.

To start getting acquainted with JavaScript, in the next exercise you will add a click action to `<h1>` elements, so that clicking them toggles the background and text colors.

EXERCISE 1-7: Programming the `onclick` action with JavaScript

To carry out this task, follow these steps:

1. Start with a copy of the `Exercise-01-06` folder, `Exercise-01-06`, and use the files within the copied folder.

2. In the code editor, delete the `h1:hover` definition from `style.css`. Add a new definition, as highlighted in the following code, to the CSS file, which represents the style of a clicked `<h1>` element:

```css
body {
  font-family: Verdana, Arial, sans-serif;
}
h1 {
  color: white;
  background-color: navy;
}
h1.clicked {
  color: navy;
  background-color: lightgray;
}
h2 {
  color: green;
  margin-left: 40px;
  border-bottom: 4px dotted black;
}
```

3. In the `index.html` file, add the following JavaScript code snippet enclosed within the `<script>` tags right after the last `<h2>` element, just before the closing `</body>` tag:

```
<script>
  function handleClick(node) {
    var value = node.getAttribute('class') || '';
    value = value === '' ? 'clicked' : '';
    node.setAttribute('class', value);
  }
</script>
```

4. Add the `onclick="handleClick(this)"` attribute to each `<h1>` element. After these changes the `index.html` file should look like this:

```
<!DOCTYPE html>
<html>
<head>
  <title>Table of Contents</title>
  <link href="style.css" rel="stylesheet" />
</head>
<body>
  <h1 onclick="handleClick(this)">
    Introduction
  </h1>
  <h2>Whom this book is for?</h2>
  <h2>Errata</h2>
  <h1 onclick="handleClick(this)">
    Chapter 1
  </h1>
  <h2>What you will learn in this chapter</h2>
  <h2>Summary</h2>
  <h1 onclick="handleClick(this)">
    Chapter 2
  </h1>
  <h2>Recap</h2>
  <h2>Conclusion</h2>

  <script>
    function handleClick(node) {
      var value = node.getAttribute('class') || '';
      value = value === '' ? 'clicked' : '';
      node.setAttribute('class', value);
    }
  </script>
</body>
</html>
```

5. Display the page, and then click several times to any of the first level headings. You'll experience that the both the text and background colors change.

HOW IT WORKS

The key of the behavior is the `handleClick` function you added to `index.html` in step 3. When loading a page, the browser recognizes the `<script>` sections, and immediately executes the code within. Here, the `<script>` contains a function definition, and executing the code means that the definition is hoisted into the current page's JavaScript context. Let's have a look at what this function does.

```
1   function handleClick(node) {
2       var value = node.getAttribute('class') || '';
3       value = value === '' ? 'clicked' : '';
4       node.setAttribute('class', value);
5   }
```

Line 1 defines the function that accepts a single parameter—which is assumed to be an HTML element in the following code, although nothing marks this fact. Line 2 gets the value of those element's `class` attribute, or result an empty string, if there is no such attribute defined within the element. The third line toggles this value between "clicked" and empty, and Line 4 assigns the toggled value to the `class` attribute of the element passed in the input argument.

The `handleClick` function is triggered by the `onclick` event handler (`onclick="handleClick(this)"`) so that the element receiving the click event is passed as the input of `handleClick`. As a result, when you click an `<h1>` element, the class attribute of that will be changed from nothing or empty string to "clicked", and from "clicked" to empty string. The `h1.clicked` style selector (you added its definition to `style.css` in step 1) represents the style of all `<h1>` elements that have a `class` attribute with the value `clicked`.

Changing the class attribute to `clicked` triggers the rendering engine of the browser to apply the `h1.clicked` style, which results an inversion of the original text and background colors.

This very short JavaScript code carried out a simple action. Due to the power of JavaScript, you can do much more with only a few lines of code. There are many typical tasks that can easily be done with JavaScript, so the community created great libraries such as jQuery, Bootstrap, AngularJS, Knockout.js and many, many more.

As this exercise suggested, with JavaScript you can change the structure of the page—or, more technically, the DOM (*Document Object Model*) behind the page. When you toggled the class attribute of `<h1>` elements in the exercise, you actually changed the DOM. This feature of JavaScript is a powerful tool, the cornerstone of interactive and spectacular web sites.

Discovering the Document Object Model

You can learn a lot from looking into the source code of existing web pages. Practically all web browsers support viewing that. However, when using JavaScript, the DOM of the page may change at run time, and its source does not reflect the current structure of the page. Most browsers provide tools built directly into the browser to allow developers to examine the momentary state of the page structure. However, these tools are a bit different depending on your preferred browser.

In this exercise, you will learn using the Developer Tools window of Chrome to examine the DOM of the current page. Microsoft Edge and Firefox also have their own tools to discover the DOM.

EXERCISE 1-8: Discovering the Changes of the Document Object Model

To get acquainted with this great tool, follow these steps:

1. In this exercise, you do not need to create a new folder, you can work with the page in the `Exercise-01-07` folder.

2. Display the page in the Exercise-01-07 folder. If you're using Chrome, you can go to step 4.

3. Start Chrome, and navigate to the `http://127.0.0.1:8080` URL to display the page.

4. To display the Developer Tools pane, press F12 or Ctrl+Shift+I. When you select the element tab, the DOM view appears, displaying the structure of the `index.html` page. This view shows that the `<h1>` node does not have a `class` attribute (Figure 1-9).

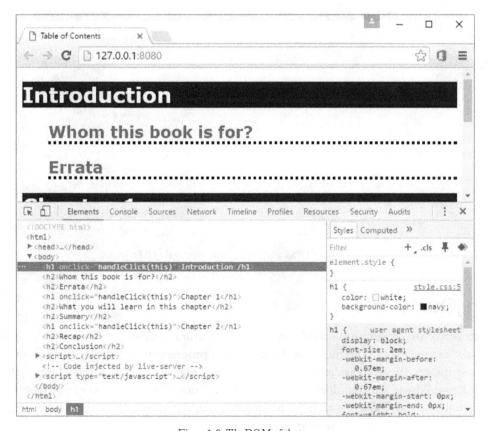

Figure 1-9: The DOM of the page

4. Now, in the page—and not in the DOM pane—, click the "Introduction" heading. This click action—as you learned in the previous exercise—adds a `class` attribute to the corresponding `<h1>` element with a value of "clicked". With the help of the DOM view you can check that this change of structure really happens. Figure 1-10 shows that the attribute has been added to the element.

5. Click the "Introduction" header again. Now you can check that the `class` attribute is toggled from `clicked` to empty, as shown in Figure 1-11.

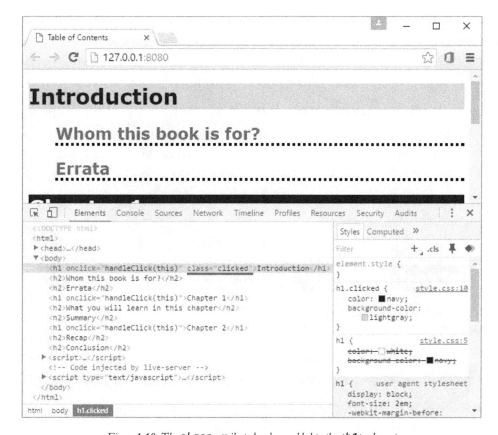

Figure 1-10: The `class` *attribute has been added to the* `<h1>` *element*

Using jQuery

JavaScript is a relatively simple, versatile, dynamic programming language. Code libraries and frameworks can help you to be more productive with a programming language—this is the same with JavaScript, too. If you'd ask rabid fans of JavaScript to name indispensable libraries, jQuery would be among them, without doubt. Instead of buckle down and spend weeks or months learning about the ways JavaScript can be used, you can add jQuery to your page, and use it. It's very simple, as you will learn in the next exercise.

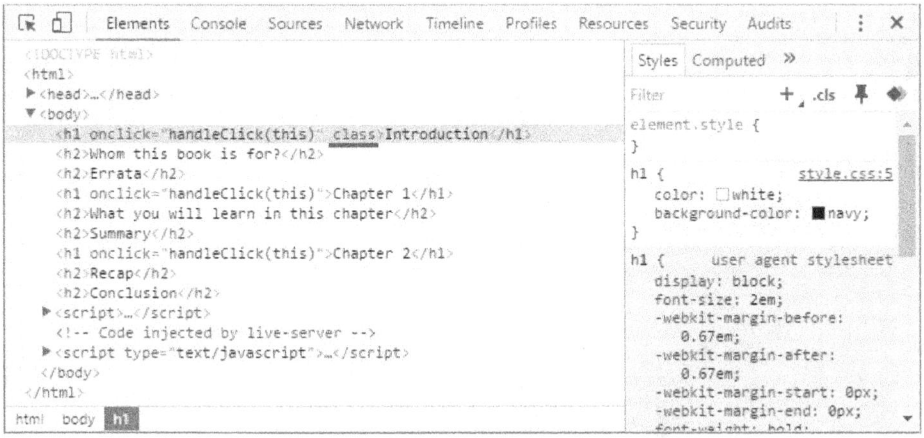

Figure 1-11: The class *attribute has been set to empty*

EXERCISE 1-9: Adding jQuery to the Page

In this exercise you will change the index.html page so that when you click on a first level heading, which is expanded or collapsed, showing or hiding embedded headings, respectively. You will achieve this with jQuery which will change the DOM of the page as soon as it loads into the browser.

To implement this action with jQuery, follow these steps:

1. Copy of the Exercise-01-07 folder to Exercise-01-09, and use the files within this new folder.

2. In the index.html file, remove the <script> block from <body>, and also delete the onclick attribute from each <h1> element. Your HTML markups should look simple like this:

```
<!DOCTYPE html>
<html>
<head>
  <title>Table of Contents</title>
  <link href="style.css" rel="stylesheet" />
</head>
<body>
  <h1>Introduction</h1>
  <h2>Whom this book is for?</h2>
  <h2>Errata</h2>
  <h1>Chapter 1</h1>
  <h2>What you will learn in this chapter</h2>
  <h2>Summary</h2>
  <h1>Chapter 2</h1>
  <h2>Recap</h2>
  <h2>Conclusion</h2>
</body>
</html>
```

2. Surround the `<h2>` elements belonging to an `<h1>` with a `<div>` block, as shown in the following code snippet. This block defines the content of the `<h1>` block preceding `<div>`, so when the user clicks the first level heading, this content will be collapsed or expanded.

```
<body>
  <h1>Introduction</h1>
  <div>
    <h2>Whom this book is for?</h2>
    <h2>Errata</h2>
  </div>
  <h1>Chapter 1</h1>
  <div>
    <h2>What you will learn in this chapter</h2>
    <h2>Summary</h2>
  </div>
  <h1>Chapter 2</h1>
  <div>
    <h2>Recap</h2>
    <h2>Conclusion</h2>
  </div>
</body>
```

3. Start a command prompt, and select the Exercise-01-09 folder as the current working folder. Install jQuery with this command:

```
npm install jquery --save
```

This command downloads the **jquery** package from the web, and stores it within the **node_modules** folder, and saves a dependency in **project.json**.

5. Add the following script elements before the closing `</body>` tag:

```
<script src="node_modules/jquery/dist/jquery.js"></script>
<script>
  $(document).ready(function () {
    $('h1').prepend('<span class="node">-</span>');
    $('h1').click(
        function () {
          var node = $(this).children('.node');
          $(this).next().fadeToggle(500, 'swing',
              function () {
                var mark = node.text();
                mark = mark === '-' ? '+' : '-';
                node.text(mark);
              });
        })
  });
</script>
```

6. Add the following style definition to **style.css**:

```
h1 .node {
    font-family: monospace;
}
```

7. Display the page in the browser. Click a first level heading a couple of times, and you can see it collapse or expand while fading out or in, respectively. You can also observe that headings now have a plus or minus sign indicating the collapsed or expanded state of the heading, as shown in Figure 1-12.

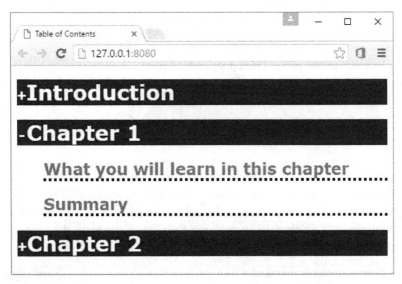

Figure 1-12: First level headings now can be collapsed and expanded.

HOW IT WORKS

The key of the behavior you experienced is the script you added in step 5. This script carries out two things. First, it extends each `<h1>` element with a `<span>` tag that holds the plus or minus sign indicating the collapsed or expanded state of the heading, respectively. Second, it describes the function that responds to the click events.

The script is very concise due to jQuery. The first `<script>` element in you added in step 5 loads jQuery. The second script contains the magic. Let's see how it works line by line.

```
1   $(document).ready(function () {
2     $('h1').prepend('<span class="node">-</span>');
3     $('h1').click(
4        function () {
5          var node = $(this).children('.node');
6          $(this).next().fadeToggle(500, 'swing',
7             function () {
8               var mark = node.text();
9               mark = mark === '-' ? '+' : '-';
10              node.text(mark);
11           });
12       })
13  });
```

The $ symbol used in this script is an alias to (a representation of) the jQuery JavaScript object that can be used to access the functions and variables defined in the library. The first line defines a function that is executed when the page is entirely loaded by the browser, and is ready for rendering. Line 13 closes this declaration, so eventually the code between line 2 and line 12 are executed as soon as the page is loaded.

Line 2 is responsible for adding a <span> element with the minus sign to each <h1> elements. The $('h1') expression retrieves a set of DOM elements that match the 'h1' selector, and it retrieves the list of <h1> elements in the page. The .prepend(…) method nests the <span> elements within <h1>. After this line has run, the Introduction heading looks like this:

```
<h1>
  <span class="node">-</span>
  Introduction
</h1>
```

NOTE: The <span> element defines an inline block, and that is why the plus or minus sign appears right before the text of the <h1> element (Figure 1-12). You can take it into account as a logical markup to set the visual properties of the embedded elements. The <span> element in the code snippet above simply says that the minus sign should use the node class for its appearance and visual behavior.

Line 3 defines a function that is invoked when you click an <h1> element. Similarly to line 2, the $('h1') expression retrieves the list of <h1> elements in the page, and .click(…) assigns a function to each <h1> to execute when the corresponding node is clicked. The body of the function that is carried out as a response for the click event that is defined between line 5 and 11.

The variable declaration in line 5 assigns the object behind the <span> element nested into the <h1> element—into the one clicked—to the node variable. The $(this) expression stands for the clicked <h1>, and .children('.node') gets all nested elements of <h1> with the class attribute set to 'node', which happens to be the single <span> element created in line 2.

Line 6 instructs the jQuery engine—through the fadeToggle function—that the node directly following <h1> should be faded out if its visible, or faded in if its hidden; and the whole action should take 500 milliseconds using the 'swing' easing (slow start and slow end). The third parameter of fadeToggle is a function to be executed when the appropriate fading animation has completed, and it is defined between line 8 and 10. Because the node directly following an <h1> is a <div> enclosing second level headings, the whole content of that <div> is faded in or out.

NOTE: The <div> element defines a block of content in the page. Although <div> is a logical container too, just like <span>; in contrast to <span>, <div> is not inline. It will start a new block, just as <p> starts a new paragraph.

When the fading animation has completed, the code between line 8 and 10 toggles the plus and minus signs. Line 8 reads the text of the <span> node into the mark variable (with the text() function), line 9 toggles the value, and line 10 writes back that value to the node. The triple equation mark in Line 9 is not a typo, it is a valid JavaScript equality operator.

The style definition you added in step 6 defines that all elements that are embedded into <h1> and have a class attribute with value node should use monospace font. These elements happen to be the <span> elements.

This short script may demonstrate the power of jQuery. JavaScript is often mentioned the facto assembly of the Web. Using this metaphor, if JavaScript is the assembly language, then jQuery is the C programming language. There are at least a dozen great JavaScript libraries used by the majority of Web developers, and many of them are built with (or built on) jQuery.

NOTE: Examine the DOM of the page with your browser's Developer Tools, and check how the short JavaScript code changes the DOM of the page, as you click the first level headings. It gives you a great understanding of the mechanisms that make your web page interactive.

Debugging JavaScript

When you add JavaScript code to the web page, you add code that—as Murphy's law says—can go wrong, and it will. Finding the bug in any code is much easier if you can use a debugger. The major web browsers provide tools for debugging JavaScript code while its executing.

The next exercise demonstrates a few of these debugging features—using Chrome and the jQuery code developed in the previous exercise. You will stop the execution in the function that is executed when the fading animation has been completed.

EXERCISE 1-10: Debugging JavaScript with Chrome

To discover the simplicity of JavaScript debugging in Chrome, follow these steps:

1. Display your page in Chrome (the page you created in the previous exercise), and turn on the Developer Tools pane (with F12 or Ctrl+Shift+I). Select the Source tab, and in the source file hierarchy, click (**index**). To the right from the source file hierarchy, the index.html file is displayed. Scroll down to the **var mark** line, and click the line number to set a breakpoint, as shown in Figure 1-13.

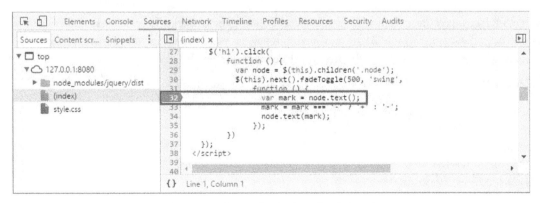

Figure 1-13: Setting a breakpoint on JavaScript code

2. Click one of the first level headings. As soon as the nested content is faded out, Chrome suspends the code execution, because the execution flow reaches the breakpoint you set. This is indicated by the border around the shaded code line, as shown in Figure 1-14.

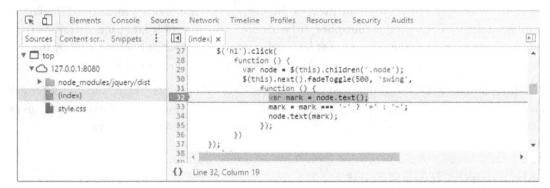

Figure 1-14: The execution flows reaches the breakpoint

3. Move the mouse over the `mark` variable name in the highlighted line. Chrome shows in a tooltip that its value is undefined (Figure 1-15), because the breakpoint stopped right before the value of the variable has been set.

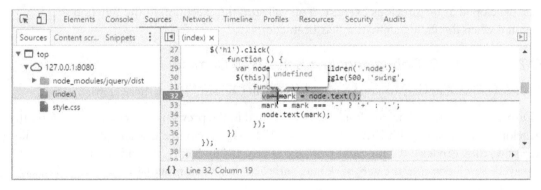

Figure 1-15: The value of mark is undefined.

4. Press F10 to execute the current line. Now the debugger stops at the next code line. Move the mouse over the `mark` variable name, and you can see, its initial value is "–" (Figure 1-16), indicating the expanded state of the first level heading.

5. Press F10 again, and check the value of mark again. Now, it is toggled from "–" to "+".

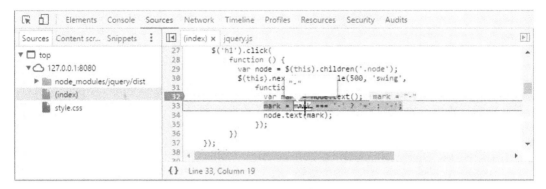

Figure 1-16: The value of mark is set to "–"

Summary

To create web pages with great design, interactivity, and maintainability, the trinity of HTML, CSS, and JavaScript provides you a powerful toolset. Each contributor adds a precious piece to the result.

HTML describes the *content* of your web pages. Using the *Hypertext Markup Language*, you can build up the structure of the page—without defining its exact visual properties, typography, and layout. Although you can utilize the **style** attribute of HTML elements to express appearance, you'd better not do this. Mixing content and style in HTML markup would definitely jeopardize the maintainability of your page's source code.

Style is where *CSS* comes into the picture. With *Cascading Style Sheets,* you can describe the visual attributes of your page, clearly separated from its content. It not only provides you more readable and maintainable code, but also enables you to deal with the design of your web pages as a different role that can be totally disconnected from managing the content.

JavaScript is the secret sauce that empowers your pages with interactivity. This dynamic programming language provides full control over your page, allows changing its content, responding to events, communicating with the server, and much more. In real webpages you can use great JavaScript libraries such as jQuery to solve common tasks.

Chapter 2:
Getting to Know HTML5

WHAT YOU WILL LEARN IN THIS CHAPTER

Getting to know the brief history of HTML

Understanding the basic structure of an HTML document, and fundamental syntax of HTML markup

Creating text content in your web pages

Adding links and images to an HTML document

The Unordinary Story of HTML5

HTML is an acronym for Hypertext Markup Language. Although it had started its life as a document description language for sharing research papers at CERN (European Organization for Nuclear Research), it became the basic technology of rendering web pages. Since its emerge in 1980, it went through many modifications, while it reached the HTML 4.0 state at the end of 1997, when it was published as an official W3C (World Wide Web Consortium) Recommendation.

From HTML to XHTML

Even W3C did not believe that HTML will survive the next century, so instead of moving forward with HTML, they stopped working on it. W3C bet on HTML's renovated successor, XHTML (Extensible Hypertext Markup Language) that was to be built on XML. The main reason behind this decision was to enforce stricter syntax rules than required by HTML. For example, the following markup that makes the second word boldfaced is totally valid in HTML:

```
<p>Hello <b>HTML!</p></b>
```

Browsers accept it, and display exactly what the creator of this markup is intended to show, although its perfunctory syntax is not valid. The right—and so valid—version was where the closing `</p>` and `</b>` tags would follow the proper nesting:

```
<p>Hello <b>HTML!</b></p>
```

This second style follows the strict XML syntax rules, required by XHTML. Just think over the advantages what an XML-compliant markup such as XHTML could result. XML can be easily parsed and processed—without dealing with the quirks of HTML (such as the nesting issue in the "Hello HTML!" markup), easy integration with XML tools, portability to different devices including mobile, and so on.

Well, at the beginning XHTML seemed to be the right direction, because more and more professional developers and web designers accepted it as a standard. Of course, browsers also parsed it, and displayed XHTML pages as demanded by the standard. However, browsers did more: they did not enforce the very strict rules, and instead spitting out error messages, they simply rendered the web page autocorrecting the improper markup—such as exchanging the `</b>` and `</p>` tags in the sample above.

This kind of deliberate behavior torpedoed the XHTML standard, because browsers processed old-fashioned HTML pages called XHTML. W3C thought that tightening up the strict rules and requiring browsers to reject invalid pages in XHTML 2 would solve the issues with standardization. Well, they were wrong. Not only the too many small—actually logical—changes in the standard made it fail, but the extremely slow cadence of getting forward turned developers away from it. After five years, in 2004, XHTML 2 seamed to reach a dead-end.

The Emerging HTML5

In the very same year, a group of enthusiastic people at Mozilla Foundation and Opera Software—the creators of Firefox and Opera browser, respectively—tried to lobby for transforming XHTML into a standard that provides much more development-oriented features. They intended to position the markup—that was originally created for describing documents—into a great tool for developing web applications, but they failed the W3C voting for this change. With Apple, they established the Web Hypertext Application Technology Working Group (WHATWG) within W3C. The most important goal of this group was to extend the existing HTML standard with developers in mind—and still keeping backward compatibility. First they worked on add-in specifications (Web Applications 1.0, Web Forms 2.0).

In 2007, W3C indirectly admitted its failure when it disbanded the group working on XHTML2, and they commenced formalizing a new standard, HTML5—based on the work of WHATWG.

HTML Forever?

While today W3C is responsible for the official HTML5, WHATWG have not stopped visioning new HTML features. They imagine HTML as a living standard (visit `http://developers.whatwg.org` for details), and the markup itself as a living language. According to this vision, HTML pages won't have a version number, and a previously created HTML page will never become obsolete. As time goes on, and technology evolves, HTML will introduce new element and support new features. It's up to browser vendors and developers to choose whether they will use a certain new feature or not.

Although this "living thing" seems weird—just imagine how developers would respect a moving target as new features are added to the language—, it's actually not different what we have today with the hodgepodge of HTML features supported by different browsers. So, will it work? Time will tell.

What Behind the Term HTML5 Is

Although HTML is a markup language, HTML5 is not only about the fifth version of that markup, it is much more:

1. It is still a markup language that describes documents, and this markup has new elements to accommodate the expectations of modern web apps. For example, it supports multimedia elements such as `<video>` and `<audio>`.

2. Related technologies—such as CSS3 (Cascading Style Sheets 3), and JavaScript—add power to the development of spectacular web applications. There are other great technologies, such as Web Open Font Format (font format to use in web pages), SVG (a vector image format markup)—and many more—, which modernize the HTML5 ecosystem.

3. HTML5 modules and APIs: HTML5 specifies a number of scripting APIs that can be used with JavaScript. Many of them were initiated by WHATWG, and are now the part of the W3C HTML5 specification, and there are new ones still in working draft phase. Just to mention a few APIs: Web Workers, Web Storage, Navigation Timing, Canvas, Web Sockets, Geolocation.

In this chapter you will get acquainted with the HTML5 markup, and subsequent chapters will provide you more details about technologies and APIs.

HTML5 Markup Basics

In the first chapter you have already examined a simple HTML document:

```
<html>
<head>
  <title>HTML page written in Notepad</title>
</head>
<body>
  <p>I would not have thought it is easy!</p>
</body>
</html>
```

To tell your browser this document uses HTML5 markup, add the highlighted line to the top:

```
<!DOCTYPE html>
<html>
<head>
  <title>HTML page written in Notepad</title>
</head>
<body>
  <p>I would not have thought it is easy!</p>
</body>
</html>
```

Document Types

The `<!DOCTYPE>` tag announces to the reader—and, of course, to the browser—the type of markup to be used when parsing and displaying the document. The `<!DOCTYPE html>` code says that the remainder of the document is to be read as HTML5. The codes for previous markup types were considerably longer, and more complex to write and remember, for example:

XHTML 1.0 Strict:

```
<!DOCTYPE html PUBLIC "-//W3C//DTD XHTML 1.0 Strict//EN"
  "http://www.w3.org/TR/xhtml1/DTD/xhtml1-strict.dtd">
```

HTML 4.01 Transitional:

```
<!DOCTYPE HTML PUBLIC "-//W3C//DTD HTML 4.01 Transitional//EN"
  "http://www.w3.org/TR/html4/loose.dtd">
```

NOTE: This chapter will focus on HTML5 markup and does not deal with the historical overview of older markup formats. If you are interested in all `<!DOCTYPE>` tags, visit `http://www.w3schools.com/tags/tag_doctype.asp`.

Slackened Structure and Syntax Rules

HTML5 allows being perfunctory, so you can omit many HTML tags and the markup is still valid:

```
<!DOCTYPE html>
<title>HTML page written in Notepad</title>
<p>I would not have thought it is easy!
```

Here not only the `<html>`, `<head>`, and `<body>` tags have been omitted, but as you may observe, the closing `</p>` tag is missing, too.

HINT: Although in HTML5 `<html>`, `<head>`, and `<body>` are optional, as a rule of thumb, always use them. As you already know, `<body>` and `<head>` elements separate the page content and other details. As you'll learn later, `<html>` is a convenient place to define the natural language of the page's content.

Because HTML5 is not case-sensitive, you can mix lowercase and uppercase letters in tag and attribute names, so the following declaration is still valid:

```
<!DOCTYPE html>
<html>
<HEAD>
  <title>HTML page written in Notepad</title>
</HEAD>
<bODy>
  <p>I would not have thought it is easy!</P>
</BodY>
</HTML>
```

HINT: Always use lowercase letters as a convention. It makes reading the code easier—it is not as disturbing as mixing uppercase with lowercase—, and it also means, you do not need to use the Shift key when typing code.

HTML5 also loosens the syntax to be used for attributes. Unless you use a restricted character in attribute values (such as ">", "<", "=", space, and a few others) you can omit quotation marks. For example, instead of writing

```
<h2 class="special" />
```

You can define the class attribute like this:

```
<h2 class=special />
```

HINT: Well, this rule seems comfortable, but in my opinion, it's a wrong one. If you use a wrong character in an attribute value without quotation marks, it may break your whole page. So, as a rule of thumb, always use quotation marks in attributes, do not care whether those could be omitted or not.

You can also make your code simpler by using attributes with no values. In this case the attribute presents some default value that is interpreted by the context the attribute is used in. For example, traditionally you could use the following markup to define a checkbox with checked state:

```
<input type="checkbox" checked="checked" />
```

With the loosened syntax you can write it shorter:

```
<input type="checkbox" checked />
```

Well, you can question if the slackened structure and syntax rules are really useful. To be honest, I guess, in many situations they help add inconsistencies, moreover they raise issues—of course, there are exceptions.

Comments

Just as programming languages support comments, so does HTML. You can use the `<!-- … -->` tag to put comment in your markups, as shown in this code snippet:

```
<!-- Display the "see also" section -->
<p>You can find more information on this topic:</p>
```

Of course, comments are not displayed by the browser.

Using HTML <head>

The `<head>` tag is an important part of HTML. It is a container of non-content elements that belong to the whole page. It must contain the `<title>` element, and may contain one of the following additional elements as well: `<style>`, `<link>`, `<script>`, `<noscript>`, `<meta>`, and `<base>`.

`<title>` is required, and it provides the title of the page that is displayed in the browser toolbar, in favorites—provided the page is added to Favorites—, and also used by search engines to display the headline when the page is in within the search results.

In *Chapter 1: A Short Tour of HTML, CSS, and JavaScript*, you already met the `<style>` element describing a style sheet. This element is also nested in `<head>`:

```
<head>
  <title>Table of Contents</title>
  <style>
    body {
      font-family: Verdana, Arial, sans-serif;
    }
  </style>
</head>
```

As you remember, when you moved a style sheet into a separate file, you tied that file to the page with the `<link>` tag:

```
<head>
  <title>Table of Contents</title>
  <link href="style.css" rel="stylesheet" />
</head>
```

In this definition, the `href` attribute names the document, while `rel` describes the relationship between the page and the linked document. The only clue to understand the role of the document is `rel`, this attribute is required.

Defining Scripts

In *Chapter 1*, you also met with the `<script>` tag that defined a JavaScript code snippet, however, that time `<script>` was nested into `<body>`. Well, you can add one or more `<script>` tags both to `<head>` and `<body>`. You should know that the browser processes a `<script>` section as soon as it is read. So, if you use `<script>` in `<head>`, the code within will be executed before any real content is read.

NOTE #1: The `<script>` tag allows you to specify the `type` attribute, which declares the MIME-type of the script. If you omit `type`, the "text/javascript" default MIME-type is used, so the script is taken into account as JavaScript. You can use other MIME-types, depending what is supported by your browser.

NOTE #2: The `<script>` tag also lets you to refer external script files with the `src` (source) attribute. You will learn more about this tag later, in the chapters treating JavaScript.

The `<script>` tag has a pair, `<noscript>`, usually used only in tandem with `<script>`. When your browser does not support scripts—or scripts are disabled because of security reason—, this tag defines the alternate content. For example, the following script displays a message when the page cannot use JavaScript:

```
<head>
  <script>
    document.write("Hello from JavaScript");
  </script>
  <noscript>Sorry, your browser does not support JavaScript</noscript>
</head>
```

Specifying Metadata

Surfing the web is unimaginable without search. Search engines examine the content of a page, but also use metadata, such as keywords, the name of the page's author, and so on. You can assign metadata to your web pages with the `<meta>` tag. The following sample shows, how you can add additional information to your page—extracted and used by search engines:

```
<head>
  <title>My book's Table of Contents</title>
  <meta name="description" content="This page provides you the TOC"/>
  <meta name="author" content="Istvan Novak"/>
  <meta name="keywords" content="html,css,javascript" />
</head>
```

You can provide `name` and `content` attribute pairs with `<meta>`, where `name` describes the type of metadata, and `content` provides the related value.

Using `<meta>`, you can also describe the character encoding of the page:

```
<meta charset="utf-8" />
```

NOTE: The character encoding is the standard that tells how to convert your text into a sequence of bytes (when it's stored in a disk file), and how to convert it back (when the disk file is read). For historical and cultural reasons, there are many different character encodings in use. Most English websites use the UTF-8 encoding, which is compact, fast, and supports all the non-English characters you'll ever need. Other frequently used encodings are—among many others—Windows-1251 (Cyrillic scripts like Russian, Bulgarian, Serbian), Windows-1252 (Latin alphabet), EUC-JP (Extended Unix Code for Japanese, Korean and simplified Chinese).

Defining Text Content

As you already learned, HTML is about defining the content of your web pages, and it is specified between the `<body>` and `</body>` elements.

```
<!DOCTYPE html>
<html>
<head>
  <title>Defining HTML Content</title>
</head>
<body>
  This is a part of this page's content
  <p>This is a paragraph</p>
```

```
</body>
</html>
```

This content can be text, images, audio, video, drawings, forms, tables, links, and other elements; and they can be combined into compound elements, too. For example, you can create a table of videos and images forming a gallery, or make an article with multiple columns of text that embed related links and figures.

When the browser renders the content, it automatically adjusts that content to the size of your browser window—following the styling rules that define the layout. For example, if you define a long text, it is broken down into multiple lines. Have a look at the markup in Listing 2-1.

Listing 2-1: Exercise-02-01/index.html

```
<!DOCTYPE html>
<html>
<head>
  <title>Rendering long text</title>
</head>
<body style="font-family: Verdana; font-size:x-large;">
    This is a long text that is broken down into
    multiple lines, and the width of lines
    varies according to the current width of
    your browser        window.
</body>
</html>
```

The browser renders the text in a flow layout. Using different browser window widths results in different displays, as shown in Figure 2-1 and Figure 2-2.

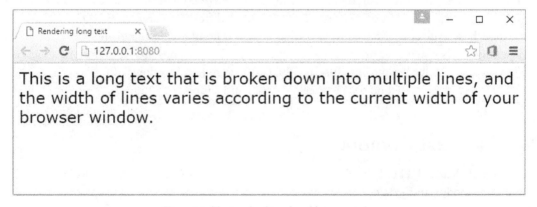

Figure 2-1: Text rendered in a broad browser window

If you look back to Listing 2-1, you can observe that each line of the text starts with a couple of spaces, and there are a number of spaces in the last line between "browser" and "window". The rendering engine ignores extra space characters, and replaces line breaks with a simple space.

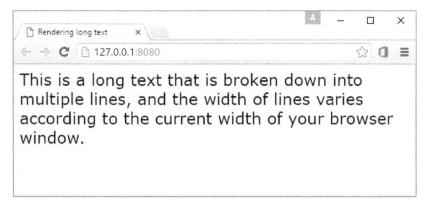

Figure 2-2: The same text rendered in a narrower browser window

Content and Structure

HTML defines a few dozen markup elements. Most of the define content, while other elements define logical containers. For example, the `<h1>` elements define content, and the markup that signs that the content within should be rendered as a first level heading. In contrast, the `<section>` element is a logical container. It tells the browser that the nested content defines a section of the document (e.g. a sidebar, a part of a chapter, etc.).

Inline and Block Content

The elements that provide content can be inline or block elements. Inline elements render their content so that the content goes on the same "line" as the previous markup, while block elements start a new block from the beginning of a new line. To make it easier to understand, Listing 2-2 shows a simple examples of inline and block elements.

Listing 2-2: Exercise-02-02/index.html

```
<!DOCTYPE html>
<html>
<head>
    <title>Rendering inline and block content</title>
</head>
<body>
  <strong>This strong text</strong>
  goes inline with this
  <em>emphasized text.</em>
  <p>
    Because &lt;p&gt; defines block content,
    this text goes into a separate paragraph.
  </p>
  <div>
    &lt;div&gt; always starts a new block,
    <span style="font-weight: bold">
```

```
      however &lt;span&gt; defines a
      logical container for inline text.
    </span>
  </div>
</body>
</html>
```

When you check how this markup is rendered in a browser, you'll see the page displayed like in Figure 2-3.

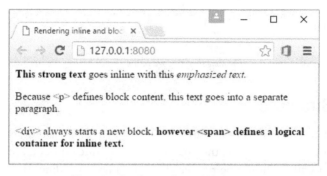

Figure 2-3: Rendering inline and block content

This page contains three blocks represented by the three paragraphs in Figure 2-3. The first block is rendered according to the content of the three lines directly following the <body> tag. It is assembled from three parts, the <strong> element, the plain text (starting with "goes") and the <em> element. Because all of them are inline elements, they are rendered as a single line.

The <p> markup defines a paragraph that holds block content by definition (that's what is expected from a paragraph), so that is why it is started in a new line, and does not go on the same line as the previous markup.

The third block is rendered as it is, because <div> defines a block, while <span> defines inline content.

The default behavior can be changed through the display property of the style attribute. For example, in Listing 2-3, adding the "display: block" property to the <em> element's style forces starting a new block. The result of this slight change is shown in Figure 2-4.

Listing 2-3: Exercise-02-03/index.html

```
<!DOCTYPE html>
<html>
<head>
    <title>Changing the default rendering style</title>
</head>
<body>
  <strong>This strong text</strong>
  goes inline with this, but
```

```
<em style="display: block">
   emphasized text goes in its own block.
</em>
</body>
</html>
```

Figure 2-4: The rendering style of <em> has been changed to "block".

Rendering Text

No doubt, even in our multimedia-biased web era text is an indispensable part of web pages. As you already saw in Listing 2-1, plain text without any markup is understood by the browser and rendered with replacing multiple spaces (including white space characters, such as tab) and line breaks with a single space character. As you experienced, Listing 2-2 used a few special markups—such as <strong> and <em>—to add special importance to their content, and let the browser represent them with some kind of highlighting, such as bold and italic formatting.

HTML5 defines a number of tags that add some kind of emphasis to your text:

- <abbr>: Indicates an abbreviation or an acronym, like "WWW" or "SOA". By marking up abbreviations you can give useful information to browsers, spell checkers, translation systems and search-engine indexers.
- <b>: Renders bold text. Use <strong> instead of <b> to indicate important text.
- <bdo>: This tag is used to override the current text direction. It has a dir attribute that can be set to ltr (from left to right) or rtl (from right to left).
- <big>: Defines bigger text (that uses larger font than its environment)
- <code>: This tag is used for indicating a piece of code. The code being marked up could represent an XML element name, a filename, a computer program, or any other string that a computer would recognize.
- <del>: Defines text that has been deleted from a document
- <dfn>: Defines a definition term
- <em>: Renders an emphasized text
- <i>: Defines a part of text in an alternate voice or mood. The content of this tag is usually displayed in italic.
- <ins>: Defines text that has been inserted into a document
- <kbd>: Defines keyboard input

- `<mark>`: This tag defines marked text. Use it if you want to highlight parts of your text.
- `<pre>`: Text enclosed in this element preserves both spaces and line breaks—it is usually displayed in a fixed-width font (such as Courier).
- `<q>`: Defines a short quotation
- `<s>`: This tag specifies text that is no longer correct, accurate or relevant. The `<s>` tag should not be used to define replaced or deleted text, use the `<del>` tag to define replaced or deleted text.
- `<samp>`: Defines sample output from a computer program
- `<small>`: Defines smaller text (that uses smaller font than its environment)
- `<strong>`: Defines important text
- `<sub>`: Defines subscripted text
- `<sup>`: Defines superscripted text
- `<u>`: This tag represents some text that should be stylistically different from normal text, such as misspelled words or proper nouns in Chinese.
- `<var>`: Defines a variable that could be part of an application, mathematical expression, or a placeholder in prose (phrase).

A number of tags described above have a different semantics in HTML 4.01 markup than in HTML5. Here is a list of tags with their meaning in HTML 4.01

- `<abbr>`: HTML 4.01 defines an `<acronym>` tag that is not supported in HTML5. Use the `<abbr>` tag instead of `<acronym>` in HTML5.
- `<cite>`: Defines a citation
- `<i>`: Renders text in italic
- `<mark>`: This tag is new in HTML5, it is not defined in HTML 4.01.
- `<s>`: Defines strikethrough text
- `<strong>`: Defines strong emphasized text
- `<u>`: Defines underlined text

Let's create a few samples!

Listing 2-4 demonstrates a few markups used in technical texts (Figure 2-5). You can see that different tags, such as `<dfn>` and `<em>` use the same visual style. The `<abbr>` markup does not change the visual properties of the embedded text at all.

Listing 2-4: Exercise-02-04/index.html

```
<!DOCTYPE html>
<html>
<head>
  <title>Common text markups</title>
</head>
<body>
  <strong>HTML5</strong>
  is a <dfn>markup language</dfn>
```

```
   for structuring and presenting content for the
   World Wide Web (<abbr>WWW</abbr>)
   and a core technology of the <em>Internet</em>.
</body>
</html>
```

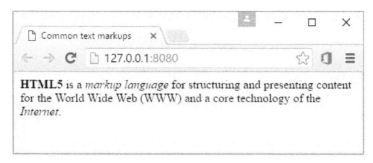

Figure 2-5: Common text markups

When you create text with markup, take care that you use the appropriate markup to tell the browser about the semantics of the highlighted text. According to Listing 2-4, the "markup language" expression is a term definition, while Internet is an emphasized text, even if both are displayed in italic. You could have used the markup shown in Listing 2-5 to get exactly the same result as shown in Figure 2-5.

Listing 2-5: Exercise-02-05/index.html

```
<!DOCTYPE html>
<html>
<head>
   <title>Common text markups</title>
</head>
<body>
   <b>HTML5</b>
   is a <i>markup language</i>
   for structuring and presenting content for the
   World Wide Web (WWW)
   and a core technology of the <i>Internet</i>.
</body>
</html>
```

The main difference between the two listings is that while Listing 2-4 adds semantics to the page (such as definition, abbreviation, etc.), while Listing 2-5 rather adds styling and does not mark semantic differences.

Wherever possible, use rich semantics instead of simple styling markups. It gives you two immediate advantages. First, semantics adds more information to your pages. Second, using CSS you can set how a certain semantic meaning should be visually represented. For example, you can change definitions to use different background color, while emphasized text still could be shown in italic.

You can easily display technical text with source code, just use the `<pre>`, `<code>`, `<var>`, and `<kbd>` tags, as shown in Listing 2-6.

Listing 2-6: Exercise-02-06/index.html

```
<!DOCTYPE html>
<html>
<head>
  <title>Common text markups</title>
</head>
<body>
  <p>
    The following definition describes the
    <code>ILoggable</code> interface that
    should be implemented by loggable
    data structures. <var>Timestamp</var>
    holds the exact time point of the
    event to be logged.
  </p>
  <pre>using System;
namespace Logging
{
  // This interface represent log data.
  public interface ILoggable
  {
    // Gets or sets the time of the event
    DateTime Timestamp { get; set; }
  }
}</pre>
  <p>
    Surround your code with
    <kbd>&lt;pre&gt;</kbd>
    to preserve spacing.
  </p>
</body>
</html>
```

This markup renders the source code with monospace font, as it is shown in Figure 2-6. You can observe that spaces and line breaks are preserved by `<pre>`. As you can see, the content directly follows the opening tag, and the closing tag is put directly after the last character to display. Should you put a line break after `<pre>` and before `</pre>` would cause an extra line break before and after the rendered source code.

Figure 2-6: The markup renders the source code with monospace font

With the `<del>` and `<ins>` tags, you can display a reviewed document with changes—such as deleted and inserted parts—shown. Listing 2-7 demonstrates these markups.

Listing 2-7: Exercise-02-07/index.html

```html
<!DOCTYPE html>
<html>
<head>
  <title>Common text markups</title>
</head>
<body>
  <del cite="http://mybooks.com/Windows8"
    datetime="2012-06-22T08:45:13">
    Windows Vista, r</del>
  <ins cite="http://mybooks.com/Windows8"
    datetime="2012-06-22T08:45:15">R</ins>eleased
    in November, 2006,
  <ins cite="http://mybooks.com/Windows8"
    datetime="2012-06-22T08:45:15">
    Windows Vista</ins>
  appeared with a brand-new design, and it
  offered a very improved security—in contrast
  to XP, which required three service packs
  to remove its security issues and pains.
</body>
</html>
```

As shown in Figure 2-7, deleted text is represented with strikethrough characters, inserted text with underlined characters by default.

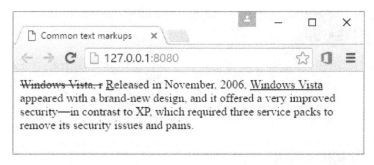

Figure 2-7: A reviewed document

The `<ins>` and `<del>` tags provide the `cite` and `datetime` attributes to give you extra information about the modification of the text. The `cite` attribute (it is a URL) refers to a document that explains why the text was deleted or inserted, while `datetime` specifies the date and time when the text was modified. Although the information in these attributes is not rendered in the browser; there are techniques to display them. For example, with CSS and JavaScript (as you will learn later in this book) you can write code that pops up a little tooltip when the mouse moves over the modified text, and in the tooltip the information stored in these attributes is revealed.

Using Reserved Characters and Symbols in HTML

In a few listings you have already met with a strange set of character literals, such as in this snippet:

```
<div>
  &lt;div&gt; always starts a new block,
  <span style="font-weight: bold">
    however &lt;span&gt; defines a
    logical container for inline text.
  </span>
</div>
```

In those listings I ignored to explain what they are, but it is time to get acquainted with them.

There are characters that are reserved in HTML and XHTML. For example, the "<" and ">" signs are reserved, because they are used by the HTML (XHTML) scanner to recognize the beginning and end of tags. However, these are characters that also could be part of the page's content.

Also, there are non-printable characters, and ones that cannot easily be entered with the keyboard, but still should be rendered when displaying a page. HTML provides a simple way displaying reserved characters and other special symbols (such as Greek letters) with *entities*. Entities have two formats; they can use codes or names. All entities start with an ampersand (&) character, and are closed with a semicolon (;), such as `&copy;` (the © symbol), `&pound;` (the £ symbol), or `&#09;` (the horizontal tab). Coded and named entities differ in the literals typed between the delimiting characters. Coded entities use a number sign (#) and a sequence of decimal digits to define the code of the entity. Named entities use a predefined name that is understood by the browser.

All characters can be described as coded entities; but only a few hundred have names. Table 2-1 summarizes the reserved characters, while Table 2-2 lists several frequently used symbols.

Table 2-1: Reserved Characters in HTML

Code	Name	Description
&#34;	&quot;	quotation mark (")
&#39;	&apos;	apostrophe (')
&#38;	&amp;	ampersand (&)
&#60;	&lt;	less-than (<)
&#62;	&gt;	greater-than (>)

Table 2-2: Frequently used symbols in HTML

Code	Name	Symbol
		non-breaking space
&#162;	&cent;	cent (¢)
&#163;	&pound;	pound (£)
&#165;	&yen;	yen (¥)
&#167;	&sect;	section (§)
&#169;	&copy;	copyright (©)
&#171;	&laquo;	angle quotation mark (left, «)
&#174;	&reg;	registered trademark (®)
&#176;	&deg;	degree (°)
&#182;	&para;	paragraph (¶)
&#182;	&middot;	middle dot (·)
&#187;	&raquo;	angle quotation mark (right, »)
&#192;	&Agrave;	capital a, grave accent (À)
&#193;	&Aacute;	capital a, acute accent (Á)
&#199;	&Ccedil;	capital c, cedilla
&#8719;	&prod;	prod (∏)
&#8721;	&sum;	sum (Σ)
&#8730;	&radic;	square root (√)
&#8734;	&infin;	infinity (∞)
&#8747;	&int;	integral (∫)
&#915;	&Gamma;	capital Greek letter gamma (Γ)
&#945;	&alpha;	Greek letter alpha (α)

&#946;	&beta;	Greek letter beta (β)
&#947;	&gamma;	Greek letter gamma (γ)
&#8592;	&larr;	left arrow ($\leftarrow$)
&#8594;	&rarr;	right arrow ($\rightarrow$)

Using entities, you can easily provide the markup (see in Listing 2-8) for the expression shown in Figure 2-8.

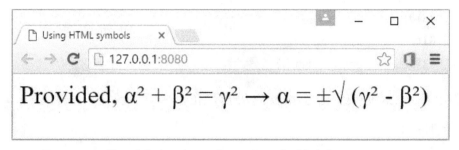

Figure 2-8: A mathematical expression rendered in the browser

Listing 2-8: Exercise-02-08/index.html

```html
<!DOCTYPE html>
<html>
<head>
  <title>Using HTML symbols</title>
</head>
<body style="font-size: 2em">
  Provided, &alpha;&sup2; + &beta;&sup2;
  = &gamma;&sup2;
  &rarr;
  &alpha; = &plusmn;&radic;
  (&gamma;&sup2; - &beta;&sup2;)
</body>
</html>
```

Paragraphs and Text Breaks

As you have already learned, when rendering the HTML markup, the browser ignores line breaks in the page's source code. It behaves as if line breaks were single space characters. In many cases you want to control explicitly where to break lines. HTML provides two tags for this purpose.

The `<p>` markup designates a paragraph. It surrounds the text (and other markups) that should be rendered as a single paragraph. The `<br/>` markup causes the browser to start a new line. The HTML page shown in Listing 2-9 helps you compare the effect of `<p>` and `<br/>`.

Listing 2-9: Exercise-02-09/index.html

```
<!DOCTYPE html>
<html>
<head>
    <title>Using &lt;p&gt; and &lt;br;/&gt;</title>
</head>
<body>
  <p>
    This long sentence is a single paragraph
    because it is enclosed between &lt;p&gt;
    and &lt;/p&gt; tags.
  </p>
  This long text contains several lines
  <br />
  that have line breaks (represented by
  the &lt;br /&gt;) markups
  <br/>
  among them.
</body>
</html>
```

The browser calculates the positions where lines should be broken in a paragraph so that the lines fill up the width of the browser window correctly. The **
** markup is an explicit instruction to break the line, and as you see in Listing 2-9, it can be nested in a paragraph as well. You can look at the rendered page in Figure 2-9.

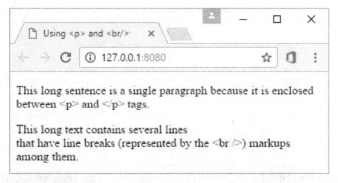

Figure 2-9: Rendering paragraphs and line breaks

Figure 2-9 may suggest that the second text block is an implicit paragraph (even if its corresponding markup is not enclosed within **<p>**). Well, if you intend it to be a paragraph, mark it explicitly so. Otherwise, styles applied to paragraphs won't be applied to this "orphaned" text. With Listing 2-10, you can examine what it means.

Listing 2-10: Exercise-02-10/index.html

```
<!DOCTYPE html>
<html>
<head>
  <title>
    Using &lt;p&gt; and &lt;br;/&gt; with styles
  </title>
  <style>
    p {
      margin-top: 1em;
      margin-bottom: 2em;
      line-height: 1.8em;
    }
  </style>
</head>
<body>
  <p>
    #1: This long sentence is a single paragraph
    because it is enclosed between &lt;p&gt;
    and &lt;/p&gt; tags.
  </p>
  <p>
    #2: This is another paragraph
  </p>
  #3: This long text contains several lines
  <br />
  that have line breaks (represented by
  the &lt;br /&gt;) markup
  <br/>
  among them.
  <p>
    #4: This is a paragraph with explicit
    <br/>
    line break within.
  </p>
</body>
</html>
```

The page displays four text blocks, as shown in Figure 2-10. The style assigned to the `<p>` tag sets the space before and after the paragraph, as well as the line spacing through `margin-top`, `margin-bottom`, and `line-height` properties, respectively. You can see that the spacing values have been properly applied for blocks #1, #2, and #4, but not for #3—as this one is not a paragraph, just a block of plain text with line breaks.

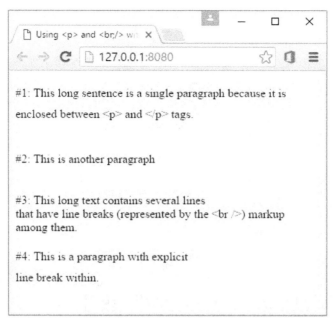

Figure 2-10: Block #3 is a non-paragraph

The HTML5 markup provides a new tag, `<wbr/>`, which specifies a position where in a text it would be okay to add a line break. This feature is great when you have a long text that could be broken during rendering. Listing 2-11 shows an example of using this tag.

Listing 2-11: Exercis-02-11/index.html

```
<!DOCTYPE html>
<html>
<head>
    <title>Using &lt;wbr&gt;</title>
</head>
<body>
  <p>ThisIsAVeryLongTextWrittenAsOneWord</p>
  <p>ThisIsAVeryLong<wbr />TextWrittenAs<wbr />OneWord</p>
</body>
</html>
```

NOTE: Internet Explorer does not support the `<wbr/>` tag.

When this page is displayed in a narrow browser window, as shown in Figure 2-11, the long word without `<wbr/>` is displayed in one line, while the one with `<wbr/>` tags is displayed as expected— the long word is broken at one of the suggested positions.

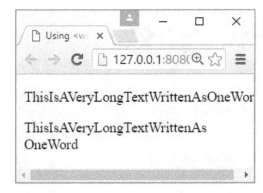

Figure 2-11: Using `<wbr/>` to suggest line break position

It is time to learn some new HTML features that open the way to create more visual, hyperlinked pages.

Enriching Web Pages with Headings, Lists, Links, and Images

Although you can create compound text document with HTML text formatting tags, the experience your users got would be really poor and sullen. To set your web pages to show signals of life, you need to get acquainted with a few more HTML tags. With adding more structure and formatting to your texts transform your page into a more realistic document. Adding images and links to other pages opens a new world for the viewers of your page.

Adding Headings

In *Chapter 1: A Short Tour of HTML, CSS, and JavaScript* you have already met with the `<h1>` and `<h2>` tags that represent first and second level headings, respectively. These headings give a structure to your document, namely second level headings with their related content are logically nested to their parent (first level) heading. HTML allows you to use six levels of headings with the `<h1>`, `<h2>`, `<h3>`, `<h4>`, `<h5>`, and `<h6>` tags. Listing 2-12 demonstrates using them; the page rendered from this markup is shown in Figure 2-12.

Listing 2-12: Exercise-02-12/index.html

```html
<!DOCTYPE html>
<html>
  <head>
    <title>Using headings</title>
  </head>
  <body>
    <h1>First Level Heading</h1>
    <p>This text follows H1</p>
    <h2>Second Level Heading</h2>
```

```html
    <p>This text follows H2</p>
    <h3>Third Level Heading</h3>
    <p>This text follows H3</p>
    <h4>Fourth Level Heading</h4>
    <p>This text follows H4</p>
    <h5>Fifth Level Heading</h5>
    <p>This text follows H5</p>
    <h6>Sixth Level heading</h6>
    <p>This text follows H6</p>
  </body>
</html>
```

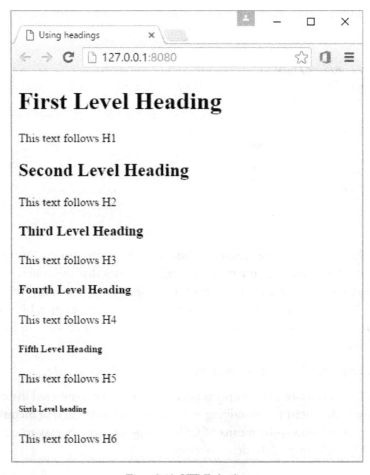

Figure 2-12: HTML headings

Using HTML Lists

HTML provides you two tags for organizing your text into lists. These tags are <ul> and <ol>, and they display unordered and ordered lists, respectively. Each of these tags represents a single block of list items designated by nested <li> items, as shown in Listing 2-13.

Listing 2-13: Exercise-02-13/index.html

```
<!DOCTYPE html>
<html>
<head>
  <title>Using HTML Lists</title>
</head>
<body>
  <p>This is an <em>unordered</em> list:</p>
  <ul>
    <li>Apple</li>
    <li>Banana</li>
    <li>Pear</li>
  </ul>
  <p>This is an <em>ordered</em> list:</p>
  <ol>
    <li>Open the door</li>
    <li>Step out</li>
    <li>Start your journey</li>
  </ol>
  <p>This ordered list is customized</p>
  <ol start="5" reversed type="I">
    <li>Roman 5</li>
    <li>Roman 4</li>
    <li>Roman 3</li>
  </ol>
</body>
</html>
```

The <ol> allows customizing the appearance of lists with three attributes. The start attribute sets the starting counter of list numbers, the reverse attribute states that the counter is decreased for each list item. The type attribute sets up the kind of the marker to use in the list. It can be one of the "1", "A", "a", "I", "i" values which represent numeric, uppercase letter, lowercase letter, uppercase Roman number, lowercase Roman number formats, respectively. In Figure 2-13, you can check how these tags work.

NOTE: Internet Explorer does not support the reverse attribute in <ol>.

The role of HTML lists is more than simply rendering bulleted or numbered list of texts. Unordered lists are widely used for describing navigation structures such as menus and toolbars. With a very little customization—by means of CSS styling—it is pretty easy to turn a list into a menu as Listing 2-14 and Figure 2-14 demonstrates.

Figure 2-13: Using HTML lists

Listing 2-14: Exercise-02-14/index.html

```html
<!DOCTYPE html>
<html>
<head>
  <title>Simple menu with lists</title>
  <style>
    ul {
      font-family: "Verdana", sans-serif;
      background-color: red;
      color: white;
      padding: 8px 0;
    }
    li {
      padding: 8px 20px;
      display: inline;
    }
    li.active {
      background-color: black;
    }
  </style>
</head>
<body>
  <ul>
    <li class="active">Home</li>
    <li>Products</li>
    <li>About</li>
  </ul>
</body>
</html>
```

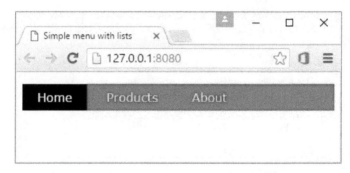

Figure 2-14: A simple menu described with an HTML list

NOTE: Do not feel intimidated if you do not understand how the style definitions in Listing 2-14 works! You will learn about it in the chapters treating CSS3. Right now, only remember the fact that a list can be easily turned into a menu by using styles.

Adding Links

No doubt, the power of World Wide Web is in links that allow web pages to link to other pages. The HTML <a> tag adds this power to pages. You can surround parts of the HTML markup to link them to other pages, or to bookmarks within your page, as Listing 2-15 demonstrates.

Listing 2-15: Exercise-02-15/index.html

```
<!DOCTYPE html>
<html>
<head>
  <title>Using links</title>
  <style>
    .rectangle {
      width: 200px;
      height: 100px;
      margin: 100px 20px;
      text-align:center;
      color: white;
    }
    .red {
      background-color: red;
    }
    .green {
      background-color: green;
    }
    .blue {
      background-color: blue;
    }
  </style>
</head>
<body>
  <p>
```

```
    Go to <a href="http://en.wikipedia.org/wiki/HTML">
    This page</a> for more info about HTML.
  </p>
  <p>
    Open this
    <a href="http://en.wikipedia.org/wiki/Markup_language"
       target="_blank">link</a> in a new tab
  </p>
  <ul>
    <li><a href="#red">Red</a></li>
    <li><a href="#green">Green</a></li>
    <li><a href="#blue">Blue</a></li>
  </ul>
  <div id="red" class="rectangle red">Red</div>
  <div id="green" class="rectangle green">Green</div>
  <div id="blue" class="rectangle blue">Blue</div>
</body>
</html>
```

The <a> tag surrounds the HTML markup that represents the link on the screen. When the user clicks to the area of a link, the browser navigates to the page or bookmark specified in the href attribute. In Listing 2-15, the first two links point to pages of Wikipedia.org, while the unordered list at the bottom contains links within the page (indicated by the "#" preceding the name of the corresponding bookmark). Bookmarks are marked with the id attributes of the three <div> sections.

NOTE: The style section in Listing 2-15 defines the layout of the red, green, and blue rectangles. Later in this book you will learn how it works. Right now, just accept that it does its job.

The page is simple, as shown in Figure 2-15. You can see the top part of the "red" section, but to discover the "green" and "blue" sections, you have to scroll down. Instead of scrolling, you can use the "Red", "Green", and "Blue" links that immediately reveal the corresponding area of the page. Figure 2-16 shows the same browser window after the "Green" link has been selected.

The second link opens the corresponding page in a new window. This is due to the target="_blank" attribute that instructs the browser to open the link in a new tab or window.

The <a> tag defines a few other useful attributes beside href and target. The hreflang attribute can be used to specify the language of the linked document, media tells what type of media or device the linked document is optimized for. Search engines may use the rel attribute that specifies the relationship between the current and target document. The MIME type of the linked document can be set with type—provided href is set—, but this attribute is purely advisory.

Figure 2-15: Links in a page

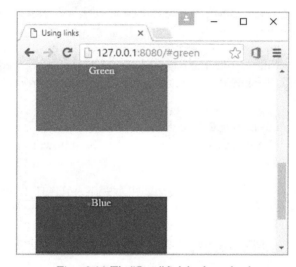

Figure 2-16: The "Green" link has been selected

Enriching Your Page with Images

"A picture is worth a thousand words"—says the truism. It's especially true for web pages.

HTML provides the `<img>` tag to display images in your pages. The `src` attribute of `<img>` describes the URL—relative to the current page—where the picture can be loaded from. For example, if you have two image files named `picture1.png` and `picture2.jpg` stored in the `content\images` folder, and your document is in the root web folder, you can use the following markup to display them:

```
<img src="content/images/picture1.png" />
<img src="content/images/picture2.jpg" />
```

Image files should be in a format supported by your browser—otherwise they would not be shown. If an image cannot be displayed, the browser generally displays a placeholder. With the `alt` attribute you can specify an alternate text for the image to be displayed in the placeholder. Let's assume, your image is defined like this:

```
<img src="boat.png" alt="This is a boat" />
```

If your browser cannot download the `boat.png` image, it will display a placeholder with the alternate text, as shown in Figure 2-17.

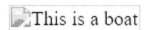

Figure 2-17: Image placeholder in Chrome

You can explicitly set the size of the image with the `width` and `height` attributes (specified in pixels), and the picture will be stretched to the specified size.

In the next exercise you will add existing pictures to a web page. To save time, you will start from a prepared project that can be found in the `Exercise-02-16-Begin` folder.

EXERCISE 2-16: Adding Images to a Web Page

To decorate the webpage with images, follow these steps:

1. Copy the `Exercise-02-16-Begin` folder into a new one, `Exercise-12-16`, and work within this new folder. The prepared project an `index.html` file and several `.jpg` file in the `Images` folder, as shown in Figure 2-18.

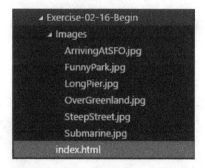

Figure 2-18: The structure of the exercise folder

2. Open the `index.html` file. Its body section looks like this, and contains two placeholder comments:

```
<body>
  <p>
    Hey dude, I'd taken these pictures during
    my San Francisco trip, while I was there for
    the BUILD 2013 conference!
  </p>
```

```
<h2>#1: On the way, over Greenland</h2>
<!-- Put OverGreenland.jpg here -->

<p>
   Can you see the signs of global climate change?
</p>
<h2>#2: I arrived to SFO in the evening</h2>
<!-- Put drop ArrivingAtSFO.jpg here -->

<p>
   I really liked the style of this building.
</p>
</body>
```

3. When you display the page, you see exactly what you expect (Figure 2-19).

Figure 2-19: The page displayed by the original `index.html`

4. Replace the placeholders with these `<img>` tags, respectively:

```
<img src="Images/OverGreenland.jpg"
  width="426" height="240" />

<img src="Images/ArrivingAtSFO.jpg"
    width="426" height="240" />
```

The size of the pictures would be too big to fit in the browser windows, so the `width` and `height` attributes of the `<img>` tags specify the display size of these images in pixels.

5. Turn back to the browser. Now, you can see the pictures inserted into the page, as shown in Figure 2-20.

Figure 2-20: Pictures inserted into the page

It's great that now you can see the pictures, but in the current implementation those are shrunk to the one third of their original size. I know my pals, and I'm sure they'd like to see all pictures with full size.

Well, it's pretty easy to implement by combining links and images, as you will learn from the next exercise.

EXERCISE 2-17: Displaying images with full size

The obvious solution would be to remove the `width` and `height` attributes of `<img>` tags, but in this case the page would display both images in full size. A more practical approach is to show thumbnails of pictures and to pop up a full size image when the user clicks on a thumbnail. Well, this is exactly what you will do, so follow these steps:

1. Create a copy of the previous exercise, put it into the `Exercise-02-17` folder. In the code editor, and open the copied `index.html` file.

2. Surround each `<img>` tag with an `<a>` tag, using the `href` attribute with the value of `src` attribute belonging to the nested `<img>`—as the highlighted code in the following code snippet shows:

```
. . .
<h2>#1: On the way, over Greenland</h2>
<a href="Images/OverGreenland.jpg">
   <img src="Images/OverGreenland.jpg"
     width="426" height="240" />
</a>
<p>
   Can you see the signs of global climate change?
</p>
<h2>#2: I arrived to SFO in the evening</h2>
<a href="Images/ArrivingAtSFO.jpg">
   <img src="Images/ArrivingAtSFO.jpg"
     width="426" height="240" />
</a>
<p>
   I really liked the style of this building.
</p>
. . .
```

3. Display the page in the browser. When you move the mouse over any picture, you can see that the cursor's shape changes a pointing hand, indicating that you're over a clickable link, as shown in Figure 2-21.

4. Click the picture. Because you clicked on a link, the browser navigates you to the target document specified by the href attribute of <a>. This is the picture file itself, as shown in Figure 2-22.

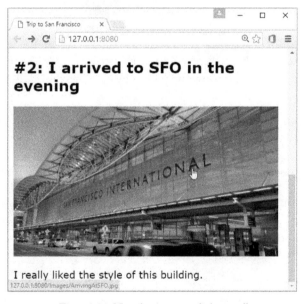

Figure 2-21: Now the pictures are links as well

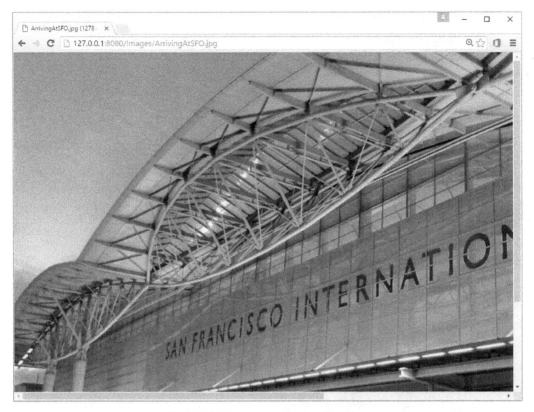

Figure 2-22: The browser shows the full size picture

Summary

The HTML (Hypertext Markup Language) went through many changes—not free from political debates—while it reached the "living HTML" state as promised today by HTML5. While the original HTML was a tool to share documents, HTML5 is not only a markup language, but rather a collection of related technologies—including CSS3 and JavaScript—to support efficient web development.

The structure of an HTML5 document can be described with a simple skeleton:

```
<!DOCTYPE html>
<html>
  <head>...</head>
  <body>...</body>
</html>
```

The `<head>` section describes all non-content page data (such as title and other metadata), `<body>` contains the content of the document.

Literal text written between the opening and closing `<body>` text is displayed by the browser in a flow layout. Line breaks and multiple white spaces within the text are translated to single space characters. Explicit line breaks can be placed with the `<br/>` tag. The `<p>` tag handles the enclosed text as a paragraph. There are about two dozen tags for formatting text, such as `<strong>`, `<sup>`, `<em>`, `<cite>`, `<code>`, and many more. With the `<h1>`, `<h2>`, ..., `<h6>` tags headings can be defined from level one to level six.

The `<ul>` and `<ol>` tags render unordered and ordered lists, respectively. Use the nested `<li>` tags to define list items.

You can add images to your web pages with the `<img>` HTML tag. To define hyperlinks to other pages (or within your current page), use the `<a>` tag.

By now, you learned the basic constructs of HTML. In Chapter 3, you will learn new tags and markup patterns that help you add richer user experience by extending the types and layout of the HTML content.

Chapter 3:
Achieving Richer User Experience with HTML

WHAT YOU WILL LEARN IN THIS CHAPTER

Understanding how HTML5 semantic elements change the way web pages are structured and styled

Getting to know using headers, footers, figures and sidebars

Establishing tables for displaying tabular data and reports

Getting acquainted with the basics of adding multimedia to your pages with new HTML5 markup elements

Before HTML5, web page developers and designers had to use the constrained toolset of HTML to provide great-looking web pages. It led to unordinary solutions that were often hard-to-read, and laborious-to-maintain. For example, designers used tables to position standard elements, such as headers, footers, navigation bars, sidebars, etc. Video and audio were not the standard parts of the markup language (can you imagine any great websites today without providing video at all?) they had to be "hacked" into web pages with the `<object>` and `<embed>` tags.

HTML5 brings new colors to the markup. It adds many new tags to make web developers and designers more productive by expressing their intention more explicitly than they could do it with previous HTML versions. It also provides tags that help establish richer user experience. Beside new tags, HTML5 also bares the existing tags by means of semantic accuracy and deprecating obsolete or unnecessary attributes—including those that can be better described with CSS.

In this chapter, you will learn about the most significant features of HTML that provide this kind of clear-cut characteristics. Although the emphasis is on treating HTML5, for the sake of getting into the proper context, sometimes you'll find sections that mention the old markup.

Old Style: The Omnipotent <div>

It's amazing, how much the web changed in the last decade! In contrast to this, it's surprising how prehistoric HTML remained for a long time, how verbose and ambiguous markup was created by developers in response to new challenges. Undoubtedly, the reason for this ancient style was the semantic weakness of HTML. With the emerge of CSS the conciseness of webpages improved—

styling attributes left the content and moved to the style section of the page—, but the HTML content of complex pages stayed messier than justifiable by the sheer page structure.

The ultimate weapon of web designers was the `<div>` tag, which defines a division or section in HTML. If they had any part of the content that constituted a logical block with their own visual properties, they used the following pattern:

```
<!-- … -->
<head>
  <title>Sample</title>
  <style>
    #myBlock {
      <!-- Style description of the block -->
    }
  </style>
</head>
<body>
  <div id="myBlock">
    <!-- Content of the block -->
  </div>
</body>
```

This pattern assigns an identifier (`myBlock`) to the section, and a style (here `#myBlock`) that describes the appearance of the `<div>`. It's simple, but the `<div>` itself does not help to understand the meaning of the section, nor does it tell the intention of the designer.

NOTE: In *Chapter* 1, you already met exercises using the `<div>` tag.

While there are only a few `<div>` tags in the code, those may be easily understandable and maintainable. However, as the size of the markup grows, designers and developers feel being lost in the complexity of the page. It's not easy to find whether a `<div>` is a header, a section of the main document, a sidebar, a part of the navigation structure, or whatever else. It's just because `<div>` has only poor semantic: it's just a generic block.

For example, Figure 3-1 shows an article in a web page. The structure of the article is typical: it contains a header, the main content, a footer; the main content is divided further into sections.

According to the listings and exercises you already went through, you can easily draft the skeleton of such a webpage. One example is shown in Listing 3-1.

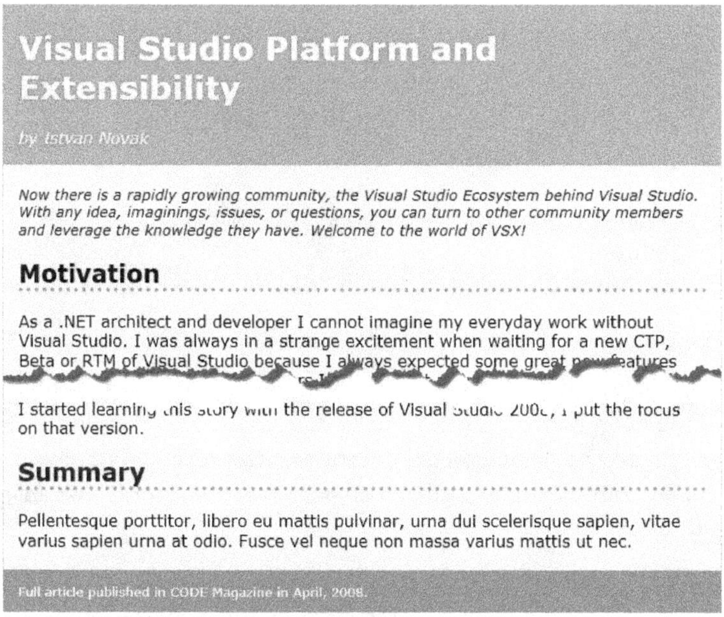

Figure 3-1: An article shown in a web page

Listing 3-1: Exercise-03-01/index.html

```html
<html>
<head>
  <title>Old Style Article</title>
  <style>
    <!-- Omitted for the sake of brevity -->
  </style>
</head>
<body>
  <div class="header">
    <h1>Visual Studio Platform and Extensibility</h1>
    <p class="byLine">by Istvan Novak</p>
  </div>
  <div class="mainContent">
    <p>
      <span class="abstract">
        <!-- ... -->
      </span>
    </p>
    <h2>Motivation</h2>
    <p>
      <!-- ... -->
    </p>
    <h2>Visual Studio: Extensible Platform</h2>
    <p>
      <!-- ... -->
    </p>
```

```
    <h2>Summary</h2>
    <p>
      <!-- ... -->
    </p>
  </div>
  <div class="footer">
    <p>
      Full article published in CODE Magazine
      in April, 2008.</p>
  </div>
</body>
</html>
```

Although this skeleton uses `<div>` tags to define document sections, it's pretty easy to find the header, footer, and the main content—due to deliberate naming conventions. The `class` attributes adorning the `<div>` tags exactly tell the roles of the corresponding sections. Well, it's easy for a human reader, but what about search engines and other tools that analyze the structure of the page?

If I used "*fejléc*", "*lábléc*", "*tartalom*" for class names instead of "header", "footer", and "mainContent", respectively, would a human reader know their role? Not unless she speaks Hungarian!

It's a big issue with the good old `<div>` tag that is misses any extra meaning that would help in analyzing and understanding the role of page sections.

Structure and Semantics

HTML5 changes this ancient plight significantly. It adds new *semantic elements* to the markup, which provide the missing meaning of the embedded content. Listing 3-2 shows the skeleton of the same page of article as drafted in Listing 3-1, but it uses new semantic elements.

Listing 3-2: The skeleton of an article—with HTML5

```
<!DOCTYPE html>
<html>
<head>
  <title>New Style Article</title>
  <style>
    <!-- Omitted for the sake of brevity -->
  </style>
</head>
<body>
  <article>
    <header>
      <h1>Visual Studio Platform and Extensibility</h1>
      <p class="byLine">by Istvan Novak</p>
    </header>
    <div class="mainContent">
```

```
        <p>
          <span class="abstract">
            <!-- ... -->
          </span>
        </p>
        <section>
          <h2>Motivation</h2>
          <p>
            <!-- ... -->
          </p>
        </section>
        <section>
          <h2>Visual Studio: Extensible Platform</h2>
          <p>
            <!-- ... -->
          </p>
        </section>
        <section>
          <h2>Summary</h2>
          <p>
            <!-- ... -->
          </p>
        </section>
      </div>
    </article>
    <footer>
      <p>
      Full article published in CODE Magazine
      in April, 2008.</p>
    </footer>
</body>
</html>
```

Without knowing *anything* about these new elements, you can intuitively understand the structure of the document: it contains an article that is composed from a header and a number of sections; and it also has a footer. Comparing the two code listings (the old-school style with HTML5), you can easily state that the second one (HTML5 style) is easier to read, and it's easier to maintain.

If you think about how a search engine works, you can imagine that this information helps a lot to separate the more important information in this page from the less important. For example, an occurrence of a certain word in the header may have a higher rank than the same word in a section, or in a footer.

Semantic elements may empower tools that analyze or change the page on-the-fly. For example, you can generate an automatic navigation bar for the page that displays the structure of sections. The great thing is, that you can even create a library (in JavaScript, for example), which prepares this structure and automatically attaches it to a page. Third parties can load your library and generate the content structure for their own pages.

HTML5 defines nine semantic elements that behave exactly like the good old `<div>` tag, but add some extra meaning to your pages. These elements are summarized in Table 3-1.

NOTE: There are a few more semantic tags that are related to text elements. For example, the `<mark>` and `<wbr>` tags treated in *Chapter 2* are such ones. As you already learned, those are inline elements, and so they are not the semantic extensions of `<div>` by any means.

Table 3-1: Semantic elements of page structure

Element	Description
`<article>`	This element defines an independent, self-contained content, such as a blog entry, a newspaper article, a forum post, a CV, an author biography, a story, etc.—anything that you think of as an article.
`<aside>`	This element defines content that is separate from the other (surrounding) content of the page—aside from the content it is placed in. It is frequently used to create sidebars related to an article.
`<figure>`	Represents a figure that is—in contrast to traditional images—a self-contained content, such as an illustration, diagram, photo, etc. The `<figure>` element is a wrapper for this content, including the `<img>` for the figure, as well as the caption nested into a `<figcaption>` element. The aim is to indicate the relation between the image and its associated caption.
`<figcaption>`	This element defines a caption for the `<figure>` element.
`<footer>`	Defines a footer for a document or section, so this element should contain information about its container element. It can be a set of important links, a copyright notice, terms of use, contact information, etc.
`<header>`	This element represents an enhanced heading for a document or a section. It should be a container for introductory content, and may contain logo, byline, set of navigational links, etc.
`<hgroup>`	This element defines an enhanced heading that groups two or more heading elements without any additional content. Its purpose is to make a title and a subtitle (or subtitles) stand together.
`<nav>`	Defines a major block of links on a page. These links may point to topics on the current page, or to other pages on the website. Not all links of a document must be in a `<nav>` element. A page may have multiple `<nav>` sections.
`<section>`	This element defines logical sections in a document. These sections can be headers, footers, chapters, sections of chapters, etc. Use `<section>` only if other semantic elements do not apply. As a rule of thumb, the content `<section>` holds always should begin with a heading (`<h1>`, ..., `<h6>`)

All these elements behave exactly like `<div>`. They only enclose a markup block, and provide a logical container that can be used to apply formatting (through styling), or to add behavior by means of a script language (JavaScript).

It's time to see these semantic elements in action.

Headers

There are two ways you can use headers in HTML5. First, the header can be used as the title of your web page. Second, you can use a header as a title of some content—and in this context you can have multiple headers, each associated with its related content. You can even combine these aspects, so in a web page you may apply a single header for the page, and multiple headers for separate content sections.

HINT: If your page has a simple (ordinary) title, you do not need to use the `<header>` tag. Simply use the `<h1>` tag with the title text. Apply `<header>` when you want to display a compound header with multiple parts of the title. Nonetheless, if you plan to redesign your header later, you may wrap the single `<h1>` tag into a `<header>`.

In Listing 3-2, the `<header>` tag was used as a content-related header. It was nested into the `<article>` tag, as this code snippet shows:

```
<body>
  <article>
    <header>
      <h1>Visual Studio Platform and Extensibility</h1>
      <p class="byLine">by Istvan Novak</p>
    </header>
    <!-- ... -->
  </article>
  <!-- ... -->
</body>
```

If it were a page with multiple articles, you could create a separate header for each article plus a page header, as shown in Listing 3-3.

Listing 3-3: Exercise-03-03/index.html

```
<!DOCTYPE html>
<html>
<head>
  <title>Using Page Headers (no style)</title>
</head>
<body>
  <header class="pageHeader">
    <h1>Articles about Visual Studio</h1>
    <p class="byLine">edited by Istvan Novak</p>
  </header>
  <article>
    <header class="articleHeader">
      <h2>Visual Studio Platform and Extensibility</h2>
      <h3>April, 2008</h3>
    </header>
    <div class="mainContent">
      <p>
        Sed tincidunt hendrerit iaculis. Phasellus eget
        dolor ac nisi porttitor porta. Integer tortor sem,
```

```
            condimentum a auctor ac, interdum eget.
        </p>
      </div>
    </article>
    <article>
      <header class="articleHeader">
        <h2>Creating Visual Studio Packages</h2>
        <h3>June, 2009</h3>
      </header>
      <div class="mainContent">
        <p>
          Phasellus condimentum suscipit molestie. Praesent
          volutpat nunc orci, rhoncus accumsan nunc sodales
          molestie. Proin quis risus eget mauris ultricies tempor.
        </p>
      </div>
    </article>
  </body>
</html>
```

As you see, this code sample does not contain any style information, so displaying it (Figure 3-2) produces the same result as if you omitted the semantic tags (`<article>`, `<header>`) from the page source.

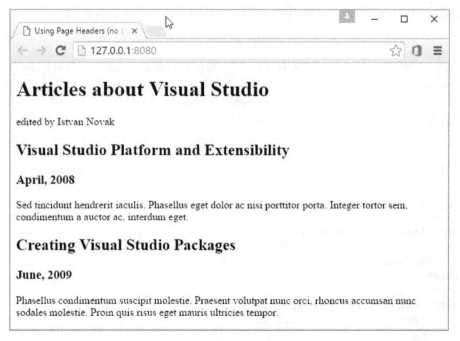

Figure 3-2: Using headers with no style information

NOTE: Although you can create a page title with the `<header>` tag, it does not substitute the `<title>` tag in the HTML markup. The page title is a part of the content, `<title>` is a kind of metadata—and it is mandatory by the HTML standard.

As Figure 3-2 shows, you have no visual clue about headers, and so you can distinguish between the page title and article title information only by the text size. To emphasize headers visually, you must provide styling information. Listing 3-3 is prepared for styling simply by using semantic elements. However, the page designer must be able to assign separate style for page header and article headers, so those are distinguished with the value of the `class` attribute:

```
<body>
  <header class="pageHeader">...</header>
  <article>
    <header class="articleHeader">...</header>
      <!-- ... -->
  </article>
  <!-- ... -->
</body>
```

With styling applied, you can visually distinguish between page and article headers, as shown in Figure 3-3.

Figure 3-3: Using headers with style information

NOTE: You can find the complete code that renders Figure 3-3 in the `Exercise-03-04` folder.

If you have a closer look at article headers, you can see that they are composed from a title and a subtitle:

```
<header class="articleHeader">
  <h2>Creating Visual Studio packages</h2>
  <h3>June, 2009</h3>
</header>
```

This markup is a bit confusing, because it suggests that the article has a title (the `<h2>` tag) that is immediately followed by an embedded section (the `<h3>` tag). Let's assume that an external entity or service want to generate an outline of your page. Should it use only the `<h2>` heading, or the `<h3>` heading as well in the outline? Is `<h3>` a subtitle, or a title of a subsection?

The `<hgroup>` HTML tag helps answering this question. By surrounding the title part of the header with `<hgroup>` you can sign that only the top-level heading should be taken into account as a title:

```
<header class="articleHeader">
  <hgroup>
    <h2>Creating Visual Studio Packages</h2>
    <h3>June, 2009</h3>
  </hgroup>
</header>
```

Well, at the first sight `<hgroup>` seems just to complicate the code, because you may think it only adds a new level of nesting. But examine this markup:

```
<header class="articleHeader">
  <hgroup>
    <h2>Creating Visual Studio Packages</h2>
    <h3>June, 2009</h3>
  </hgroup>
  <p class="author">John Doe</p>
</header>
```

This code helps to highlight the part of the header that should be taken into account in outline generation, and separates the part that are just descriptive information in your header.

NOTE: HTML5 defines a set of rules that describe exactly what do you mean by the outline of a page. Browsers actually do not care about these rules, but thinking about design tools, you may get excited. With these tools you may easily refactor your pages (for example, you may change the order or nesting or article sections), or create a navigation bar (or overlay) to quickly surf within a document. You can find a great and practical article about HTML5 outlines at `http://html5doctor.com/outlines/`.

Footers

Just as you can create headers for a page and document sections, HTML5 allows you to apply footers, too. As the HTML5 specification says (`http://www.w3.org/html/wg/drafts/html/master/sections.html#the-footer-element`), "A footer typically contains information about its section such as who wrote it, links to related documents, copyright data, and the like". For example, you can extend the page in Listing 3-3 with footers, as shown in Listing 3-4 (styles are omitted for the sake of brevity).

Listing 3-4: Exercise-03-05/index.html

```
<!DOCTYPE html>
<html>
<head>
  <title>Using Page Headers (no style)</title>
  <style>
    <!-- Omitted for the sake of brevity -->
  </style>
</head>
<body>
  <header class="pageHeader">
    <h1>Articles about Visual Studio</h1>
    <p class="byLine">edited by Istvan Novak</p>
  </header>
  <article>
    <header class="articleHeader">
      <h2>Visual Studio Platform and Extensibility</h2>
      <h3>April, 2008</h3>
    </header>
    <div class="mainContent">
      <p>
        Sed tincidunt hendrerit iaculis. Phasellus eget
        dolor ac nisi porttitor porta. Integer tortor sem,
        condimentum a auctor ac, interdum eget.
      </p>
    </div>
    <footer class="articleFooter">
      <p>Viewed: 12,419</p>
    </footer>
  </article>
  <article>
    <header class="articleHeader">
      <h2>Creating Visual Studio Packages</h2>
      <h3>June, 2009</h3>
    </header>
    <div class="mainContent">
      <p>
        Phasellus condimentum suscipit molestie. Praesent
        volutpat nunc orci, rhoncus accumsan nunc sodales
        molestie. Proin quis risus eget mauris ultricies tempor.
      </p>
    </div>
    <footer class="articleFooter">
      <p>Viewed: 18,048</p>
    </footer>
  </article>
  <footer class="pageFooter">
    <p>&copy; Super Visual Studio Articles Community, 2013</p>
  </footer>
</body>
</html>
```

When showing the page in a browser, footers are rendered as expected (Figure 3-4).

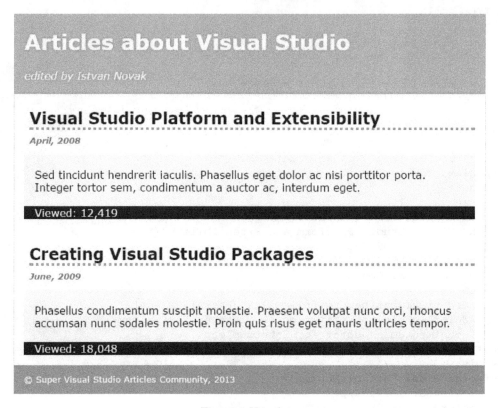

Figure 3-4: Using footers

Your footers can be fat footers, so they can contain a set of links, logos, images, etc.

Sections

With the `<section>` tag, you can mark parts of your web page as a section. Well, this tag seems to be a kind of jolly joker, depending on what you take into account as a section. In case of a book, each chapter and subchapter can be a section, as well as sidebars or emphasized notes and hints. If the webpage displays a report, it also can have sections, for example, each region in a sales report. Let's assume, you create a news site. In the home page, each article may have its own section, as well as a collection of highlighted articles can be put in a separate section.

It seems that a section does not have a pretty clear identity. It's up to you how you define it. The creators of HTML5 could have crafted at least two different kinds of section-like tags (for example, one for single items, and another one for a collection of items, etc.), but they created only one for the sake of simplicity.

Let's have a look at a web page that displays an e-book. Listing 3-5 shown the skeleton of the web page—using `<section>` tags.

Listing 3-5: Exercise-03-06/index.html

```html
<!DOCTYPE html>
<html>
<head>
  <title>Sections</title>
</head>
<body>
  <header class="pageHeader">
    <h1>Unraveling HTML5</h1>
    <p class="byLine">&mdash; with Visual Studio 2013</p>
  </header>
  <section>
    <h1>Introduction</h1>
  </section>
  <section>
    <h1>A Short Tour of HTML</h1>
    <p>...</p>
    <section>
      <h2>Creating a Basic HTML Page</h2>
      <p>...</p>
    </section>
    <section>
      <h2>Formatting the HTML Page</h2>
      <p>...</p>
    </section>
    <section>
      <h2>...</h2>
      <p>...</p>
    </section>
  </section>
  <section>
    <h1>Getting to Know HTML5</h1>
    <p>...</p>
    <section>
      <h2>The Unordinary story of HTML5</h2>
      <p>...</p>
    </section>
    <section>
      <h2>What Behind the Term HTML5 Is</h2>
      <p>...</p>
    </section>
    <section>
      <h2>...</h2>
      <p>...</p>
    </section>
  </section>
  <footer class="pageFooter">
    <p>&copy; Istvan Novak, 2013</p>
  </footer>
</body>
</html>
```

As you see from this Listing 3-5, each chapter of the book, and each subchapter is in its own section, so actually <section> tags are nested in each other. As you already learned, <section> tags do not affect the rendering of the page, they are just simple semantic containers.

However, the extra semantics are very useful for tools. For example, if you use Google Chrome, you can add an extension named HTML5 Outliner by *Dominykas Blyžė*. This tool puts a small icon in the address bar, and clicking it displays the outline of the currently loaded document. HTML5 Outliner utilizes the semantic information to create the outline, as shown in Figure 3-5.

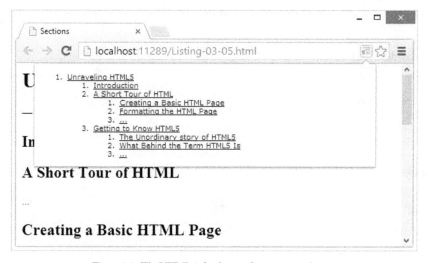

Figure 3-5: The HTML5 Outliner utilizes semantic elements

Figure 3-6: The page outline when no semantic elements are used

This tool uses the outlining rules defined by the HTML5 specification. If you do not use sections, the tool still understands the structure of the document using the headings (<h1>, ..., <h6>), but in this case the outline is a bit different, as shown in Figure 3-6. Since there is no section information, the `<h1>` tag in the `<header>` is taken into account as a top level outline entry with all other `<h1>` tags.

Now, if you turn back to Listing 3-5, and change all `<h2>` tags to `<h1>`, the document will contain only first level headings. Nonetheless, because the `<section>` tags still define the document structure properly, the HTML5 Outline tool will display the same outline, as shown in Figure 3-5.

Figures in the Page

In *Chapter 2*, you have already met with images, and the usage of `<img>` tag. You may ask yourself, why HTML5 has another tag for figures. The reason behind this fact is that figures have another semantic than images. A figure is a self-contained content that is related to the main flow of a document, but it can be placed anywhere in the page, or even can be removed without affecting the main flow of the document. For example, in Figure 3-7, you can see such a page. The figure in this article can be moved anywhere in the page without breaking the main flow of the document.

Visual Studio Platform and Extensibility

by Istvan Novak

Thousand ways of extension

Well I know, it is an exaggeration to tell about "a thousand ways" when treating Visual Studio extensibility, but I'd like to point out that you have many choices. In this part I show you how many options you have when dealing with adding some extra stuff to Visual Studio. Reference materials, books, and articles generally enumerate about a dozen options. Instead of simply telling you what they are I would like to methodize them. The key to understand extensibility options is the architecture of the Visual Studio IDE (Figure 1)

When running the Visual Studio IDE we start the devenv.exe file. However, the IDE we see and work with is not just a simple monolithic .exe file or an executable divided into a few .dll files. It is a shell that provides a graphical environment to host functional units, called packages. What we perceive is a cooperation of the shell and hosted packages. The core functions of the IDE are

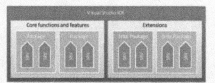

Figure 1: Visual Studio IDE

also implemented in packages including the C# or Visual Basic project types, testing features, and many more. The majority of third-party extensions loaded into Visual Studio are also implemented in packages. Just to give you a feeling about how many of them are used: in my notebook I counted 129 packages including those installed with Visual Studio 2008 and third-parties.

Full article published in CODE Magazine in April, 2008.

Figure 3-7: A web page with a figure

HTML5 provides the `<figure>` and `<figcaption>` tags to define such a figure. Listing 3-6 shows the skeleton of the page in Figure 3-7, highlighting the tags that are related to the figure.

Listing 3-6: Exercise-03-07/index.html

```html
<!DOCTYPE html>
<html>
<head>
  <title>Using Figures</title>
  <style>
    <!-- Omitted -->
  </style>
</head>
<body>
  <article>
    <header>
      <h1>Visual Studio Platform and Extensibility</h1>
      <p class="byLine">by Istvan Novak</p>
    </header>
    <div class="mainContent">
      <section>
        <h2>Thousand ways of extension</h2>
        <p>
          <!-- Omitted -->
        </p>
        <figure id="figure1">
          <a href="Figure1.gif" target="_blank">
            <img src="Figure1.gif" width="307" height="118" />
          </a>
          <figcaption>
            Figure 1: Visual Studio IDE
          </figcaption>
        </figure>
        <p>
          <!-- Omitted -->
        </p>
      </section>
    </div>
  </article>
  <footer>
    <p>
      Full article published in CODE Magazine
      in April, 2008.
    </p>
  </footer>
</body>
</html>
```

As you see, the definition of this figure is pretty simple. The `<figure>` tag defines the whole construct, marking the nested markup as a self-contained content that is related to the document, but it's still independently positioned. The corresponding caption is defined with `<figcaption>`, and without doubt, it is the part of the figure. The image of the figure is defined by the `<a>` and `<img>` tags, but it could be anything else that represent the illustration.

As Figure 3-7 shows, the illustration is positioned aside of the main document flow. This can be quite easily achieved with CSS styling, as you will learn it later. The `<figure>` is defined right before the second paragraph, so that the text wraps it—due to this simple CSS rule:

```
figure {
  float: right;
  margin: 0 0 16px 16px;
}
```

Sidebars

Your web page may have content that is only tangentially related to the main flow of the content, and can be positioned actually everywhere near to the related content—such as a sidebar. HTML5 provides the `<aside>` semantic tag to define this "tangentially related" section. You can put anything in `<aside>` that you would put into a sidebar, including text, image, a set of navigation links, header, footer, and so on. Listing 3-7 shows you the skeleton of a web page that contains two small sidebars.

Listing 3-7: Exercise-03-08/index.html

```
<!DOCTYPE html>
<html>
<head>
  <title>Using Figures</title>
  <style>
    <!-- Omitted -->
  </style>
</head>
<body>
  <article>
    <header>
      <h1>Visual Studio Platform and Extensibility</h1>
      <p class="byLine">by Istvan Novak</p>
    </header>
    <div class="mainContent">
      <section>
        <h2>When to use macros, add-ins and packages?</h2>
        <p>...</p>
        <aside class="rightBar">
          &quot;...macros are your best friends.&quot;
        </aside>
        <p>...</p>
        <aside class="leftBar">
          Few extensibility options are not available
          through automation model
        </aside>
        <p>...</p>
```

```
      </section>
    </div>
  </article>
  <footer>
    <p>
      Full article published in CODE Magazine
      in April, 2008.
    </p>
  </footer>
</body>
</html>
```

This listing shows that the sidebars belong to the section describing the main content. With a few style rules (one for the `<aside>` tag, and two others for the `leftBar` and `rightBar` classes) you can transform the `<aside>` sections into real sidebars, as shown in Figure 3-8.

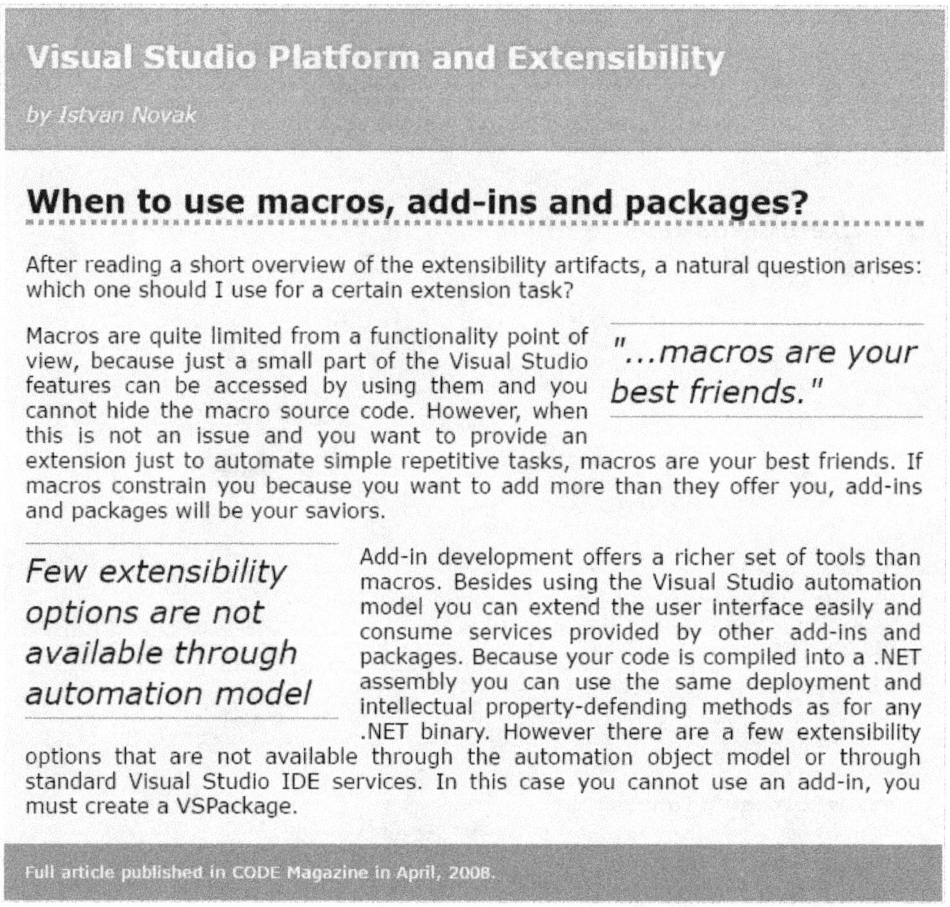

Visual Studio Platform and Extensibility

by Istvan Novak

When to use macros, add-ins and packages?

After reading a short overview of the extensibility artifacts, a natural question arises: which one should I use for a certain extension task?

Macros are quite limited from a functionality point of view, because just a small part of the Visual Studio features can be accessed by using them and you cannot hide the macro source code. However, when this is not an issue and you want to provide an extension just to automate simple repetitive tasks, macros are your best friends. If macros constrain you because you want to add more than they offer you, add-ins and packages will be your saviors.

"...macros are your best friends."

Few extensibility options are not available through automation model

Add-in development offers a richer set of tools than macros. Besides using the Visual Studio automation model you can extend the user interface easily and consume services provided by other add-ins and packages. Because your code is compiled into a .NET assembly you can use the same deployment and intellectual property-defending methods as for any .NET binary. However there are a few extensibility options that are not available through the automation object model or through standard Visual Studio IDE services. In this case you cannot use an add-in, you must create a VSPackage.

Full article published in CODE Magazine in April, 2008.

Figure 3-8 `<aside>` tags styled to sidebars

Navigation

You may have many links placed in a web page with the `<a>` tag. Most websites contain a set of navigation links that are the essential links within the site (or within the page). With the help of the `<nav>` semantic element, you can place these links into a specific section. A page can have more than one set of navigation links. Quick links are quite often put into an `<aside>` section, as the page skeleton in Listing 3-8 shows.

Listing 3-8: Exercise-03-09/index.html

```html
<!DOCTYPE html>
<html>
<head>
  <title>Using Figures</title>
  <style>
    <!-- omitted -->
  </style>
</head>
<body>
  <article>
    <header>
      <h1>HTML5 Semantic Elements</h1>
    </header>
    <div class="mainContent">
      <section>
        <h2>What Semantic Elements Are</h2>
        <aside>
          <h3>Quick Links</h3>
          <nav>
            <ul>
              <li><a href="#article">&lt;article&gt;</a></li>
              <li><a href="#aside">&lt;aside&gt;</a></li>
              <li><a href="#figure">&lt;figure&gt;</a></li>
              <li><a href="#figcaption">&lt;figcaption&gt;</a></li>
              <li><a href="#footer">&lt;footer&gt;</a></li>
              <li><a href="#header">&lt;header&gt;</a></li>
              <li><a href="#hgroup">&lt;hgroup&gt;</a></li>
              <li><a href="#nav">&lt;nav&gt;</a></li>
              <li><a href="#section">&lt;section&gt;</a></li>
            </ul>
          </nav>
        </aside>
        <p class="hilited">To improve the structure ...</p>
      </section>
      <section>
        <h3 id="article">&lt;article&gt;</h3>
        <p>This element defines ...</p>
      </section>
      <section>
        <h3 id="aside">&lt;aside&gt;</h3>
        <p>This element defines ...</p>
```

```
      </section>
      <!-- Other sections omitted for the sake of brevity -->
    </div>
  </article>
  <footer>
    <p>
      Full article published in CODE Magazine
      in April, 2008.
    </p>
  </footer>
</body>
</html>
```

As you can see, the <nav> element contains only hyperlinks embedded into an unordered list. With simple styling, this markup is rendered as shown in Figure 3-9.

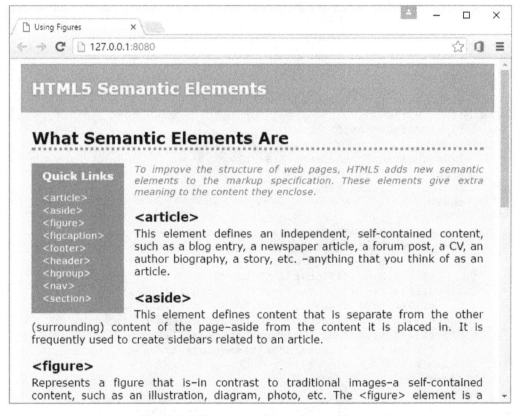

Figure 3-9: Adding navigation links to the page with <nav>

Other Semantic Elements

By now, you have got acquainted with semantic tags related to page structure. There are other semantic elements that do not influence the structure of the page, but still add extra semantic meaning to the content. The <mark> element mentioned in *Chapter 2, Rendering Text*, and <wbr>

treated in *Chapter 2, Paragraphs and Text Breaks* are text level semantic elements (defined so by the HTML5 specification).

The `<time>` tag signifies its content as one that specifies time related value. It can be either a time using a 24-hour clock, a date in the Gregorian calendar that optionally has a time and a time-zone offset.

Is there any benefit from marking a value as `<time>`? Yes, definitely! User agents (scripts) can understand this markup, and because dates and times are there in a machine-readable format, they can utilize it. For example, a user agent can offer to add meetings and other scheduled events, flights, birthday reminders to the user's calendar. Knowing that certain values define time, search engines can produce better results. It's very easy to use `<time>`, as the following code snippet shows:

```
<p>Do not forget, Henriett's birthday is on <time>1969-09-07</time><p>
```

NOTE: HTML5 provides three related tags, `<ruby>`, `<rt>`, and `<rp>` to render Ruby annotations, which are used for East Asian typography, to show the pronunciation of East Asian characters. To be honest, I'm not familiar with any of these languages. If you're interested, you'll find more information on Wikipedia (`http://en.wikipedia.org/wiki/Ruby_(annotation_markup)#HTML`).

Tables

HTML5 has versatile support for tabular data. The markup language always treated tables as first-class citizens when rendering content, but for a long time tables had been considered by web designers mainly as tools for establishing the layout of a web page. For example, a page with a standard header, footer, navigation bar and content pane (as shown in Figure 3-10) was defined with tables, as shown in Listing 3-9.

Listing 3-9: Exercise-03-10/index.html

```
<html>
<head>
  <title>Page Layout with Tables</title>
</head>
<body>
  <table border="1" width="720px">
    <tr height="80px">
      <td colspan="2">
        <!-- Header placeholder-->
        <p>Header</p>
      </td>
    </tr>
    <tr height="600px">
      <td width="200px">
        <!-- Navigation placeholder-->
        <p>Navigation</p>
      </td>
```

```
      <td>
        <!-- Main Content placeholder-->
        <p>Main Content</p>
      </td>
    </tr>
    <tr height="60px">
      <td colspan="2">
        <!-- Footer placeholder-->
        <p>Footer</p>
      </td>
    </tr>
  </table>
</body>
</html>
```

Table definitions use the `<table>` tag that encloses a number of `<tr>` tags—each of them representing a table row. Rows contain cells—defined by the `<td>` tag—, and these cells contain the actual content. This sample contains only placeholders, but real websites put long markup in each table cell to define their content. As you see, `height` and `width` attributes are used to specify table row and cell dimensions; the `colspan` attribute defines that the table cell for Header and Footer should span two columns (the Navigation Bar and Main Content).

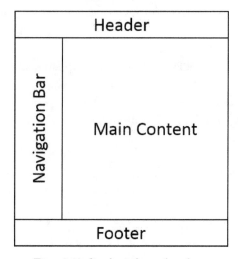

Figure 3-10: Simple wireframe of a web page

With HTML5, forget about this practice! The styling capabilities provided by CSS3 offer much intuitive and flexible solutions to establish the layout of a great web page. Just think about how difficult it could be to rearrange such a table layout where hundreds of markup lines could be located between `<td>` and `</td>`. Another big bottleneck of table-based layout is that providing dynamic layout (for example, selecting a skin from a variety of predefined themes) could be challenging.

So, in HTML5 uses tables only for their real application: presenting tabular data.

Table Content, Style, and Semantics

The old school sample you saw in Listing 3-9 used a few attributes (dimensions) to define a very basic style for the table defined in the markup. In contrast to that, HTML5 explicitly separates the content of a table from its style. The tags defining the structure of your table focus on the content and layout, and you must use separate styling rules to establish the visual properties of the tabular data. HTML5 allows you to use simple cell semantic, or compound table semantic.

In the simpler case, your table is built up from cells organized in rows and columns. It best fits for presenting simple tabular data, such as a contact table where rows describe a single contact with columns for contact name, mobile phone end email.

The compound tables have the power to describe complex reports with headers, tabular details, footers, and help defining UI that accommodates to browsing table data, for example allows scrolling table details while freezing the header and footer of the table.

Simple Table Markup

Let's have a quick overview of the simple table markup (cell semantic).

A table definition is managed by the `<table>` tag that encloses other elements defining the table content. The content is built from table rows—zero, one or more `<tr>` tag nested in `<table>`—, and rows are built from cells (details) that contain zero, one or more `<td>` tags with cell content. Listing 3-10 demonstrates the markup.

Listing 3-10: Exercise-03-11/index.html

```
<!DOCTYPE html>
<html>
<head>
  <title>Simple Table (no styling)</title>
</head>
<body>
  <table border="1">
    <tr>
      <td>North</td>
      <td>12%</td>
    </tr>
    <tr>
      <td>East</td>
      <td>42%</td>
    </tr>
    <tr>
      <td>South</td>
      <td>27%</td>
    </tr>
    <tr>
      <td>West</td>
      <td>19%</td>
```

```
    </tr>
  </table>
</body>
</html>
```

As the markup shows, this table has four rows with two cells in each. The `<table>` tag has only one attribute in HTML5, `border`; its value of "1" specifies that the table should have a drawn border. This table is displayed in your browser as shown in Figure 3-11.

Figure 3-11: A simple table rendered in Internet Explorer

Spanning Rows and Columns

Creating matrix-like tables is easy, but sometimes you need to create tables with more complex layout. Two attributes of `<td>`, `colspan` and `rowspan`, allows you to specify the number of columns and rows a cell should span, respectively. Let's assume, you want to create a table, as shown in Figure 3-12.

North	12%	$38.64m
Top 3		
Chicago		$20.09m
Cleveland		$12.24m
Minneapolis		$3.53m
East	42%	$135.24m
Top 3		
???		$34.52m
		$23.09m
		$12.64m
South	27%	$86.94m
West	19%	$61.18m

Figure 3-12: A table with colspan and rowspan attributes

108

This table contains twelve rows and three columns. When you set the `colspan` attribute of `<td>`, the cell you specify spans the number of specified columns. When you set the `rowspan` attribute of `<td>`, the corresponding cell spans the number of specified rows. So, to define the table in Figure 3-12, you need use the markup shown in Listing 3-11.

Listing 3-11: Exercise-03-12/index.html

```
<!DOCTYPE html>
<html>
<head>
  <title>Using rowspan and colspan</title>
</head>
<body>
  <table border="1">
    <!-- Row 1 -->
    <tr>
      <td>North</td>
      <td>12%</td>
      <td>$38.64m</td>
    </tr>
    <!-- Row 2 -->
    <tr><td colspan="3">Top 3</td></tr>
    <!-- Row 3 -->
    <tr>
      <td colspan="2">Chicago</td>
      <td>$20.09m</td>
    </tr>
    <!-- Row 4 -->
    <tr>
      <td colspan="2">Cleveland</td>
      <td>$12.24m</td>
    </tr>
    <!-- Row 5 -->
    <tr>
      <td colspan="2">Minneapolis</td>
      <td>$3.53m</td>
    </tr>
    <!-- Row 6 -->
    <tr>
      <td>East</td>
      <td>42%</td>
      <td>$135.24m</td>
    </tr>
    <!-- Row 7 -->
    <tr><td colspan="3">Top 3</td></tr>
    <!-- Row 8 -->
    <tr>
      <td rowspan="3" colspan="2">???</td>
      <td>$34.52m</td>
    </tr>
    <!-- Row 9 -->
```

```
    <tr><td>$23.09m</td></tr>
    <!-- Row 10 -->
    <tr><td>$12.64m</td></tr>
    <!-- Row 11 -->
    <tr>
      <td>South</td>
      <td>27%</td>
      <td>$86.94m</td>
    </tr>
    <!-- Row 12 -->
    <tr>
      <td>West</td>
      <td>19%</td>
      <td>$61.18m</td>
    </tr>
  </table>
</body>
</html>
```

The second and seventh row (the ones with "Top 3" text) specify `colspan="3"`, so the cell occupies the full row. The first cells of the third, fourth and fifth row use `colspan="2"` (each row specifies a second cell, too), and so the first cells takes up the space of the second column as well.

The eighth row specifies `rowspan="3"` and `colspan="2"`, so the cell with "???" text spans three rows (the eighth, ninth, and tenth rows), and two columns. According to this definition, the eighth row has one more cell beside "???", but the ninth and tenth rows have only one cell, as their first two columns are taken by the spanning "???" cell.

Markup for Table Headers

Most tables have headers (either columns or rows, sometimes both). HTML table definitions allow you to specify cells as headers with the `<th>` tag. A `<th>` tag can be used exactly as the `<td>` tag, so it can use the `colspan` and `rowspan` attributes as well. Listing 3-12 demonstrates tables with header cells.

Listing 3-12: Exercise-03-13/index.html

```
<!DOCTYPE html>
<html>
<head>
  <title>Header Cells</title>
</head>
<body>
  <table border="1">
    <tr>
      <th>Category</th>
      <th>Points</th>
    </tr>
    <tr>
      <td>Gold</td>
```

```
      <td>15000</td>
    </tr>
    <tr>
      <td>Silver</td>
      <td>8000</td>
    </tr>
    <tr>
      <td>Bronze</td>
      <td>3000</td>
    </tr>
  </table>
</body>
</html>
```

Table headers are displayed in most browsers with boldfaced font (Figure 3-13), and normally, this is the only visual clue that tells you they are header cells.

Category	Points
Gold	15000
Silver	8000
Bronze	3000

Figure 3-13: Table with header cells

NOTE: Of course, with styling you can make more visual distinction between headers and normal cells, as you will learn later in this chapter.

You can use header cells not only in the first row, but actually in any rows. Listing 3-13 demonstrates this fact. It defines a table that describes the behavior of the logical XOR (logical eXclusive OR) operation, and defines two row and two column header cells. The rendered markup is shown in Figure 3-14.

Listing 3-13: Exercise-03-14/index.html

```
<!DOCTYPE html>
<html>
<head>
  <title>Header Cells</title>
</head>
<body>
  <table border="1">
    <tr>
      <td>XOR</td>
      <th>false</th>
      <th>true</th>
    </tr>
    <tr>
      <th>false</th>
      <td>false</td>
```

111

```
      <td>true</td>
    </tr>
    <tr>
      <th>true</th>
      <td>true</td>
      <td>false</td>
    </tr>
  </table>
</body>
</html>
```

XOR	false	true
false	false	true
true	true	false

Figure 3-14: Table with multiple header cells

In this chapter, you already learned that HTML5 provides new semantic elements for page structure (such as `<aside>`, `<footer>`, etc.) and for text (such as `<time>`, `<mark>`, etc.). Tables have new attributes in HTML5 just for the sake of additional semantics.

If you use multiple header cells, attributes assigned to `<th>` can provide more semantic value, which could be leveraged by browser extensions, such as screen readers. Listing 3-14 extends Listing 3-13 with new header cells, and demonstrate the extra semantic offered by the `headers` and `scope` attributes of `<th>`.

Listing 3-14: Exercise-03-14/index.html

```
<!DOCTYPE html>
<html>
<head>
  <title>Header Cells</title>
</head>
<body>
  <table border="1">
    <tr>
      <td rowspan="2" colspan="2">XOR</td>
      <th id="input" colspan="2">Input</th>
    </tr>
    <tr>
      <th headers="input" scope="col">false</th>
      <th headers="input" scope="col">true</th>
    </tr>
    <tr>
      <th id="output" rowspan="2">Output</th>
      <th headers="output" scope="row">false</th>
      <td>false</td>
      <td>true</td>
    </tr>
```

```
    <tr>
      <th headers="output" scope="row">true</th>
      <td>true</td>
      <td>false</td>
    </tr>
  </table>
</body>
</html>
```

Take a look at Figure 3-15 which shows how the markup in Listing 3-14 is rendered. Just as most of the semantic elements do not provide any visual properties in regard to the extra semantic meaning, you cannot see any additional clue that would describe new semantics. Well, those are invisible for human readers, but not for browser plug-ins accessing the page structure.

XOR		Input	
		false	**true**
Output	**false**	false	true
	true	true	false

Figure 3-15: Table with extra semantic

The first row's `<th>` tag has an id attribute with the value of "input". This cell not only visually nests the "false" and "true" cells directly beneath it in Figure 3-15, but as the second row's definition shows, those cells are semantically connected to the "input" `<th>` tag through their `headers="input"` attribute:

```
    <tr>
      <th headers="input" scope="col">false</th>
      <th headers="input" scope="col">true</th>
    </tr>
```

Both tags' `scope` attributes are set to "col", and this setting tells that the corresponding `<th>` cells are headers for a column.

The similar relationship is built up for the "Output" cell and its related "false" and "true" cells, using the "output" id value. As their `scope="row"` settings tell, these cells are headers for rows.

Defining Styles for Tables

NOTE: This book dedicates several chapter to styling with CSS, but here you will learn a few details in advance.

HTML markups prior HTML5 defined dozens of attributes for table related tags that were responsible for setting up the visual properties of tabular data. For example, the `<table>` tag had attributes, such as `align`, `bgcolor` (background color), `cellpadding` (space between the cell wall and the cell content), `cellspacing` (space between cells), `summary`, `width` to let designers style the visual appearance. Other tags had their own styling attributes, too.

HTML5 got rid of these attributes, and allows setting up table appearance only through styles. So, when you need to apply table styles, use CSS style sheets. Let's assume, you would like to add styles to the table defined in Listing 3-14, so that it is rendered, as shown in Figure 3-16. One possible solution is the set of style rules in this code snippet:

```
<style>
  body {
      font-family: Tahoma, Arial, sans-serif;
  }

  table {
    background-color: aliceblue;
    border: 4px solid dimgray;
    border-collapse: collapse;
  }

  td, th {
    padding: 4px 8px;
    text-align: center;
    border: 2px solid dimgray;
  }

  th {
    font-weight: normal;
    background-color: cornflowerblue;
    color: white;
  }

  td {
    color: dimgray;
    font-weight: bold;
  }

  .origin {
    background-color: navy;
    color: lightgoldenrodyellow
  }
</style>
```

Without going into details about CSS, here are a few things to understand how styling works:

When a part of your HTML document is rendered, the browser applies the visual properties of the element being rendered. By default, each element has a default style (a set of visual properties) that can be modified by a style associated with that element, and with the `style` attribute. Certain visual properties are inherited by nested elements.

The style sheet in the code snippet above does the following things:

1. The `body` rule sets the default font face of the entire page to Tahoma, or Arial provided Tahoma is not found, or to the default san-serif font, if neither font is available. The `font-family` property is inherited in every nested element of `<body>`, so it will be the font of all elements, unless one of them overrides this setting.

2. The `table` rule sets up the background color of the table and applies a thick border with solid line around it. The `border-collapse` property is set so that the table borders are collapsed into a single border.

3. There are two rules defined for table cells (`td`), the first is related to `<th>` tags as well, the second applies to `<td>` only. Both rules are applied to table cells, so each `<td>` cell has a light background and boldfaced font.

4. Similarly to `<td>` there are two rules applied for `<th>`, and as a result, header cells have a darker background with light text color.

5. The field containing "XOR" is marked with the `class="origin"` attribute, so both the `td` (this cell is a normal cell) and the `.origin` rule is applied. So, this cell gains a dark background and a yellowish text color.

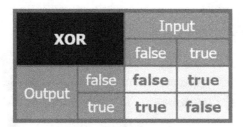

Figure 3-16: Table with styles

With CSS, you can easily define alternating row colors for a table, as shown in Listing 3-15.

NOTE: You can find the completed sample in the `Exercise-03-16` folder.

Listing 3-15: Exercise-03-17/index.html

```
<!DOCTYPE html>
<html>
<head>
  <title>Alternating Table Rows</title>
  <style>
    body {
      font-family: Verdana, Arial, sans-serif;
    }

    table {
      border-collapse: collapse;
    }

    td, th {
      padding: 4px 8px;
      border: 1px solid dimgray;
    }
```

```
    th {
       font-weight: normal;
       background-color: navy;
       color: white;
    }

    tr:nth-child(odd) {
       background-color: lightblue;
    }

  </style>
</head>
<body>
  <table>
    <tr><th>Region</th><th>Result</th></tr>
    <tr><td>North</td><td>12%</td></tr>
    <tr><td>East</td><td>42%</td></tr>
    <tr><td>South</td><td>27%</td></tr>
    <tr><td>West</td><td>19%</td></tr>
  </table>
</body>
</html>
```

The `tr:nth-child(odd)` rule is applied for all table rows with odd row index (1, 3, and 5 in this case). The first row has `<th>` elements, so the `th` rules override the style of cells set by `tr`. The result of this markup is shown in Figure 3-17.

Region	Result
North	12%
East	42%
South	27%
West	19%

Figure 3-17: Setting up alternating table rows

In HTML, the table structure is built up from rows (`<tr>`) nesting cells (`<td>` or `<th>`), so it's a bit more difficult to set up alternating columns. One solution is that you assign a different `class` attribute for each cell in alternating columns, but it adds a lot of extra markup, and so it's pretty error-prone.

To cope with this situation, HTML defines two tags, `<colgroup>` and `<col>` that can be used as shown in Listing 3-16.

Listing 3-16: Exercise-03-18/index.html

```
<!DOCTYPE html>
<html>
<head>
  <title>Alternating Table Columns</title>
  <style>
    body {
      font-family: Verdana, Arial, sans-serif;
    }

    table {
      border-collapse: collapse;
    }

    td, th {
      padding: 4px 8px;
      border: 1px solid dimgray;
    }

    th {
      font-weight: normal;
      background-color: navy;
      color: white;
    }

    .result {
      background-color: lightblue;
    }

  </style>
</head>
<body>
  <table>
    <colgroup>
      <col span="2">
      <col class="result">
    </colgroup>
    <tr>
      <th>Region</th><th>Code</th>
      <th>Result</th>
    </tr>
    <tr>
      <td>North</td><td>N</td>
      <td>12%</td>
    </tr>
    <tr>
      <td>East</td><td>E</td>
      <td>42%</td>
    </tr>
    <tr>
      <td>South</td><td>S</td>
```

```
      <td>27%</td>
    </tr>
    <tr>
      <td>West</td><td>W</td>
      <td>19%</td>
    </tr>
  </table>
</body>
</html>
```

This markup creates a table with three columns. The `<colgroup>` tag is a container that holds `<col>` tags. Each `<col>` defines the visual properties of a single column, or a span of columns. In Listing 3-16, the following definition is used:

```
<colgroup>
  <col span="2">
  <col class="result">
</colgroup>
```

The first `<col>` tag defines the style for the first two columns, because the span attribute is set to 2. This element does not have any attribute, and it means that the first column should be displayed with their calculated style, without any deviation. The second `<col>` is applied for the third column, and it says that the `.result` rule should be applied. This rule declares that the background color of this column should be light blue, and it is set so, as shown in Figure 3-18.

Region	Code	Result
North	N	12%
East	E	42%
South	S	27%
West	W	19%

Figure 3-18: Using `<colgroup>` and `<col>`

NOTE: The visual properties of `<col>` are applied only to the table cells, but not the cells' content. So, you cannot set text properties such as color, alignment, etc. through `<col>`.

Table Captions

With the help of the `<caption>` tag, you can easily add titles to your tables, as shown in Listing 3-17.

Listing 3-17: Exercise-03-19/index.html

```html
<!DOCTYPE html>
<html>
<head>
  <title>Simple Table (no styling)</title>
  <style>
    <!-- Omitted for the sake of brevity -->
  </style>
</head>
<body>
  <table>
    <caption>
      Monthly Sales<br/>(March, 2013)
    </caption>
    <tr>
      <td>Office #1942</td><td>12%</td>
    </tr>
    <tr>
      <td>Office #2612</td><td>42%</td>
    </tr>
    <tr>
      <td>Office #3125</td><td>27%</td>
    </tr>
  </table>
</body>
</html>
```

The caption of the table is displayed above the table—independently where you put the `<caption>` tag within `<table>`—, as shown in Figure 3-19.

Figure 3-19: This table has a caption

By now, you have learned all basic information about setting up and styling simple tables. It's time to build compound tables.

Compound tables

The HTML5 markup defines additional elements for describing tables. These are `<thead>`, `<tbody>`, `<tfoot>`, and they are containers for rows describing table header, table body and table footer, respectively. The easiest way to understand them is to take a look at a sample. So, examine Listing 3-18; it describes a table using these elements.

Listing 3-18: Exercise-03-20/index.html

```
<!DOCTYPE html>
<html>
<head>
  <title>Table with header and footer</title>
  <style>
    body {
        font-family: Verdana, Arial, sans-serif;
    }
    table {
      border-collapse: collapse;
    }
    th, td {
      padding: 4px 8px;
      border: 1px solid dimgray;
    }
    th, tfoot td {
      background-color: navy;
      color: white;
      text-align: left;
    }
    tr:nth-child(odd) {
      background-color: lightblue;
    }
  </style>
</head>
<body>
  <table>
    <thead>
      <tr><th>Office</th><th>Result</th></tr>
    </thead>
    <tbody>
      <tr><td>North</td><td>3.28</td></tr>
      <tr><td>East</td><td>11.23</td></tr>
      <tr><td>South</td><td>6.37</td></tr>
      <tr><td>West</td><td>10.51</td></tr>
    </tbody>
    <tfoot>
      <tr><th>Sum</th><th>3139</th></tr>
    </tfoot>
  </table>
</body>
</html>
```

As you can see, this definition separates the table rows (`<tr>` elements) that constitute the header, body, and footer of the table. They work as simple containers for rows, and they provide hooks for styling. When you display this page in the browser, you can definitely distinguish the sections of the table, as shown in Figure 3-20.

Office	Result
North	3.28
East	11.23
South	6.37
West	10.51
Sum	**31.39**

Figure 3-20: A table using `<thead>`, `<tbody>`, and `<tfoot>`

Frankly, you do not need these new tags to provide this appearance—you can set up styles that provide the same results. However, using these semantic containers, you can provide enhanced behavior to your tables, as you will learn in the next exercise.

EXERCISE 3-21: Scrolling the table body

To save time, you will start from a prepared project that can be found in the `Exercise-03-21-Begin` folder within the book's source code.

To understand the new features provided by the `<thead>`, `<tbody>`, and `<tfoot>` tags, follow these steps:

1. Open the `index.html` file (that can be found in the project folder). It contains a table definition with empty `<tbody>` and `<tfoot>` sections:

```
<table>
  <thead>
    <tr><th>Operation</th><th>Result</th></tr>
  </thead>
  <tbody>
    <!-- Filled up by JavaScript -->
  </tbody>
  <tfoot>
    <!-- Filled up by JavaScript -->
  </tfoot>
</table>
```

These sections are filled up with 100 rows in the table body, using the following jQuery script:

```
$(function () {
  var sum = 0;
  for (var i = 0; i < 100; i++) {
    var a = Math.floor(100 * Math.random());
```

```
    var b = Math.floor(100 * Math.random());
    var row = $("<tr>")
      .append($("<td>").html(a + " + " + b + " ="))
      .append($("<td>").html(a + b));
    sum += a + b;
    $("tbody").append(row);
  }
  var sumRow = $("<tr>")
    .append($("<td>").html("Sum:"))
    .append($("<td>").html(sum));
  $("tfoot").append(sumRow);
});
```

2. Display the page in the browser; it displays a long table. Use the Print Preview command of your browser, and you can observe that the page will take more than one printed page. As you browse among the previewed pages, you can see that the table header and the table footer is printed on each page, as shown in Figure 3-21.

3. Close the browser, and switch back to the IDE. Add the following style rules to the `<style>` section of `index.html`:

```
thead, tfoot, tbody {
  display: block;
}

tbody {
  height: 280px;
  overflow-y: scroll;
}
```

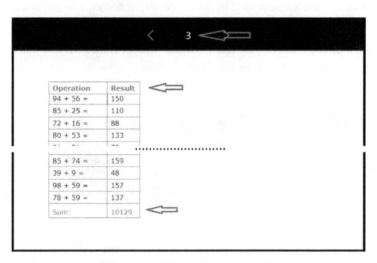

Figure 3-21: The print preview of the table

4. Save `index.html`, and run the app again. The list is as long as before, but this time the visible part of the table body is shorter, and it can be scrolled, as shown in Figure 3-22.

NOTE: Unfortunately, Google Chrome does not support putting table headers and footers automatically on each printed page. I created the figure with Microsoft Edge.

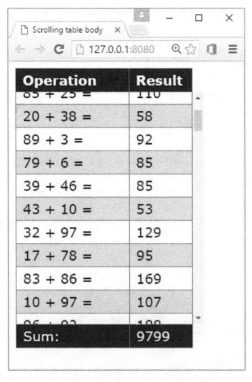

Figure 3-22: The table body can be scrolled

HOW IT WORKS

The JavaScript shown is step 2 creates 100 rows in a loop. It generates two random numbers, and adds a new table row with two columns, one with the definition of adding the two random numbers, and another one with the result, respectively. The loop also sums up the results, and at the end it adds a new summary row to the table footer. The script is bound to the event when the page is loaded, so the first time the page is shown, it already contains the randomly generated rows.

Microsoft Edge not only understands the semantics of <thead>, <tbody>, and <tfoot>, but also utilizes it when printing a page. That is why in step 3 you saw the header and the footer of the table in each page.

The style sheet snippet you added in step 4 set a fixed height for the <tbody> section, and the overflow-y property's scroll value instructed the browser to provide a vertical scrollbar so that the hidden part of the table body could be revealed by scrolling.

Using Multimedia

It's amazing how many audio, video and other means of multimedia can be found in most web pages. In social networks people communicate through photos and short videos more and more often than with traditional text messages. Even if they use text such sites are regularly adorned with funny—or sometimes brutal—pictures and video.

Old Style: Pain with Plethora of Browsers and Plug-ins

Although from users' point of view multimedia has been being a part of the web experience for a long time, from developers' angle it was one of the most annoying part of web page creation. To add video or audio to web pages, they had to use the HTML `<embed>` tag (a container for an external application, interactive content—through a browser plug-in), and the `<object>` tag (a container for an embedded object within an HTML document).

For example, Listing 3-19 inserts a Windows MediaPlayer video through an ActiveX component (plug-in) into the page.

Listing 3-19: Inserting video with `<object>` and `<embed>`—old school

```
<html>
<head>
  <title>Old style video</title>
</head>
<body>
  <h1>My Video</h1>
  <object id="MediaPlayer"
    width="394"
    height="360"
    classid="CLSID:22D6F312-B0F6-11D0-94AB-0080C74C7E95"
    standby="Loading Windows Media Player components..."
    type="application/x-oleobject">
    <param name="FileName" value="MyVideo.wmv">
    <param name="autostart" value="false">
    <param name="ShowControls" value="true">
    <param name="ShowStatusBar" value="false">
    <param name="ShowDisplay" value="false">
    <embed type="application/x-mplayer2"
      src="MyVideo.wmv"
      name="MediaPlayer"
      width="394" height="360"
      showcontrols="1"
      showstatusbar="0"
      showdisplay="0"
      autostart="0">
    </embed>
  </object>
</body>
</html>
```

This markup is not only weird, but also a playground for creating inconsistency. As you see, almost all parameters above (for example, width, height, file name, etc.) are written in two locations, too, in `<object>` and in `<embed>`.

NOTE: Do not expect Listing 3-19 to play any video, it is just for demonstration purposes.

There are many plug-ins for playing video in today's browsers, the widest-spread is Flash Player that supports many browsers, and provides a granular control over the way playback works. Other plug-ins (such as Microsoft's Silverlight Player) are not so easy-to-use with majority of browsers.

New Style: The <iframe> tag

Fortunately, the verbose markup in chaos with `<embed>` and `<object>` has been altered with a new HTML tag, `<iframe>` that specifies an inline frame within the current HTML document. Many online services, including video are available through web pages, so the `<iframe>` tag is a perfect solution to embed video into your document—assuming it comes from a remote source (from a site providing a video service). For example, the markup in Listing 3-20 plays a YouTube video.

Listing 3-20: Exercise-03-22/index.html

```
<!DOCTYPE html>
<html>
<head>
  <title>Playing Video with &lt;iframe&gt;</title>
</head>
<body>
  <h1>Walking in the Air</h1>
  <iframe width="640"
    height="360"
    src="http://www.youtube.com/embed/VOQNgUtJkKs"
    frameborder="0"
    allowfullscreen>
  </iframe>
</body>
</html>
```

Compared to Listing 3-19, this markup is not only more concise, but also easier to understand.

New HTML5 markup

HTML5 introduces new HTML tags, `<audio>` and `<video>`, to add audio and video support to your web pages, respectively. The aim of these tags is to provide that audio and video can be the part of an HTML5 web page with the same easiness as you add pictures with the `<img>` tag.

Using the <video> Tag

In the next exercise, you will learn using the `<video>` tag.

EXERCISE 3-23: Using the <video> tag

To save time, you will start from a prepared project that can be found in the `Exercise-03-23-Begin` folder within the book's source code.

To learn adding video to an HTML5 web page, follow these steps:

1. Open the `index.html` file. You will find a placeholder comment there to insert a video. Type the following markup right beneath the comment:

```
<video src="Video/Caribbean.mp4" controls autoplay>
</video>
```

After typing, the <body> section should look like this:

```
<body>
  <h1>Snorkeling in the Caribbean</h1>
  <p>
    Hey dude, In 2010 I cruised around a few great
    Caribbean islands. Here is a short video about
    my snorkeling experience.
  </p>
  <!-- Place the video here -->
  <video src="Video/Caribbean.mp4" controls autoplay>
  </video>
</body>
```

2. Display the page in the browser. When the web page is displayed, the video starts playing, as shown in Figure 3-23.

HOW IT WORKS

The `<video>` tag instructs the browser to display a video player in the page's window. The `src` attribute defines the source of the video, which is an MP4 (H.264 encoded video) file in this exercise. The `controls` attribute specifies that video controls—such as the play/pause button, the volume control, etc.—should be displayed. The `autoplay` attribute instructs the browser to start playing the video as soon as the page is loaded.

Beside the `src`, `controls`, and `autoplay` attributes, `<video>` provides a few others. The default size of the video player is aligned to the size of the source, but with the `width` and `height` attributes you can specify a custom size. The `poster` attribute allows specifying the image to be shown while the video is downloading, or until the user hits the play button. You can tell the player that your video should be `muted`; and with using `loop`, you can tell that the video should start over again, every time it's finished.

Snorkeling in the Caribbean

Hey dude, In 2010 I cruised around a few great Caribbean islands. Here is a short video about my snorkeling experience.

Figure 3-23: Using the `<video>` *tag in a web page.*

Video Formats

Although the early versions of the HTML5 recommendations suggested several specific video and audio formats that every browser should support, the standard does not require any specific format. It means that browsers are free to choose the supported video and audio formats. Supporting a certain video format actually means accommodating to three standards: the *video codec*, which is responsible for decoding the compressed video into a stream of data; the *audio codec*, which is expected to decode one of the audio tracks (a video can have more than one audio track); and the *container format*, which assembles the video, audio, and other descriptive information—such as still images and subtitles—into a single video file.

By the time of writing this book, there are three wide-spread standards used with HTML5-compliant browsers, but of course the list of them will definitely change as time passes on.

H.264 is an industry standard for video encoding (generally used for high-definition video). Most consumer devices, such as camcorders, mobile phones, and Blu-ray players support it, and it is popular in video sharing websites (like YouTube and Vimeo). This is what most users know as MP4 files, because the default file extension of this kind of video is `.mp4`, and they use the `video/mp4` MIME type.

Ogg Theora is a free, open standard for video, and although its quality and performance is not as good as H.264, this standard still satisfies most users. When you see the `.ogv` file extension, it means an Ogg Theora format, which has the `video/ogg` MIME type.

There is a new video format, *WebM* (Google purchased VP8 and transformed it into a free standard). It was designed to provide royalty-free, open video compression for use with HTML5 video. When you meet videos with the `video/webm` MIME type, or with the `.webm` file extension, you see examples of this new standard.

When you add video to your pages, you have to cope with the fact that different browsers support different formats. HTML5 provides workaround to resolve most of this issues with the help of the `<source>` tag, as you will learn in the next exercise.

EXERCISE 3-24: Supporting multiple video formats

To save time, you will start from the same prepared Visual Studio project as in the previous exercise (Exercise 3-2).

To learn new features of the `<video>` tag, follow these steps:

1. Copy the `Exercise-03-23-Begin` folder into Exercise-03-24, and work with the files in the new folder.

2. Open the `index.html` file. Add the highlighted `<video>` code snippet to the file:

```
<body>
  <h1>Snorkeling in the Caribbean</h1>
  <p>...</p>
  <!-- Place the video here -->
  <video controls
      poster="Images/VideoPoster.png">
      <source src="Video/Caribbean.webm" type="video/webm" />
    </video>
</body>
```

3. Display the page in Chrome. When the app starts, and shows you the image you set in the poster attribute, unless you click the play button, then it plays the video.

4. Open Internet Explorer, and display the page (use the `http://127.0.0.1:8080` URL). Internet Explorer does not support the WebM format, so it will display an error message, as shown in Figure 3-24.

5. Close the browser, and go back to the editor to change the `index.html` file. Add the following highlighted `<source>` tag right after the previous one:

```
<video controls
  poster="Images/VideoPoster.png">
  <source src="Video/Caribbean.webm" type="video/webm" />
  <source src="Video/Caribbean.mp4" type="video/mp4" />
</video>
```

6. Add the highlighted text right before the closing `</video>` element:

```
<video controls
  poster="Images/VideoPoster.png">
  <source src="Video/Caribbean.webm" type="video/webm" />
  <source src="Video/Caribbean.mp4" type="video/mp4" />
    Sorry, HTML5 video is not supported.
</video>
```

Figure 3-24: Internet Explorer cannot play the video file, but it still shows the poster.

7. Display the page again (using Internet Explorer, just like in step 4). When you click the play button, the video starts playing.

8. Click the Compatibility View icon in the address bar (or press Alt, and then choose Tools|Compatibility View). Add the 127.0.0.1 sites to the Compatibility View list. Internet Explorer goes into the compatibility view mode, in which it does not support HTML5 video. Instead of a video player, you'll see the text you inserted in step 7 (Figure 3-25).

Figure 3-25: Fallback, when HTML5 video is not available

HOW IT WORKS

In step 2, you used the `<source>` tag (instead of the `src` attribute of `<video>`) to specify the stream to play:

```
<video controls
    poster="Images/VideoPoster.png">
    <source src="Video/Caribbean.webm" type="video/webm" />
</video>
```

With Google Chrome (in step 3), the video played seamlessly, because Chrome supports WebM out-of-box, so it was able to play the `.webm` file. However, Internet Explorer does not support WebM (at least, not by the time of this writing), so it displayed an error message in step 4 (with the specified poster image).

When you added another source tag in step 5, the situation changed:

```
<video controls >
  <source src="Video/Caribbean.webm" type="video/webm" />
  <source src="Video/Caribbean.mp4" type="video/mp4" />
</video>
```

Internet Explorer could not play the video stream available at the first source (since that was WebM), but the second source was MP4, supported by IE, so that worked.

In step 8 you turned on the compatibility view of IE. In this view `<video>` is unsupported, so the browser renders the markup within `<video>`, which is a simple text telling that HTML5 video is not supported.

Video Resilient Web Pages

If your web browser does not support the `<video>` tag, you can fall back to the old style of embedding video:

```
<video controls >
  <source src="Video/Caribbean.webm" type="video/webm" />
  <source src="Video/Caribbean.mp4" type="video/mp4" />
  <embed>
    <!-- Old style markup for playing video -->
  </embed>
</video>
```

In the body of `<video>`, simply add the `<embed>`, `<object>`, or `<iframe>` markups to provide the non-HTML5 video.

Using the <audio> Tag

The `<audio>` tag is as simple to use as `<video>`, it follows the same pattern. The following code snippet (you can find it in the book's downloaded source code, within the `Exercise-03-25` folder):

```
<body>
  <h1>Hey dude, listen to one of my favorite ringtones!</h1>
  <audio controls>
    <source src="Audio/Good%20News.mp3" type="audio/mpeg" />
  </audio>
</body>
```

Similarly to `<video>`, the audio player is displayed in the web page, as shown in Figure 3-26.

Hey dude, listen to one of my favorite ringtones!

Figure 3-26: The audio player is displayed in the browser

You can use the `src`, `controls`, `autoplay`, `muted`, and `loop` attributes similarly to `<video>`, but `<audio>` does not have `height`, `width`, and `poster` attributes.

Similar to video, there are several audio formats. The most frequently used ones are these (of course the list is going to be longer, as new formats emerge and are being supported by browsers):

MP3 is the world's most popular audio format; it is supported by almost every browser. You can recognize this format from the `.mp3` file extension of `audio/mp3` MIME type.

The *WAV* format is the original raw format for digital audio. Unfortunately, it does not support compression, so it unsuitable for most websites—because of suboptimal (big) audio stream size. This content can be recognized from the `.wav` file extension or the `audio/wav` MIME type.

Ogg Vorbis is a free, open standard that provides high-quality audio comparable to MP3. This format supports compression, and is very popular among web site producers. When you meet with the `.ogg` file extension or `audio/ogg` MIME type, it means this standard is used.

Using <track>

HTML5 defines a new element in regard to audio and video playback. This is `<track>`, and it is used to specify subtitles, caption files or other files containing text, that should be visible when the media is playing. For example, when you have a `<video>` tag, and you would like to select between English and Hungarian subtitles, the highlighted `<track>` tags will express this intention:

```
<video>
  <!-- Source tags omitted-->
  <track src="subtitlesEn.vtt" kind="subtitles"
    srclang="en" label="English">
  <track src="subtitlesHu.vtt" kind="subtitles"
    srclang="hu" label="Hungarian">
</video>
```

The `src` attribute of `<track>` specifies the text stream, `srclang` tells the language of the text. You can define the `kind` of text track, which can be any of the followings: `captions` (translation for dialogue and sound effects suitable for deaf users), `chapters` (chapter titles suitable for navigation), `descriptions` (textual description for blind users, synthetized audio), `metadata` (invisible content used by scripts), `subtitles` (displays subtitles in video).

When `subtitles` is set for `kind`, `srclang` is required.

What You Cannot Do with <video> and <audio>

The <video> and <audio> HTML5 elements provide great solution to add multimedia to your websites when the stream is available in one of the native formats supported by the majority of browsers. However, there are situations—and most of them are very common—when you cannot use these tags:

HTML5 does not support audio or video capturing, or recording. So, you do not have HTML5 native tools to stream audio or video content from one computer (or device) to another. If you want to build web pages that use the microphone or camera, you need additional technology (most of them use JavaScript).

Most online video websites provide you adaptive streaming with different video resolution, buffering, live events, and many more; and they adjust the video quality to the available bandwidth. Well, today HTML5 does not provide these features.

Do not forget, that HTML5 does not deliver any sort of copyright protection system. So if a video or audio is available for playing with the <video> or <audio> tags, respectively, they can be simply downloaded to the users' devices.

In any case you find that HTML5 does not support a video or audio feature you need, you have to fall back to other technologies.

Summary

HTML5 provides new semantic elements that help you to structure your web pages in a more readable and maintainable way—due to the extra semantic they add to the corresponding context. They also add hooks for styling, and support search engines that may retrieve better-ranked results to you.

Tables have been the part of the HTML markup for a long time. Although the old-school of web design primarily used them as a way to establish page layout, HTML5 suggests to use them only for the aim they best serve: to display tabular data. With table-related markup elements you can easily render tabular data, even complex reports with headers, footers, and details sections.

With the <video> and <audio> elements, HTML5 enables you to add multimedia to your web pages with the same simplicity as you use the <img> element for displaying pictures. The new markup helps you manage multiple streaming formats, and so support a plethora of browsers, but there are still scenarios when you need to switch back to traditional technologies for multimedia playback.

Chapter 4:
Forms and Controls

WHAT YOU WILL LEARN IN THIS CHAPTER

Understanding the concept of web forms

Getting to know the fundamental input controls

Sending form data from the client to the server

Validating form data on the client side

Web Forms Basics

Web pages are not just about reading documents and articles, but are also for social and business applications. You can hardly imagine any kind of web app without asking some data from users—just think about the most common functions, such as login and registration.

HTML forms are the part of the markup since the earliest versions, and now, after several twists—that are related to HTML-XHTML debates—we have a refined model of forms in HTML5, which still works with older browsers.

How Web Forms Work

Figure 4-1 shows a web form in action, which contains user interface components—or, with another name, controls. Not only textboxes, checkboxes and radio buttons are controls in this form, but labels, and frames surrounding the sections, too, as well as the Register button.

To design and code web forms, you need to understand how they work. Here is a simplified overview:

When the browser displays a web form, it simply renders its controls just like any other element, such as text, menus, images, and so on. Users fill it out, and then click a button that submits the form. The submission of a form means that the browser collects the data entered by the user, puts it into an HTTP/HTTPS request, and sends it to the server. When the server side receives the request, the web server finds out the type of application or module to dispatch the request with the collected data. The entity receiving the request analyzes the information collected, and decides what to do next.

Figure 4-1: A web form in action

For example, if the request contains registration data, the web server may store it in the database and send back a message about the success of registration. Or, if the data is invalid, for example a mandatory field has not been filled out, the webserver might send back the original form with the data specified by the user, and with additional markup that summarizes the issues found by the server application.

So, this process contains these fundamental steps:

1. The browser collects the form data, and sends it to the web server.

2. The web server processes the data, and sends back the result to the browser.

3. The browser visualizes the result (which may be a web page, an error message, or some other kind of information, etc.)

Of course, the most difficult part of this process is step 2, which is carried out at the server side. There are many server technologies that can process web forms, but in this book we do not dive into them, we will only scratch the surface.

As the web evolved, and users expected fluent experience, new asynchronous technologies appeared, such as AJAX (Asynchronous JavaScript and XML). These do not expect the web server to retrieve a full web page, but only a part of the page—affected by the changes in regard to the information the users specified. This approach results in smaller network packages, and less flickering on the screen. The main virtue of the asynchronous technologies is that they can send data to—and retrieve data from—a server asynchronously in the background, without preventing user interaction.

In this chapter you will focus on building and using web forms at the client side.

Representing Web Forms in HTML

The key HTML element is `<form>` that defines a web form within a page. The simplest web form takes only a few lines of markup:

```
<form action="ProcessAtServer.html">
  <input type="submit" value="Do it!"/>
</form>
```

This `<form>` contains a single `<input>` tag that is decorated with the **type="submit"** attribute, and it represents a submit button. The action property of `<form>` is set to **ProcessAtServer.htlm**, so when the user clicks the submit button, the content of the form will be sent to that page. Of course, as shown in Figure 4-2, this form does not have any other useful element, so actually there is no information to send to the action page.

Figure 4-2: A very simple and useless web form

So, let's create a form with a few real input fields:

```
<form action="#">
  <input name="fname" />
  <br />
  <input name="lname" />
```

135

```
    <br />
    <input type="submit" value="Do it!"/>
</form>
```

This markup contains two input fields, having the names fname (first name) and lname (last name), respectively. Their corresponding <input> tags are not decorated with the type attribute, so these fields will be rendered as text boxes. The action attribute of the form is set to #, which will send the form data to the page itself.

Let's assume, you've put this code into the form.html file. When you display it in the browser, you can type data into the text boxes, as shown in Figure 4-3.

Figure 4-3: A simple form with two input fields

When you click the submit button, the form sends the data to the form.html file through a web request. The page is displayed again, with empty input fields. Only the address bar of your browser tells you that the page is displayed as a result of web request from the form, its URL is something like this:

http://127.0.0.1:8080/?fname=John&lname=Smith#

In the URL you can see the form data as ?fname=John&lname=Smith, indicating that this information was passed through the URL.

Controls Overview

In these small markup snippets above you've already seen a few controls, such as the textbox and the submit button, but there are much more. You will learn to use them through exercises, but first you'll be given a short overview of them.

So, as you already know, <form> is the markup element that encapsulates all controls. Most controls can be rendered with the <input> element that has a type attribute. This attribute specifies the type of the control, it determines how the control is rendered in the browser, and how it behaves. If you do not specify type, the control will be a textbox (and this is the same as setting type to text). You can choose from several kind of buttons, such as button (clickable button mostly used with JavaScript), checkbox, radio (radio button), submit (submits the form), image (an image as the submit button), and reset (resets all form values to their defaults).

There are several predefined textual controls with some extra semantics, such as `password` (characters are masked), `email` (defines a field for an email address), `url` (field for entering an URL), `tel` (field for a telephone number), `search` (field for search text), and `number` (field for entering a number). The type `file` provides a file-select field with a Browse button for file uploads. You can place `hidden` fields in a form, used to set form values programmatically.

HTML5 adds a number of date and time related controls to the old markup through the `type` attribute of `<input>`: `date` (date control with year, month, day, and no time), `datetime` (date and time control with the precision of fraction of a second, based on UTC time zone), `datetime-local` (date and time control with no time zone), `month` (a month and year control), `time` (a control for entering time, no time zone), and `week` (a week and year control, not time zone).

NOTE: Using date and time related controls on your web pages means you're walking on thin ice. These controls are relatively new, and—as of this writing—in most browsers they are rendered only as text boxes, and not as nice date and time pickup controls.

HTML5 also adds two other types, `color` (color picker), and `range` (a kind of slider to choose a number in a specified range).

Beside `<input>` there are a few other HTML tags to allow specifying user data. With `<select>`, you can define a dropdown list with option values. To type in longer text, use the `<textarea>` element.

The `<fieldset>` element lets you group related controls into sections, the `<legend>` element adds a caption to a `<fieldset>` element.

Input fields do not tell anything about their role to users. You can use the `<label>` element to provide appellation to input controls. Besides adding a descriptive text, `<label>` provides a usability improvement for mouse users, because if the user clicks on the text within `<label>`, it toggles the control (for example a check box, or radio button), or moves the focus to the related input field.

Used with the `button`, `submit` or `reset` types, `<input>` elements are rendered as pushbuttons. With the `<button>` element you can create clickable buttons with the same behavior, but you can create compound button content instead of a simple text.

Well, the enumeration of controls seems very long—too long to recall by heart—, so in the next section you are going to build web forms that help you to understand how they work, and in which scenarios they are useful.

Using Controls to Build Web Forms

Figure 4-1 showed you a web form with several controls, and provided a great territory to drill building web forms. Let's start with a simple exercise that creates text fields.

EXERCISE 4-1: Creating a form with textual controls

To save time, you will start from a prepared Visual Studio project that can be found in the `Exercise-04-01-Begin` folder within this chapter's source code download.

To prepare a compound web form, follow these steps:

1. Open the `index.html` file in the code editor. It contains an empty body, and refers the `style.css` file:

```
<!DOCTYPE html>
<html>
<head>
  <title>Conference Registration</title>
  <link href="style.css" rel="stylesheet" />
</head>
<body>
  <h2>
    Fill in this form to register to Visual Studio
    Smarts Conference
  </h2>
  <!-- This is where to put form -->
</body>
</html>
```

2. Add the following form definition to the markup to replace the placeholder comment:

```
<form action="#">
  <fieldset>
    <legend>Personal Data</legend>
    <label for="fname">First Name:</label>
    <input id="fname" type="text" name="fname" />
    <br />
    <label for="lname">Last Name:</label>
    <input id="lname" type="text" name="lname" />
    <br />
    <label for="email">Email:</label>
    <input id="email" type="text" name="email" />
    <br />
  </fieldset>
  <fieldset>
    <legend>Your Conference Account</legend>
    <label for="login">Login name:</label>
    <input id="login" type="text" name="login" />
    <br />
    <label for="pwd">Password:</label>
    <input id="pwd" type="password" name="pwd" />
    <br />
    <label for="pwd2">Confirm Password:</label>
```

```
    <input id="pwd2" type="password" name="pwd2" />
    <br />
  </fieldset>
  <input type="submit" value="Register" />
</form>
```

As you see from the markup, it adds a new form that sends the information to itself (**action** is set to "#"). The form contains two sections enclosed in two **<fieldset>** elements, respectively, and a submit button. These sections contain only textboxes, and each field has a corresponding label.

3. Start the app. When the form is displayed, click the "First Name" label. The related text box receives the focus, and the caret starts blinking there. Fill in the First Name, Last Name, Email, Login Name, Password, and Confirm Password fields. As you can see (Figure 4-4), passwords are masked.

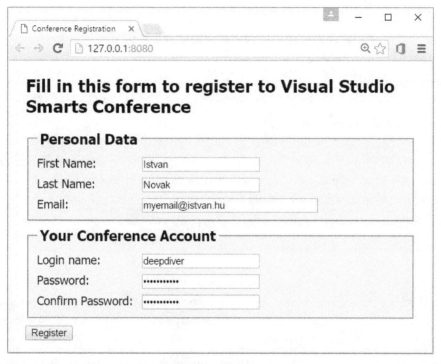

Figure 4-4: The form in action

4. Turn back to the code editor, and add the following markup between the last closing **</fieldset>** tag and the **<input>** following it:

```
<fieldset>
  <legend>Sessions</legend>
  <p>What do you expect from sessions?</p>
  <textarea id="comments" rows="3" cols="50"
    name="comments">
  </textarea>
</fieldset>
```

7. Now, the web form has a third section with a multi-line text box, as shown in Figure 4-5. Type something into this textbox, and close the browser.

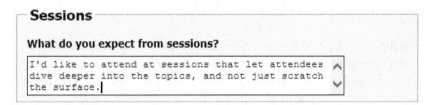

Figure 4-5: Textbox rendered by `<textarea>`

HOW IT WORKS

In this exercise you added a number of text controls to the form. The markup you inserted in step 2 contained two `<fieldset>` sections, each having its own `<legend>`. The first section had `<input>` tags with "text" type. The second one has two fields with "password" type, and that is why the related textboxes masked the text typed in.

When in step 3 you clicked the "First Name" label, the focus jumped to the next textbox, just as if you had clicked the textbox itself. This is due to the behavior of the `<label>` control:

```
<label for="fname">First Name:</label>
<input id="fname" type="text" name="fname" />
```

Here, the `for` attribute of `<label>` refers to the `id` attribute of the subsequent `<input>`, and that allows the browser to behave like this. Even if `<input>` would not be adjacent with `<label>`, the match between the identifiers would specify this behavior.

In step 4 you added a multi-line textbox with this definition:

```
<textarea id="comments" rows="3" cols="50"
  name="comments">
</textarea>
```

The `rows` and `cols` attribute set the size of this textbox so that it contains three rows and 50 characters per row. These parameters set only the display size of the field, and do not constrain the number of characters you can type in.

Each control that holds input data, has a `name` attribute with a unique value. This is crucial: when the form is sent to the `action` page, form values are sent as key and value pairs, where `name` is used as the key. If a control has no `name` attribute, its value will not be sent!

In complex web forms, you generally use not only text boxes, but also other controls that provide more intuitive input for users. In the next exercise you will extend the form to learn a few of these controls.

EXERCISE 4-2: Using controls that allow specifying options

To add new controls to the form you created in the previous exercise, follow these steps:

1. Copy the `Exercise-04-01` folder into `Exercie-04-02`, and work with this new folder. Open the `Registration.html` file, and add the `autofocus` attribute to the input field with the `fname` identifier:

```
<input id="fname" type="text" name="fname"
  autofocus />
```

2. Insert the following markup right after the "Personal Data" `<legend>`:

```
<label for="salutation">Salutation</label>
<select id="salutation" name="salutation">
  <option label="" value="" />
  <option label="Mr." value="Mr." selected />
  <option label="Mrs." value="Mrs." />
  <option label="Ms." value="Ms." />
  <option label="Dr." value="Dr." />
</select>
<br />
```

3. Run the app. When the form is displayed, the caret is automatically positioned into the First Name field. Right above this field there is a dropdown list with the item "Mr." selected, as shown in Figure 4-6.

Figure 4-6: A dropdown list added to the form

4. Turn back to the code editor, and add this markup right before the first closing `</fieldset>` tag of the "Personal Data" section:

```
<p>Your Smarts Membership status</p>
<label class="memberoption">
  <input type="radio" name="membership"
    value="none" />
  Not a member
</label>
<label class="memberoption">
  <input type="radio" name="membership"
    value="silver" />
  Silver member
</label>
<label class="memberoption">
```

```
    <input type="radio" name="membership"
      value="gold" checked />
    Gold member
  </label>
  <br />
  <a href="#">Read more about Smarts membership</a>
```

5. As a result of this markup, you can observe three membership options, with the third one checked (Figure 4-7).

Figure 4-7: Radio buttons that specify membership options

6. Insert this markup right after the `<legend>` of the last (third) `<fieldset>`:

```
<p>What are the tracks you are interested in?</p>
<label>
  <input type="checkbox" name="dev" />
  Development
</label>
<label>
  <input type="checkbox" name="alm" />
  ALM
</label>
<label>
  <input type="checkbox" name="aspnet" />
  ASP.NET
</label>
<label>
  <input type="checkbox" name="csharp" />
  C#
</label>
<label>
  <input type="checkbox" name="vb" />
  Visual Basic
</label>
<label>
  <input type="checkbox" name="sql" />
  SQL
</label>
```

7. Run the app again, and take a look at the six checkboxes in the Sessions section (Figure 4-8). Check a few of them.

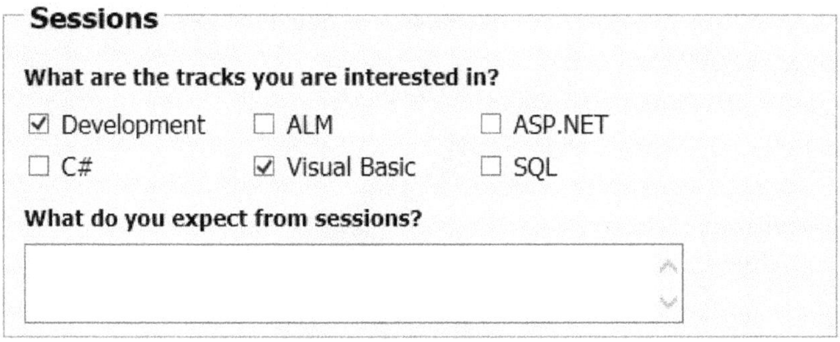

Figure 4-8: Checkboxes

8. Add the checked attribute to the markup of the first checkbox:

```
<label for="dev">
  <input id="dev" type="checkbox" name="dev" checked />
  Development
</label>
```

9. Turn back to the browser, and observe that now the first checkbox in the Session section is checked. Close the browser.

HOW IT WORKS

The autofocus attribute you inserted in the first step instructed the browser to set the focus to the specified control (first name) automatically after the page is loaded.

NOTE: Before HTML5, you had to use a short JavaScript snippet to achieve the same result.

In the rest of this exercise you applied three different ways to allow users to select an option (or multiple options).

In step 2 you inserted a dropdown list with this code:

```
<select id="salutation" name="salutation">
  <option label="" value="" />
  <option label="Mr." value="Mr." selected />
  <option label="Mrs." value="Mrs." />
  <option label="Ms." value="Ms." />
  <option label="Dr." value="Dr." />
</select>
```

Here, the <select> tag defines a dropdown list control, and each <option> tags describes—*nomen est omen*—an option the user can select. The label attribute defines the text of an option that should be displayed in the dropdown list; value specifies the value that should be sent when the form is posted to the action page. The selected attribute of the "Mr." option states that this should be selected when the form is displayed.

NOTE: In a real web page you should not suggest a default value for a salutation, here it is used for demonstration only.

In step 4, you added three radio buttons that allow selecting a membership option:

```
<label class="memberoption">
  <input type="radio" name="membership"
    value="none" />
  Not a member
</label>
<label class="memberoption">
  <input type="radio" name="membership"
    value="silver" />
  Silver member
</label>
<label class="memberoption">
  <input type="radio" name="membership"
    value="gold" checked />
  Gold member
</label>
```

Each `<input>` tag has a `type` of `radio`, and uses different `value` attribute than the others. The `name` of each control is the same, and this setting provides that these radio buttons are in the same group, so you can choose only one of them at the same time. The `checked` attribute of the third button instructs the browser to set that option automatically when the form is displayed. When the form is posted, the `value` of the radio button checked at that time will be sent.

In this set of controls, you used a different markup to label radio buttons:

```
<label class="memberoption">
  <input type="radio" name="membership"
    value="silver" />
  Silver member
</label>
```

Here, as you see, `<input>` is nested into `<label>`. Instead, you could use a `<label>` following the `<input>`, or vice versa (depending on whether you want to put the label to the left or to the right of the button). However, in the code snippet above you do not have to specify the `for` attribute of `<label>` to point to the corresponding `<input>`, because the nesting gives the same semantic.

In step 6, you added six checkboxes to the form that allowed you to provide six options that can be set independently from each other:

```
<label>
  <input type="checkbox" name="dev" />
  Development
</label>
<label>
  <input type="checkbox" name="alm" />
  ALM
</label>
```

```
<label>
  <input type="checkbox" name="aspnet" />
  ASP.NET
</label>
<!-- Other checkboxes omitted -->
```

Each checkbox has a different **name** attribute. When the form is about to send, this **name** is used to specify whether a checkbox is selected or not.

The previous exercises demonstrated that it's pretty easy to build HTML forms. However, building nice and intuitive forms requires styling—of course, with CSS. The form you saw in Figure 4-1 utilizes a simple style sheet, but without it the form would be really poor. Figure 4-9 shows how the same form would be displayed with no style sheet.

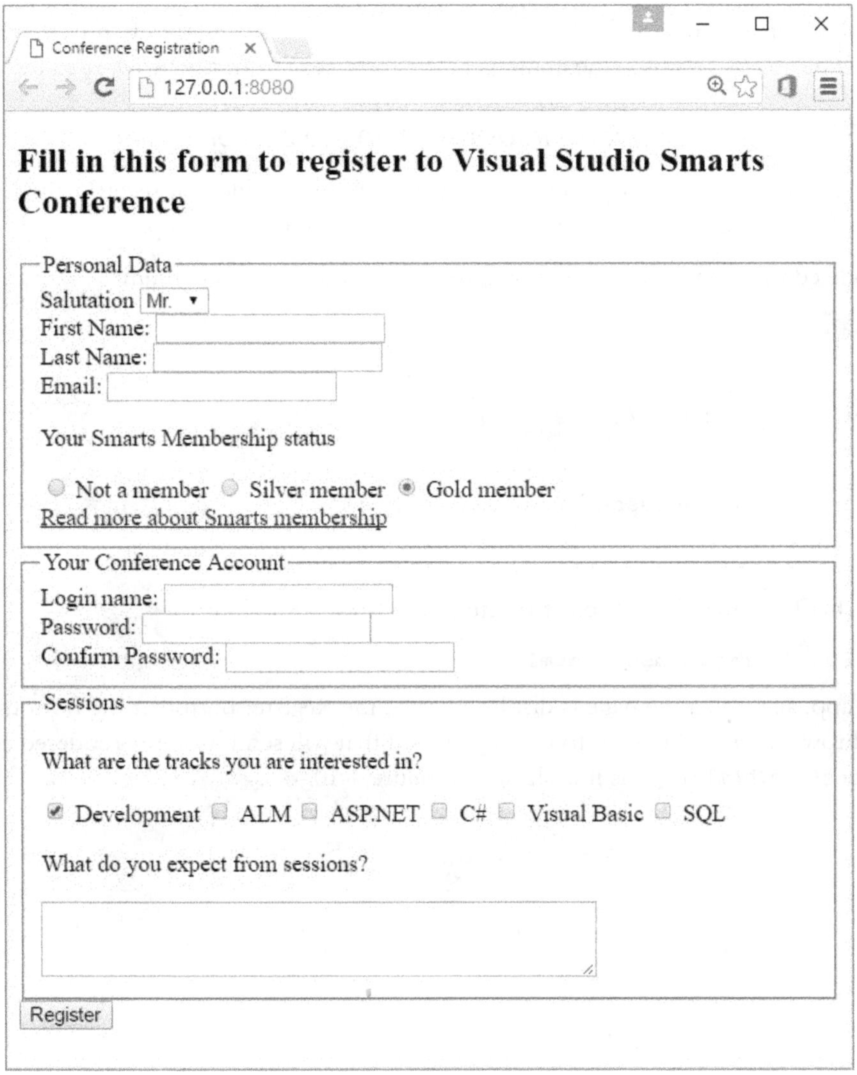

Figure 4-9: The form without the style sheet

Later in this book you will learn more details about CSS, and there you'll understand how the ugly duckling in Figure 4-9 became the beautiful swan in Figure 4-1.

Nonetheless, there are more important things in regard to forms. You already learned that the information collected from a form is sent to a page on the server, and that page can process this information. In the next section you will understand what it means.

Sending and Processing Form Data

To leverage the information posted by a form, the server side must extract this data from the request sent. You already know that the form information is sent to the server as a set of key and value pairs, where the key is the name of a specific form element, and the value represents the content of the corresponding field. In the following exercise you will modify the registration page so that you'll be able to examine the content of the form sent from the browser to the server.

EXERCISE 4-3: Sending form information to the server

In this exercise you are going to create a new page at the server side that receives the form information from the browser. To carry out this activity, follow these steps:

1. In the code editor, create a new file, formprocessor.html with this content:

```
<!DOCTYPE html>
<html>
<head runat="server">
  <title>Form Processor</title>
</head>
<body>
  <h1>This page was accessed from a form.</h1>
</body>
</html>
```

2. In `index.html`, change the `action` attribute of the form definition:

```
<form action="formprocessor.html">
```

3. Start the app, and when the page is displayed, click the Register button at the bottom of the form. The browser sends the form to the server, and that will send back the rendered content of the `formprocessor.html` page, as it is shown in Figure 4-10.

Figure 4-10: The form was sent to the server, to the formprocessor.html page

HOW IT WORKS

This exercise demonstrated that your form is really sent to the server page specified in the action attribute of the form. In the first step you defined the server page, and in step 2 you directed the registration form to this page. Right now, the server page did not extract any form information, it simply indicated that it received the form from the browser.

Catching Data at the Server

It is good to know that the server receives the form data, but it would be even greater to visualize it. In the next exercise you will change the formprocessor.html file so that it will display the data received by the server page.

EXERCISE 4-4: Visualizing form data

In this exercise, you will use a prepared project that can be found in the Exercise-04-04 folder. Although this exercise uses client-side JavaScript to extract the form parameters, it mimics the same operation the server side can carry out.

To display form data, follow these steps:

1. Open the project in Exercise-04-04 folder in your code editor. The extraction of form parameters is handled by the getFormParameters() JavaScript method. Do not feel intimidated, if you do not understand how the code works, just accepts that it does what its name says. A short jQuery code snippet turns the form parameter key-value pairs into an HTML table.

```
...
<body>
  <h1>Form Data</h1>
    <table>
    <thead>
      <tr><th>Property</th><th>Value</th></tr>
    </thead>
    <tbody>
      <!-- Filled up by JavaScript -->
    </tbody>
  </table>
  <script src="scripts/jquery.min.js"></script>
```

```
<script>
  $(function () {
    var params = getFormParameters();
    for (var parName in params) {
      var row = $("<tr>")
        .append($("<td>").html(parName))
        .append($("<td>").html(params[parName]));
      $("tbody").append(row);
    }
  });

  function getFormParameters() {
    var uri = window.location.search;
    var result = {};
    if (uri.indexOf("?") === -1) {
      return {};
    }
    var query = uri.slice(1);
    var params = query.split("&");
    var i = 0;
    while (i < params.length) {
      var parameter = params[i].split("=");
      result[parameter[0]] = parameter[1];
      i++;
    }
    return result;
  }
</script>
</body>
...
```

2. Start the app. When the registration form is displayed, simply click Register. The form is posted to the server, and the browser will display the form data, as shown in Figure 4-11. As you see, the form contains empty strings for all text fields, "Mr." for the **salutation** field, and "gold" for the **membership** field, and signs that the dev checkbox is turned on.

3. Use the Back button of the browser to go back to the index.html page. In the code editor change the option values of the **salutation** field, and remove the **selected** attribute from the second option:

```
<select id="salutation" name="salutation">
  <option label="" value="" />
  <option label="Mr." value="mrval" />
  <option label="Mrs." value="mrsval" />
  <option label="Ms." value="Ms." />
  <option label="Dr." value="Dr." />
</select>
```

4. Remove the checked attribute from the "gold" membership option, and from the "dev" checkbox.

Form Data

Property	Value
salutation	Mr.
fname	
lname	
email	
membership	gold
login	
pwd	
pwd2	
dev	on
comments	

Figure 4-11: Form data—default values

5. Turn back to the browser, and click Register again. Now, you see the form data as shown in Figure 4-12. The salutation field is empty, and there is no membership value.

Form Data

Property	Value
salutation	
fname	
lname	
email	
login	
pwd	
pwd2	
comments	

Figure 4-12: Form data—No salutation and membership option specified

6. Use the Back button of the browser to go back to the form. Fill each text field, specify a membership option, and check at least two checkboxes in the Sessions section. Click Registration, and take a look at the form data. Figure 4-13 shows the data I have specified. Now, you can see a selected membership option ("silver"), the dev and csharp fields with the value set to "on" (I checked the "Development" and "C#" options in Sessions).

Form Data

Property	Value
salutation	mrval
fname	Istvan
lname	Novak
email	myemail@mycompany.hu
membership	silver
login	istvan
pwd	secret
pwd2	secret
dev	on
csharp	on
comments	Surprise me!

Figure 4-13: Form Data—all fields have values

7. Close the browser.

HOW IT WORKS

This exercise demonstrated how different kinds of form data are sent to the server. As you saw in the figures, there was always a data entry sent for each text field, however, empty fields contained empty values. The content of password fields is displayed in their clear form—otherwise how would you be able to process them?

When the dropdown list (represented by the <select> tag) was sent, you could see the value of the selected option in the form data. The first time (Figure 4-11) the salutation field was sent with its default option, "Mr.". The second time (Figure 4-12) the field was sent with the first (empty) option value, because you removed the selected attribute in step 3. The third time (Figure 4-13) "mrval" was sent, because in step 3 you modified the value attribute of the "Mr." option to "mrval", and in step 6, I selected the "Mr." salutation.

Radio button values—such as membership in this exercise—are sent to the server only when there is an option selected. In step 4 you removed the checked attribute from the "gold" option, so when you posted the form in step 5, no membership option was selected, and so no membership property was specified in the form. Please note that a non-specified (missing) property is very different from a property with empty value!

Checkboxes are sent to the server only when they are checked. In this case "on" value is posted in pair with the name of the checked control. That is why you saw the data for the two checked options in Figure 4-13.

Using GET and POST

Sending the form data to the server in the way Exercise 4-4 did has a big issue. It's privacy. The content of the form is sent as the part of the URL, which can be copied from the address line of the browser. For example, when you copy the request belonging to Figure 4-13, you'll see this:

```
http://localhost:8467/FormProcessor.aspx
  ?salutation=mrval
  &fname=Istvan
  &lname=Novak
  &email=myemail%40mycompany.hu
  &membership=silver
  &login=istvan
  &pwd=secret
  &pwd2=secret
  &dev=on&csharp=on
  &comments=Surprise+me%21
```

NOTE: In the real URL there are no line breaks and indentations. Here I used them only for the sake of readability.

Here you can see my password strings! Even if you would use HTTPS, these passwords were the part of the URL, so anyone could read it!

HTTP and HTTPS provides a way to solve this issue. When you send a request to a server, you can send it with any either the GET or the POST verb, and each has its own semantic.

By default, when sending form data, the browser uses the GET verb. The HTML specification says that GET should be used when the form "has no lasting observable effect on the state of the world". This is the plight—for example—when you send query parameters to the server that does not change anything in a database, but only retrieves query results. The POST verb should be used if the request sent to the server carries out some permanent change. The conference registration is a typical example where you should use POST, because your intention is to save a registration, and it is definitely a change in the application's state.

When you use the GET verb, form data is passed in the URL—just as you saw in the code snippet earlier. It means, it can be seen by anyone. When the POST verb is used, the form data is send in the body of the message—and it cannot be directly seen in the browser's address bar.

Of course, the server side also has to be prepared to extract the form data either from the message URL, or from the message body, depending on whether GET or POST was used.

You can specify the verb to use when sending form data with the `method` attribute of the `<form>` element:

```
<form action="formprocessor.html" method="post">
```

As you remember, the `formprocessor.html` page in Exercise-04-04 uses client-side JavaScript to display form parameters. If you use the POST method, the parameters posted to the server won't be displayed by the JavaScript code.

There are many important and subtle differences between GET and POST in regard to web forms, and you'll definitely need to learn more about them when you're about to create web applications using heavy logic on the server side. Now the most important things to remember are these:

1. GET verb transfers the form information in the URL, and so it is directly visible to users. Use GET only when you send query parameters to the server—and these parameters do not contain any sensitive data.

2. POST verb transfers the form data in the request body, so it is not directly visible for users—however can be easily read with simple monitoring tools, which are often built in the browsers. Use POST when sending information to the server that will trigger data changes.

3. If you have sensitive data in your web forms, use HTPPS with POST.

In these exercises, you learned the basics of creating web forms that use text, dropdown list, options represented by radio buttons and checkboxes. It is time to take a look at other controls.

More Controls

There are several controls you can use to provide rich user experience. In this section, you will learn a few of them.

Using Data Lists

HTML5 defines a new tag, `<datalist>`, which can be used to provide input suggestions to ordinary text boxes. On its own, a data list is invisible, but you can bind it to text controls. The next exercise demonstrates how to use it.

EXERCISE 4-5: Using Data Lists

In this exercise you will start from a prepared project that can be found in the `Exercise-04-05-Begin` folder. The project contains a simplified version of the conference registration page, as shown in Figure 4-14. This uses a textbox for the Salutation field—instead of a dropdown list.

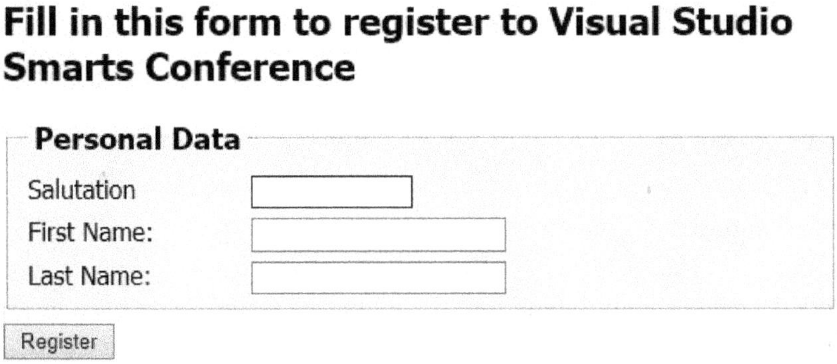

Fill in this form to register to Visual Studio Smarts Conference

Personal Data

Salutation	
First Name:	
Last Name:	

Register

Figure 4-14: Simplified registration form.

This form is represented by the following markup:

```
<form action="FormProcessor.aspx" method="post">
  <fieldset>
    <legend>Personal Data</legend>
    <label for="salutation">Salutation</label>
    <input id="salutation" type="text"
      name="salutation" autofocus />
    <br />
    <label for="fname">First Name:</label>
    <input id="fname" type="text" name="fname"
           autofocus />
    <br />
    <label for="lname">Last Name:</label>
    <input id="lname" type="text" name="lname" />
    <br />
  </fieldset>
  <input type="submit" value="Register" />
</form>
```

To create a data list, follow these steps:

1. Create a copy of the **Exercise-04-05-Begin** folder (**Exercise-04-05**), and work with the files in this new folder. Open **index.html** in the code editor, and insert the highlighted markup:

```
<form action="FormProcessor.aspx" method="post">
  <fieldset>
    <legend>Personal Data</legend>
    <datalist id="salutationlist">
        <option value="mrval">Mr.</option>
        <option value="mrsval">Mrs.</option>
        <option value="Ms." />
        <option value="Dr." />
    </datalist>
    <label for="salutation">Salutation</label>
    <input id="salutation" type="text"
      name="salutation" autofocus />
    <br />
```

```
    <label for="fname">First Name:</label>
    <input id="fname" type="text" name="fname" />
    <br />
    <label for="lname">Last Name:</label>
    <input id="lname" type="text" name="lname" />
    <br />
  </fieldset>
  <input type="submit" value="Register" />
</form>
```

2. You have added a data list, but to bind it to the salutation textbox, you must insert the list attribute, as this markup snippet highlights:

```
<input id="salutation" type="text"
  list="salutationlist"
  name="salutation" autofocus />
```

3. Run the app. When the form opens, the Salutation field receives the focus. Depending on your browser, the list may be opened automatically (Internet Explorer/Edge, Figure 4-15) or a dropdown arrow can be displayed (Chrome, Figure 4-16).

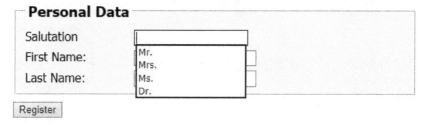

Fill in this form to register to Visual Studio Smarts Conference

Figure 4-15: The data list in action (Edge)

Fill in this form to register to Visual Studio Smarts Conference

Figure 4-16: The data list in action (Chrome)

4. As you type (for example type "m", and then "r") the content of the list is filtered (to "Mr." and "Mrs.", as shown in Figure 4-17 and Figure 4-18.

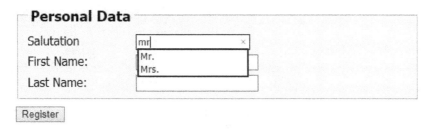

Figure 4-17: The filtered data list (Edge)

Figure 4-18: The filtered data list (Chrome)

5. Click the Register button, and the contents of the form is posted to the server. If you select the "Mr." item, the corresponding value, "mrval" is posted, as shown in Figure 4-19.

Form Data

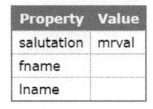

Property	Value
salutation	mrval
fname	
lname	

Figure 4-19: The form data posted to the server

6. Click the Back button of the browser, and type "Prof." into the Salutation field, then click Register. Now, the form is posted with the "Prof." value in `salutation`.

HOW IT WORKS

In the first step you added the `<datalist>` element to the form definition. It used a number of `<option>` tags to define suggestions that can be offered by textboxes. The `value` attribute of each option defined the text that was to be posted to the backend. The first and the second `<option>` items defined text values that can be used by the browser to when rendering the item. Figure 4-17 and Figure 4-18 demonstrated that browsers use different style to display a data list item.

In step 2, you assigned the list (through its identifier, `suggestionlist`) to the `salutation` textbox. In step 4 you experienced how the list of suggestions is filtered as you typed. Finally, in step 5, you could see that selecting "Mr." set the textbox value to "mrval", because the `value` attribute of the "Mr." option was defined as "mrval".

Although the Salutation field had an associated data list, it allowed typing any free text, not only the predefined suggestions. This is how "Prof." was set in step 6.

NOTE: You can put the `<datalist>` tag technically anywhere in the page. Nonetheless, it is a good practice to put it in the form, close to a text box it is attached to.

Using Hidden Fields

You can set the type of an `<input>` element to "hidden", to provide a form field that is never shown to the user. Of course, you should set the value of such a field either to a static value in the markup, or from a script.

In the next exercise you'll use a hidden field to allow sending a return URL data.

EXERCISE 4-6: Using hidden fields

To use a hidden field in a web form, follow these steps:

1. Create a copy of the project in the previous exercise, name the new folder `Exercise-04-06`. Open `index.html` in the code editor, and add the following hidden field right before the submit button:

```
<input type="hidden" name="caller" value="index.html" />
```

2. Open the `formprocessor.html` file, and add this snippet right after the closing `</table>` tag:

```
<br/>
<a id="back" href="#">Back to the caller</a>
```

3. Modify the second `<script>` element, as highlighted in this code snippet:

```
...
$(function () {
    var params = getFormParameters();
    for (var parName in params) {
      var row = $("<tr>")
        .append($("<td>").html(parName))
        .append($("<td>").html(params[parName]));
```

```
    $("tbody").append(row);
  }
  $("#back").attr("href", getFormParameters()["caller"])
});
...
```

4.Start the app, and click the Register. You can see that not only the form data will be displayed, but also a link back to the previous page, as shown in Figure 4-20.

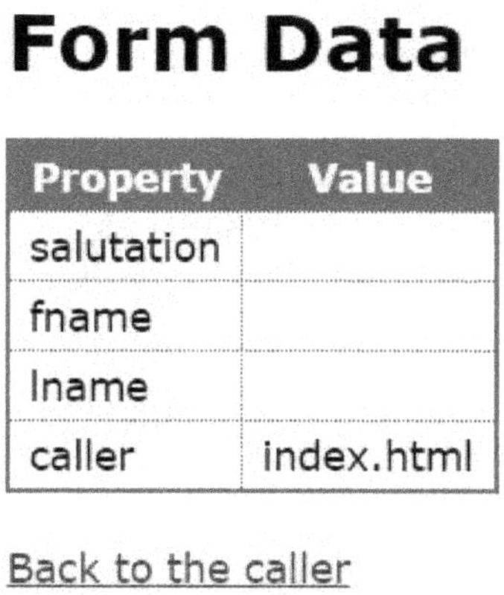

Form Data

Property	Value
salutation	
fname	
lname	
caller	index.html

Back to the caller

Figure 4-20: The hidden field value and the return link is displayed

5. Click the link under the table, and you'll get back to the original form. Close the browser.

HOW IT WORKS

In the first step you added a hidden field with the name `caller` and value of "index.html" to the form. As you could see in Figure 4-20, this hidden value was sent with the form data. The code you added to the `formprocessr.html` page in step 2 and 3 rendered a HTML markup to display a link according to the value of the `caller` field. That is why clicking it in step 5 redirected you to the `index.html` page.

Using <optgroup> in Dropdown Lists

The `<select>` tag allows you to use the `<optgroup>` tag to create groups of options, as an example is shown in Figure 4-21. In order to create these groups, surround the specific options with `<optgroup>`. Listing 4-1 demonstrates this concept, it shows the markup that creates Figure 4-21.

Listing 4-1: Exercise-04-07/index.html

```
<!DOCTYPE html>
<html>
<head>
  <title>Conference Registration</title>
  <style>
    <!--Omitted for the sake of brevity -->
```

```
    </style>
  </head>
  <body>
    <h3>Select a Car for the report</h3>
    <form action="#">
      <label for="car">Car: </label>
      <select id="car">
        <optgroup label="Japanese Cars">
          <option value="honda">Honda</option>
          <option value="toyota">Toyota</option>
          <option value="lexus">Lexus</option>
        </optgroup>
        <optgroup label="German Cars">
          <option value="audi">Audi</option>
          <option value="vw">Volkswagen</option>
          <option value="mercedes">Mercedes</option>
        </optgroup>
      </select>
      <br />
      <input type="submit" value="Report" />
    </form>
  </body>
</html>
```

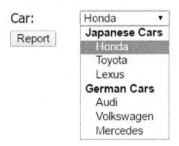

Figure 4-21: Using <optgroup>

NOTE: You cannot use the `<optgroup>` element with `<datalist>`, and cannot nest it into another `<optgroup>`.

Using Buttons

In the previous form examples, you only used one kind button, submit button, which was represented by an `<input>` tag with **type** set to "submit". You have other options to use buttons in your forms, here you will overview them. In the **Exercise-04-08** folder within the source code download of the chapter, you'll find a project that includes a number of HTML files.

When you work with forms, you do not have to send the form back to the server, you may run a JavaScript function to respond to the event when the user submits the form. Listing 4-2

demonstrates this; it shows that every time the user clicks the submit button, the changeBy()
JavaScript method is called with "1" passed as the function argument.

Listing 4-2: Exercise-04-08/index.html

```
<!DOCTYPE html>
<html>
<head>
  <title>Range Sample #1</title>
  <link href="style.css" rel="stylesheet" />
  <script src="changeby.js"></script>
</head>
<body>
  <ul>
    <li><a href="index.html">Sample #1</a></li>
    <li><a href="sample2.html">Sample #2</a></li>
    <li><a href="sample3.html">Sample #3</a></li>
    <li><a href="sample4.html">Sample #4</a></li>
    <li><a href="sample5.html">Sample #5</a></li>
  </ul>
  <form action="javascript:changeBy(1)">
    <label>
      Number of Machines:
      <input id="noMachines"
             type="range" min="1" max="8" value="2" />
    </label>
    <br />
    <input type="reset" value="Reset" />
    <button>
      <img src="images/plus.png" />
      <br />
      Increment
    </button>
  </form>
</html>
```

This form uses a range control (observe, the type of <input> is set to "range") with the initial
value of two (value="2"), and clicking the submit button increments the control's current value.
After clicking the button twice, the control has a value of four, as shown in Figure 4-22.

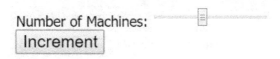

Figure 4-22: Form using a JavaScript action

When you use <input> with the type of "reset", clicking this button resets the form data—
including the value of each control—to its initial state. Listing 4-3 extends Listing 4-2 with a reset
button. When you display the page, after two increments it reaches the value of four, and then
clicking Reset will set the range back to its initial value, 2.

Listing 4-3: Exercise-04-08/Sample2.html

```
...
<form action="javascript:changeBy(1)">
  <label>
    Number of Machines:
    <input id="noMachines"
      type="range" min="1" max="8" value="2" />
  </label>
  <br />
  <input type="reset" value="Reset" />
  <input type="submit" value="Increment" />
</form>
...
```

You can use images instead of buttons. Use the "image" type of `<input>`, as Listing 4-4 shows. In this case, you need to specify the source of the image in the `src` attribute, and you may use the `width` and `height` attributes, too. Figure 4-23 shows the submit button represented by an image.

Listing 4-4: Exercise-04-08/Sample3.html

```
...
<form action="javascript:changeBy(1)">
  <label>
    Number of Machines:
    <input id="noMachines"
           type="range" min="1" max="8" value="2" />
  </label>
  <br />
  <input type="reset" value="Reset" />
  <input type="image"
    src="Images/plus.png"
    height="32" width="32" />
</form>
...
```

Number of Machines:

Reset

Figure 4-23: Now, the submit button is represented by an image

You are not constrained to apply a simple button or an image, you can create compound markup to represent a clickable area—with the `<button>` element. Listing 4-5 composes an image and a text into a button (with a little styling help—see the `button` rule in `style.css`); the result is shown in Figure 4-24.

Listing 4-5: Exercise-04-08/Sample4.html

```
...
<form action="javascript:changeBy(1)">
  <label>
    Number of Machines:
    <input id="noMachines"
           type="range" min="1" max="8" value="2" />
  </label>
  <br />
  <input type="reset" value="Reset" />
  <button>
    <img src="Images/plus.png" />
    <br />
    Increment
  </button>
</form>
...
```

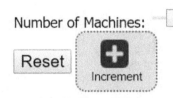

Figure 4-24: A submit `<button>` *is used*

Fifth, you can use more submit buttons, each having its own action. Earlier you learned that a `<form>` has only one `action` attribute that describes what to do when the submit button is clicked. How can a single attribute describe multiple actions so that each submit button can have its own? It cannot. Submit buttons may have a `formaction` attribute that overrides the `action` attribute of the form. Listing 4-6 demonstrates this feature with three new buttons (Figure 4-25). Observe that all new `<button>` elements have a `formaction` attribute.

Listing 4-6: Exercise-04-08/Sample5.html

```
...
<form action="javascript:changeBy(1)">
  <label>
    Number of Machines:
    <input id="noMachines"
           type="range" min="1" max="8" value="2" />
  </label>
  <br />
  <input type="reset" value="Reset" />
  <button>
    <img src="Images/plus.png" />
    <br />
    Increment
  </button>
```

```
<button formaction="javascript:changeBy(-1)">
  <img src="Images/minus.png" />
  <br />
  Decrement
</button>
<button formaction="javascript:changeBy(2)">
  <img src="Images/right.png" />
  <br />
  Add 2
</button>
<button formaction="javascript:changeBy(-2)">
  <img src="Images/left.png" />
  <br />
  Subract 2
</button>
</form>
...
```

Figure 4-25: Four submit buttons on the same form

NOTE: Beside the `formaction` attribute, `<input>` offers you the `formmethod` attribute to override the `method` attribute of the `<form>` element. For example, if the form's method suggests a GET verb, in the `formmethod` that belongs to a submit button you can change it to POST.

By now, you have learned many important things about forms. However, one pivotal thing is really missing: validation. It's time to get acquainted with this concept.

Form Validation

When you collect information in a web page, nothing prevents your users to provide something different than you ask for. For example, they may leave a textbox empty, type names where you expect numbers, provide a phone number instead of an e-mail address, and so on. When they click the submit button, all data goes to the server as it is filled out.

If your server side would not validate the data, it might get wrong information, and that leads to errors and confusion. It is very trivial that the server side *must* check all data coming from the browser—the server side *must not trust* that the client side sends valid data.

However, sending invalid data to the server side consumes resources: the form data goes to the network, it reaches the server, the server carries out validation procedures, and it sends back an answer telling that something is wrong with the input.

162

Resources consumed at the server side costs more—at least from the aspect of the service provider—than resources spent at the client (browser) side. If invalid data could be held back and not sent to the server, it would save resources. That is the idea behind client side validation.

NOTE: I should emphasize again that the server must validate all data, even if the client does it, too. So, when client side validation is mentioned, it means validation in two places: at the client and at the server.

Client side validation is not a new idea. It existed before HTML5 as well, and it required JavaScript. The creators of HTML5 recognized the importance of this topic, and they provided a way to free web developers from writing most of the validation scripts. They achieved this aim with HTML5 markup, and with a set of JavaScript functions.

Informing Users

In many cases users type invalid data, because they do not exactly know what a specific form field expects. The `<input>` element has an attribute, `placeholder`, which specifies a short hint that describes the expected value of the field. With using `placeholder`, you can help the user to guess out what you expect. Listing 4-7 shows you an example. When the page is displayed, you can see that each input field shows the placeholder text (Figure 4-26). The placeholder (often called watermark) is a bit dimmed to tell the user it is not the actual content of the field, only a hint. When you type data into a field, the placeholder is removed and the real content is shown (Figure 4-27).

Listing 4-7: Exercise-04-09/index.html

```html
<!DOCTYPE html>

<html>
<head>
  <title>Using placeholder</title>
</head>
<body>
  <h2>Specify your booking info</h2>
  <form>
    <label>
      First name:
      <input type="text"
        placeholder="John" />
    </label>
    <br />
    <label>
      Last name:
      <input type="text"
        placeholder="Smith" />
    </label>
    <br />
    <label>
```

```
      Membership ID:
      <input type="text"
        placeholder="ABC-123" />
    </label>
    <br />
    <input type="submit" value="Query" />
  </form>
</body>
</html>
```

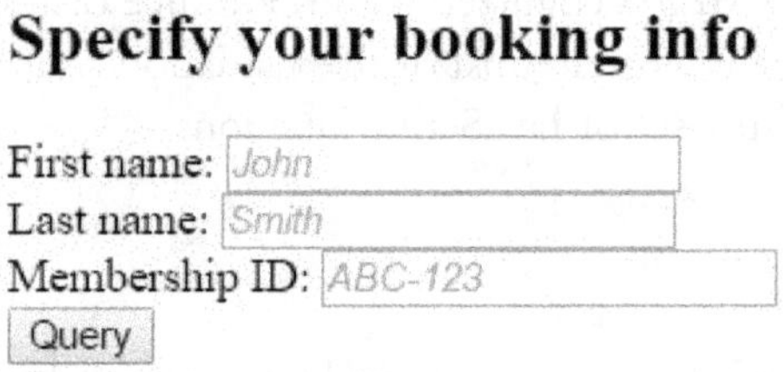

Specify your booking info

First name: *John*
Last name: *Smith*
Membership ID: *ABC-123*
Query

Figure 4-26: Placeholders help users to guess out the content and format of a field.

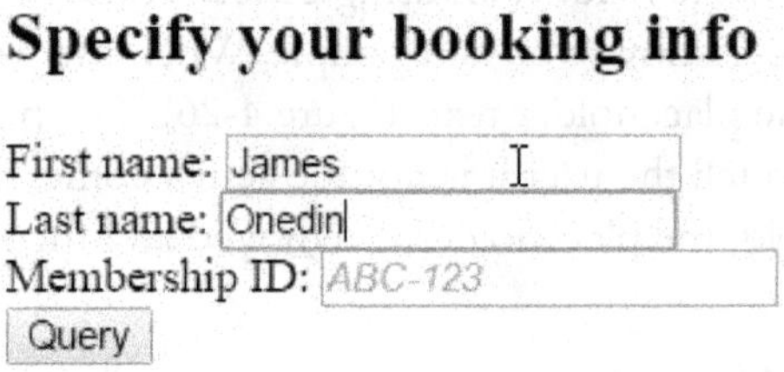

Specify your booking info

First name: James
Last name: Onedin
Membership ID: *ABC-123*
Query

Figure 4-27: Placeholders are removed when you specify the value of a field

With properly designed placeholders you can even suggest the format of an input. For example, the Membership ID's "ABC-123" placeholder implicitly tells the user that this field expects an ID that starts with three letters, goes on with a dash, and concludes with three digits.

In Listing 4-7, I made a little styling trick that italicizes the font of the placeholder, and added the following style definition to the **<head>** section:

```
<style>
  ::-webkit-input-placeholder {
    font-style: italic;
  }

  :-moz-placeholder { /* Firefox 18- */
    font-style: italic;
  }

  ::-moz-placeholder { /* Firefox 19+ */
    font-style: italic;
  }

  :-ms-input-placeholder {
    font-style: italic;
```

```
  }
</style>
```

Later in this book you'll learn how it works.

NOTE: The `<input>` element has an attribute, `autocomplete`, which allows the browser to predict the value. When a user starts to type in a field, the browser can display options to fill in the field—based on earlier typed values. Generally, you have to allow this option in your browser's settings.

Validation Attributes

HTML5 extended the `<input>` tag with new attributes that specify different kind of automatic validation. With the `required` attribute you can specify that an input field must be filled out before submitting the form. When you work with text input, use `maxlength` to define the maximum number of characters allowed in the field.

In case of numeric values (number, range, and date related input fields) you can specify an acceptable range with the `min` and `max` attributes, and optionally define the legal number intervals with the `step` attribute. For example, the following markup defines a numeric field that can have only the -3, 1, 5, and 9 values:

```
<input type="number" min="-3" max="9" step="4">
```

In Listing 4-7, the Membership ID field's placeholder with the value of "ABC-123" suggested a special format. You can use the `pattern` attribute to specify a regular expression that the field's value is checked against. For example, to validate Membership ID, you should add the following attribute to the corresponding `<input>` markup:

```
pattern="[A-Za-z]{3}-\d{3}"
```

Before submitting a form, the browser checks if all fields are valid. If not, it changes the appearance of invalid fields, and provides some information about what the source of invalidity is. In most cases, you can use the `title` attribute to provide extra information about the expected value and format of the field.

NOTE: Different browsers may provide different ways to sign invalid content.

Listing 4-8 provides you an example that demonstrates these validation attributes.

Listing 4-8: Exercise-04-10/index.html

```
<!DOCTYPE html>

<html>
<head>
  <title>Using placeholder</title>
<!--Style omitted for the sake of brevity -->
</head>
<body>
```

```
<h2>Specify your booking info</h2>
<form>
  <label>
    First name:
    <input type="text"
      placeholder="John"
      maxlength="20"
        />
  </label>
  <br />
  <label>
    Last name*:
    <input type="text"
      placeholder="Smith"
      title="Please, specify the last name"
      required />
  </label>
  <br />
  <label>
    Membership ID*:
    <input type="text"
      placeholder="ABC-123"
      required
      title="Three letters, dash, three digits"
      pattern="[A-Za-z]{3}-\d{3}" />
  </label>
  <br />
  <label>
    Number of passengers*:
    <input type="number"
      placeholder="1-8"
      required
      min="1"
      max="8" />
  </label>
  <br />
  <input type="submit" value="Query" />
</form>
</body>
</html>
```

As you can see from the markup, all fields except First name are required. Last name and Membership ID defines a helping title that is displayed when the field is found invalid. The Number of passengers field expects a numeric value between 1 and 8.

Browsers display this form differently. For example, Edge renders the last field as a simple textbox, while Google Chrome provides a numeric control with up and down arrows, as shown in Figure 4-28, and Figure 4-29, respectively.

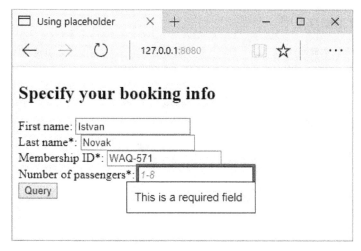

Figure 4-28: The form in Internet Explorer

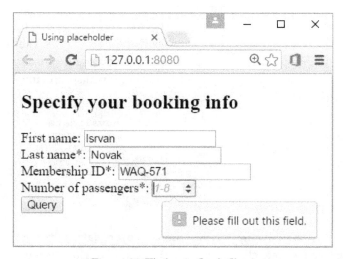

Figure 4-29: The form in Google Chrome

Validation and JavaScript

Although validation attributes help you in many situations, in complex systems you cannot avoid writing your own JavaScript validation code, or using a validation framework. Browsers apply form validation only when you click a submit button.

Great web applications with enhanced user experience validate fields as soon as you leave them, or sometimes as you type. In these situations, you cannot leverage validation attributes only, you also need to create custom validation code. When the validation logic does not fit into the frame provided by the validation attributes, you also fall back to writing JavaScript.

NOTE: Custom validation is a quite complex topic and often bound to server-side frameworks.

Turning Validation Off

There might be situations when you need to turn off form validation. For example, if you have a long form with many inputs, you need to provide a way users can save the input already typed in, without validating the data—in order to go on filling out the form later. You can add a second submit button that saves the form. Append the `formnovalidate` attribute to the submit button to avoid form validation before submission, such as in the following example:

```
<form action="processform.html" method="post" >
  <!-- Input fields -->
  <input type="submit" value="Process" />
  <input type="submit" value="Save"
    formaction="SaveForm.aspx"
    formnovalidate />
</form>
```

You already learned that the server side must always validate data received from the client side. When you want to test whether the validation at the server side works as you expect, you need to transfer invalid data to the server side. Adding the `novalidate` attribute to the `<form>` tag turns the validation off. It provides you a context to prove that the server side validation logic is invoked properly, and this logic can be triggered from the browser. For example, the following code snippet turns off the client side form validation—so, if you specify invalid data, you can be sure the wrong information will reach the server side:

```
<form action="processform.html" method="post" novalidate >
  <!-- Input fields -->
  <input type="submit" value="Process" />
</form>
```

New HTML5 Input Types

The HTML5 markup defines new input types, such as `color`, `date`, `datetime`, `datetime-local`, `email`, `month`, `number`, `range`, `search`, `tel`, `time`, `url`, `week`. Unfortunately, they have different support in different browsers, which means that some of them are not supported in certain browsers, or different browsers render the same control with totally diverse appearance. When creating web pages, check that the input type you intend to use is supported by the set of browsers utilized by you or your customers.

Summary

HTML provides you a set of controls to create forms on web pages, collect the data your users specify, and send that information to a web page that can process them. The key element is `<form>` that wraps all fields to be sent to the server side. Most form elements can be defined with the `<input>` tag, and you can specify the `type` attribute to describe the kind of control, such as text, number, file, email, checkbox, and many more. With `<select>`, you can define dropdown lists. The `<fieldset>` element provides a way to organize controls within your form into logical groups.

The form is sent to the server as a collection of name and value pairs. Only those inputs are sent to the server side that provide a `name` attribute. The form data can be sent to the server either with GET or POST verb. The GET verb puts the data into the request URL (so it is apparently visible to users), unlike POST, which adds form data to the request body (so it's hidden from the user).

Before sending the data to the server side, the browser can validate input fields. Should the form have any invalid information, the data would not be sent. HTML5 specifies several validation attributes, so you can avoid writing validation code (JavaScript) in most common situations.

Chapter 5: A Few More Things about HTML

WHAT YOU WILL LEARN IN THIS CHAPTER

Getting to know a few more HTML elements

Understanding URL formats and custom attributes

Getting acquainted with the `<canvas>` element

Using a few HTML5 tools

Other HTML Elements

In the previous chapters you have learned—or at least have met—the majority of HTML elements. However, there are a few untouched tags left, and here you will get acquainted with them.

Definitions

In *Chapter 2 (Using HTML Lists)*, you already touched unordered lists (`<ul>`), and ordered lists (`<ol>`). Well, HTML provides you a third type of lists. With the `<dl>` element, you can create a list of definitions. The `<dl>` tag is a container that embeds definition terms (or names), and definition descriptions, using the `<dt>`, and `<dd>` tags, respectively, as shown in Listing 5-1.

Listing 5-1: Exercise-05-01/index.html

```
<!DOCTYPE html>
<html>
<head>
  <title>Definition Lists</title>
</head>
<body>
  <p>A Few .NET CLR Intrinsic Types:</p>
  <dl>
    <dt>System.Byte</dt>
    <dt>byte</dt>
    <dd>8-bit unsigned integer</dd>
    <dt>System.SByte</dt>
    <dt>sbyte</dt>
    <dd>8-bit signed integer</dd>
```

```
    <dt>System.Boolean</dt>
    <dd>1 bit; represents true or false</dd>
    <dt>System.Char</dt>
    <dd>16-bit Unicode character</dd>
    <dd>(no 8-bit character type is supported)</dd>
  </dl>
</body>
</html>
```

While both `<ul>` and `<ol>` embed `<li>` tags, the definition list uses terms (`<dt>`), and description tags (`<dd>`). When you take a look at the rendered page, you see that the definition list is rendered very similarly to normal text; except that the `<dd>` element is indented (Figure 5-1).

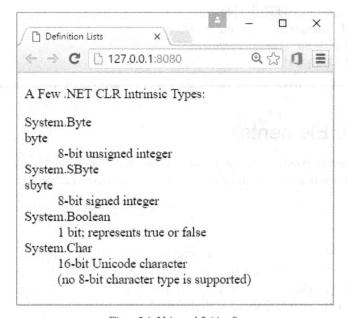

Figure 5-1: Using a definition list

As you can see from the code and the rendered page, you can mix terms and descriptions within definition lists. Nonetheless, use one name and one description for each term, unless you have a strong reason to do otherwise.

Thematic Break

The `<hr>` tag defines a thematic break that is used to separate content in a web page. Although originally in HTML 4.01 it was defined as simple visual element (horizontal rule), HTML5 defines it as a semantic term. Listing 5-2 shows an example of applying the `<hr>` tag.

Listing 5-2: Exercise-05-02/index.html

```
<!DOCTYPE html>
<html>
<head>
  <title>Thematic Break</title>
</head>
<body>
  <h2>First Topic</h2>
  <p>
    Pellentesque habitant morbi tristique
    senectus et netus et malesuada fames
    ac turpis egestas. Maecenas auctor
    ipsum ut lectus sodales pharetra.
  </p>
  <hr />
  <h2>Change in Topic</h2>
  <p>
    Integer ultricies tempor imperdiet.
    Vestibulum at elit enim. Suspendisse
    pellentesque mollis tincidunt. Mauris
    felis velit, aliquam sit amet varius in.
  </p>
  <hr />
</body>
</html>
```

The <hr> tag is represented as a horizontal line, as shown in Figure 5-2.

Figure 5-2: Using thematic break

Quotes

In documents—especially in publications—we often use and quote external sources. In HTML, two tags, <q> and <blockquote> can be used to mark these citations. In *Chapter 2 (Rendering Text)*, you tangentially learned about the <q> tag, as a way of formatting text. To be more precise, <q> is more—and in this nature it is very similar to most HTML5 tags—than simple text formatting, as this tag adds a special semantic to its content: this is a quotation that comes from another source.

While <q> is an inline tag, <blockquote> defines a block (section) of citation. Both elements have a cite attribute that specifies the URL pointing to the source of quotation. Listing 5-3 shows a short example of these tags.

Listing 5-3: Exercise-05-03/index.html

```
<!DOCTYPE html>
<html>
<head>
  <title>Using Quotes</title>
  <style>
    body {
      font-family: Verdana, Arial, sans-serif
    }
    q {
      font-style: italic;
    }
    blockquote {
      background-color: #cccccc;
      padding: 4px 8px;
    }
  </style>
</head>
<body>
  <h2>Visual Studio Extensibility</h2>
  <p>
    I have read a great article about
    Visual Studio Extensibility. What into
    my brain have come after reading this
    article was the
    <q cite="http://magazine.com/Article.html">thousand
      ways of extension</q>
    that Visual Studio Provides.
  </p>
  <p>I've found this especially important:</p>
  <blockquote cite="http://magazine.com/Article.html">
    Because Visual Studio has been architected
    with extensibility in mind, the question
    is not whether there are appropriate
    extension points for a feature of your imagination.
    The real question is what those points are and
    how you can add your features.
  </blockquote>
```

```
</body>
</html>
```

From this listing you can see that I've added a few style rules to give the quotations more emphasis. Figure 5-3 shows how this page is rendered.

Figure 5-3: Using quotes

The `<q>` tags have been set to display in italic, while `<blockquote>` has a light shade. Observe, I have not used quotation marks around the text enclosed between `<q>` tags, the browser automatically rendered them.

Images and Mappings

In *Chapter 2 (Exercise 2-3)* you have learned how you can turn your images into links by surrounding an `<img>` tag with an `<a>` tag. Images provide another great feature, the ability to define a number of hot-spots, each of them having a link of its own. For example, you can display a color picker image (as shown in Figure 5-4) where each separate color is a hot-spot, and when the user clicks any of them, you'll use the link to pick up the appropriate color. Another example is a map of the world, where you use each country as a hot-spot to show related sales information.

Figure 5-4: A color picker defined as a single image

To achieve this behavior, you need to define a map, and assign it to an image, as shown in this markup snippet:

```
<img src="myimage.png" usemap="#mymap" />
<map name="mymap">
  <area ... />
  <area ... />
  <!-- More area tags -->
  <area ... />
</map>
```

The `<map>` tag embeds one or more `<area>` elements, and each defines a hot-spot. A `<map>` has a `name` attribute that can be used to assign the map to an image with the `<img>` tag's `usemap` attribute. As the markup snippet shows, you need to put a number mark (#) in front of the map's name when referring it from `usemap`.

A hot-spot definition contains a clickable (or touchable) region within the image, and—of course—the hyperlink information. The `shape` and `coords` attributes of `<area>` hold the information about the hot-spot's region. The value of `shape` can be any of "rect", "circle", or "poly" to define the area as a rectangle, circle, or polygon, respectively. Depending on `shape`'s value, `coords` define a sequence of coordinate information separated with a comma. If `shape` is set to "rect", `coords` contains two points in form of "x_1, y_1, x_2, y_2". Use two points and a radius value for `coords` (in form of "x, y, rad") when `shape` is set to "circle". If the area is defined as a polygon (`shape` is set to "poly"), you need to specify all points of the polygon, in form of "$x_1, y_1,..., x_n, y_n$". The lines of the following snippet define a rectangle, a circle (with a radius of 28), and a polygon (triangle), respectively:

```
<area shape="rect" coords="10,10,54,86" />
<area shape="circle" coords="102,43,28" />
<area shape="poly" coords="84,16,21,38,114,38
" />
```

To demonstrate using image maps, Listing 5-4 shows you an HTML page definition. This listing can be found in the `Exercise-05-04` folder within this chapter's source code download. Open the project within this folder to try how it works.

Listing 5-4: Exercise-05-04/index.html

```html
<!DOCTYPE html>
<html>
<head>
  <title>Images and mappings</title>
  <link href="style.css" rel="stylesheet" />
</head>
<body>
  <h2>A few things about scuba diving</h2>
  <p>
    Click on the picture to get some more
    information about what you see.
  </p>
  <img src="Images/MappedPictureWithOverlay.JPG"
    usemap="#scubamap"/>
  <map name="scubamap">
    <area shape="rect" coords="668,25,723,93"
      title="Tiger" href="#Tiger" alt="Tiger" />
    <area shape="circle" coords="553,122,71"
      title="Istvan" href="#Istvan" alt="Istvan" />
    <area shape="circle" coords="299,121,57"
      title="Eszter" href="#Eszter" alt="Eszter" />
    <area shape="circle" coords="555,210,26"
      title="Second Stage"
      href="#SecondStage" alt="Second Stage" />
    <area shape="poly"
      coords="524,509,558,598,609,578,582,490"
      title="Decompression Buoy"
      href="#DecoBuoy" alt="Deco buoy" />
  </map>
  <h2 id="Istvan">Istvan</h2>
  <p>
    Istvan is a NASE Dive Master with more than 400
    registered underwater dives.
  </p>
  <h2 id="Eszter">Eszter</h2>
  <p>
    Eszter is a PADI Open Water Diver with about 20
    registered underwater dives.
  </p>
  <h2 id="Tiger">Tiger</h2>
  <p>
    Tiger is Istvan's underwater buddy escorting
    him tied to his tank.
  </p>
  <h2 id="SecondStage">Second Stage</h2>
  <p>
    The second stage is an important part of the
    scuba equipment, you breath the air through it.
  </p>
  <h2 id="DecoBuoy">Decompression Buoy</h2>
```

```
<p>
    Decompression buoy is used to send to the surface
    while you are under water for your safety stop.
  </p>
</body>
</html>
```

This code uses an image with marked hot-spots (so that you can find them easily). When you move the mouse pointer above any hot-spot, the pointer changes to a hand, and a tooltip shows the title of the corresponding hot-spot (the title attribute of the related `<area>` element). When you click a hot-spot, it takes you to the part of the page that describes germane details. Figure 5-5 shown this sample page in action.

Figure 5-5: An image with hot-spots

The `<area>` tag defines a few attributes that describe the related hyperlink. These are `alt`, `href`, `hreflang`, `media`, `rel`, `target`, and `type`; they have the same semantic as the same tags of `<a>`—just as described in *Chapter 2 (Adding Links)*.

NOTE: You can easily get coordinates with the help of drawing or image processing programs. As you move the cursor while drawing a rectangle, a circle, or a polygon, these apps generally display your coordinates. Put down these coordinates, and when your finished drawing all shapes, use your notes to specify the coords attributes of <area> tags.

Visualizing Progress

HTML5 defines a new tag, <progress>, which can be used to represent the progress of a task. It has only two attributes, max, and value, which specify the amount of work a task requires in total, and amount of units the task has been completed, respectively. For example, if the task requires 25 work units in total, with three already completed, it can be represented with this markup:

```
<progress max="25" value="3" />
```

In the source code download of this chapter you find the Exercise-05-05 folder with a sample web application. Listing 5-5 shows how it allows you to display and manage a progress bar. It uses the same technique to change the value of the current progress, as you already learned in *Chapter 4 (Using Buttons)*. This app displays a page, as shown in Figure 5-6.

Listing 5-5: Exercise-05-05/index.html

```html
<!DOCTYPE html>
<html>
<head>
  <title>Visualizing Progress</title>
  <link href="style.css" rel="stylesheet" />
  <script src="Scripts/changeby.js"></script>
</head>
<body>
  <p>
    Survey progress:
    <progress id="progress" max="100" value="10" />
  </p>
  <form>
    <button formaction="javascript:changeBy(-10)">
      <img src="Images/minus.png" />
      <br />
      Decrement
    </button>
    <button formaction="javascript:changeBy(10)">
      <img src="Images/plus.png" />
      <br />
      Increment
    </button>
  </form>
</body>
</html>
```

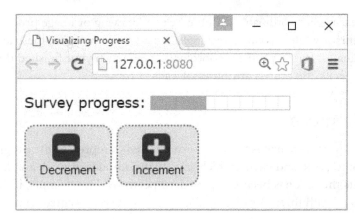

Figure 5-6: Displaying a progress bar

By now, you have learned almost all HTML5 markup elements. Before going on to the missing ones, it is time to look back and refine important details on elements and attributes.

Refining Markup Details

In the chapters you have already gone through, you have seen a number of HTML elements, and you have utilized them in exercises and samples. Most exercises had a "How It Works" section that explained important details, however, there were important subtleties not treated there. In this section you will learn the most important nitty-gritty markup details that are crucial to know before diving into deeper subjects.

Working with URLs

When creating an HTML page, there are many markup elements that require you to specify URLs (where URL stands for *Uniform Resource Locator*). The first that probably jumps into your mind is the `<a>` element's `href` attribute, which contains a link to a target page. There are other elements where URLs play important role, and we can divide them into groups just to see that there are different situations where you can meet URLs:

You can use them to link to other documents and resources. The previously mentioned `<a>` tag is one example, but you can also use the `<link>` tag in this context, for example, when you use it to point to the next document, provided the current document is a part of a series.

You often link external style sheets and scripts with the `<link>` and `<script>` tags, and here you refer those external files with URLs. Your web page may cite an external reference, such as the `<q>`, `<blockquote>`, `<ins>`, and `<del>` elements, and they use—as you can guess—URLs.

To provide rich user experience, you often include images, audio and video resources in your pages, and all related markup elements specify the source of these media through URLs.

Forms are submitted to web servers, and their target is defined with URLs, too.

It is time to examine how you can access resources through URLs with the markup. The resources can be within your website, can point to external websites somewhere in the intranet of your company, or even can address other locations in the internet. To reach all kind of resources, you can use absolute and relative URLs that might be extended with an optional fragment identifier.

An absolute URL is independent from any relationship, when you use it, you point directly to a resource. For example, the following URL is an absolute one: `http://othercompany.com/pages/catalog.html`. It does not matter in which page do you use it, this resource identifier undoubtedly names the resource it wants to use.

In contrast, relative URLs always specify resources in relation to the current location of the web page that refers to the resource. For example, let's assume, that a page is in the `http://mycompany.com/Admin` folder (the name of the page is irrelevant). If this page uses the `/Images/logo.png` resource identifier, it is a URL relative to the page location, so it will be reached at the `http://mycompany.com/Images/logo.png` address. Should this page use the `HowTo/Login.mp4` resource in a `<video>` tag, this resource would be loaded from the `http://mycompany.com/Admin/HowTo/Login.mp4` URL.

NOTE: Folders mirrored by a URL do not need to specify physical folders, they can be virtual ones as well. So, for example the `http://mycompany.com/Admin` address does not mean that there must be an `Admin` folder physically on the web server serving `mycompany.com`—or that this folder is in the root,—it just means that the web server understands that there are resources in the server that can be addressed with the `/Admin` route.

The concept of absolute and relative URLs is pretty easy to understand, especially if you try using them. In the source code download of this chapter, you find a sample in the `Exercise-05-06` folder. When you load it into the code editor (Visual Studio Code), it displays the folder structure, as shown in Figure 5-7.

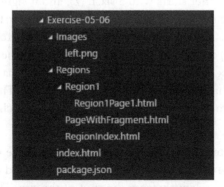

Figure 5-7: The structure of the sample project

The `index.html` page is directly within the root of this web site, its markup is shown in Listing 5-6.

Listing 5-6: Exercise-05-06/index.html

```
<!DOCTYPE html>
<html>
<head>
  <title>URL Sample</title>
</head>
<body>
  <p>The following links use relative URL:</p>
  <a href="/Regions/Region1/Region1Page1.html">
    /Regions/Region1/Region1Page1.html
  </a>
  <br />
  <a href="Regions/RegionIndex.html">
    Regions/RegionIndex.html
  </a>
  <br />
  <a href="UsingBase.html">
    UsingBase.html
  </a>
  <p>The following links contain absolute URLs:</p>

  <a href="http://www.w3.org">
    World Wide Web Consortium
  </a>
  <br />
  <a href="http://visualstudiogallery.msdn.microsoft.com">
    Visual Studio Gallery
  </a>
</body>
</html>
```

The first three links in the page specify relative URLs, while the last two define absolute ones. The first relative resource identifier starts with a slash (/), and it signs that this resource should be accessed from the root, under the Regions folder, within the Region1 subfolder, and the resource is named Region1Page1.html. The second URL starts with the Regions folder name, and because the current page (index.html) is in the root, it will be resolved to the RegionIndex.html file in the Regions folder. Because index.html is in the web root, you could have started this resource with a slash too, and it would still have resolved to the very same page. The third URL is a simple page name, so it will be served from the same folder as index.html, which happens to be the root folder.

Observe that the slash character at the beginning of the first relative URL is very important. It provides that moving the index.html to another folder will still find the Region1Page1.html resource, because it is specified relatively from the root of the site. The second relative link would not survive the movement of the page, since it accesses the RegionIndex.html file relatively from the current page. So moving index.html, and leaving RegionIndex.html in its place would definitely break the link.

The `Region1Page1.html` file contains a link pointing back to the index page, as shown in Listing 5-7. It displays the `left.png` image that can be found in the `Images` folder.

Listing 5-7: Exercise-05-06/Region1Page1.html

```
<!DOCTYPE html>
<html>
<head>
  <title>Region1/Page1</title>
</head>
<body>
  <h1>This is Page #1 of Region #1.</h1>
  <a href="/index.html">
    <img src="../../Images/left.png" />
    Back to the index page
  </a>
</body>
</html>
```

As the markup shows, the "`../../Images/left.png`" relative URL is specified to reach the image file. The "`../`" means a step up in the folder hierarchy, so the "`../../`" path means step up to the root of the site. This image can be accessed with the "`/Images/left.png`" relative URL, too.

When you refer to a page, the browser loads it, and displays the page from its top. You can use fragment identifiers to instruct the browser to scroll down to a specified fragment of the page when displaying it. Listing 5-8 shows you the `PageWithFragment.html` that demonstrates this feature.

Listing 5-8: Exercise-05-06/PageWithFragment.html

```
<!DOCTYPE html>
<html>
<head>
  <title>Page with Region</title>
</head>
<body>
  <h1>This is Page #2 of Region #1.</h1>
  <a href="/Regions/PageWithFragment.html#date">
    Fragment within this page #1
  </a>
  <br />
  <a href="#date">
    Fragment within this page #2
  </a>
  <br />
  <a href="/index.html">
    <img src="/Images/left.png" />
    Back to the index page
  </a>
  <p id="date"></p>
  <script>
```

```
      var dateElement = document.getElementById("date");
      dateElement.innerHTML = new Date();
   </script>
</body>
</html>
```

There's a `<p>` tag with "date" identifier, and the first two links point to this tag with the `#date` fragment id. The very first link uses a relative URL that addresses the page itself, and the `#date` fragment within. The second link uses only the "#date" URL, and that points to the very same fragment. The page contains a script that writes the current date into the `<p>` tag while the page is being load.

Figure 5-8 shows the page displayed in a short browser window. The date information cannot be seen, because that overflows the bottom of the window.

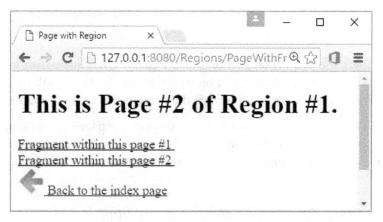

Figure 5-8: The date information cannot be seen

When you click any of the first two links, the browser navigates to the date information. Figure 5-9 shows this situation.

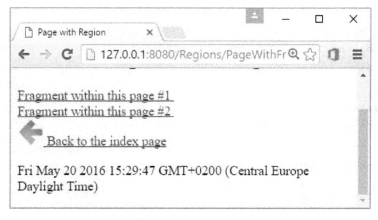

Figure 5-9: The browser displays the date information

This sample also demonstrates that the browser does not load the page from the web server again when you click any of the links pointing to the `date` fragment. The date information displayed remains exactly the same after clicking the links as at the initial load. However, refreshing the page (with F5) changes the date information, and indicates that the page has been reloaded from the server.

There is an HTML element, `<base>`, which specifies the default URL and target for all relative URLs in a page. Listing 5-9 shows an example of using this tag.

Listing 5-9: Exercise-05-07/index.html

```
<!DOCTYPE html>
<html>
<head>
  <title>Using &lt;base&gt; sample</title>
  <base href="http://www.w3.org/" target="_blank" />
</head>
<body>
  <a href="standards/webdesign/htmlcss">
    Click to access the HTML &amp; CSS Standard pages
  </a>
  <br />
  <a href="html/wg">
    Click to access the HTML Working Group page
  </a>
</body>
</html>
```

The `<base>` tag must be in the `<head>` section, and may occur up to once. Its `href` attribute defines the default URL, `target` specifies the default target for all hyperlinks and forms in the page. When you run Listing 5-9, and click the links, the corresponding pages of the `www.w3.org` web site appear—in a new browser tab.

Inline Frames

In *Chapter 2 (Using Multimedia)*, you already used the `<iframe>` tag to insert an inline video into a sample page. It's pretty easy to insert an inline frame into your web page, but before doing so, there are a few things you need to think over, and most of them are security considerations.

You know—because you have already tried—that you can add JavaScript code to your page, which runs when a web page is loaded, or as you interact with the page. This code can do many things in your browser (everything that the browser's current security configuration allows). If the inline page contains malicious code, that may run in your page.

You can use the `sandbox` attribute of `<iframe>` to specify extra security restrictions for the content of the inline frame. If you omit this attribute, your browser's default security restrictions are applied. When you set it to an empty string, all extra security restrictions are forced. To constrain the inline frame in a more granular manner, you can add one or more restriction values to sandbox, and separate these values by spaces. HTML5 defines the following constraints:

The allow-scripts enables the page to run scripts defined in the inline page. The inline content can submit forms only when allow-forms is set. With the allow-same-origin setting the content is treated as being from the same origin as the containing document. By default, the frame's content can navigate only within itself, but applying the allow-top-navigation setting enables it to navigate (load) content from the containing document.

In the source code download of this chapter, you find a sample in the Exercise-05-08 folder. This project demonstrates the sandbox attribute. It contains a DisplayTitle.html file (Listing 5-10) that represents the content of an inline frame, and the index.html file (Listing 5-11) which is a container that embeds frames.

Listing 5-10: Exercise-05-08/DisplayTitle.html

```
<!DOCTYPE html>
<html>
<head>
  <title>This is the title of this page!</title>
</head>
<body style="background-color: #dddddd">
  <button onclick="displayTitle()">
    Action!
  </button>
  <p id="output"></p>
  <script>
    function displayTitle() {
      var outputPar = document.getElementById("output");
      outputPar.innerHTML = document.title;
    }
  </script>
</body>
</html>
```

DisplayTitle.html has only a simple button. When you click it, the displayTitle() JavaScript function shows the title of this page.

Listing 5-11: Exercise-05-08/index.html

```
<!DOCTYPE html>
<html>
<head>
  <title>Using &lt;frame&gt;</title>
  <style>
    .seamless {
      border: none;
    }
  </style>
</head>
<body>
```

```
<h3>No restriction</h3>
<iframe src="DisplayTitle.html"
  width="200" height="88">
</iframe>
<h3>All restrictions</h3>
<iframe src="DisplayTitle.html"
  width="200" height="88"
  sandbox="">
</iframe>
<h3>Scripts allowed</h3>
<iframe src="DisplayTitle.html"
  width="200" height="88"
  sandbox="allow-scripts"
  seamless
  class="seamless">
</iframe>
</body>
</html>
```

This page embeds the `DisplayTitle.html` file three times, with no restrictions, with all restrictions, and with allowing the scripts to run, respectively. When the browser renders this file, only the first and third frame outputs the title of the embedded page, because the second runs in a sandbox that does not allow running scripts.

Listing 5-11 demonstrates another feature of `<iframe>`. By default, it draws a border around the inline frame. This behavior can be turned off with the `seamless` attribute. However, `seamless` works only with Safari and Chrome. With the little styling trick applied for the third frame, you can easily emulate `seamless`, as shown in Figure 5-10.

Figure 5-10: Inline frame without the default border

Custom Attributes

HTML5 adds many new elements and changes the definition of old ones to support semantic web development. An important step toward this paradigm is that HTML5 allows using custom attributes. This is very important, because you can use them to provide your own semantic to your own markup building blocks. To understand the way HTML5 defines and utilizes custom attributes, take a look at Listing 5-12.

Listing 5-12: Exercise-05-09/index.html

```
<!DOCTYPE html>
<html>
<head>
  <title>Custom attributes</title>
</head>
<body>
  <h3>Product details</h3>
  <div id="computer"
    data-product-cpu="4th generation Intel Core i5"
    data-product-ssd="128/256/512 GB">
    <h4>Surface 3 Pro</h4>
    <p>CPU: <span id="s2ProCpu"></span></p>
    <p>SSD: <span id="s2ProSsd"></span></p>
    <button onclick="getDetails('computer',
      's2ProCpu', 's2ProSsd')">
      Get Details
```

```
    </button>
  </div>
  <script>
    function getDetails(prod, label1, label2) {
      var prodNode = document.getElementById(prod);
      var l1 = document.getElementById(label1);
      var l2 = document.getElementById(label2);
      l1.innerText =
        prodNode.getAttribute('data-product-cpu');
      l2.innerText = prodNode.dataset.productSsd;
    }
  </script>
</body>
</html>
```

Here, the `<div>` element with "computer" identifier defines two custom attributes, `data-product-cpu`, and `data-product-ssd`, respectively. When the user clicks the Get Details button, the `getDetails()` function reads the attribute values and displays them on the screen. The first attribute is read with the `getAttribute()` function, while the second one uses the `dataset` property of the `<div>` node. This property-based style uses naming conventions to translate the 'data-product-ssd' attribute name to 'productSsd'.

NOTE: Do not feel intimidated if it is not really clear for you how `getDetails()` does its magic. In Part II you will learn the basics of JavaScript and you'll understand the mechanisms behind this code.

Painting the Canvas

Today online games infest the web. Without downloading and installing any application, you can directly go to a web page and immediately start an on-line game. Most of them have amazing graphics, and is totally competitive with many simple games that require local installations. These games are generally implemented with Flash, Silverlight, or other plug-ins that support the hardware acceleration available in your computer.

HTML5 provides a new element, `<canvas>`, which is a place where you can draw. The standard defines a canvas API with operations supporting web applications that demand high performance, and low-overhead graphics. Instead of using markup, you describe your drawing as a set of instructions—JavaScript function calls to the canvas API—, and it provides a great flexibility. In this section you will only scratch the surface of the possibilities made available by `<canvas>` and its accompanying API, but it will be enough to understand the concept behind this new HTML5 element.

NOTE: To use the canvas API, you must have a basic understanding of JavaScript. Do not feel intimidated, if you did not use JavaScript before, the samples in this section are easy to read with assuming you have ever used C, C++, C#, VB, or any other imperative programming languages. There are no tricks utilizing any very JavaScript-specific features.

Say Hello To <canvas>

There is no shorter way to understand <canvas> than creating your first page utilizing this element. In the next exercise you will learn how easy painting the canvas is. You are going to create a simple animation that shows the trajectory of a flung ball. A momentary snapshot of your final application is shown in Figure 5-11.

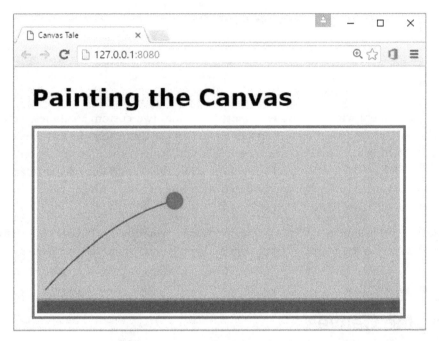

Figure 5-11: A snapshot of the final application

The algorithm behind the application is very simple. The trajectory of the ball is calculated from the previous position and the momentary speed of the ball. The ball has an initial speed—a vector combined from its horizontal and vertical speed. The horizontal speed of the ball is constant; however, its vertical speed is continuously changed by the gravity.

To save time, you are going to start from a prepared Visual Studio solution that can be found in the Exercise-05-10-Begin folder.

EXERCISE 5-10: Painting the canvas area

In this exercise you are going to paint only a static picture of the animation's scene, including the sky, the soil, the grass, and the ball. To carry out this simple activity, follow these steps:

1. Create a copy of the Exercise-05-10-Begin folder (Exercise-05-10), and use this new folder.

2. In the code editor, open index.html. It contains this markup:

```
<!DOCTYPE html>
<html>
<head>
  <title>Canvas Tale</title>
  <link href="style.css" rel="stylesheet" />
  <script src="drawing.js"></script>
</head>
<body>
  <h1>Painting the Canvas</h1>
  <!-- Put the canvas here -->
</body>
</html>
```

This file loads the `drawing.js` script file and links the style sheet to the page. The real "engine" behind the app can be found in `drawing.js`, which contains a few JavaScript constants, variables, and functions:

```
// --- Constants
const HEIGHT = 250;
const WIDTH = 500;
const BALL = 12;
const SOIL = 17;
const GRASS = 3;
const BALLCOLOR = '#CC333F';
const SKYCOLOR = '#9CC4E4';
const SOILCOLOR = '#6A4A3C';
const GRASSCOLOR = '#93A42A';

// --- Drawing context
var ctx;
var ballX;
var ballY;

function initDraw(elemId) {
  ctx = document.getElementById(elemId).getContext('2d');
  ballX = BALL;
  ballY = HEIGHT - BALL - SOIL - GRASS;
  draw();
}

function drawArea() {
  // Draw sky
  ctx.fillStyle = SKYCOLOR;
  ctx.beginPath();
  ctx.rect(0, 0, WIDTH, HEIGHT - SOIL - GRASS);
  ctx.fill();

  // Draw soil
  ctx.fillStyle = SOILCOLOR;
  ctx.beginPath();
  ctx.rect(0, HEIGHT - SOIL, WIDTH, SOIL);
  ctx.fill();
```

```
  // Draw grass
  ctx.fillStyle = GRASSCOLOR;
  ctx.beginPath();
  ctx.rect(0, HEIGHT - SOIL - GRASS, WIDTH, GRASS);
  ctx.fill();
}

function draw() {
  drawArea();

  // Draw ball
  Ctx.fillStyle = BALLCOLOR;
  ctx.beginPath();
  ctx.arc(ballX, ballY, BALL, 0, Math.PI * 2);
  ctx.closePath();
  ctx.fill();
}
```

At the end of this exercise I will explain how this script works. Right now it is enough to know that the `initDraw()` function is responsible to paint the canvas.

3. Display the page. As you expect, it displays only the "Paint the Canvas" heading, and nothing else.

4. Switch to the `index.html` file, and change the placeholder comment to the markup highlighted in this snippet:

```
<!DOCTYPE html>
<html>
<head>
  <title>Canvas Tale</title>
  <link href="style.css" rel="stylesheet" />
  <script src="drawing.js"></script>
</head>
<body>
  <h1>Painting the Canvas</h1>
  <canvas id="myCanvas"
    width="500" height="250">
  </canvas>
  <script>
    initDraw('myCanvas');
  </script>
</body>
</html>
```

The `<canvas>` tag defines the drawing area. It specifies its identifier as "myCanvas", and sets its width and height to 500 and 250 pixels, respectively. The `<canvas>` tag is followed by a `<script>` that invokes the `initDraw()` function passing the identifier of the canvas as its input argument.

5. Turn back to the browser. Now, it displays the canvas with the scenery already drawn, as shown in Figure 5-12.

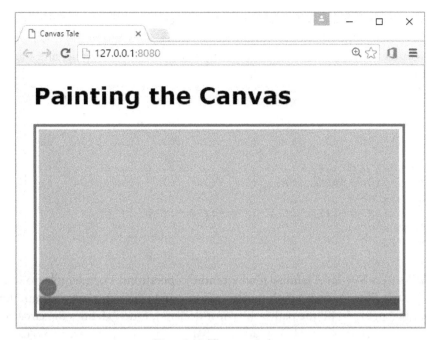

Figure 5-12: The scenery is drawn

HOW IT WORKS

In step 4, you defined the <canvas> tag and set it up with the "myCanvas" identifier. The page loads the drawing.js file in its <head> section, so the <script> placed right after the canvas knows the initDraw() function, and invokes it with the id of the canvas passed.

The initDraw() function does all initialization, and it invokes the draw() method to paint the scenery:

```
1 function initDraw(elemId) {
2     ctx = document.getElementById(elemId).getContext('2d');
3     ballX = BALL;
4     ballY = HEIGHT - BALL - SOIL - GRASS;
5     draw();
6 }
```

Line 2 is the most important, as it sets up the context object (ctx), which can be used to draw shapes on the canvas. First, using document.getElementById(), it retrieves the object representing the "myCanvas" element in the page. By invoking getContext('2d'), it obtains a context object that allows drawing to a two-dimensional surface, and stores it in ctx.

NOTE: You probably ask yourself whether there is a three-dimensional drawing context—based on the fact that a two-dimensional drawing context is used ("2d" in the code). Not yet, but the creators of HTML5 have left space for one in the future. There are frameworks using canvas with three-dimensional rendering, such as *Babylon.js*.

The `<canvas>` element uses a coordinate system that designates its top-left corner as the point **(0, 0)**. The canvas used in `index.html` has a width of 500 pixels, and a height of 250 pixels, so its bottom-right corner is the point **(499, 249)**. Using this coordinate mapping, line 3 and 4 initialize the position of the ball, and then Line 5 calls the `draw()` function.

It is worth the time to examine `draw()`, since it tells a lot about the canvas API:

```
 1 function draw() {
 2    drawArea();
 3
 4    // Draw ball
 5    ctx.fillStyle = BALLCOLOR;
 6    ctx.beginPath();
 7    ctx.arc(ballX, ballY, BALL, 0, Math.PI * 2);
 8    ctx.closePath();
 9    ctx.fill();
10 }
```

The canvas API offers low-level (and so low-overhead) operations. For example, to draw the ball, you set up a fill style (line 5), start a path (line 6), draw a circle (line 7), close the path (line 8), and finally instruct the engine to fill the path you've just declared. Line 7 defines the circle as an arc with a center point of **(ballX, ballY)**, a radius of **BALL**, and starting the arc at 3 o'clock on a dial **(0)**, and moving clockwise it goes back to 3 o'clock (**Math.PI*2**).

NOTE: Angles in the canvas API use radians (rad). So 0 rad (0°) is at 3 o'clock, PI/2 rad (90°) at 6 o'clock, PI rad (180°) at 9 o'clock, 3*PI/2 rad (270°) at 12 o'clock, and finally, 2*PI rad (360°) is at 3 o'clock, again.

The `drawArea()` function is used to draw the sky, soil, and grass. It uses a similar approach to paint rectangular areas, as `draw()` does to paint the ball. The following code snippet uses the `rect()` operation to create the soil:

```
ctx.fillStyle = SOILCOLOR;
ctx.beginPath();
ctx.rect(0, HEIGHT - SOIL, WIDTH, SOIL);
ctx.fill();
```

Here `rect` uses the **(0, HEIGHT-SOIL)** point as the top-left corner of the rectangle, the third and fourth arguments define its width and height, respectively.

As Exercise 5-10 demonstrated, it's pretty easy to create a static canvas. When you create real apps (games) you definitely use a canvas that displays animations. Thanks to the low-level graphic primitives of the canvas API, animations are simple to create—as you will learn in the next exercise.

Vivifying the Canvas

The ball still stays on the surface, so we need to add calculations that move it as time goes on, and redraw the ball periodically in its new position.

EXERCISE 5-11: Moving the ball

In this exercise you add the calculation that will compute the new position of the ball. This uses the current position and velocity of the ball, calculates the new ball coordinates, and modifies the vertical velocity component with the effect of gravity. To implement these changes, follow these steps:

1. Turn back to the code editor, and carry on from the point you completed the previous exercise. Open the drawing.js file, and add new constant and variable declarations, as the highlighted code shows in this snippet:

```
// --- Constants
const HEIGHT = 250;
const WIDTH = 500;
const BALL = 12;
const SOIL = 17;
const GRASS = 3;
const BALLCOLOR = '#CC333F';
const SKYCOLOR = '#9CC4E4';
const SOILCOLOR = '#6A4A3C';
const GRASSCOLOR = '#93A42A';
const GRAV = 0.02;

// --- Drawing context
var ctx;
var ballX;
var ballY;
var vX = 2.0;
var vY = 2.25;
```

GRAV is a constant representing the force of gravity, vX and vY stand for the horizontal and vertical components of the ball's initial velocity.

2. Add the highlighted computations to the draw() function:

```
function draw() {
  drawArea();

  // Draw ball
  ctx.fillStyle = BALLCOLOR;
  ctx.beginPath();
  ctx.arc(ballX, ballY, BALL, 0, Math.PI * 2);
  ctx.closePath();
  ctx.fill();

  // Calculate the next ball position
  ballX += vX;
  ballY -= vY;
  vY -= GRAV;
}
```

3. Modify the drawInit() function to calculate the 25th ball position, as highlighted here:

```
function initDraw(elemId) {
  ctx = document.getElementById(elemId).getContext('2d');
  ballX = BALL;
  ballY = HEIGHT - BALL - SOIL - GRASS;
  for (var i = 0; i < 25; i++) {
      draw();
  }
}
```

4. Display the page. Now, as shown in Figure 5-13, the flung ball advanced.

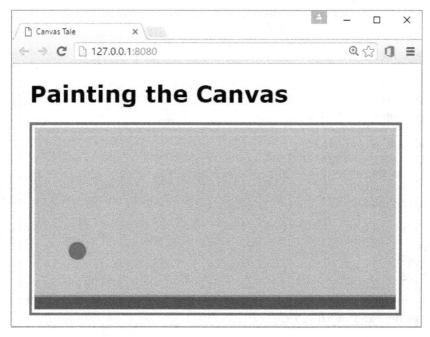

Figure 5-13: Now, the flung ball advanced

5. There is still no visible animation. Modify the section of variables by adding these definitions right after the declaration of vY:

```
var timerHandle;
var initialBallY;
```

6. Remove the **for** loop from **drawInit()**, and change it as highlighted in this code snippet:

```
function initDraw(elemId) {
  ctx = document.getElementById(elemId).getContext('2d');
  ballX = BALL;
  ballY = HEIGHT - BALL - SOIL - GRASS;
  initialBallY = ballY;
  timerHandle = setInterval(draw, 10);
}
```

7. Turn back to the browser, and refresh the page. This time you can see that the ball flies on its trajectory. Nonetheless, it does not stop when reaches the grass again.

NOTE: If you do not refresh the page manually, you may miss how the ball is animated.

8. Add the following lines at the beginning of the body of **draw( )**:

```
// Stop ball
if (ballY > initialBallY) {
  clearInterval(timerHandle);
}
```

10. Go back to the browser, and refresh the page. This time the ball not only flies on its trajectory, but stops when landing on the grass.

HOW IT WORKS

In step 1 and 2, you implemented the single calculation that computes the new ball coordinates. The **for** loop you added in step 3 calculated the 25th position of the ball, but it did it so fast that you could not see the ball is being animated.

In step 6, you implemented a timer with the **setInterval(draw, 10)** operation. The **setInterval** method starts a timer that invokes the **draw( )** function in every 10 milliseconds. It retrieves a handle that can be utilized to interact with the timer, you stored it in **timerHandle**. That time the animation went on smoothly, as you expected, but the ball did not stop.

In step 8 you added a condition to **draw( )**, which checked if the ball had landed, and then stopped the timer by invoking **clearInterval( )**. The **clearInterval( )** function accepts a handle pointing to a timer, so here you passed **timerHandle** set up when you created the animation timer.

NOTE: You can find the completed code for this exercise in the **Exercise-05-11** folder.

This exercise moved the ball. To complete the original task, you need to draw the trajectory. In the next exercise, you are going to create this drawing code.

EXERCISE 5-12: Drawing the trajectory

To complete the task, follow these steps:

1. Switch back to the code editor, and carry on from the point you completed the previous exercise. Open the **drawing.js** file, and add the following variable declaration to the code, right after the declaration of the **vY** variable:

```
var trajectory = [];
```

2. Modify the body of **draw( )** as shown highlighted in this code snippet:

```
function draw() {
  // Stop ball
  if (ballY > initialBallY) {
    clearInterval(timerHandle);
  }

  drawArea();
```

```
// Save the current position
trajectory.push({ x: ballX, y: ballY })

// Draw trajectory
ctx.strokeStyle = 'black';
ctx.beginPath();
ctx.moveTo(trajectory[0].x, trajectory[0].y);
for (i = 1; i < trajectory.length ; i++) {
  ctx.lineTo(trajectory[i].x, trajectory[i].y);
}
ctx.stroke();

// Draw ball
ctx.fillStyle = BALLCOLOR;
ctx.beginPath();
ctx.arc(ballX, ballY, BALL, 0, Math.PI * 2);
ctx.closePath();
ctx.fill();

// Calculate the next ball position
ballX += vX;
ballY -= vY;
vY -= GRAV;
}
```

3. Turn back to the browser. Now, this time you can see the trajectory, as shown in Figure 5-14. Close the browser.

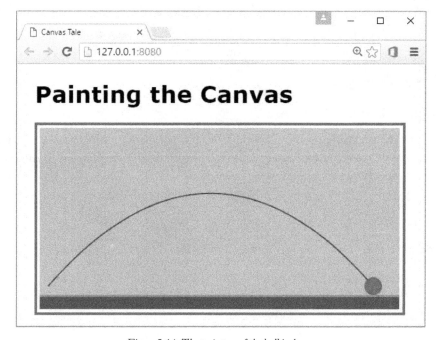

Figure 5-14: The trajectory of the ball is drawn

NOTE: You can find the completed code for this exercise in the `Exercise-05-12` folder.

HOW IT WORKS

The `trajectory` variable you added in step 1, represents an empty array. In step 2, you saved the current ball position with the following code:

```
trajectory.push({ x: ballX, y: ballY })
```

This code—the invocation of `push()`—added a new object to the `trajectory` array. This object is created with JavaScript's object notation as a tuple of two coordinates, x and y, respectively. With this instruction `ballX` was saved as the x, `ballY` as the y coordinate.

The code drawing the trajectory is very similar to the code responsible for painting the scenery:

```
1 ctx.strokeStyle = 'black';
2 ctx.beginPath();
3 ctx.moveTo(trajectory[0].x, trajectory[0].y);
4 for (i = 1; i < trajectory.length ; i++) {
5   ctx.lineTo(trajectory[i].x, trajectory[i].y);
6 }
7 ctx.stroke();
```

The `strokeStyle` property of the drawing context sets the color of the line. First, a new path is started (line 2), and then the starting point is moved (line 3) to the very first point stored in `trajectory`—which happens to be the starting position of the ball. The `for` loop between line 4 and 6 appends a new line segment to this path according to the stored coordinates. When all segments are added, the `stroke()` method draws them.

NOTE: Taking a closer look at the code reveals that actually every pixel of the canvas is redrawn for every animation frame, because `draw()` invokes the `drawArea()` function that repaints the sky, soil, and grass, too. You can optimize this code, for example, you need to draw the soil and grass only once, at the very beginning of the canvas setup.

What Else You Can Do with a Canvas

The canvas is a much more powerful tool than demonstrated by these short exercises. The canvas API contains many operations to draw, and it leverages the hardware acceleration—provided your browser supports it. The canvas handles fractional pixels, can use antialiasing, and many other features to ensure a great user experience.

You can combine a canvas with other HTML markup, and so you can create overlapping layers in your page. This hybrid solution is often useful, because in this way you use both HTML markup and canvas where they are the most powerful. Canvas is very strong in managing graphics, while HTML is great in displaying text layout. For example, when you create a game, graphics can be arranged by a canvas object, while text (e.g. scores and statistics) can be managed with HTML markup.

CSS provides you properties to absolutely position page elements, and arrange their z-order (virtual depth on the page). With them you can easily create hybrid (combined) pages. For example, if you change the style.css file of Exercise-05-12 to this one, you can create a page with a canvas overlaid by the heading element:

```
body {
  font-family: Verdana, Arial, sans-serif;
  margin-top: 48px;
  margin-left: 48px;
}

#myCanvas {
  border: 4px solid dimgray;
  position: absolute;
  z-index: -1;
  padding: 4px;
  top: 24px;
  left: 24px;
}
```

This modification alters the page as shown in Figure 5-15.

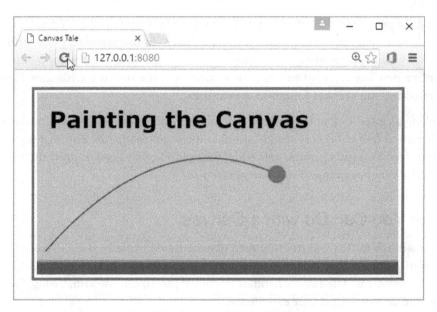

Figure 5-15: Canvas overlaid with HTML text

Facing with the Past and Future of HTML5

By now, you learned about HTML5, and you had to think of older HTML versions only tangentially. However, in real life, you often meet old HTML dialects, including XHTML and other old HTML versions. They are very close to HTML5 you learned in this book, but they may use HTML elements and attributes you do not know yet. On the other hand, HTML5 defines new elements that are not supported by all browsers, or not fully, but partially.

This section gives you a few tips to learn how to live together with this phenomenon.

Old HTML Dialects

At the very beginning of your first exercises, you met the `<!DOCTYPE>` tag that instructs the web browser about the version—dialect—of HTML the page is written in. Since that you have applied this tag many times in the form of `<!DOCTYPE html>`, which refers to HTML5. You have already learned about the "living standard" approach the creators of HTML5 follow, so you know that next markup versions (e.g. HTML5.1) will use exactly the very same `<!DOCTYPE html>` tag.

So, if you read HTML source and you find a different `<!DOCTYPE>`, you can be sure the page was written with an older version of HTML. Older does not necessary mean obsolete, or outdated, just as using HTML5 does not mean that your pages are modern. You must learn to live together with older markup, and be prepared to understand page structures written with them—and it is not difficult at all. Here is a list of older document types:

HTML 4.01 was the last published ISO/IEC international standard of the markup before HTML5. This standard provides three flavors, Strict, Transitional, and Frameset, respectively. These flavors use the following `<!DOCTYPE>` designations:

HTML 4.01 Strict—the standard contains all HTML elements and attributes, but does not include presentational or deprecated elements (like `<font>`); framesets are not allowed.

```
<!DOCTYPE HTML PUBLIC "-//W3C//DTD HTML 4.01//EN"
"http://www.w3.org/TR/html4/strict.dtd">
```

HTML 4.01 Transitional— the standard contains all HTML elements and attributes, and in contrast to HTML 4.01 Strict, it includes presentational or deprecated elements; but still, framesets are not allowed.

```
<!DOCTYPE HTML PUBLIC "-//W3C//DTD HTML 4.01 Transitional//EN"
"http://www.w3.org/TR/html4/loose.dtd">
```

HTML 4.01 Frameset—equals to HTML 4.01 Transitional, and additionally allows using framesets.

```
<!DOCTYPE HTML PUBLIC "-//W3C//DTD HTML 4.01 Frameset//EN"
"http://www.w3.org/TR/html4/frameset.dtd">
```

XHTML 1.0 uses markup written as well-formed XML (each opening tag must have a proper closing tag). Similar to HTML 4.01, XHTML 1.0 has Strict, Transitional, and Frameset flavors.

XHTML 1.0 Strict:

```
<!DOCTYPE html PUBLIC "-//W3C//DTD XHTML 1.0 Strict//EN"
"http://www.w3.org/TR/xhtml1/DTD/xhtml1-strict.dtd">
```

XHTML 1.0 Transitional:

```
<!DOCTYPE html PUBLIC "-//W3C//DTD XHTML 1.0 Transitional//EN"
"http://www.w3.org/TR/xhtml1/DTD/xhtml1-transitional.dtd">
```

XHTML 1.0 Frameset:

```
<!DOCTYPE html PUBLIC "-//W3C//DTD XHTML 1.0 Frameset//EN"
"http://www.w3.org/TR/xhtml1/DTD/xhtml1-frameset.dtd">
```

XHTML 1.1—this markup is equal to XHTML 1.0 Strict, but it allows you to add modules.

```
<!DOCTYPE html PUBLIC "-//W3C//DTD XHTML 1.1//EN"
"http://www.w3.org/TR/xhtml11/DTD/xhtml11.dtd">
```

The original HTML markup defined several elements that did not have any special semantic; they simply set up visual appearance of documents. Such elements were `<basefont>` (default font color and font size), `<center>` (a tag used to center-align text), and a few more. The Strict mode does not allow using them, while the Transitional mode does.

HTML 4.01 and XHTML 1.0 defines elements that help displaying multiple web pages within a browser window, organized into rectangular frames. These elements are `<frameset>` and `<frame>`. Using multiple pages in this way is obsolete, and has potential security consequences, too. You must use the Frameset mode (either HTML 4.01 or XHTML 1.0) to leverage this old method. In all other flavors—including HTML5—you can use the `<iframe>` tag instead.

Issues with New HTML5 Tags

The nightmare of web page designers and developers is the plethora of browsers they need to prepare their apps to work with. At the first sight the world of HTML seems easy to understand and apply. However, when you assemble complex web pages with styles and JavaScript code snippets, different browsers make your development diverge. The root of this divergence is that browsers provide separate feature sets, and implement standards in—sometimes only slightly, but—different ways. For a long time, the black sheep of browsers was Internet Explorer (especially IE6) that required its own separate code branch for almost every app.

HTML5 has brought a kind of balance, because browser vendors try to accommodate the standard continuously as much as they can. Nonetheless, there are still differences in the features sets of browsers. There are a few HTML5 elements that are not supported by any browsers, as of this writing, for example `<command>`, and `<menu>`. There are elements where attributes are not fully supported by all browsers, for example the `reversed` attribute of `<ol>` is not handled by Internet Explorer (still not in version 11).

By means of uniformity, the most disturbing part of HTML5 is the `<input>` element. There are a few new HTML5 input types that are supported by most major browsers (but not all of them yet), such as `number`, `email`, `url`. There are many types scarcely implemented, such as `color`, `search`, and date-related input. As you learned in Chapter 4, the appearance of form controls in different browsers is far from being uniform, and the plight is the same with form validation messages, too.

NOTE: To overcome this mess, the best way is to use JavaScript UI libraries, such as jQuery UI, Bootstrap, Kendo UI, etc. These libraries handle the variegation of browsers, and free developers from managing them manually.

HTML5 Tools

HTML development would not be really productive without great tools that help you solve common issues and overcome frequently occurring situations, such as managing browser-independency. In this section you will learn a few tools that make your everyday work with HTML easier, and let you focus on your goals instead of coping with small, but time-wasting details.

HTML Validation

You learned that browsers pamper you by means of skimming over the typos and semantic inaccuracies of your web page. Sometimes you do not even know that there are issues with a web page. But there's a potential problem with relying the browser to fix up your faulty markup. The standard defines what to do with proper markup, but does not specify how to overcome with wrong one. It might happen that wrong markup causes mystic issues that behave very differently depending on the browser in which you display the page.

HTML validation tools are to observe the anomalies coming from using an invalid markup. The W3C consortium, who leads the standardization process of HTML5, provides a validation service (`http://validator.w3.org/`) that allows you to check HTML content by its URI, by file upload, or even by directly typing it. Figure 5-16 shows this tool with a small HTML page typed in as direct input.

If you do not see what is wrong with this markup, just click the Check button, and the tool instantly tells you that you forgot to add a `<title>` tag to the `<head>` section, as shown in Figure 5-17. Besides errors, this validator tool also checks for potential issues and raises warnings. One of the best virtues of this tool is that it provides links to the appropriate sections of the standard, and so you can immediately navigate to it.

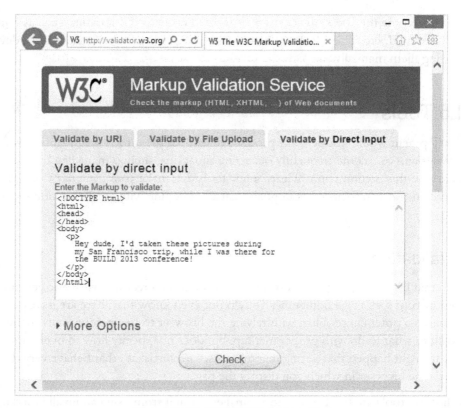

Figure 5-16: The W3C HTML Validator Tool

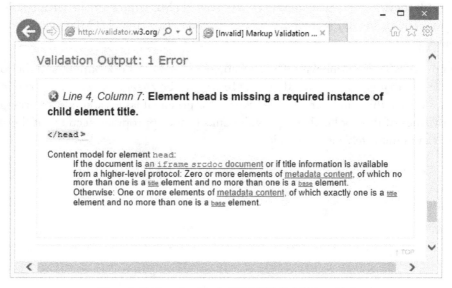

Figure 5-17: Error found by the W3C HTML Validator Tool

Checking HTML5 compatibility

The HTML5 standard reached the recommendation phase (you can take into account as an approved standard) on 28th October, 2014. Before creating a web application, it is worth it to check how certain browsers support the HTML5 markup set you intend to use. There are many tools and web sites providing information about it. One of my favorites is `http://html5test.com/`, which allows you compare browsers as well as focus on specific features, such as audio codec support, semantic elements, and many others. Figure 5-18 shows a view that compares Chrome 45, Internet Explorer 11, Edge, and Firefox 40 by means of field type support.

forms	73	34	49	62
Field types				
▶ input type=text	Yes ✓	Partial ○	Yes ✓	Yes ✓
▶ input type=search	Yes ✓	Yes ✓	Yes ✓	Yes ✓
▶ input type=tel	Yes ✓	Yes ✓	Yes ✓	Yes ✓
▶ input type=url	Yes ✓	Yes ✓	Yes ✓	Yes ✓
▶ input type=email	Yes ✓	Yes ✓	Yes ✓	Yes ✓
▶ input type=date	Yes ✓	No ✕	No ✕	Yes ✓
▶ input type=month	Yes ✓	No ✕	No ✕	Yes ✓
▶ input type=week	Yes ✓	No ✕	No ✕	Yes ✓
▶ input type=time	Yes ✓	No ✕	No ✕	Yes ✓
▶ input type=datetime	No ✕	No ✕	No ✕	No ✕
▶ input type=datetime-local	Yes ✓	No ✕	No ✕	Yes ✓
▶ input type=number	Yes ✓	Yes ✓	Yes ✓	Yes ✓
▶ input type=range	Yes ✓	Yes ✓	Yes ✓	Yes ✓
▶ input type=color	Yes ✓	No ✕	Yes ✓	No ✕

Figure 5-18: The html5test.com sites comparing field types in Chrome 44 (first column), Internet Explorer 11 (second column), Edge (third column), and Firefox 40 (fourth column)

Another great chart is available at `http://fmbip.com/litmus/` (by FindMeByIP.com), that summarizes not only HTML5 markup compatibility, but also CSS3 information, too, as shown in Figure 5-19.

205

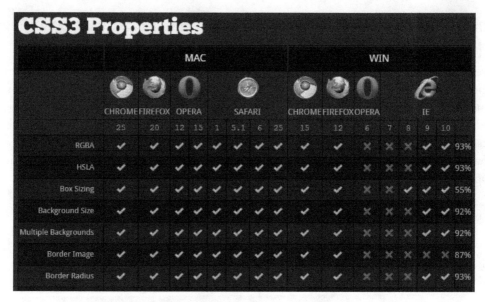

CSS3 Properties

	MAC								WIN						
	CHROME	FIREFOX	OPERA	OPERA	SAFARI	SAFARI	SAFARI	SAFARI	CHROME	FIREFOX	OPERA	IE	IE	IE	IE
	25	20	12	15	1	5.1	6	25	15	12	6	7	8	9	10	
RGBA	✓	✓	✓	✓	✓	✓	✓	✓	✓	✓	✗	✗	✗	✓	✓	93%
HSLA	✓	✓	✓	✓	✓	✓	✓	✓	✓	✓	✗	✗	✗	✓	✓	93%
Box Sizing	✓	✓	✓	✓	✓	✓	✓	✓	✓	✓	✗	✗	✓	✓	✓	55%
Background Size	✓	✓	✓	✓	✓	✓	✓	✓	✓	✓	✗	✗	✗	✓	✓	92%
Multiple Backgrounds	✓	✓	✓	✓	✓	✓	✓	✓	✓	✓	✗	✗	✗	✓	✓	92%
Border Image	✓	✓	✓	✓	✓	✓	✓	✓	✓	✓	✗	✗	✗	✗	✗	87%
Border Radius	✓	✓	✓	✓	✓	✓	✓	✓	✓	✓	✗	✗	✗	✓	✓	93%

Figure 5-19: Chart showing CSS3 Properties compatibility of major browsers

These tools are crucial, because you can assess the potential issues you'll face when using a particular set of HTML5 elements with a set of preferred browsers. You can adjust your software design to the findings you read from these charts, or you can utilize the information to decide whether you really want to support a specific browser—according to your budget.

HINT: Do not forget that the standard may slightly change, and new browsers may support additional features compared to previous versions. Check these charts regularly to keep your apps up-to-date.

Summary

Beside the fundamental elements you already learned in previous chapters, HTML defines several useful markup tags, such as thematic break (`<hr>`), quotes (`<q>` and `<blockquote>`), progress bar (`<progress>`). To specify hot-spots in images, HTML adds a mapping mechanism that allows assigning separate hyperlinks to different image regions (`<map>`, `<area>`).

The concept of `<canvas>`, a new element in HTML5, opens a new horizon of web applications that can use a two-dimensional drawing surface with hardware-accelerated graphics. The `<canvas>` uses an API—it is the part of the standard, too—that allows using simple, but powerful graphic primitives, which are suitable to write even performance-demanding applications, such as games.

Although more and more browsers support HTML5, there are—sometimes subtle, occasionally more significant—differences in the feature set they provide. The best way to overcome these deviations is to use predefined JavaScript libraries and tools, which allow you to create your browser-independent pages.

Chapter 6:
Exploring the Document Object Model

WHAT YOU WILL LEARN IN THIS CHAPTER

Understanding what the Document Object Model is
Navigating the document tree
Changing your page programmatically with the help of the Document Object Model
Getting to know the global attributes and events of HTML

By now, you already understand how HTML, CSS, and JavaScript connect to each other to provide fully functional web pages. The structure of the page is built on HTML markup that provides the content. The typography, the visual appearance of the page—that makes it attractive—is made complete by CSS that assigns style to the structure. JavaScript brings interactivity, motion, and dynamism to the page. In the exercises and listings of the previous chapters you often see HTML markup mixed with styles and scripts, so you probably got used to the phenomenon that these three technologies work together.

Besides the role-based connection among HTML, CSS, and JavaScript, there is another point of gravity that attracts and binds them: the Document Object Model, or shortly, DOM. In this chapter you will learn why it is important in creating your web pages.

DOM Basics

The structure of HTML markup evidently provides a hierarchy of elements, similarly as any programming language provides a syntax tree and a semantic tree. For example, take a look at this very simple markup:

```
<html>
  <head>
    <title>Simple web page</title>
  </head>
  <body>
    <p>This is a paragraph</p>
  </body>
</html>
```

The natural hierarchy of the components of the page is easy to understand. The `<html>` element directly embeds two other elements, `<head>`, and `<title>`, respectively, and each of them nests another element, `<title>`, and `<p>`, as shown in Figure 6-1. As you can see from this figure, texts enclosed by `<title>` and `<p>` are also the part of this structure.

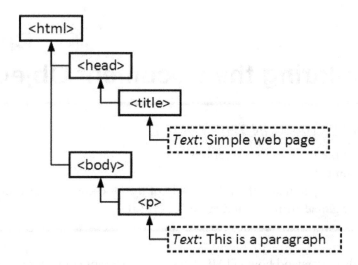

Figure 6-1: The structure of a simple HTML markup

If you try to think as the rendering engine of the browser does, this object model is indispensable to display the page. Right before showing the page, the browser must build up the structure of the page. This step generally starts parsing the HTML source, and ends with a structure of the page represented as a tree (or tree-like) structure in the memory. Different browsers may—and definitely do—use separate implementations to express this structure, but all representations must use the same semantic; otherwise they would render different pages—by means of page structure.

After having prepared this model in the memory, rendering engines utilize it to display the page according to the HTML standard.

Ubiquitous Language of Page Representation

For a moment, try to think with the head of the HTML standard creators'. The standard defines more than hundred markup tags with their semantics, properties, and behavior—including the visual appearance. How would you describe them in a formal way so that all browser vendors can understand them, without any ambiguities?

For each element, you need to create a definition that explains the things the certain element represents, or with other words, you need to describe the semantic of the element. You cannot put elements everywhere in the markup arbitrarily, they all have a well-defined context where they can be put in. For example, the `<title>` element can be placed only within the `<head>` element. You also need to define the content model of an element, and describe what other elements it can embed. Most markup elements have attributes, so you need to explain their usage as well.

As you see, the description of markup elements needs a kind of object model. The browser also need this model to render an HTML page based on the behavior (or definition) of the fundamental elements. The creators of HTML5 put the Document Object Model into the standard as its backbone, as a ubiquitous language for standard designers and implementers (browser vendors).

NOTE: The term *ubiquitous language* comes from the world of modeling. It is used to characterize a common language used by business analysts and developers on the same way to avoid ambiguities. The main virtue of a ubiquitous language is that it avoids the abstraction gap that would otherwise exist between the domain language used by analysts, and the language used by developers.

Cornerstone of Interactions

Do not think that DOM is great only for standardizers and browser vendors. Developers are the real winners of DOM's existence! Almost every interaction between a user and a web page is built on DOM. When you click a component of a page, a node of the DOM hierarchy receives the event and responds by executing some code. Most interactive user interface elements change the DOM dynamically to provide a UI effect. Web pages that keep the UI responsive while running queries against the server in the background, use the DOM to update the page when results arrive, too.

Many pages generate additional UI components at the client side—right after the page is loaded—, such as thumbnails, quick links, table of contents, or other elements helping page navigation. The scripts behind these activities also utilize the DOM. Moving charts, animated figures, interactive footers and banners all leverage the DOM.

The DOM Defined by the W3C Standard

The World Wide Web Consortium's standard defines the DOM like this (source: `http://www.w3.org/DOM/`):

"The Document Object Model is a platform- and language-neutral interface that will allow programs and scripts to dynamically access and update the content, structure and style of documents. The document can be further processed and the results of that processing can be incorporated back into the presented page."

This standard separates the DOM definition into three different parts. It contains an abstract *Core DOM* description, which is a model for any structured document. This abstraction is taken on to an *XML DOM* (standard model for XML documents), and to an *HTML DOM* (standard model for HTML documents).

The DOM Application Programming Interface

Besides describing a standard object model for HTML, the DOM standard defines an Application Programming Interface (API) to manage this model. The available functionality of this API is defined as a set of abstract interfaces, such as `HTMLDocument` (describes the behavior of an HTML document behind a web page), `HTMLElement` (a single instance of a markup element within a document), `HTMLCollection` (a collection of `HTMLElement` instances), and others. These abstract interfaces are implemented in multiple places to support all DOM related operations.

First, the browser implements them so that it can display the web page—based on the HTML markup requested from a server. Often the browser proffers this interface to plug-ins so that those can leverage the DOM to analyze and transform a loaded page. A good example of plug-in analyzing the page is the HTML5 Outliner tool you already met in *Chapter 3 (Sections)*. Skype and other VOIP apps often install browser plug-ins that recognize phone numbers in the web page and surround them with a context-specific markup that allows starting calls. These use the DOM to transform the loaded web page.

Second, these abstract interfaces are implemented in the JavaScript engines of browsers so that page developers will be able to write scripts interacting with this model.

In this book I will cover only the JavaScript implementation of DOM interfaces (partially), and do not treat plug-in development, which is very browser-specific.

The HTML DOM API standardizes the properties and operations that can be used on specific objects of the model. Nonetheless, many—but not all—browser vendors extend this API with extra operations. These may provide you a simpler way to carry out certain tasks, but you may create a page that does not work on every browser.

What the DOM Covers

In Figure 6-1, you saw the graphical representation of a web page's structure—or using the HTML terminology, the structure of an HTML document. The DOM API allows full control (both querying and altering the DOM), and you have practically full support in the API to leverage all features provided by the HTML markup. The best way to understand what the DOM API covers is to look at examples, but before doing this, let's have a short overview of what this API proffers to developers.

First of all, it allows accessing a certain part of the document (the HTML markup). You can access a certain markup element using its identifier, or a collection of elements by their name, class type (according to the values of the elements' `class` attribute), their tag name (for example all `<h1>` elements), and by several other aspects. You can query the metadata of a document, including its URL, character set, last modification date, etc.

When you obtain a collection of HTML elements, you can iterate them and carry out some operation with chosen items.

If you obtain an instance of a markup element (for example, an `<img>` element), you can access the content of that element, including the full markup they embed, the embedded text, as well as the values of the element's attributes. Moreover, you can modify both the content and the attributes—with only a few exceptions, where a certain attribute or property of an element is read-only. Each element instance has global attributes—by now, I have not explicitly mentioned them yet—, for example the id attribute, which has been used in many listings and exercises earlier.

There are a few common operations on every markup element that you can use. For example, you may set the focus to the specified element, or ask the browser to scroll it into view, and so on.

You already learned that JavaScript is the cornerstone of web page interactivity; when you interact with a page (or a component on the page), a script is triggered. This behavior is based on the DOM. Each markup element can respond dozens of events that can be accessed through the DOM. You can define a response for an event, and you can trigger events as well.

At the document level, DOM provides you information that allows carrying out a number of document operation, such as opening an HTML document, close the current document, writing content directly to the document, and so on.

Now, you probably have a basic understanding of the DOM API, so it is time to take a closer look through several code listings and exercises.

NOTE: In the next exercises you will use JavaScript to understand how the DOM works. Just like in the previous exercises, you are not assumed to know JavaScript, you will understand all programs with the help of explanations. You do not have to wait very long for getting closer to JavaScript programming: in the next chapter, *Chapter 7: Getting to Know JavaScript* you will learn every nitty-gritty detail you may miss now.

In the remaining part of this section you will transform a static web page into an interactive one. This page has this simple markup, as shown in Listing 6-1.

Listing 6-1: Exercise-06-01-Begin/index.html

```
<!DOCTYPE html>
<html>
<head>
  <title>Hide And Seek</title>
  <link href="style.css" rel="stylesheet" />
</head>
<body>
  <h2>First Secret</h2>
  <div>
    <p>
      Cras ullamcorper nisi id imperdiet
      suscipit. Interdum et malesuada fames
      ac ante ipsum primis in.
    </p>
  </div>
  <h2>Second Secret</h2>
  <div>
    <p>
      Integer pellentesque, augue nec faucibus
      dapibus, ipsum nisl euismod massa, quis
      dictum nisl arcu vel.
    </p>
```

```
    <p>
       Mauris faucibus tortor neque, quis
       fermentum sapien egestas sit amet.
    </p>
  </div>
  <h2>Third Secret</h2>
  <div>
    <p>
       Nulla a orci mi. Pellentesque facilisis
       elementum facilisis. Vivamus porta mauris
       et posuere bibendum. Fusce.
    </p>
  </div>
</body>
</html>
```

This page displays three headings with associated content (with a simple style sheet), as shown in Figure 6-2. With a few steps you will transform it into an interactive page that allows collapsing and expanding the content of headings, as shown in Figure 6-3.

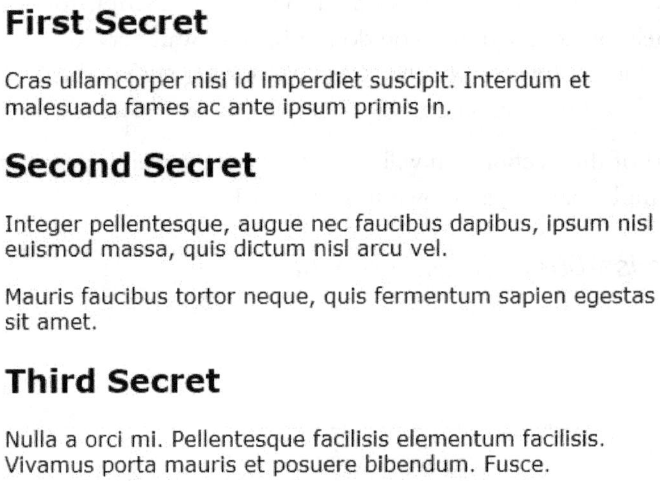

First Secret

Cras ullamcorper nisi id imperdiet suscipit. Interdum et malesuada fames ac ante ipsum primis in.

Second Secret

Integer pellentesque, augue nec faucibus dapibus, ipsum nisl euismod massa, quis dictum nisl arcu vel.

Mauris faucibus tortor neque, quis fermentum sapien egestas sit amet.

Third Secret

Nulla a orci mi. Pellentesque facilisis elementum facilisis. Vivamus porta mauris et posuere bibendum. Fusce.

Figure 6-2: A simple static page

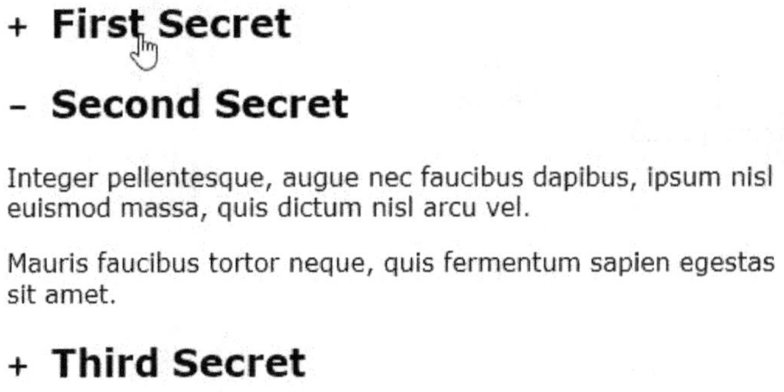

+ First Secret

− Second Secret

Integer pellentesque, augue nec faucibus dapibus, ipsum nisl euismod massa, quis dictum nisl arcu vel.

Mauris faucibus tortor neque, quis fermentum sapien egestas sit amet.

+ Third Secret

Figure 6-3: The page turned into an interactive one

To carry out this transformation, you will insert an extra `<span>` element into each `<h2>` heading, which represents the plus or minus sign to expand or collapse the heading, respectively. You will also add an event to each `<h2>` element, which is triggered when the user clicks the heading, and it will expand or collapse the `<div>` element that holds the related content. This event handler takes care about exchanging the plus or minus signs accordingly.

Querying the Document

The first thing you should focus is to query the document model. In the next exercise you will learn how to do.

EXERCISE 6-1: Querying the DOM

To save time, you will start from a prepared Visual Studio project that can be found in the `Exercise-06-01-Begin` folder within the book's source code.

To query the DOM, follow these steps:

1. Copy the `Exercise-06-01-Begin` folder to `Exercise-06-01`, and use this new folder. The project contains an `index.html` file, a simple style sheet, and an empty JavaScript file named `hideandseek.js`. The `index.html` file contains the code shown in Listing 6-1, with one addition, it includes `hideandseek.js`:

```
<!DOCTYPE html>
<html>
<head>
  <title>Hide And Seek</title>
  <link href="style.css" rel="stylesheet" />
</head>
<body>
  <h2>First Secret</h2>
  <!-- Omitted for the sake of brevity -->
  <script src="hideandseek.js">
  </script>
</body>
</html>
```

2. Run the app. The web page displayed in your browser will be similar to Figure 6-2; it represents the original state of the page.

3. Open the `hideandseek.js` file. It is empty now. Type in the following code:

```
var titles = document.getElementsByTagName('h2');
for (var i = 0; i < titles.length; i++) {
  var title = titles[i];
  document.write('<h3>' + title.textContent + '</h3>');
}
```

4. Turn back to the browser. This time the page displays three more lines (third level headings) at the end of the page, as highlighted in Figure 6-4.

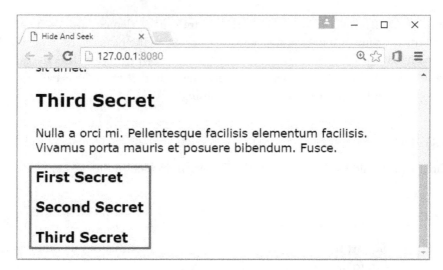

Figure 6-4: The script added extra output to the page

HOW IT WORKS

Because originally `hideandseek.js` was empty, including it in `index.html` did not actually run any JavaScript code. However, when in step 3, you added code to this file, it was executed, and that is how the output in Figure 6-4 was created. You added this code:

```
1  var titles = document.getElementsByTagName('h2');
2  for (var i = 0; i < titles.length; i++) {
3    var title = titles[i];
4    document.write('<h3>' + title.textContent + '</h3>');
5  }
```

The key operation is in line 1. The `document` object represents the current document in the browser. Because the `hideandseek.js` file is loaded at the end of the `<body>` section, the real content of the document is already loaded. The `getElementsByTagName()` function queries the DOM of the loaded document, and retrieves a list of elements that match the argument of the function. This time "h2" is passed as the argument, so this invocation retrieves the collection of all `<h2>` instances in the DOM.

The `for` loop enclosed between line 2 and 5 iterates through the items of this list (item indexes start at 0). Line 3 puts the current item into the `title` variable. Line 4 uses the `write()` method of `document`, which appends the argument's text at the end of the document markup. The code above creates `<h3>` headings with the text of the markup element represented by `title`. The value of `title` is the current `<h2>` heading, and its embedded text can be accessed through the `textContent` property. Because the `for` loop's body is executed for each `<h2>` tag, you see three new `<h3>` tag added to the page.

As you see, querying the DOM is pretty easy. Besides the `getElementsByTagName()` function, document provides a few more query methods, such as `getElementById()`, and `getElementsByClassName()`. Their names indicate what they retrieve; later in this section you'll learn a bit more about each of them.

Changing the DOM

The previous exercise did not carry out any useful activity that gets us closer to the page functionality—it only demonstrated that you can easily query the DOM. To achieve our goal, we need to extend the current document with plus and minus signs that indicate the state of a heading (collapsed, or expanded, respectively). The markup of the first header looks like this:

```
<h2>First Secret</h2>
```

Instead, we'd like to have this:

```
<h2><span class="mono">- </span>First Secret</h2>
```

Here, the "mono" value of the `class` attribute is used to specify that the marker should be displayed with monotype font—through the `.mono` style rule in `style.css`:

```
.mono {
  font-family: monospace;
}
```

We also would like add an event handler to the `<h2>` elements so that they could respond when the user clicks them. In the next exercise you will learn how to carry out these activities.

EXERCISE 6-2: Changing the DOM

To add the markers and the event handlers to the document, follow these steps:

1. Switch back to the code editor. Open `hideandseek.js`, remove the line that invokes the `document.write()` method, and replace it with the highlighted code:

```
var titles = document.getElementsByTagName('h2');
for (var i = 0; i < titles.length; i++) {
  var title = titles[i];
  title.innerHTML = '<span class="mono">- </span>'
    + title.innerHTML;
  title.addEventListener('click', onClick, true);
}
```

2. Append the following code to the end of `hideandseek.js`:

```
function onClick(evt) {
  var headerClicked = evt.currentTarget;
  headerClicked.setAttribute("style",
    "background-color: red;");
}
```

3. Turn back to the browser. When the page is displayed in the browser, you can see that a dash is shown in each heading. When you click a heading, its background color changes to red (Figure 6-5).

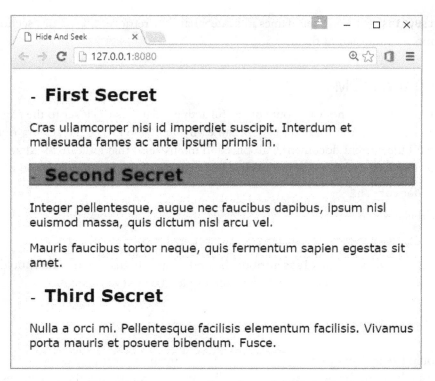

Figure 6-5: Now, you can see the markers, and click the headings

HOW IT WORKS

The marker is added to the heading with this code line:

```
title.innerHTML = '<span class="mono">- </span>'
  + title.innerHTML;
```

Here, **title** represents the heading. The **innerHTML** property can be used to access and set the content of an HTML element using textual HTML markup. Most HTML element may nest other markup elements. Although using the DOM operations, you can navigate from a parent element to its child or children, in many situations, it's much easier to access the nested content as HTML text, and this is exactly what **innerHTML** does. The code above shows that you add a **<span>** tag to the headings content, so that it precedes the original text.

In the first step you added another code line to the script file:

```
title.addEventListener('click', onClick, true);
```

This line is responsible for creating an event handler (or with other words, an event listener) and by invoking **addEventListener()** it attaches the handler to the **onclick** event (it is named by the first argument, "click") of the heading element represented by **title**. The second argument specifies the function that should be executed when the heading has been clicked. This is the **onClick()** function you added in step 2:

```
1  function onClick(evt) {
2    var headerClicked = evt.currentTarget;
3    headerClicked.setAttribute("style",
4      "background-color: red;");
5  }
```

This function has a single argument, **evt**, which holds information about the event raised. In line 2, you use its **currentTarget** property that contains the element (in this case the corresponding <h2> instance) that has been clicked. In line 3 and 4 you use the **setAttribute()** method of the clicked element to set its "style" attribute to "background-color: red;".

The browser catches all changes of the DOM, and updates its UI immediately to apply modifications. So, as soon as you added the markers to the DOM, or set the background color of the heading clicked, the browser immediately showed the results of these alterations.

NOTE: You can find the completed sample in the `Exercise-06-02` folder.

Completing Event Handling

The previous exercise showed that you can easily change an element in the DOM. However, instead of setting the background color of headings to red, the <div> section adjacent with the <h2> should be hidden, or shown again. In the next exercise, you will learn how to do it with the operations of the DOM.

EXERCISE 6-3: Completing event handling

To change the event handler method, follow these steps:

1. Switch back to the code editor, and open `hideandseek.js`. Remove the body of the `onClick()` function, and change it to this:

```
function onClick(evt) {
  var headerClicked = evt.currentTarget;
  var relatedDiv = headerClicked.nextElementSibling;
  var collapseMark = headerClicked.firstChild;
  var isCollapsed = collapseMark.innerText[0] == "+";
  collapseMark.innerText = isCollapsed ? "- " : "+ ";
  relatedDiv.setAttribute("style",
    isCollapsed ? "" : "display: none");
}
```

2. Take a look at the page in the browser. When you click any of the headings, now the related details are collapsed, as shown in Figure 6-6.

Figure 6-6: The code collapsed or expands the heading clicked

3. When the page appears, it would be better if all headings were collapsed by default. Add the highlighted lines to the `for` loop in `hideandseek.js`:

```
var titles = document.getElementsByTagName('h2');
for (var i = 0; i < titles.length; i++) {
  var title = titles[i];
  title.innerHTML = '<span class="mono">- </span>'
    + title.innerHTML;
  title.addEventListener('click', onClick, true);
  var relatedDiv = title.nextElementSibling;
  var collapseMark = title.firstChild;
  collapseMark.innerText = "+ ";
  relatedDiv.setAttribute("style", "display: none");
}
```

4. Turn to the browser again. This time all headings are collapsed. Try that you can expand and collapse the headings.

5. If you take a look at the highlighted code lines in the previous step, you can observe that those lines carry out exactly the same operations as if you clicked the heading. Instead of repeating these operations, you can instruct the DOM to fire the click event. Change the highlighted lines in the previous step to these ones:

```
var evt = document.createEvent("mouseEvent");
evt.initEvent("click", true, false);
title.dispatchEvent(evt);
```

6. Check the page again. It will start and work exactly the same was as in step 4. Close the browser.

HOW IT WORKS

In the first step you added this code to handle the click event of a heading:

```
1  var headerClicked = evt.currentTarget;
2  var relatedDiv = headerClicked.nextElementSibling;
3  var collapseMark = headerClicked.firstChild;
4  var isCollapsed = collapseMark.innerText[0] == "+";
5  collapseMark.innerText = isCollapsed ? "- " : "+ ";
6  relatedDiv.setAttribute("style",
7    isCollapsed ? "" : "display: none");
```

Line 1 stores the clicked element instance in the `headerClicked` variable. The `nextElementSibling` property evaluated on `headerClicked` (in line 2) navigates to the subsequent `<div>` element directly following the `<h2>` represented by `headerClicked`. The `firstChild` property retrieves the first child element of the node it is evaluated on, so line 3 it will retrieve the marker of the clicked heading.

Let's assume that the first `<h2>` element has been clicked. In this case the variables will hold the DOM elements shown in Figure 6-7.

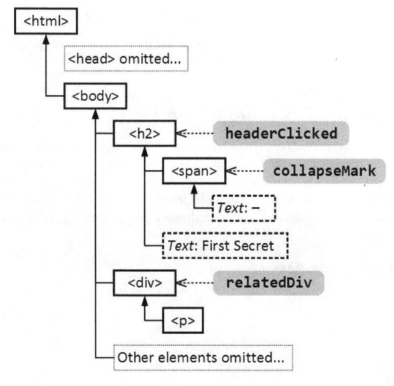

Figure 6-7: The document structure of the clicked heading

Line 4 sets the flag indicating whether the clicked heading is collapsed. This flag is used in line 5 to switch the marker between the plus sign and the dash, which represent the collapsed and

219

expanded states, respectively. Line 6 uses the same flag to set the style attribute to "display: node" (it hides the <div> tag), or to an empty string (it shows the <div> tag).

The code the added in step 3 uses the same navigation logic to set the default state of headings when the page is being loaded.

In step 5 you used this code to fire a click event:

```
1   var evt = document.createEvent("mouseEvent");
2   evt.initEvent("click", true, false);
3   title.dispatchEvent(evt);
```

When the user clicks an element in the page, the browser creates an event object, and sends it to the event handler method set for the onclick event. In line 1, you use the createEvent() function of the document object to create a generic mouse event. The initEvent() function invoked on this new event object—with "click" as its first argument—specifies that this event should be triggered as if the mouse button has been clicked. The other arguments of the method are not relevant in this context. Line 3 sends this event to the clicked heading with the dispatchEvent() method. As the final result, these three lines force the click event to fire on the heading, just as if the user clicked the corresponding <h2> element.

NOTE: You can find the completed sample in the Exercise-06-03 folder.

These exercises gave you a very brief overview about the functionality covered by the Document Object Model. It is time to dive a bit deeper into the details.

Navigating in the Document Tree

As it is obvious, the whole document—that represents a web page—can be depicted as a tree. This tree is built up from nodes, where each node has exactly one parent—except the root node that has no parent—, and each node may have zero, one or even more child nodes. HTML elements, texts, attributes of elements are all nodes in this tree. Figure 6-1 already showed you a simple HTML markup as a hierarchy. Figure 6-8 shows a bit more compound markup; its source is detailed in Listing 6-2.

Listing 6-2: Exercise-06-04/index.html

```
<!DOCTYPE html>
<html>
<head>
  <title>DOM Tree</title>
</head>
<body>
  <h1>Chapter <strong>#1</strong>: HTML Basics</h1>
  <p class="firstPara">
    This is the first paragraph of this chapter
  </p>
  <ul>
    <li>Item #1</li>
```

```
   <li>Item #2</li>
  </ul>
</body>
</html>
```

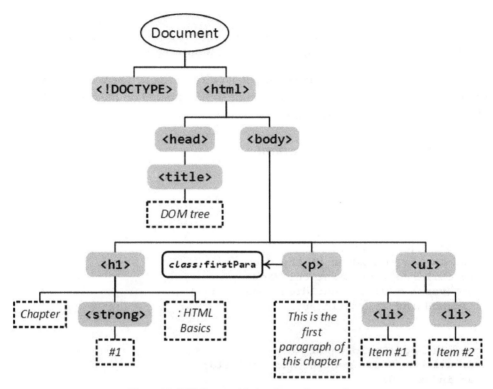

Figure 6-8: HTML tree with elements, attributes, and texts

The representation in Figure 6-8 helps you to understand the basic concepts related to the document tree. If you do not see this figure, you may think that the root of this tree is the <html> node. Nonetheless, the root of this tree is the document itself, drawn as an ellipse. Nodes with shaded background represent HTML elements. Rectangles with dashed border depict text embedded into HTML elements, and the single rectangle with rounded corners and solid border marks the attribute belonging to its parent markup element.

Nodes can have child nodes (direct descendants), and each child node has a parent (direct ancestor). For example, the Document node's child nodes are <!DOCUMENT> and <html>, similarly, the two <li> nodes are the child nodes of <ul>. This relationship means that <!DOCUMENT> and <html> have the same parent, the Document node; the two <li> nodes' parent is the <ul> node.

Although an attribute node is associated with an HTML element node, this is not a parent-child relationship, but rather a directed association from the element to the attribute. In Figure 6-8, <p> has only one child, the "This is..." text, the "class: firstPara" node is an attribute.

Just as in a real family, where children of the same parents are siblings; in the document tree, nodes belonging to the same parent are said siblings. So <head> and <body> are sibling nodes, their common direct parent is <html>. Similarly, <h1>, <p>, and <ul> are siblings, and their parent is <body>.

Node Navigation Basics

The concept of root node, parent, child, and sibling nodes, text nodes, and attributes is very important, because the navigation in the tree is based on these ideas.

The document tree is represented by the **document** JavaScript object. There are a number of **document** operations dedicated to navigation. Listing 6-3 (it is based on the markup shown in Listing 6-2) demonstrates a few methods of navigation.

Listing 6-3: Exercise-06-05/index.html

```
<!DOCTYPE html>
<html>
<head>
  <title>DOM Tree</title>
  <script>
    function logNavigation() {
      console.log('Children of the document')
      var children = document.childNodes;
      for (var i = 0; i < children.length; i++) {
        logNodeInfo(i, children[i]);
      }

      console.log('Children of <body>')
      var current = document.body.firstChild;
      var index = 0;
      while (current != null) {
        logNodeInfo(index, current);
        index++;
        current = current.nextSibling;
      }

      console.log('Children of <p>')
      children = document.getElementsByTagName('p')[0]
        .childNodes;
      for (var i = 0; i < children.length; i++) {
        logNodeInfo(i, children[i]);
      }

      console.log('Parent of <li>');
      var parent = document.getElementsByTagName('li')[0]
        .parentNode;
      logNodeInfo(0, parent);
    }

    function logNodeInfo(index, node) {
      var nodeVal = node.nodeValue == null
```

```
      ? '{empty}'
      : node.nodeValue.replace('\n', '{nl}');
    console.log('  ' + index + ': ('
      + node.nodeType + ') '
      + node.nodeName + ' | '
      + nodeVal);
    }
  </script>
</head>
<body onload="logNavigation()">
  <h1>Chapter <strong>#1</strong>: HTML Basics</h1>
  <!-- This is a comment -->
  <p class="firstPara">
    This is the first paragraph of this chapter
  </p>
  <ul>
    <li>Item #1</li>
    <li>Item #2</li>
  </ul>
</body>
</html>
```

The JavaScript code in this listing uses the `console.log()` method to add diagnostic messages to the console of the browser you use. Using the F12 key in Google Chrome or Edge, or Ctrl+Shift+K in Firefox will show you the developer tools, where you can find the console. When displaying the page in Listing 6-3, the console will display this output:

```
Children of the document
  0: (10) html | {empty}
  1: (1) HTML | {empty}
Children of <body>
  0: (3) #text | {nl}
  1: (1) H1 | {empty}
  2: (3) #text | {nl}
  3: (8) #comment |  This is a comment
  4: (3) #text | {nl}
  5: (1) P | {empty}
  6: (3) #text | {nl}
  7: (1) UL | {empty}
  8: (3) #text | {nl}

Children of <p>
  0: (3) #text | {nl}    This is the first paragraph of this chapter

Parent of <li>
  0: (1) UL | {empty}
```

NOTE: Earlier, in Exercise 6-2 you have already used the `document.write()` method. Because this method changes the document body itself, it would cause issues with navigating the page structure while altering it. Using `console.log()` avoids this potential problem.

The <script> section of the page (nested in <head>) contains only function definitions. The onload attribute of <body> is set to "logNavigation()", so when the loading of the page has been completed, the logNavigation() method is immediately invoked; this carries out the navigation operations logged in the console output.

This method contains four chunks of operations that query the children of the document, of the <body> element, of the <p> element, and last, the parent of the <li> element, respectively. To display node details, it utilizes the logNodeInfo() method.

Before going on to examine the output, let's see what logNodeInfo() does:

```
function logNodeInfo(index, node) {
  var nodeVal = node.nodeValue == null
    ? '{empty}'
    : node.nodeValue.replace('\n', '{nl}');
  console.log('  ' + index + ': ('
    + node.nodeType + ') '
    + node.nodeName + ' | '
    + nodeVal);
}
```

This method receives an index (order) value, and a tree node object. It displays the nodeType, nodeName, and nodeValue properties of the node passed as an argument. Each node in the tree has a node type (nodeType), such as element, text, comment, <!DOCTYPE> node, and a few others. These are represented by integer values, as displayed in the output within parentheses. Nodes have a name (nodeName) that varies according to the node type. Text node names are always set to "#text". Comments use the "#comment" constant as their name. HTML elements use the name of related markup tag, using uppercase letters. To help reading the console output, the logNodeInfo() method replaces the empty nodeValue texts with the "{empty}" text, and new line characters within the text with the "{nl}" literal.

The children of the document node are listed with this code snippet:

```
console.log('Children of the document')
var children = document.childNodes;
for (var i = 0; i < children.length; i++) {
  logNodeInfo(i, children[i]);
}
```

This code is straightforward. The document.childNodes property retrieves the collection of child nodes, and the subsequent for loop iterates through them. This snippet generates the following output:

```
Children of the document
  0: (10) html | {empty}
  1: (1) HTML | {empty}
```

The (10) integer refers to the <!DOCTYPE html> node. Its name, "html" covers the document type (HTML5 document) and not the <html> node of the markup. Just as shown in Figure 6-8, the document node has two children, the second one is the <html> node, at index 1 in the output. As you see, both nodes have empty values.

The same code could be used to display the children of <body>, however the code listing uses a different approach:

```
console.log('Children of <body>')
var current = document.body.firstChild;
var index = 0;
while (current != null) {
  logNodeInfo(index, current);
  index++;
  current = current.nextSibling;
}
```

It uses the document.body property, which represents the <body> node of the document. To access the first child node of <body>, the code uses the firstChild property. The while loop displays the information about the current node, and after incrementing the node index, it uses the nextSibling method of the node—and not the one of the document!—to get to the next child of the parent, which is the sibling of the previously touched child. So, this loop gets the first child and iterates through that child's siblings. Figure 6-8 indicates that <body> has only three children, <h1>, <p>, and <ul> respectively. However, the console output shows much more:

```
Children of <body>
  0:  (3)  #text    |  {nl}
  1:  (1)  H1       |  {empty}
  2:  (3)  #text    |  {nl}
  3:  (8)  #comment |  This is a comment
  4:  (3)  #text    |  {nl}
  5:  (1)  P        |  {empty}
  6:  (3)  #text    |  {nl}
  7:  (1)  UL       |  {empty}
  8:  (3)  #text    |  {nl}
```

Listing 6-3 includes and additional comment, it is shown in the output at index 3. But where are the extra five text nodes coming from? As the output shows, they come from the line breaks between markup elements. For example, the text at index 1 comes from the line break between <body> and <h1>:

```
<body onload="logNavigation()">
  <h1>Chapter <strong>#1</strong>: HTML Basics</h1>
```

When you remove the line break in the original markup, and go on with <h1> right after the closing ">" of <body> (without spaces), the text node at index 0 will disappear.

All other text nodes come from other line breaks within <body>.

A third approach is used to display the children of <p>:

```
console.log('Children of <p>')
children = document.getElementsByTagName('p')[0]
  .childNodes;
for (var i = 0; i < children.length; i++) {
  logNodeInfo(i, children[i]);
}
```

Unraveling HTML5, CSS3, and JavaScript

Now, the `document.getElementsByTagName()` method is used with "p" as its input argument. This call retrieves a collection of all `<p>` tags in the document. Using the `[0]` indexing tag gets the first item from this collection, and evaluating the `childNodes` property of this item returns all child nodes of the first `<p>` element in the document. The subsequent `for` loop iterates through the child nodes.

NOTE: The code above assumes that there is at least one `<p>` tag in the markup, by using the [0] indexing expression. Of course, we know that it's true, but in real life the code should check if there is any child before referring the first one.

There is one very important thing the output of this code snippet indicates:

```
Children of <p>
  0: (3) #text | {nl}     This is the first paragraph of this chapter
```

The output does not display the `class` attribute of `<p>` which is set to "firstPara". Of course, the attribute node is the part of the document tree, *but it is not a child node* of `<p>`!

The last code segment is so easy to understand that it does not need extra explanation:

```
console.log('Parent of <li>');
var parent = document.getElementsByTagName('li')[0]
  .parentNode;
  logNodeInfo(0, parent);
}
```

The `parentNode` property of a node simply retrieves its parent node object.

As mentioned earlier, element attributes are document tree nodes, too. Because attributes are not children of their container node, they cannot be accessed by any child-related operations. The document object has attribute-related navigation operations and properties, as Listing 6-4 demonstrates.

Listing 6-4: Exercise-06-06/index.html

```
<!DOCTYPE html>
<html>
<head>
  <title>DOM Tree</title>
  <style>
    .redcolor {
      color: red;
    }
  </style>
  <script>
    function logAttributes() {
      console.log('item1 attributes:');
      logElementAttrs('item1');

      console.log('item2 attributes:');
      logElementAttrs('item2');
```

```
      console.log('item3 attributes:');
      logElementAttrs('item3');

      console.log('item2 "class" attribute:');
      var attr = document.getElementById('item2')
        .getAttributeNode('class');
      logNodeInfo(0, attr);
    }

    function logElementAttrs(id) {
      var attrs = document.getElementById(id)
        .attributes;
      for (var i = 0; i < attrs.length; i++) {
        logNodeInfo(i, attrs[i]);
      }
    }

    function logNodeInfo(index, node) {
      console.log('  ' + index + ': ('
        + node.nodeType + ') '
        + node.nodeName + ' | '
        + node.nodeValue);
    }
  </script>
</head>
<body onload="logAttributes()">
  <p>This is an ordered list</p>
  <ol start="1">
    <li id="item1">Item #1</li>
    <li id="item2" class="redcolor">Item #2</li>
    <li id="item3" invalid="wrong"
        data-myAttr="custom">Item #3</li>
  </ol>
</body>
</html>
```

This markup displays a paragraph and an ordered list. The attached script works with the same approach as the one in Listing 6-3, but this time it traverses through element attributes. It displays all attributes of elements with "item1", "item2", and "item3" identifiers, respectively. Additionally, the scripts display information on the class attribute of "item2".

The logNodeInfo() method works exactly the same way as in the previous listing, except that it does not transform the input node's value. The lion's share of the work is done by logElementAttrs() that accepts an id argument, and displays the attributes of the node specified by the identifier passed in. The key is this code snippet:

```
var attrs = document.getElementById(id)
  .attributes;
```

The attributes property of an element—which is obtained by `document.getElementById()`—retrieves a collection of attribute nodes. The subsequent `for` loop in `logElementAttrs()` iterates through all attributes and displays their details.

When you display the page, it produces the following output:

```
item1 attributes:
  0: (2) id | item1
item2 attributes:
  0: (2) id | item2
  1: (2) class | redcolor
item3 attributes:
  0: (2) id | item3
  1: (2) invalid | wrong
  2: (2) data-myattr | custom
item2 "class" attribute:
  0: (2) class | redcolor
```

There are important things this output shows you. Attributes are nodes with type 2, as the (2) value in the output indicates. The **attribute** property retrieves all attributes, including valid (such as `id`, `class`), custom (`data-myattr`), and invalid (`invalid`) attributes as well. The DOM does not care whether the browser can display the markup or not, it provides every detail of the document tree.

The last chunk of the script accesses the `class` attribute of "item2" directly:

```
var attr = document.getElementById('item2')
  .getAttributeNode('class');
```

This is the task of `getAttributeNode()`, which navigates to the attribute specified by its name as the argument of the function.

NOTE: The element object provides another method, `getAttribute()`, to access an attribute by its name. Although `getAttributeNode()` retrieves a node object, `getAttribute()` retrieves the attribute's value (a string) only.

Accessing Element Content

To implement useful functionality, it is not enough to navigate to a document tree node. You often need to query the content of a specific node, or a set of nodes. The DOM provides three simple ways to access node content.

The first—and most obvious—way is that you use the HTML element and attribute navigation methods to access child elements and attributes. Sooner or later you reach a node that does not have any child. The second way is to use the `textContent` property of the node you have grasped. It retrieves the concatenated text within the element—excluding all other nodes. The third way—and this is the most frequently used—is to obtain the value of the `innerHTML` property, which retrieves the textual representation of the HTML markup embedded within the element. Listing 6-5 demonstrates using the `textContent` and `innerHTML` properties.

Listing 6-5: Exercise-06-07/index.html

```html
<!DOCTYPE html>
<html>
<head>
  <title>DOM Tree</title>
  <script>
    function logContent() {
      console.log('paragraph content:');
      var para = document
        .getElementById('para');
      console.log('text:' +
        '"' + para.textContent + '"');
      console.log('HTML:' + para.innerHTML);

      console.log('ol content:');
      var ol = document
        .getElementsByTagName('ol')[0];
      console.log('text:' +
        '"' + ol.textContent + '"');
      console.log('HTML:' + ol.innerHTML);
    }
  </script>
</head>
<body onload="logContent()">
  <p id="para">
    This is an
    <strong>ordered</strong> list
  </p>
  <ol start="1">
    <li id="item1">Item #1</li>
    <li id="item2">Item #2</li>
    <li id="item3">Item #3</li>
  </ol>
</body>
</html>
```

This script's code queries the text and HTML content of the `<p>` tag and the `<ol>` tag, respectively, and produces this console output:

```
paragraph content:
text:"
    This is an
    ordered list
  "
HTML:
    This is an
    <strong>ordered</strong> list

ol content:
text:"
    Item #1
    Item #2
```

```
    Item #3
  "
HTML:
    <li id="item1">Item #1</li>
    <li id="item2">Item #2</li>
    <li id="item3">Item #3</li>
```

This output clearly shows that the innerHTML property retrieves the full HTML markup of the elements, while textContent omits all HTML elements and their attributes. The output highlights the HTML tags. If you omit them, you get exacly the output produced by textContent.

You can observe another important thing. The <p> element has a child element, <strong>:

```
<p id="para">
  This is an
  <strong>ordered</strong> list
</p>
```

The value of textContent recursively obtains text nodes within all child nodes, and this is why the output includes "ordered" which is not a child node of <p>, but the child of <strong> (so, actually the "grandchild" node of <p>).

A Brief Navigation Reference

Now, it is time to summarize the operations you can use for navigation. Generally, you start with querying the document object for a single node, or a collection of nodes. For this activity, you can use the operations summarized in Table 6-1.

Table 6-1: Document operations to query nodes

Operation	Description
getElementById()	This method returns the element that has the id attribute with the specified value. It is one of the most commonly used methods in the HTML DOM, and is invoked almost every time you want to manipulate, or get info from, an element on your document. Returns null if no elements with the specified id exists.
getElementsByName()	This method retrieves a collection of all elements that have their name attribute with the specified value. Returns an empty collection if no elements with the specified name exists.
getElementsByTagName()	This method returns a collection of all elements in the document with the specified tag name. Passing the value "*" to this method returns all elements in the document.

In Listing 6-3, you already used the **body** property of **document** as a shortcut to access the **<body>** tag. The document object provides a number of properties to access frequently used nodes and node collections, as summarized in Table 6-2:

Table 6-2: Document properties to access nodes

Property	Description
anchors	This property returns an array of all the anchors (**<a>** tags) in the current document.
body	Returns the body element of the document.
doctype	Returns the **<!DOCTYPE>** of the HTML document.
documentElement	This property returns the document, as an Element object. Using this property, you can access HTML element operations on the document node.
forms	This property returns an array of all the forms (**<form>** tags) in the current document.
images	This property returns an array of all the images (**<img>** tags) in the current document.
links	This property returns an array of all the links in the current document. As you learned, not only the **<a>** tag, but also the **<area>** tag can define links to other documents. This property retrieves all of them.

When you grab a node representing an HTML element, you can use the navigation methods and properties summarized in Table 6-3. If you have a collection of HTML elements, you can iterate through them, and apply the operations in Table 6-3 on each collection item, or on selected ones.

Table 6-3: HTML element navigation methods and properties

Method/Property	Description
attributes	Returns a collection of the element's attributes.
childNodes	Returns a collection of child nodes for an element.
firstChild	Returns the first child node of the specified node. Do not forget, in HTML, the document itself is the parent node of the **<html>** element, **<head>** and **<body>** are child nodes of **<html>**.
getAttribute()	Returns the specified attribute value of the element node
getAttributeNode()	Returns the specified attribute node
getElementsByTagName()	Returns a collection of all child elements with the specified tag name
hasAttribute	Returns **true**, if an element has the specified attribute; otherwise, **false**.
hasAttributes()	Returns **true**, if an element has any attributes; otherwise, **false**.

231

Method/Property	Description
hasChildNodes()	Returns true, if an element has any child nodes; otherwise, false.
innerHTML	This property sets or returns the inner HTML of the element. Yes, it not only retrieves, but allows changing the content of the element.
lastChild	Returns the last child node of the specified node.
nextSibling	Returns the node immediately following this node, in the same tree level.
ownerDocument	Returns the root element (document object) for this element.
parentNode	Returns the parent node of the element.
previousSibling	Returns the previous node of this node, in the same tree level.
textContent	This property sets or returns the textual content of the specified node, and all its direct and indirect descendants. This property not only retrieves the textual content, it allows changing it.

Element specific properties

DOM elements are represented by JavaScript objects. When you access an element through the document tree, you can access the properties of that specific JavaScript object. Depending on what HTML element is behind the specific object, you can work with different property sets. For example, when you work with an <ol> element, you can refer properties that are <ol>-specific, as shown in Listing 6-6.

Listing 6-6: Exercise-06-08/index.html

```
<!DOCTYPE html>
<html>
<head>
  <title>Element properties</title>
  <script>
    function logProperties() {
      console.log('ol properties:');
      var ol = document
        .getElementsByTagName('ol')[0];
      console.log('start: ' + ol.start);
      console.log('type: "' + ol.type + '"');
      console.log('reversed: ' + ol.reversed);
      console.log('reversed attr: "' +
        ol.getAttribute('reversed') + '"');
    }
  </script>
</head>
<body onload="logProperties()">
  <ol start="3" reversed>
```

```
      <li id="item1">Item #1</li>
      <li id="item2">Item #2</li>
      <li id="item3">Item #3</li>
    </ol>
  </body>
</html>
```

This code obtains a reference to the `<ol>` element in the HTML markup, and then logs the `start`, `type`, and `reversed` properties of that object, respectively. The code logs the value of the `reversed` attribute node with the `getAttribute()` function.

NOTE: If you do not remember, the `<ol>` element may have `start`, `type`, and `reversed` attributes to define the starting number, the type of number format, and the flag specifying that list order should be descending.

When you display this page with Google Chrome, it will generate this log output:

```
ol properties:
start: 3
type: ""
reversed: false
reversed attr: ""
```

Internet Explorer will produce a different output:

```
ol properties:
start: 3
type: ""
reversed: undefined
reversed attr: ""
```

As you already learned, Internet Explorer does not support the `reversed` attribute of `<ol>`, so when you query it, it retrieves "undefined". In spite of the missing `reversed` support, the document tree contains the `reversed` attribute, because it is specified in the HTML markup.

Generally, all attributes of a node can be accessed through properties. Those that are not specified in the HTML markup will be set to their default value—unless you change them programmatically. Those that are not implemented by the browser (even if specified in the markup) will return "undefined".

NOTE: In *Chapter 7: Getting to Know JavaScript*, you will learn more about the "undefined" value.

Changing the Document Tree

It is great that you can traverse through the document tree, and access its content. However, it is just a single step toward creating interactive pages. The more exciting thing is to change the structure and content of the tree, and it opens totally new horizons to vivify your web pages.

The DOM contains about a dozen useful operations that allow you to change the document tree. Among the others, you can insert new elements, remove existing ones, and replace the content and attributes of existing elements. In this section you will learn these concepts through simple coding examples.

Changing the Content of Elements

You already used the `textContent` and `innerHTML` properties, and the `getAttributes()` function to query the content of the document tree. The very same properties can be used to set the content of elements, too, and `setAttribute()`, the pair of `getAttribute()`, is the one you can use to set or change the value of an element's attribute. Listing 6-7 shows an example with three short JavaScript methods, each demonstrates a way to change document tree content.

Listing 6-7: Exercise-06-09/index.html

```html
<!DOCTYPE html>
<html>
<head>
  <title>Changing content</title>
</head>
<body>
  <p id="para">These are items:</p>
  <ol id="list" start="1">
    <li id="item1">Item #1</li>
    <li id="item2">Item #2</li>
    <li id="item3">Item #3</li>
  </ol>
  <button onclick="changeContent()">
    Change content
  </button>
  <br />
  <button onclick="incrementStart()">
    Increment start
  </button>
  <br />
  <button onclick="decrementStart()">
    Decrement start
  </button>
  <script>
    function changeContent() {
      var para = document.getElementById('para');
      var item = document.getElementById('item1');

      para.innerHTML = 'These are '
        + '<strong>new </strong> items:';

      item.textContent = "First item";
      item = item.nextElementSibling;
      item.textContent = "Second item";
      item = item.nextElementSibling;
      item.textContent = "Third item";
    }
```

```
   function incrementStart() {
     var list = document.getElementById('list');
     var start = parseInt(list.getAttribute("start"));
     start++;
     list.setAttribute("start", start);
   }

   function decrementStart() {
     var list = document.getElementById('list');
     list.start--;
   }
 </script>
</body>
</html>
```

When the page is displayed, it shows the original content (Figure 6-9). The three buttons in the page are assigned to the `changeContent()`, `incrementStart()`, and `decrementStart()` methods, respectively.

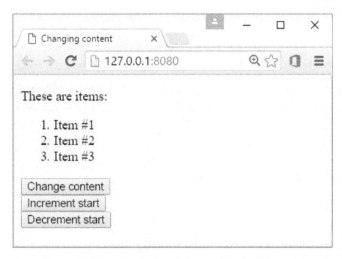

Figure 6-9: The original content of the page defined in Listing 6-7

The `changeContent()` method uses the `innerHTML` property to change the text assigned to the `<p>` tag at the top of the screen. It uses the `textContent` property to change the textual content of each list items—and uses the `nextElementSibling` property to navigate from one list item to the subsequent one.

The `incrementStart()` method leverages `getAttribute()` to obtain the current content of the `<ol>` tag's `start` attribute. It is a string, so the method uses the `parseInt()` method to convert it to an integer number, then increments is values and stores this value back to start with `setAttribute()`.

Instead of reading, incrementing and writing back the `start` attribute's value, you can simply change the `start` property of the `list` object (it represents the `start` attribute of `<ol>`), as implemented by the decrementStart() method. The effect of these methods is shown in Figure 6-10.

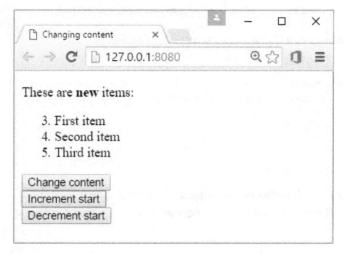

Figure 6-10: The original content of the document tree has been changed

Adding New Child Elements to the Document

After you have grabbed a document element, you can add child elements to it with the appendChild(), and beforeInsert() methods. The first appends a new child to the end of the list of exiting children, the second allows to specify the position of insertion. Listing 6-8 demonstrates using them.

Listing 6-8: Exercise-06-10/index.html

```
<!DOCTYPE html>
<html>
<head>
  <title>Add new elements</title>
</head>
<body>
  <p>These are items:</p>
  <ol id="list" start="1">
    <li id="item1">Item #1</li>
    <li id="item2">Item #2</li>
    <li id="item3">Item #3</li>
  </ol>
  <button onclick="addToTop()">
    Add new item to top
  </button>
  <br />
  <button onclick="addAfterFirst()">
    Add new item after the first child
  </button>
```

```
<br />
<button onclick="addToBottom()">
  Add new item to bottom
</button>
<script>
  function addToTop() {
    var list = document.getElementById('list');
    var firstItem = list.firstElementChild;
    var newNode = createNewNode("addToTop");
    list.insertBefore(newNode, firstItem);
  }

  function addAfterFirst() {
    var list = document.getElementById('list');
    var firstItem = list.firstElementChild;
    var secondItem = firstItem.nextElementSibling;
    var newNode = createNewNode("addAfterFirst");
    list.insertBefore(newNode, secondItem);
  }

  function addToBottom() {
    var list = document.getElementById('list');
    var newNode = createNewNode("addToBottom");
    list.appendChild(newNode);
  }

  function createNewNode(message) {
    var item = document.getElementById('list');
    var count = item.childElementCount;
    var newNode = document.createElement('li');
    newNode.textContent =
      "item #" + (count + 1) + " ("
      + message + ")";
    return newNode;
  }
</script>
</body>
</html>
```

The original page rendered by this markup is shown in Figure 6-11. The three buttons activate the addToTop(), addAfterFirst(), and addToBottom() methods, respectively. Each method gets the <ol> tag, invokes the createNewNode() method, and then inserts the new child node.

In order you can add a new element to the document tree, you need to create one. The createNewNode() uses the createElement() method of document. This is the way to create a new element, and this new object can be assigned only to the document tree it has been created in. You have to pass the type of the element as the argument of createElement(), and it retrieves the object that represents the new node. The implementation in createNewNode() accepts a message that is added to the textual content of the new <li> element, together with an item number based on the count of child elements.

237

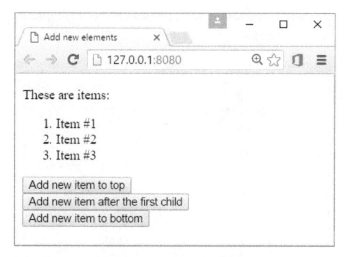

Figure 6-11: The original content of the page defined in Listing 6-8

The `addToBottom()` method uses the `appendChild()` method, while `addAfterFirst()` and `addToTop()` leverage the `beforeInsert()` method. Observe that all of them use the `<ol>` node (through the `list` object) to add the new child element to, however, each of them uses a different way. When calling `beforeInsert()`, the first argument is the new node, the second one identifies the reference element to add the new child before.

Figure 6-12 shows how the list is expanded after adding five new list items. Using the item numbers and messages written between parentheses, you can guess out the order of operations invoked.

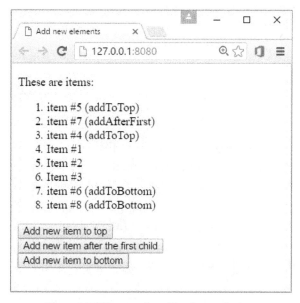

Figure 6-12: The page after adding five new list items

Adding Adjacent Elements

To extend the document tree, it is not enough to add child nodes to HTML elements. You also need to add sibling elements—and very often—text to existing HTML tags. Unfortunately, the HTML DOM standard does not contain any method that can be used to add sibling nodes directly before or after a certain document tree node.

A few browser vendors extend the standard DOM API with extra operations. For example, Google Chrome, Opera, Safari, and Internet Explorer provide three additional methods, `insertAdjacentText()`, `insertAdjacentElement()`, and `insertAdjacentHTML()`, which can be used for this task. Firefox does not implement these operations. In this section you will learn using them.

Listing 6-9 demonstrates using `insertAdjacentText()`. This code wraps every link in the page with square brackets, adding a "[" character before, and another "]" character after the link with `insertAdjacentText()`.

Listing 6-9: Exercise-06-11/index.html

```
<!DOCTYPE html>
<html>
<head>
  <title>Add new elements</title>
  <base href="http://www.w3schools.com" />
</head>
<body onload="decorateLinks()">
  <p>
    In this chapter you already met with many DOM
    manipulation methods including
    <a href="/jsref/met_node_appendchild.asp">
      appendChild()
    </a>,
    <a href="/jsref/met_node_insertbefore.asp">
      insertBefore()
    </a>, and
    <a href="/jsref/met_element_setattribute.asp">
      setAttribute().
    </a>
  </p>
  <script>
    function decorateLinks() {
      for (i = 0; i < document.links.length; i++) {
        var link = document.links[i];
        link.insertAdjacentText('beforeBegin', '[');
        link.insertAdjacentText('afterEnd', ']');
      }
    }
  </script>
</body>
</html>
```

As the onload attribute of <body> shows, the decorateLinks() method is invoked as soon as the page has been loaded. It iterates through all links declared in the document (using the document.links property), and calls the insertAdjacentText() method twice on the link element. The first argument of this method is a string that specifies where to insert the text. The listing uses the "beforeBegin", and "afterEnd" values that instruct the method to add the text before the opening tag, and the after the closing tag of the corresponding node, respectively. Beside these values, you can use "beforeEnd", and "afterBegin" to add the text before the closing tag, or after the opening tag, respectively.

When you display the page, you can immediately observe the result of this short code snippet, as shown in Figure 6-13.

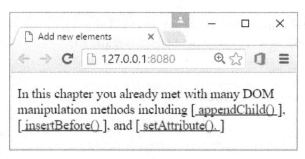

Figure 6-13: The code in Listing 6-9 wraps links into square brackets

If you want to apply your own style settings on square brackets, you'd better wrap them into a <span> tag. You can immediately try this approach with the decorateLinks2() method:

```
function decorateLinks2() {
  for (i = 0; i < document.links.length; i++) {
    var link = document.links[i];
    var openSpan = document.createElement('span');
    openSpan.textContent = '[';
    var closeSpan = document.createElement('span');
    closeSpan.textContent = ']';
    link.insertAdjacentElement('beforeBegin', openSpan);
    link.insertAdjacentElement('afterEnd', closeSpan);
  }
}
```

As you see in the highlighted part of this code, it creates an openSpan and a closeSpan object to represent two <span> elements, and uses the textContent to set them to the appropriate square bracket. Instead of utilizing the insertAdjacentText() method, this code leverages insertAdjacentElement(). The first method argument specifies the insert position—just like insertAdjacentText()—, and in the second argument you pass the object representing the element to insert.

To try decorateLinks2(), do not forget to change the onload attribute of <body>:

```
<body onload="decorateLinks2()">
```

You can implement adding `<span>` tags easier with the help of `insertAdjacentHTML()`, as shown in this code snippet:

```
function decorateLinks3() {
  for (i = 0; i < document.links.length; i++) {
    var link = document.links[i];
    link.insertAdjacentHTML('beforeBegin',
      '<span>[</span>');
    link.insertAdjacentHTML('afterEnd',
      '<span>]</span>');
  }
}
```

The `insertAdjacentHTML()` method has the same semantic as the other two `insertAdjacent...()` method, but here you have to pass an HTML markup string in the second argument.

To try `decorateLinks3()`, do not forget to alter the `onload` attribute of `<body>`:

```
<body onload="decorateLinks3()">
```

Removing and Replacing Elements

The DOM API provides a few operations that allow you to remove existing elements, or replace a node of the document tree with another one. In this section you will learn to use these operations.

Earlier you learned that Firefox does not support the `insertAdjacent...()` operations, which are not the part of the DOM API standard—although all other major browsers support it. To wrap all links with square brackets, you can find a general solution instead of the one demonstrated in Listing 6-9, which uses the script in Listing 6-10.

Listing 6-10: Browser independent way fixing issues with Listing 6-9

```
<!-- Other markup elements are omitted -->
<script>
  function decorateLinks() {
    for (var i = 0; i < document.links.length; i++) {
      var link = document.links[i];
      var span = document.createElement('span');
      span.appendChild(document.createTextNode('['));
      span.appendChild(link.cloneNode(true));
      span.appendChild(document.createTextNode(']'));
      link.parentNode.replaceChild(span, link);
    }
  }
</script>
```

This code simply replaces the links with a `<span>` that contains three children, the text for "[", the original link element, and the text for "]", respectively. The code snippet uses the `replaceChild()`

method of the link's parent node, and passes two arguments, the new child node (span), and the old child node to replace (link).

However, to make it work, another important thing should be done. The original link node cannot be at two places simultaneously (in its original location and within the newly created `<span>` element). You cannot append it to the `<span>`, but you can add the clone of the original node. This is exactly what the cloneNode() method does in the second invocation of appendChild(). Its argument with the true value indicates that the node should be cloned together with all of its children.

Let's see a more complex sample that not only replaces, but removes document tree nodes, too. Figure 6-14 displays a simple web page that works as a simple to-do-list application. You have tasks that can be moved between two lists, important, and low priority tasks, respectively. Each task can be marked as completed with clicking the Done button.

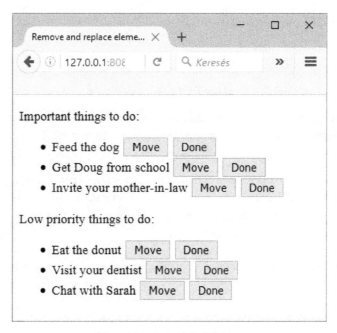

Figure 6-14: A simple to-do-list page

Listing 6-11 shows the complete HTML markup of the page. As you expect, it contains two unordered list, but the original markup does not declare buttons. The Move and Done buttons are created at page load time, with the decorateItems() method (observe, the onload attribute of `<body>` is set to invoke this method).

Listing 6-11: Exercise-06-12/index.html

```
<!DOCTYPE html>
<html>
<head>
  <title>Remove and replace elements</title>
```

```
</head>
<body onload="decorateItems()">
  <p>Important things to do:</p>
  <ul id="high">
    <li>Feed the dog</li>
    <li>Get Doug from school</li>
    <li>Invite your mother-in-law</li>
  </ul>
  <p>Low priority things to do:</p>
  <ul id="low">
    <li>Eat the donut</li>
    <li>Visit your dentist</li>
    <li>Chat with Sarah</li>
  </ul>
  <script>
    function moveItem(node) {
      var divNode = node.parentNode;
      var liNode = divNode.parentNode;
      var ulNode = liNode.parentNode;
      var fromUl = ulNode.id;
      var toUl = fromUl == 'high'
        ? document.getElementById('low')
        : document.getElementById('high');
      var clone = liNode.cloneNode(true);
      toUl.appendChild(clone);
      ulNode.removeChild(liNode)
    }

    function closeItem(node) {
      var divNode = node.parentNode;
      var liNode = divNode.parentNode;
      var ulNode = liNode.parentNode;
      ulNode.removeChild(liNode)
    }

    function decorateItems() {
      var liNodes = document.getElementsByTagName('li');
      for (i = 0; i < liNodes.length; i++) {
        var liNode = liNodes[i];
        liNode.innerHTML = '<div>' + liNode.textContent
          + ' <button onclick="moveItem(this)">'
          + 'Move</button> '
          + '<button onclick="closeItem(this)">'
          + 'Done</button></div>';
      }
    }
  </script>
</body>
</html>
```

There is nothing new in `decorateItems()`, you can understand it according to what you have already learned. After the page has been loaded and `decorateItems()` gets completed, a list item's markup looks like this:

```
<li>
  <div>
  Feed the dog
  <button onclick="moveItem(this)">
    Move
  </button>
  <button onclick="closeItem(this)">
    Done
  </button>
  <div>
</li>
```

When the Move, or Done buttons are clicked, `moveItem()`, or `closeItem()` are invoked, respectively. Both methods receive the object representing the appropriate `<button>` tag, and both initializes variables for nodes in this hierarchy:

```
var divNode = node.parentNode;
var liNode = divNode.parentNode;
var ulNode = liNode.parentNode;
```

To remove the `<li>` node, `moveItem()` and `closeItem()` both use the `removeChild()` method:

```
ulNode.removeChild(liNode)
```

Before removing a task, `moveItem()` adds a clone of that task to the other list:

```
var toUl = fromUl == 'high'
  ? document.getElementById('low')
  : document.getElementById('high');
var clone = liNode.cloneNode(true);
toUl.appendChild(clone);
```

As this code snippet shows, first it obtains the object representing the target list (`toUl`), then uses the `cloneNode()` method to create a full deep copy of the source `<li>` node. Finally, leveraging `appendChild()`, the code appends the cloned node to the target list.

Figure 6-15 shows this web page in action. As you see, a few tasks have been moved between the priority lists, and one task has already been completed.

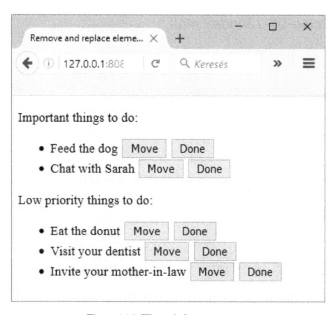

Figure 6-15: The to-do-list page in action

Changing Attributes and Element Style

Modifying the document tree allows you to change not only elements, but also attributes (with the `setAttribute()` method), and so, it provides a couple of ways to change the appearance of the web page on-the-fly. In *Chapter 3 (Listing 3-14)*, you displayed a table that defines the logical XOR operation, as shown in Figure 6-16. Listing 6-12 adds two buttons to the markup that can be used to change the table background from its original color to green, and red, respectively.

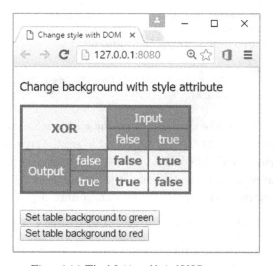

Figure 6-16: The definition of logical XOR operation

Listing 6-12: Exercise-06-13/index.html

```
<!DOCTYPE html>
<html>
<head>
  <title>Change style with DOM</title>
  <style>
    <!-- Markup omitted for brevity -->
  </style>
</head>
<body>
  <p>Change background with style attribute</p>
  <table id="table" border="1">
    <!-- Markup omitted for brevity -->
  </table>
  <br />
  <button onclick="toGreen()">
    Set table background to green
  </button>
  <br />
  <button onclick="toRed()">
    Set table background to red
  </button>
  <script>
    function toGreen() {
      var tableDef = document
        .getElementById('table');
      table.setAttribute('style',
        'background-color: lightgreen');
    }

    function toRed() {
      var tableDef = document
        .getElementById('table');
      table.style.backgroundColor = 'orangered';
    }
  </script>
</body>
</html>
```

The script in this code uses the `style` attribute to set the table background to green, and red. The `toGreen()` method utilizes the `setAttribute()` method to set the style attribute's value to "`background-color: lightgreen`". In contrast, `toRed()` leverages a simpler way: it uses the `style` property of the object that represents the table node to access the `style` attribute, and uses its `backgroundColor` sub-property to change the table background.

If you have an inline style sheet, you can use the DOM to change a style. Listing 6-13 shows how you can carry out this task.

Listing 6-13: Exercise-06-14/index.html

```
<!DOCTYPE html>
<html>
<head>
  <title>Change style with DOM</title>
  <style>
    <!-- Markup omitted for brevity -->
    table {
      border: 4px solid dimgray;
      border-collapse: collapse;
    }
  </style>
  <style id="tableStyle">
    table {
      background-color: aliceblue;
    }
  </style>
</head>
<body>
  <p>Change style with CSS manipulation</p>
  <table border="1">
    <!-- Markup omitted for brevity -->
  </table>
  <br />
  <button onclick="toGreen()">
    Set table background to green
  </button>
  <br />
  <button onclick="toRed()">
    Set table background to red
  </button>
  <script>
    function toGreen() {
      setBackgroundTo('lightgreen');
    }

    function toRed() {
      setBackgroundTo('orangered');
    }

    function setBackgroundTo(color) {
      var styleDef = document
        .getElementById('tableStyle');
      styleDef.innerHTML = "table { "
        + "background-color: "
        + color + "; }";
    }
  </script>
</body>
</html>
```

247

In this listing, toGreen() and toRed() delegate the task to the setBackgroundTo() method. It navigates to the <style> node with "tableStyle" identifier, and directly changes its HTML content. The inline style sheet contains two definitions for the table rule, this code sets the second one to use the background color passed to setBackgroundTo(). CSS merges the two table rules, and applies this merged result to the table.

Global Attributes and Events

The HTML DOM defines global attributes that you can assign to every document node, and it also specifies events that the browser fires either as a result of a user interaction, or as a page lifecycle event. You already used the id attribute, as one example of global attributes. HTML5 adds a number of new global attributes to the markup, and new events, too.

NOTE: In this section you will learn many new attributes that can be attached to HTML elements. However, here you will not see them in action. The aim of this section is that you get acquainted with these attributes and events, and not to learn all nitty-gritty details of them.

Global Attributes

HTML attributes extend the meaning and context of elements. Many attributes, called global attributes, can be used on any HTML elements, and they define comprehensive meaning. Table 6-4 summarizes these global attributes.

Table 6-4: HTML5 global attributes

Attribute	Description
accesskey	This attribute specifies a shortcut key to activate or focus an element. You can provide a single character as the value of the attribute. When using the page, press down the Alt key or the Alt+Shift keys with the shortcut key to activate or focus the element.
class	Specifies one or more class names for an element. Multiple class names must be separated with space characters.
contenteditable	This attribute specifies whether the content of an element is editable or not (its value can be set to true or false). When the attribute is not set on an element, the element will inherit it from its parent.
contextmenu	This attribute specifies a context menu for an element. The context menu appears when a user right-clicks on the element. The value of the attribute is the id of the <menu> element to open. As of this writing, no major browser supports the <menu> elements and the contextmenu attribute.
dir	Specifies the text direction of the element's content. Its value can be ltr (left-to-right), rtl (right-to-left), or auto (let the browser figure out the text direction, based on the content).

Attribute	Description
draggable	Specifies whether the element can be dragged or not. The attribute's value can be true, false, or auto (uses the default behavior of the browser)
dropzone	This attribute specifies whether the dragged data is copied, moved, or linked, when it is dropped on an element. As of this writing, no major browser supports this attribute.
hidden	When this attribute is present, it specifies that an element is not yet, or is no longer, relevant. Browsers do not display elements that have the hidden attribute specified.
id	Specifies the unique identifier for an HTML element; the value must be unique in the HTML document.
lang	Specifies the language of the element's content. The value of the attribute uses ISO 639-1 language codes. For more details, see http://www.iso.org/iso/home/standards/language_codes.htm
spellcheck	This attribute specifies whether the element is to have its spelling and grammar checked or not. The following can be spellchecked: text values in input elements (not password), text in <textarea> elements, and text in editable elements.
style	Specifies an inline style for an element. The value of style attribute will override any style set globally, e.g. styles specified in the <style> tag or in an external style sheet.
tabindex	This attribute specifies the tab order of an element (when the "tab" button is used for navigating).
title	Specifies extra information about an element. The information is most often shown as a tooltip text when the mouse moves over the element.
translate	This attribute specifies whether the content of an element should be translated or not. Its value can be yes or no. As of this writing, no major browser supports this attribute.

Global Events

You already used a few events in exercises, such as the onload event (when you set the onload attribute of the <body> tag), or the onclick event (when you set the onclick attribute of a <button> element). HTML5 defines dozens of events that are triggered either as a result of user interactions, or as a result of state changes in the document's lifecycle. You can attach event handler scripts to HTML elements. These handlers are fired when the specific event is triggered.

NOTE: You can easily distinguish event attributes from other ones, as their name always begin with the on prefix, such as onclick, onload, onblus, etc.

The scripts you set as the value of an event attribute can be any valid JavaScript, a sequence of statements as well as a single call. Listing 6-14 shows an example, where you assign event handler code to two buttons, using their `onclick` event attribute.

Listing 6-14: Exercise-06-15/index.html

```
<!DOCTYPE html>
<html>
<head>
  <title>Simple event handler</title>
</head>
<body>
  <button onclick="this.textContent='Clicked.'">
    Click me!
  </button>
  <br />
  <button onclick="nowMe()">
    Now, click me!
  </button>
  <script>
    function nowMe() {
      document
        .getElementsByTagName('button')[0]
        .setAttribute('hidden', true);
    }
  </script>
</body>
</html>
```

The first button's `onclick` attribute uses a single inline statement that sets the `textContent` property of the button to "Clicked.", while the second buttons `onclick` attribute simply invokes the `nowMe()` method.

HINT: You can use both approaches. If the activity you want to carry out is longer than a few statements, or it contains compound execution flow, you'd better put it into an individual method, and invoke that method.

There are events that are triggered by the `window` object (this object represents the browser window the current page is displayed in). You can apply the attributes representing these events to the `<body>` tag only. Table 6-5 summarizes these events.

Table 6-5: Windows event attributes

Event	It fires (when)...
onafterprint	After the document is printed
onbeforeprint	Before the document is printed
onbeforeunload	Before the document is unloaded (when you close the browser, navigate to another page, etc.)

Event	It fires (when)...
onerror	An error occurs
onhaschange	The document has changed
onload	The page is finished loading
onmessage	The message is triggered
onoffline	The document goes offline (the internet connection gets broken)
ononline	The document goes online (the internet connection gets restored)
onpagehide	The window that contains the document gets hidden
ompageshow	The window that contains the document becomes visible
onpopstate	The window's history changes
onredo	The document performs a redo
onresize	The browser window is resized
onstorage	A web storage area is updated
onundo	The document performs an undo
onunload	The page has unloaded, or the browser window has been closed

As Table 6-6 shows, you can catch keyboard events. These events can be attached to any element, except <style>, <script>, <title>, <head>, <param>, <meta>, <br>, <base>, and <html>.

Table 6-6: Keyboard event attributes

Event	It fires (when)...
onkeydown	A user is pressing a key
onkeypress	A user presses a key
onkeyup	A user releases a key

These events follow this order: onkeydown, onkeypress, onkeyup.

Elements that can accept keyboard events, can accept user interactions triggered by a mouse, or similar pointing devices (including pen, or touch), too. Table 6-7 shows these event attributes.

Table 6-7: Mouse event attributes

Event	It fires (when)...
onclick	On a mouse click on the element
ondblclick	On a mouse double-click on the element
ondrag	An element is dragged
ondragend	At the end of a drag operation

251

Event	It fires (when)...
ondragenter	An element has been dragged to a valid drop target
ondragleave	An element leaves a valid drop target
ondragover	An element is being dragged over a valid drop target
ondragstart	At the start of a drag operation
ondrop	The dragged element is being dropped
onmousedown	A mouse button is pressed down on an element
onmousemove	The mouse pointer moves over an element
onmouseout	The mouse pointer moves out of an element
onmouseover	The mouse pointer moves over an element
onmouseup	A mouse button is released over an element
onmousewheel	The mouse wheel is rotated
onscroll	An element's scrollbar is being scrolled

There are events that can be used within HTML forms, Table 6-8 summarizes them. Although they apply to almost all HTML elements, generally they are used in forms.

Table 6-8: Form event attributes

Event	It fires (when)...
onblur	The moment the element loses the focus
onchange	The moment when the value of an element is changed
oncontextmenu	A context menu is triggered. As of this writing, no major browser supports this event attribute.
onfocus	The element gets focus
onformchange	A form changes
onforminput	A form gets user input
oninput	An element gets user input
oninvalid	An element is invalid
onselect	After some text has been selected in an element
onsubmit	A form is submitted

As you learned in *Chapter 3 (Using Multimedia)*, HTML5 introduces new tags to handle audio and video. It is not surprising that you can use media events, as summarized in Table 6-9. Most of these events can be used on almost all HTML elements, but they are most common in media elements, like <audio>, <embed>, <img>, <object>, and <video>.

Table 6-9: Media event attributes

Event	It fires (when)...
onabort	Loading of media (such as an image or a video) has been aborted
oncanplay	A file is ready to start playing (when it has buffered enough to begin)
oncanplaythrough	A file can be played all the way to the end without pausing for buffering
ondurationchange	The length of the media changes
onemptied	Something bad happens and the file is suddenly unavailable (like unexpectedly disconnects)
onended	The media has reach the end
onerror	An error occurs while the media file or stream is being loaded
onloadeddata	Media data is loaded
onloadedmetadata	Meta data (like dimensions and duration) are loaded
onloadstart	Just as the file begins to load before anything is actually loaded
onpause	The media is paused either by the user or programmatically
onplay	The media is ready to start playing
onplaying	The media actually has started playing
onprogress	The browser is in the process of getting the media data
onratechange	Each time the playback rate changes (like when a user switches to a slow motion or fast forward mode)
onreadystatechange	Each time the ready state changes (the ready state tracks the state of the media data)
onseeked	The seeking attribute is set to false indicating that seeking has ended
onseeking	The seeking attribute is set to true indicating that seeking is active
onstalled	The browser is unable to fetch the media data for whatever reason
onsuspend	Fetching the media data is stopped before it is completely loaded for whatever reason
ontimeupdate	The playing position has changed (like when the user fast forwards to a different point in the media)
onvolumechanged	Each time the volume is changed which (includes setting the volume to "mute")
onwaiting	The media has paused but is expected to resume (like when the media pauses to buffer more data)

Using Event Parameters

Most events have parameters that you can use in event handlers. For example, when you catch the onmousedown event, you may utilize the mouse pointer coordinates. When you pass the event object to the handler method, you can access the parameters of an event. Listing 6-15 shows an example.

Listing 6-15: Exercise-06-16/index.html

```
<!DOCTYPE html>
<html>
<head>
  <title>Catching event parameters</title>
  <style>
    #rectangle {
      position: absolute;
      left: 24px;
      top: 24px;
      width: 200px;
      height: 100px;
      background-color: navy;
      color: white;
    }

    #pos {
      text-align: center;
    }
  </style>
</head>
<body>
  <div id="rectangle" onmousedown="handler(event)">
    <p id="pos">(?, ?)</p>
  </div>
  <script>
    function handler(event) {
      var pos = document.getElementById('pos');
      pos.textContent = '(' + event.x + ', ' + event.y + ')';
    }
  </script>
</body>
</html>
```

Here, the onmousedown attribute contains the "handler(event)" value, so when you click the mouse button while the pointer is over the rectangle represented by the <div> tag, the event parameters are passed to the handler() method. In the body of handler() you can access the properties of the event. Among the others, x indicates the horizontal, y the vertical coordinate of the mouse pointer. The current coordinates are displayed in the paragraph nested into the rectangle, as shown in Figure 6-17.

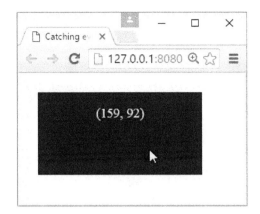

Figure 6-17: The event parameters can be caught

NOTE: Later in this book you will learn more about events and their parameters.

Summary

The HTML markup provides a hierarchy of elements—following the nesting of HTML elements and attributes in the page's markup. The web page is called document in the HTML standard, and its structure is represented by an abstract hierarchy, called Document Object Model—often referred as DOM.

The DOM is a very important representation of the page. It is used by the browser to embody the page in its memory, and also by browser plug-ins to allow queries and changes within this model. From the page creator's point of view, DOM can be used in scripts programmatically to access and alter document elements, and so it is the base of creating interactive web pages.

The DOM is represented as a document tree where HTML elements, texts, and attributes all are the nodes of the tree. Each node may have zero, one, or more child nodes; and each child node has exactly one parent node. DOM has a JavaScript API that supports navigation and changes through the `document` object.

With a few methods—such as `getElementById()`, `getElementsByTagName()`, `getElementsByName()`—, and a number of useful properties—including `anchors`, `forms`, `images`, `links`—you can access single nodes representing HTML elements, or a collection of HTML elements. When you grab an element, you can navigate to its children, siblings, or attributes.

The DOM API provides simple methods to insert, replace, or remove elements in the document tree. You can add event handler methods to the page, and in these methods you can change the tree—providing interactive user experience without round-tripping to the web server.

Chapter 7:
Getting to Know JavaScript

WHAT YOU WILL LEARN IN THIS CHAPTER

Facing the peculiarities of JavaScript

Understanding the syntax basics and the fundamental constructs of the language

Using primitive value types and objects

Getting to know a few special object types, such as `Boolean`, `Number`, `String`, `Date`, and `Array`

Working with the JavaScript operators and flow-control statements

You may find the approach of this book interesting. This is the seventh chapter, titled "Getting to Know JavaScript", nevertheless, you already faced with JavaScript very close to the beginning of this book. Moreover, the previous two chapters were packed with JavaScript code snippets. Was the author whacky, and did he shuffled the parts of the book?

No, absolutely not! I guess the basic knowledge of programming you definitely have—hey, you're going to create and program web pages!—must have been enough to understand the concept of using scripts in web pages. Nonetheless, to progress forward and master web page programming, you need to learn advanced concepts, and understand JavaScript.

Learning a new programming language is easy when you do not face a real task. When it is time to solve such an issue you have never met in the context of that language, you may waste lot of time to find the appropriate language constructs, runtime libraries, objects responsible for certain operations, and so on. This is the same with JavaScript. It might take years to possess the language, and requires a lot of coding practice to collect all useful programming patterns, and to get free from anti-patterns and common mistakes.

There are a number of levels your JavaScript knowledge may achieve:

1. With basic knowledge, you can program simple user interactions in web pages. Basic knowledge means that you are self-confident with the fundamental constructs of the language, especially with those that you need to create simple functions for user interactions, and you can bind the HTML markup with the code that manages the simple logic of the UI. To achieve this level, you need to get acquainted and practiced with DOM, and BOM (Browser Object Model).

2. With advanced knowledge, you can create more complex user interactions, and utilize a number of great JavaScript libraries that make you more productive, and allow you to program

compound web applications. To obtain this kind of knowledge, you will definitely have to build upon advanced language features.

3. JavaScript gurus possess the language so that they can create components and libraries that leverage language features extremely. The artifacts they create are powerful, they support a plethora of browsers, and they often use meta-programming elements. It is never too late to become a guru, but it needs years of practice in the fields, and mostly, passion mingled with intention.

This book intends to help you get the basic knowledge, and start advancing to understand the power of JavaScript.

A Couple of JavaScript Peculiarities

JavaScript is a great and powerful scripting language that possess all characteristics of an imperative programming language. It has its own peculiarities, too, which make it especially useful for extending HTML with interactions and dynamism. In this section you'll have a brief overview about the history of the language, and get acquainted with a few of its unusual traits, which make it powerful in web programming environment.

A Brief History of JavaScript

Would you think that JavaScript is older than 20 year? That means, it is almost as old as the World Wide Web itself! It was developed by *Brendan Eich*, who worked for Netscape that time. While its first official name was LiveScript in the beta releases of Netscape Navigator, later the marketing machine of Netscape altered its name to JavaScript. This naming intentionally tried to imply some relationship with the Java programming language that was new at that time, and obviously wanted to build on the Java hype.

Just to add some piquancy to the naming, ECMA internationally published the standardized version of the language named ECMAScript. Today, browsers mostly use the fifth edition of the ECMAScript (ECMA-262) specification, which was issued in June, 2011, and many of them support (partially) ECMAScript 2015 (formerly known as ES6), the sixth major version of JavaScript.

While in the early days JavaScript also suffered from incompatibilities between the two popular browsers, Netscape Navigator and Internet Explorer, in the past several years JavaScript has reborn. Many websites, including Yahoo, Google, Microsoft, Flickr, Twitter, and many others started using it. Yahoo and Google created very complex web applications built on the power of JavaScript, and today thousands of websites are fueled by this prodigious scripting language.

Web pages are not the only opportunities to use JavaScript. You can find the language in many places. Leveraging it, you can write apps for iPhone and iPad. Adobe Flash uses ActionScript, which is based on JavaScript. Windows 8 and Windows 10 allows you to create Windows Store apps written totally in JavaScript. With Node.js you can create simple server apps with extreme performance.

JavaScript is said to be the de-facto assembly of the web. Even if the language is old, there's no better time to learn it than today.

Most programming books start introducing a new language with a kind of "Hello, world" app to demonstrate a few traits of the language. In this book you already saw so many code snippets that you would find no news in such a small program. Instead, let's peek into one of the most important concept of the language, objects.

Objects and Dynamism

In previous code examples you could already see that JavaScript works with primitive types, such as numbers or strings. However, when you worked with the DOM in the previous chapter, you saw that the language works with objects representing the document loaded into the browser, or a collection of objects that represent HTML elements.

Objects are the most important concept in the language. Everything is either an object in JavaScript, or a primitive type's instance that can work like an object. Objects can have zero, one, or more properties with their associated values, and—wait for it!—they can be extended with properties dynamically at run-time. Listing 7-1 demonstrates this concept.

Listing 7-1: Exercise-07-01/index.html

```html
<!DOCTYPE html>
<html>
<head>
  <title>Objects, objects, objects</title>
  <script>
    // Create an object for my car
    var car = new Object();

    // Set up its properties
    car.manufacturer = "Honda";
    car.type = "FR-V";
    car.regno = "ABC-123";

    // Display what you've learned
    console.log(car);

    // Oh, I forgot the year...
    car.year = 2007;

    // Now, display it again
    console.log(car);
  </script>
</head>
<body>
```

```
    Listing 7-1: View the console output
</body>
</html>
```

The script in this listing produces this console output:

```
Object {manufacturer: "Honda",
  type: "FR-V", regno: "ABC-123"}
Object {manufacturer: "Honda",
  type: "FR-V", regno: "ABC-123",
  year: 2007}
```

NOTE: I added line breaks and indents to console output to improve its readability on Kindle devices.

HINT: As you already learned in Chapter 6, the `console.log()` operation puts its output to a channel that is hidden from everyday users of the browser. All major browsers provide a way (developer tools) to display the console output, and generally you can easily access it. To show this output, in Chrome use the F12 key, and then click the Console tab—unless that is displayed. In Edge use F12, in Firefox press Ctrl+Shift+K.

How did this short code create the output?

When you initiated the `car` object with `new Object()`, it had only a few predefined properties that each object has by default. Setting explicit properties such as `manufacturer`, `type`, and `regno` (using the dot (".") notation that is very common in many programming languages) gave meaning to the `car` object. Logging the object to the output displayed the content of `car` in a syntax called JSON (JavaScript Object Notation). As you can see from the output, setting the year property immediately added it to the other properties held by `car`.

When you design software based on objects, you generally assign behavior to the object. In most programming languages with object-oriented features (such as in C++, C#, and Java) generally you define the common behavior in the source code, and specialize objects by inheriting new types from existing ones. In contrast to this approach, JavaScript uses constructors as templates to create new instances of objects, as shown in Listing 7-2.

Listing 7-2: Exercise-07-02/index.html

```
...
// Define a constructor for Car
var Car = function (manuf, type, regno) {
  this.manufacturer = manuf;
  this.type = type;
  this.regno = regno;
}

// Create a Car
var car = new Car("Honda",
  "FR-V", "ABC-123");

// Display car properties
```

```
console.log(car);

// Oh, I forgot the year...
car.year = 2007;

// Now, display it again
console.log(car);
...
```

NOTE: In this listing I omitted all wrapper HTML markup for the sake of brevity. In this chapter's source code download you will find the full markup. From now on, I will omit HTML markup from listings whenever it does not lead to ambiguity.

The constructor is defined as a function named `Car`. When you create a new `Car` instance, this constructor function is called with the `new` keyword. This instructs the JavaScript engine to create an object in the memory, and pass it to the constructor function. In this case, the constructor function uses the `this` keyword as a reference to the newly created object, and it can be used to set up object instance properties. Although the constructor function does not retrieve any value explicitly, the JavaScript engine takes the object referenced by `this` as the return value, implicitly.

NOTE: JavaScript allows you to call the constructor function without the `new` operator, but in this case it has a totally different behavior. You will learn about it later.

When you instantiate a new object with a constructor function, the JavaScript engine creates an empty "bag" and passes it to the constructor. Using the `this` operator, you can put properties into this bag, and the constructor function returns a bag full with the properties you put in. As Listing 7-2 shows, you can put more properties into this bag any time later.

This listings output is very similar to the output of Listing 7-1:

```
Car {manufacturer: "Honda",
  type: "FR-V", regno: "ABC-123"}
Car {manufacturer: "Honda",
  type: "FR-V", regno: "ABC-123",
  year: 2007}
```

The only difference in this new output is that `Car` is written as the name of the logged object, though, previously it was `Object`. Right now, I do not treat why it is so, but later, when you'll know more about types, I'll return to a full explanation.

Functions are First Class Citizens

Object instances in JavaScript can have properties that contain special objects, called functions. After you assign a function to an object, you can use the corresponding property to invoke that function, as shown in Listing 7-3.

Listing 7-3: Exercise-07-03/index.html

```
...
// Define a constructor for Car
var Car = function (manuf, type, regno) {
  this.manufacturer = manuf;
  this.type = type;
  this.regno = regno;
  this.getHorsePower =
    function () { return 97; }
}

// Create a Car
var car = new Car("Honda",
  "FR-V", "ABC-123");
console.log("Horse power: " +
  car.getHorsePower());

// It is a stronger car
car.getHorsePower =
  function () { return 127; };
console.log("Horse power: " +
  car.getHorsePower());
...
```

The `Car` constructor assigns a function to the `getHorsePower` property of a newly instantiated `Car`. This function returns 97. Later, as the highlighted code indicates, the `getHorsePower` property of `car` (a `Car` instance) is redefined to return 127. The code invokes this function twice with the `getHorsePower()` notation, first time the one defined in the constructor, second time the redefined one. This is clearly shown in the console output:

```
97
127
```

Of course, you can define functions with arguments, as shown in Listing 7-4.

Listing 7-4: Exercise-07-04/index.html

```
...
// Define a constructor for Child
var Child = function (name, born) {
  this.name = name;
  this.born = born;
  this.ageInYear = function (year) {
    return year - born;
  };
}

// Create a Child
var ester = new Child("Ester", 1996);
console.log("Ester will be "
  + ester.ageInYear(2016)
```

```
    + " years old.");
...
```

The `Child` constructor defines an `ageInYear` function that accepts a single argument. When you invoke this function on `ester` instance, you can pass the argument, as shown in the highlighted code. This short code snippet produces this output:

```
Ester will be 20 years old.
```

As you can imagine, functions may have multiple arguments, and as you will learn later, those arguments can be functions, too. You probably won't be surprise if I tell you that functions may retrieve functions. But before going toward more abstract and advanced features, let's stay still on the ground.

Regular Expression Literals

JavaScript supports regular expressions through the `RegExp` type, and provides a simple syntax to create them, as shown in Listing 7-5.

Listing 7-5: Exercise-07-05/index.html

```
...
var pattern = /[A-Z]{3}-\d{3}/gi;
var text = "AB-123 DEF-234 ert-456 -34";
console.log(pattern.test(text));
pattern.lastIndex = 0;
var matches;
do {
  matches = pattern.exec(text);
  console.log(matches);
}
while (matches != null);
...
```

NOTE: If you are not familiar with regular expression, you can skip this section. If you would like to get more information about using them, I suggest you to start at `http://www.regular-expressions.info/quickstart.html`.

The first line of this short code defines the `pattern` variable as a regular expression. The right side of the assignment statement follows the `/pattern/flags` syntax, and so the JavaScript engine infers it is a regular expression. The pattern part is `[A-Z]{3}-\d{3}`, and it matches every string that starts with three letters in the "A"-"Z" range, followed by a dash, and closed by three decimal digits. The `/gi` is the flags part, where **g** indicates global mode (the pattern will be applied to all of the string instead of stopping after the first match is found), and **i** indicates case-insensitive mode (the case of the pattern and the string are ignored when determining matches).

Invoking the `test()` method on `pattern` checks whether the `text` passed as argument matches the pattern. The text will match, because it contains two substrings, "DEF-234", and "ert-456", which match the definition of the regular expression.

Because this expression uses global mode, you can use the `exec()` method to iterate through all matches. That is exactly what the `do-while` loop does. The `pattern` variable holds the state of the last pattern matching, so each invocation of `exec()` finds a new match, if there is any more. If there is no more match, `exec()` returns a `null`. Listing 7-5 produces this output:

```
true
["DEF-234", index: 7,
   input: "AB-123 DEF-234 ert-456 -34"]
["ert-456", index: 15,
   input: "AB-123 DEF-234 ert-456 -34"]
null
```

The `index` property in output shows the index of the first matching character in the `input`. The code snippet contains a line that sets `pattern.lastIndex` to zero. This line is used to reset the pattern after the `test()` operation, for the next `exec()` invocation to start at the beginning of the text.

When you define the regular expression with a literal, the JavaScript engine instantiates a `RegExp` object behind the scene. The definition

```
var pattern = /[A-Z]{3}-\d{3}/gi;
```

could have been written with this totally equivalent way:

```
var pattern = new RegExp("[A-Z]{3}-\\d{3}", "gi");
```

As you see, the `RegExp` constructor function accepts two arguments, pattern, and flags, respectively. The "\\" part within the string signs the single backslash character in the regular expression (using escape sequence syntax).

By now, you have already seen a few peculiarities of JavaScript. It's time to dive deeper and learn the basics of the language.

Placing JavaScript in HTML

In the previous chapter, you already met the `<script>` tag that allows you to add inline or external JavaScript to the HTML page. Normally, when the browser reads the `<script>` tag, it immediately processes the JavaScript found there before reading the other parts of the HTML markup.

In *Chapter 6*, most scripts either were added just right before the closing `</body>` tag, or contained only function definitions that were invoked through the `onload` event attribute of the `<body>` tag to ensure that the content of the page is fully loaded before starting the execution of the script.

According to this behavior, the `alert()` method in this script is invoked immediately when the browser processes the `<head>` section:

```
<!DOCTYPE html>
<html>
<head>
  <title>Alert in &lt;head&gt;</title>
```

```
  <script>
    alert("Hey, I'm running now...")
  </script>
</head>
<body>
  <h1>Display me!</h1>
</body>
</html>
```

Figure 7-1 indicates this: the message is immediately popped up in the browser, before the **<h1>** tag would be rendered.

Figure 7-1: The script in the <head> section is executed immediately

This markup moves the script to the end of the page definition:

```
<!DOCTYPE html>
<html>
<head>
  <title>Alert in &lt;head&gt;</title>
</head>
<body>
  <h1>Display me!</h1>
  <script>
    alert("Hey, I'm running now...")
  </script>
</body>
</html>
```

Now, the **<h1>** tag is displayed on the screen before the script runs, as shown in Figure 7-2.

Figure 7-2: The script runs right after the content is rendered

NOTE: You can find this sample in the `Exercise-07-06` folder.

The `<script>` tag provides you two attributes, `defer`, and `async`, which instruct the browser to change the normal way of processing the `<script>` content. Both attributes can be used only with external JavaScript files—otherwise, they do not have any effect.

In the source code download of this chapter, you can find the `Exercise-07-07` folder with a project demonstrating the usage of the `defer` attribute. The project contains two files, `index.html`, and `alert.js`, as shown in Listing 7-6, and Listing 7-7.

Listing 7-6: Exercise-07-07/index.html

```
<!DOCTYPE html>
<html>
<head>
  <title>Deffered JS loading</title>
  <script defer src="alert.js"></script>
</head>
<body>
  Do you see me?
</body>
</html>
```

Listing 7-7: Exercise-07-07/alert.js

```
alert("Message from <head>");
```

According to the normal behavior, the `index.html` page should display the popup message before rendering any part of the page. However, the `defer` attribute in `<script>` tells the browser that the script will not be changing the structure of the page as it executes, and as such, the script can be run safely after the entire page has been parsed. So, it will render the text in the document body before popping up the message, as shown in Figure 7-3.

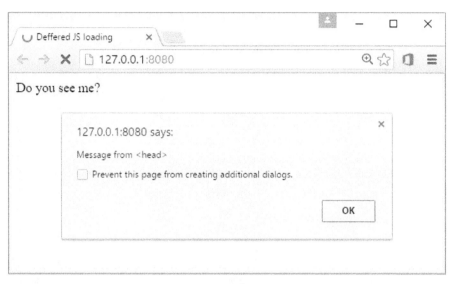

Figure 7-3: The effect of the defer attribute

The `async` attribute instructs the browser that it should load the script asynchronously, and execute the script at the first opportunity after download. Scripts loaded with `async` do not guarantee that they wait for the loading of the full HTML document. If there are more `async` scripts, the order of their execution is not guaranteed—unlike `defer`, which guaranties that scripts will follow their definition order when executing them.

HINT: Although most browsers allow use of `defer` and `async` simultaneously, the effect of such a setting is not defined, so you'd better avoid using them as a pair. If you want to be more watchful, do not assume that `defer` waits for the loading of the full document content. Use the `onload` event to trigger that the document is fully loaded.

JavaScript Syntax Basics

As every language, JavaScript has its own syntax rules. It is time to dive into details.

As you have seen in the samples of this book, JavaScript is one of the "curly-brace languages", its syntax is similar to C, C++, C#, and Java. Today, most browsers use the fifth edition of the ECMAScript standard (Ecma-262, Edition 5.1/June, 2011), so all syntax rules treated here are based on this standard. Any time JavaScript is mentioned in the context of syntax or semantic rules, the ECMAScript standard is used.

JavaScript is case-sensitive, so every token including keywords, function names, variables, object names, operators make distinction between lowercase and uppercase letters. For example, the `new` operator ("new" is a keyword) is different from `New`—which may be an identifier—, just as `myNumber` is a totally different variable name than `Mynumber`.

When the JavaScript engine parses the script, first it scans them for smaller elements, such as keywords, identifiers, operators, comments, literals, etc. To understand the rules of the languages, it is worth to start with getting to know the syntax of these smaller units.

Identifiers

Identifiers are used all-around in scripts to name variables, functions, objects, properties, or function arguments. An identifier may be one or more characters, where the first character must be a letter, a dollar sign ($), or an underscore (_), and all other characters may be letters, numbers, dollar signs, or underscores. Every letter character that can be used is taken into account in Unicode as letters, including Central European characters with accents such as "ü" or "é", as well as other letters, including the Hebrew alef or the Greek gamma.

The following strings are all valid identifiers:

```
getMyObject
$_this
Car
_transfer_24
```

NOTE: The standard allows using other Unicode characters or even Unicode escape sequences to be used in identifiers, for example, `objü\u2345` is a valid identifier (`\u2345` is a Unicode escape sequence). However, whenever it is possible, use only the letters of the English alphabet.

The language defines reserved words that cannot be used as identifiers. The reason for this restriction is that allowing reserved words to be used as identifiers would make the language parsing very complex, and sometimes it would lead to ambiguity.

HINT: You will find more information about suggested naming conventions later in this chapter.

Strict Mode

The fifth version of ECMAScript introduced a new concept, *strict mode*, which seems a bit weird at the first sight. This mode addresses some erratic behavior of the third ECMAScript edition, and it uses a different parsing and execution mode to avoid a few activities that are declared to be unsafe.

For example, strict mode does not allow you to define new variables without the `var` keyword, and also defines additional reserved words that are not allowed to be used as identifiers.

You can enable strict mode for an entire script (a `.js` file or a `<script>` section in HTML) with adding this line to the top:

```
"use strict";
```

To turn on strict mode for a single function, add the same line to the top of the function body:

```
function solveMyProblem(problem) {
  "use strict";
  // Put the function body here
}
```

At first sight this switch looks like a string that has not been assigned to any variable—well, actually, it is—, but the JavaScript engine takes it into account as a pragma to turn on strict mode. This syntax was chosen to keep compatibility with the third edition of ECMAScript.

Reserved Words

The standard defines a number of reserved words that include keywords, words reserved for future use, the null literal, true, and false (Boolean literals).

The fifth ECMAScript edition defines these keywords:

```
break
case
catch
continue
debugger
default
delete
do
else
finally
for
function
if
in
instanceof
new
return
switch
this
throw
try
typeof
var
void
while
with
```

A few other words are used as keywords in proposed extensions, and are therefore reserved to allow for the possibility of future adoption of those extensions:

```
class
consts
```

```
enum
export
extends
import
super
```

Well, strict mode extends this list with the following keywords:

```
implements
interface
let
package
private
protected
public
static
yield
```

Although you cannot use reserved words as identifiers generally, the standard allows one exception. You can use them in property names. Let's see an example:

```
var myCar = new Object();
myCar.export = true;
```

The **export** word is in the list of reserved words, however, it is still allowed to uses as an object property name. But, you cannot do this:

```
var export = 23;
```

In this context **export** is used as a variable name, and this scenario is declared being invalid by the standard.

Comments

Just as in many curly-brace languages, in JavaScript you can use single line comments, or block comments. Single line comments start with two forward-slash characters, and all characters till the end of the line are the part of the comment:

```
var x = 1; // This is a single line comment
```

Block comments start with a forward-slash immediately followed by an asterisk (/*), end with the opposite (*/), and may contain multiple lines:

```
/*
  This comment spreads
  multiple lines
*/
var x = 1;
```

Block comments cannot be nested. The highlighted part of this snippet shows what is taken into account as a block comment:

```
/*
  This comment spreads
```

```
  multiple lines
  /* and uses a wrong */
  nested block comment
*/
var x = 1;
```

Naming Conventions

APIs defined by the HTML and ECMAScript standards, as well as most JavaScript programmers follow this convention:

Identifiers in JavaScript use camel case. It means that words in the name are written with lowercase letters, the very first letter is lowercase, and each additional word is offset by a capital letter.

Constructor functions which must be used with the new operator should start with a capital letter. JavaScript issues no warning if a required new is omitted. Because odd things can happen if new is not used, this capitalization convention is indispensable. Examples:

```
Car
People
Connection
```

Variables and object properties that represent constant values are written with all capital letters, words are separated by underscore. Examples:

```
PI
MY_CONSTANT
```

Statements

JavaScript is an imperative programming language, it describes the body of a program with function declarations and statements. Statements can be expressions, variable declarations with optional initialization, the debugger statement, or flow-control statements.

Statements can be single statements, or organized into blocks that are wrapped with curly-braces ({ and } characters):

```
// This is a single statement
car.doSomethingWithMe();

// This is a statement block
if (car.wheels >= 4) {
  var cargo = new Object();
  cargo.isLarge = true;
}
```

As you can see, statements are terminated with semicolons. If you omit the semicolon, the parser determines the end of the statement:

```
var myExpr = 12 * (a + b)
```

271

```
var myVal = myExpr * 2;
```

In this short code snippet the first variable declaration statement is not terminated with semicolon, but from the context the parser decided that the statement should be terminated at the end of the first line.

HINT: Do not omit the semicolon from the end of the statement, it may lead to odd phenomena that are pretty difficult to find and troubleshoot.

By now, you possess all things you need to learn more exciting topics. Let's plunge into declaring variables and using types.

Variables, Types, and Scopes

As you learned earlier, JavaScript supports objects that can have dynamic properties, and so they can be used to represent compound things. JavaScript also supports primitive or simple value types that store irreducible values, such as numbers, strings, and Boolean flags. In this section, you will learn more about these values and types.

Variables

To store either simple values or objects, you must assign them to variables:

```
var obj = new Object();
obj.name = "Dave";
var number = 42;
var regExp = /(bat)?man/;
```

Here, `obj` and `regExp` variables hold object instances (a regular expression is represented by a `RegExp` object), `number` holds a value instance (the number 42). While many languages (C, C++, C#) are statically-typed languages—a variable can hold only the instances of a well-determined type—, JavaScript is a loosely-typed language, so the values assigned to the same variable can change its type during execution. For example, in the next code snippet, the `myValue` variable changes its type several times:

```
var myValue = new Object();
myValue.name = "Bob";
console.log(myValue);
myValue = "Bob";
console.log(myValue);
myValue = 12 + 23;
console.log(myValue);
```

The console output indicates this fact:

```
Object {name: "Bob"}
Bob
35
```

In these code snippets you can see that variables can be declared with the var keyword. In contrast to other languages, JavaScript allows you to redefine variables in the same scope, as the following code snippet indicates:

```
var myValue = new Object();
myValue.name = "Bob";
console.log(myValue);
var myValue = "Bob";
console.log(myValue);
var myValue = 12 + 23;
console.log(myValue);
```

HINT: JavaScript allows you to define variables without the var keyword. Variables declared this way are automatically created in the global context—you'll be learn about this concept soon—, so it may result in different behavior what you expect. As a best practice, always use var explicitly when you intend to introduce a new variable.

Reference Values and Primitive Values

JavaScript makes a distinction between reference values and primitive (single) values. While primitive values store simple atomic (irreducible) pieces of data, reference values are objects that may hold multiple values through properties. The distinction the language defines is very important, because reference values and primitive values are handled in different ways.

The first difference between them is the way they are stored and copied. Running the code in Listing 7-8 demonstrates it.

Listing 7-8: Exercise-07-08/index.html

```
. . .
// Define two objects
var obj1 = new Object();
obj1.name = "Steve";
var obj2 = obj1;
obj2.name = "Bob";
console.log(obj1.name
    + ", " + obj2.name);

// Define two strings
var str1 = "Steve";
var str2 = str1;
str2 = "Bob";
console.log(str1 + ", " + str2);
. . .
```

This code creates an object, sets its name property, and then stores it into the obj1 variable. After copying the value of obj1 to obj2, and updating its value, you may think you have two separate objects named Steve and Bob, respectively. However, the first console.log() produces this output, showing that you're wrong:

```
Bob, Bob
```

Objects hold reference values. When you define variables with reference values in a context, the value of the object (a set of properties it holds) is stored on the heap, separately from the context that holds only references to the value stored on the heap. Figure 7-4 shows how the context and the heap changes during the copy operation described by these four lines of code:

```
1  var obj1 = new Object();
2  obj1.name = "Steve";
3  var obj2 = obj1;
4  obj2.name = "Bob";
```

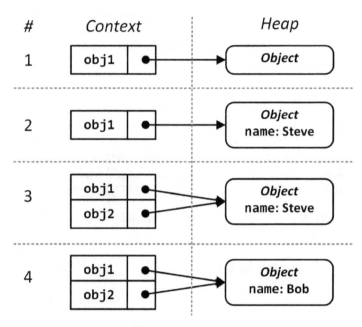

Figure 7-4: The reference value copy operation steps

As the figure indicates, at the end of the operation both `obj1.name` and `obj2.name` contain "Bob".

In contrast to reference values, primitive values are stored in the context. The second line of the console output shows this:

```
Steve, Bob
```

Figure 7-5 shows how these three code lines—which copy string values—result the console output:

```
1  var str1 = "Steve";
2  var str2 = str1;
3  str2 = "Bob";
```

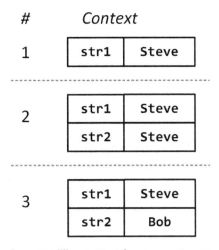

Figure 7-5: The primitive value copy operation steps

Now, you can declare variables, and know the difference of storing reference and primitive values. But what are the real types you can use in JavaScript?

JavaScript Types

Values and variables always have a concrete type that you can access with the **typeof** operator, as shown is this sample:

```
var myValue = "this is a value";
console.log(typeof new Object());
console.log(typeof myValue);
console.log(typeof (42));
```

JavaScript has only seven types—by means of the value domain of the **typeof** operator—, and these are **object**, **function**, **string**, **number**, **boolean**, **null**, and **undefined**. If the value is a string, a number, or a Boolean, evidently **string**, **number**, or **boolean** types are retrieved by **typeof**, respectively. If the value is an object, or **null** (this value represents an empty object pointer), **typeof** returns **object**. As you already learned, functions are first class citizens in JavaScript, so **typeof** retrieves **function** if you apply it on a function definition, for example, as shown in this code snippet:

```
console.log(typeof fortytwo);

function fortytwo() {
  return 42;
}
```

The **undefined** type has only one special value, **undefined**. When a variable is declared but not initialized, or you refer to a non-existing property of an object value, you get back **undefined**. This code snippet shows a few samples that all produce this value:

```
var dummy;
```

275

```
var obj = new Object();
console.log(typeof undefined);
console.log(typeof dummy);
console.log(typeof obj.name);
```

Although **typeof** never returns **null** (for **null** it gives back **object**), the ECMAScript standard defines **null** as a type, which—similarly to **undefined**—has only one special value, **null**.

Primitive Types as Objects

Earlier you already learned that you can create your own object instances with constructor functions that act as templates. JavaScript provides a few constructor functions out-of-the-box (defined by the standard). These are **Number()**, **String()**, **Boolean()**, **Object()**, **Array()**, **Function()**, **Date()**, **RegExp()**, and **Error()**.

The first three—**Number()**, **String()**, and **Boolean()**—constructors not only construct objects; but they provide a primitive value for a string, a number, and a Boolean, too. Listing 7-9 provides a little help to understand this.

Listing 7-9: Exercise-07-09/index.html

```
1   var num1 = new Number(3.14);
2   var num2 = new Number();
3   var num3 = 256;
4   console.log(typeof num1);
5   console.log(num1);
6   console.log(num1.valueOf());
7   console.log(typeof num2);
8   console.log(num2);
9   console.log(num2.valueOf());
10  console.log(typeof num3);
11  console.log(num3);
12  console.log(num3.valueOf());
```

The output of this code snippet tells a lot about **Number()**:

```
4   object
5   Number {}
6   3.14
7   object
8   Number {}
9   0
10  number
11  256
12  256
```

The first line of the code instantiates a **Number** object (**num1**) with its primitive value of 3.14. Lines 4-6 log the attributes of this **Number** instance. You can see that it is really an object, and the **valueOf()** function returns its primitive value, 3.14.

The second line of the code instantiates a `Number` object with no value specified at construction time. This kind of instantiation sets `num2` as if it were created with the 0 primitive value—as shown by the output between line 4 and line 6.

The third line initializes the `num3` variable to a number, with a primitive value of 256. The last line of the console output is a bit surprising, because it shows that `num3` has a `valueOf()` function that retrieves 256. How can it be? If `num3` is a primitive value, it should not have properties or functions!

JavaScript provides a special transition from primitive number, string, and Boolean values to corresponding `Number`, `String`, and `Boolean` object instances, and vice versa. When using literal values for a number, a string, or a Boolean, you can use the properties and operations of `Number`, `String`, and `Boolean` on these primitive values. Behind the scenes the JavaScript engine creates an appropriate wrapper object for the literal value, invokes the designated operation (or gets a property value). When the on-the-fly created wrapper object is no longer needed, the engine discards it.

So, when line 12 invoked the `valueOf()` function upon `num3`—which is a primitive value—, the JavaScript engine created a wrapper `Number` object instance, invoked the `valueOf()` function, passed the result to the `console.log()` method, and then discarded the temporary wrapper instance.

Here is another example, which displays the binary form of the value 42. It uses the `toString()` method of a `Number` object. (This method accepts a number between 2 and 36, which is used as the base of the numeric representation.)

```
var number = 42;
var other = number.toString(2);
console.log(other);
console.log((42).toString(2));
```

This sample shows that you can invoke `toString()` not only on a variable, but also on a literal value.

NOTE: In the last line, the parentheses around 42 are required, otherwise the JavaScript parser would think that "`42.`" is the beginning of a floating point number, and would give an error for `toString` that is not a valid fractional part.

Argument Passing

When you invoke functions, all arguments—independently of their type—are passed by value. The value passed to an argument is stored into a local variable that has meaning only in the scope of the function. As soon as the function returns, the local variable goes out of the scope and is discarded. It means that even if you change the value of arguments with the function, only the local copies change, and the original values remain intact. Listing 7-10 demonstrates this.

Listing 7-10: Exercise-07-10/index.html

```
...
function doubleMe(arg) {
  arg = arg + arg;
  return arg;
}

var num1 = 5;
var num2 = doubleMe(num1);
console.log(num1); // displays 5
console.log(num2); // displays 10
...
```

Although the highlighted code line in the body of doubleMe() changes the argument (arg) of the function, it changes only a local copy, it has no effect on num1 when passing this variable to doubleMe(). So, the first log output will display 5 (the original value of num1), the second will show 10 (the result of doubleMe() invoked with num1).

Passing values by arguments does not mean that functions cannot cause side effects on values passed to them. When you pass reference values (objects), you can easily check this, as shown in Listing 7-11.

Listing 7-11: Exercise-07-11/index.html

```
...
function setYearOfBirth(obj, year) {
  obj.yearOfBirth = year;
}

var me = new Object();
setYearOfBirth(me, 1968);
console.log(me.yearOfBirth); // 1968
...
```

Although the obj and year arguments are passed by values in this listing, the setYearOfBirth() function causes a side effect (setting the yearOfBirth property of the argument), and the console output displays 1968. Nonetheless, it did not change the value passed in the obj argument. The side effect is caused by the fact that objects are reference values, and even if the value is copied, the copy points to the original content of the object, which is stored on the heap.

To prove that the value of obj is really copied when it is passed to the function, add the highlighted code to setYearOfBirth(), as shown in Listing 7-12.

Listing 7-12: Exercise-07-12/index.html

```
...
function setYearOfBirth(obj, year) {
  obj.yearOfBirth = year;
  obj = new Object();
  obj.yearOfBirth = 2001;
```

```
}
var me = new Object();
setYearOfBirth(me, 1968);
console.log(me.yearOfBirth);
...
```

The first highlighted line instantiates a new object, stores it back to `obj`, and then the second line sets the `yearOfBirth` property of the newly created instance. This code snippet still displays `1968`, because the `obj` argument is a copy of the reference value (`me`) passed to the function. After the new object has been created within the body of `setYearOfBirth()`, the side effect (setting the `yearOfBirth` property affects this new object, which is definitely separate from the one passed to the function.

If the `me` instance would have been passed not by its value, but by reference, the `me` would have been automatically changed to point to the new instance created within the function, and then `me.yearOfBirth` should have been `2001`.

Understanding Scopes

JavaScript has an important concept, *execution context*, or shortly, *context*, which should be understood by all developers. The context of a function or variable defines how the function or variable behaves, as well as other data it has access to. Behind the scenes, the JavaScript engine associates a *variable object* to each execution context, and all functions and variables defined in the context exist in this variable object.

NOTE: The variable object is not accessible by code.

When a function is invoked, a new context is created for the function called, and it is pushed onto a *context stack*. After the function has been executed, this stack is popped, and the control is returned to the previously executed context.

There is a *global execution context*, it is the outermost one—the first put onto the context stack. In web browsers, the global context belongs to the `window` object (this object represents an instance of the browser). Whenever you create global functions or variables, those are created as methods or properties of the `window` object instance.

When a context has executed all of its code, it is destroyed, all of its variables and functions are discarded. Because the global context is held by the `window` object instance, it is not destroyed until the browser page is closed, or the browser application is terminated.

Scope Chain

In a complex execution flow, there can be a number of execution contexts. Each context is an individual unit by means of variables and functions, and you may declare variables and functions with the same name in separate contexts. You need a mechanism that helps to provide ordered access to all of them in a certain execution context. It is the *scope chain*. Identifiers are resolved by navigating the scope chain from its front to its tail in search of the identifier name. When the identifier is found, the search ends successfully; otherwise an error occurs.

The front of this chain is always the variable object of the currently executing context. If the context is a function, then its activation object is used as the variable object (this holds all variable and function definitions in the context). The activation object starts with an implicitly defined variable called arguments, which contains the arguments of the function. (Evidently, this doesn't exist for the global context.)

The next variable object in the chain is from the containing context, and the next after that is from the next containing context—according to the context stack. This pattern continues until the global context is reached. The global context's variable object is always the last of the scope chain.

To demonstrate the scope chain mechanism, let's see an example. At Point 3 in Listing 7-13, there are three contexts. Figure 7-6 shows a simplified view of the scope chain at Point 3.

Listing 7-13: Exercise-07-13/index.html

```
. . .
var input = "Chuck Norris";
var i = 1234;

// Point 1
function encrypt() {
  // Point 2
  var salt = "|";

  function doEncrypt(input) {
    var result = "";
    for (i = 0; i < input.length; i++) {
      // Point 3
      result += input.charAt(i) + salt;
    }
    return result;
  }
  input = doEncrypt(input);
  // Point 4
}
// Point 5
console.log(input);
encrypt();
console.log(input);
console.log(i);
. . .
```

(The sample code also demonstrates that JavaScript allows defining a function within another function definition.) This silly algorithms "encrypts" the input variable by adding "salt" (|) after each character. The outermost context (the global context) invokes the encrypt() method, which in turn calls doEncrypt() declared in its body.

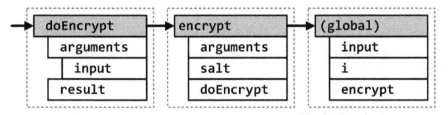

Figure 7-6: Scope chain at Point 3

This figure shows that `input` variable is declared twice, once in the `doEncrypt()`, second time in the global context. At Point 3 the identifier search starts in the `doEncrypt()` context, carries on with the `encrypt()` context, and finishes in the global context.

According to the scope chain mechanism, the "`result += ...`" statement will find the `result` variable in the `doEncrypt()` context, as well as `input`—this is the argument of the function. The `salt` variable will be found on the next scope chain element, in the `encrypt()` context. Variable `i` used in the `for` loop is held by the global context. Should an identifier named `dummy` used after point three, it would result an error, because there is no `dummy` identifier defined anywhere in the scope chain.

Variables are added to the corresponding context's variable object only when they are declared. When a script is processed, the JavaScript engine recognizes named function declarations, and it automatically adds them to the variable object—this mechanism is called *function hoisting*.

NOTE: Later, you will learn more information about named functions and function hoisting.

At Point 1, due to the function hoisting mechanism, `input`, `i` and `encrypt` identifiers are all valid, in spite of the `encrypt()` function is defined only after this point. At point 2, `input`, `i`, `encrypt` and `doEncrypt` (function hoisting!) are visible. However, `salt` is still unknown, because it is defined only after Point 2.

Well, by now you learned all the basics that you need to understand the traits of the built-in JavaScript types. Let's have an overview of each of them.

The Boolean Type

Boolean values are the basis of most flow-control statements, because they represent either `true` or `false` (as you remember, these are Boolean literals and reserved words, too). You can declare Boolean variables with these literals, or expressions resulting a Boolean value:

```
var isItValid = true;
var isTheGlobeFlat = false;
var flag = 3 < 4;
```

With the help of the `Boolean()` casting function, you can convert any value to a Boolean:

```
var thisValue = Boolean("false");
```

You must be careful with this conversion, because it follows different rules you may think of. For example, the `thisValue` variable will hold `true` after this conversion, instead of `false` suggested by the right side of the assignment statement. To understand this phenomenon, here are the conversion rules:

Boolean literals are converted to their appropriate Boolean values. Empty string is converted to `false`, but any nonempty strings will be represented with `true`. (This is why the "false" string results `true`.) Any non-zero number (including `Infinity`) results `true`, 0 and `NaN` (not-a-number) yields `false`. The `null` object is converted to `false`, while any other objects represent `true`. The `undefined` type always yields `false`.

NOTE: Soon, you will learn about `NaN` and `Infinity`.

Let's see a few examples:

```
var b1 = Boolean(undefined);    // false
var b2 = Boolean(1/0);          // true
var b3 = Boolean(0);            // false
var b4 = Boolean(null);         // false
var b5 = Boolean(new Object()); // true
```

The `1/0` expression does not raise an error, it results `Infinity`.

Be aware of that the `Boolean()` casting function is different from the `Boolean()` constructor. In the following code snippet `bool1` will be a Boolean value (`false`), while `bool2` is an object, wrapping a `true` Boolean value:

```
var bool1 = Boolean(false);
var bool2 = new Boolean(true);
```

The Number Type

JavaScript does not make distinction among different types of numbers, such as integers and floating point numbers with different length. It has only a single `Number` type that represents both integers and floating point numbers using the IEEE-754 format. You can check the `Number.MIN_VALUE` and the `Number.MAX_VALUE` constants to know this representation's limits:

```
MIN_VAULE: 5e-324
MAX_VALUE: 1.7976931348623157e+308
```

Despite of the single storage format, JavaScript provides several literal formats.

Integer Literals

Integer numbers can be represented with decimal, octal, and hexadecimal literals. Most frequently, decimal literals are used:

```
var smallInt = 73;
var longInt = 12345678901234567;
```

```
var negInt = -162;
```

When the integer literal starts with 0, it is parsed as an octal literal, unless a digit out of the 0-7 range is detected, in this case, the number is interpreted as a decimal number:

```
var octal = 046;     // decimal 38
var invOctal = 085; // decimal 85!
```

The second literal is not a valid octal number, so it is interpreted as decimal 85.

To define a hexadecimal integer literal, use the 0x prefix and use hexadecimal digits (either with lowercase or uppercase letters):

```
var hex1 = 0x3e;     // decimal 62
var hex2 = 0x2A4C; // decimal 10828
```

It does not matter which literal format you use to define an integer number; the JavaScript engine processes them the same way.

Floating-Point Literals

When you use a decimal point and at least one decimal digit after the decimal point, the number is interpreted as a floating point number. You can even omit the integer part (an implicit 0 is assumed). Alternatively, you can use the e-notation, and in this case you do not need to specify a decimal point. Here are a few samples:

```
var fl1 = 12.34;
var fl2 = .467;
var fl3 = 1.527e13;
var fl4 = 1e5;
```

According to the IEEE-754 format used to store the Number values, floating point numbers are accurate to 17 decimal places, but far less accurate in arithmetic calculations than integer numbers. As you know, internally these numbers use binary format. Because several decimal fractional numbers with final factional digits (such as 0.6) cannot be represented with final number of digits with binary base, you'd better not compare decimal numbers directly:

```
console.log(0.3 + 0.3 == 0.6); // true
console.log(0.5 + 0.1 == 0.6); // true
console.log(0.2 + 0.4 == 0.6); // false
```

NOTE: As another consequence of the IEEE-754 format, it is possible in JavaScript to have positive zero (+0) and negative zero (-0) values. These are considered to be equivalent.

Infinity

Calculations with numbers may result a value that is out of the range the Number type—the IEEE-754 format utilized in the background—can represent. In this case, the result automatically gets a special value, Infinity, or -Infinity, provided the calculation yields a negative number that cannot be represented in the allowed range. These short calculations show you examples:

```
// Results Infinity
var pInf = Number.MAX_VALUE * 2;

// Results -Infinity
var nInf = Number.MAX_VALUE * -1.2 - 100;
```

HINT: You can access the `Infinity` and `-Infinity` special values with
`Number.POSITIVE_INFINITY` and `Number.NEGATIVE_INFINITY`, respectively.

As it was mentioned earlier, dividing by 0 also results `Infinity` or `-Infinity` (depending on the sign of the dividend):

```
console.log(1/0);   // Infinity
console.log(1/-0);  // -Infinity
console.log(-1/0);  // -Infinity
```

Not-A-Number

There are operations in JavaScript, where a numeric value is expected in the result. However, these operations may not provide a numeric result, such as this:

```
var int = parseInt("q123");
```

The `parseInt()` method cannot interpret "q123" as a valid integer. Instead of raising an error, it gives back `NaN`, a special value representing "not-a-number". `NaN` shows unique behavior. Any calculations involving `NaN` always return `NaN`. Sounds odd, but `NaN` is not equal with any values, including `NaN` itself.

To check whether a certain operation results `NaN`, JavaScript provides the `isNaN()` function:

```
console.log(isNaN(NaN));        // true
console.log(isNaN("23.3e45"));  // false
console.log(isNaN(1/0));        // false
console.log(isNaN("Linux"));    // true
```

The `isNaN()` function can be applied upon objects as well—although, this is not a typical use:

```
console.log(isNaN(null));             // false
console.log(isNaN(new Number(123)));  // false
console.log(isNaN(new String("3")));  // false
console.log(isNaN(new String("q")));  // true
```

If the argument of `isNaN()` is an object, first it checks if it can be converted to a number. If it does not work, it uses the `valueOf()` method of the object to check whether that can be converted to a number. Should this check fail, `isNaN()` uses the `toString()` method to check if the string representation of the object can be converted to a number. If all conversion steps fail, the object is `NaN`.

So `isNaN(null)` returns `false`, because `null` can be converted a number (0, as you will learn soon). `IsNaN(new String("q"))` yields `true`, because all conversion attempts fail.

Converting Numbers

JavaScript provides three functions to convert non-numeric values into numbers: the `Number()` casting function, `parseInt()`, and `parseFloat()`. While `Number()` is used to convert any data to numbers, `parseInt()` and `parseFloat()` are used specifically to convert strings to numbers.

The `Number()` function uses these rules:

An `undefined` value returns `NaN`; `null` is converted to 0. When the argument is a number, it is simply passed through and returned. Boolean values, `true` and `false`, are converted to 1 and 0, respectively. String values are converted to numbers according to the following cases:

1. An empty string is converted to 0.

2. If the string contains only numbers, optionally preceded by a plus or minus sign, it is always converted to a decimal number. Leading zeros are ignored.

3. If the string contains a valid floating-point format, it is converted into the appropriate floating-point numeric value. Leading zeros are ignored.

4. If the string contains a valid hexadecimal format (with a "0x" prefix followed by one or more hexadecimal digits), it is converted into an integer that matches the hexadecimal value.

5. If the string contains anything other than these previous formats, it is converted into `NaN`.

You can apply `Number()` to objects. In this case, the `valueOf()` method of the object instance is called and the returned value is converted based on the previously described rules. If that conversion results in `NaN`, the `toString()` method is called and the rules for converting strings are applied.

Here are a few examples:

```
var n1 = Number(null);        // 0
var n2 = Number(undefined);   // NaN
var n3 = Number(true);        // 1
var n4 = Number(26.78);       // 26.78
var n5 = Number("014");       // 14
var n6 = Number("0x3e");      // 62
var n7 = Number("");          // 0
var n8 = Number("qwe");       // NaN
var strObj = new String("34.5");
var n9 = Number(strObj);      // 34.5
```

If you work with integer numbers, `parseInt()` is a more flexible solution than `Number()`. When examining a string value, `parseInt()` skips leading whitespaces, and checks the first useful (non-whitespace) character. If this character isn't a number, the minus sign, or the plus sign, `parseInt()` returns `NaN`. This behavior implies that the empty string returns `NaN`. If the first character is a number, plus, or minus, then the conversion goes on to the second character and continues on until either the end of the string is reached or a non-numeric character is found.

Provided that the first useful character is a number, the `parseInt()` function also recognizes all hexadecimal numbers (they begin with "0x"). Examine these examples:

```
var n1 = parseInt("");          // NaN
var n2 = parseInt("  -12.4");   // -12
var n3 = parseInt("238bla");    // 238
var n4 = parseInt("047");       // 47
var n5 = parseInt("0x41");      // 65
var n6 = parseInt("42");        // 42
```

NOTE: While ECMAScript 3 recognized integers starting with "0" as octal numbers, ECMAScript 5 interpret them as decimal numbers.

To be more accurate, `parseInt()` provides a second optional argument, the `radix` (base of conversion, must be between 2 and 36) to use. It makes the conversion more explicit:

```
var n1 = parseInt("1001001", 2); // 73
var n2 = parseInt("124", 5);     // 39
var n3 = parseInt("238", 10);    // 238
var n4 = parseInt("41", 16);     // 65
var n5 = parseInt("54", 8);      // 44
```

Even if you convert strings holding decimal numbers, use the `radix` argument (10) explicitly:

```
var number = parseInt("281", 10);
```

The `parseFloat()` function provides similar flexibility as `parseInt()` by means of skipping leading whitespaces and stopping at the first non-float-number character. Evidently, `parseFloat()` does not support hexadecimal format, or the `radix` argument. When you provide a string representing an integer, then an integer number will be returned. Here are a few examples:

```
var n1 = parseFloat("12.34e4bla"); // 123400
var n2 = parseFloat("  -0012");    // -12
var n3 = parseFloat("0x4f");       // 0
var n4 = parseFloat("3.14");       // 3.14
```

Number Methods

The `Number` type has several specific instance methods, as summarized in Table 7-1.

Table 7-1: Number instance methods

Method	Description
`toExponential()`	Returns a string representing the `Number` object in exponential notation. This method accepts an optional integer that specifies the number of digits after the decimal point.
`toFixed()`	This method formats a number using fixed-point notation. You can pass an integer that specifies the number of digits to appear after the decimal point. This value may be between 0 and 20. If this argument is omitted, it is treated as 0.

Method	Description
toLocaleString()	Returns a string with a language sensitive representation of this number. The method accepts two optional arguments. The first describes the locale information; the second provides an object describing options. For more information, see toLocaleString() reference on Mozilla Developer Network (MDN).
toPrecision()	Returns a string representing the Number object to the specified precision. Accepts an optional integer that specifies the number of significant digits.

Examples:

```
var num = 12.5345128;
console.log(num.toExponential(2));// 1.25e+1
console.log(num.toFixed(6));       // 12.534513
console.log(num.toPrecision(6));   // 12.5345
console.log(num.toLocaleString(
  "hu",
  { style: "currency",
    currency: "HUF" }));           // 12,535 Ft
```

NOTE: The toLocaleString() call uses JavaScript Object Notation. You will learn about it later.

The String Type

When you intend to work with text or characters, you should use the String type. This data type represents a sequence of 16-bit Unicode characters, including the empty string with zero length. JavaScript allows you to define strings enclosed between two single quotes (') or two double quotes ("). So the following string declarations are all valid:

```
var name1 = 'Steve';
var name2 = "Jane";
```

Nonetheless, quotes must match, so these are invalid declarations:

```
var name1 = "Steve';
var name2 = 'Jane";
```

When you need to specify characters that are not available on the keyboard, or are non-printable, you can use character escape sequences that begin with a backslash (\) character. Table 7-2 summarizes the available escape sequences.

Table 7-2: Character escape sequences

Sequence	Description
\n	New line character (U+000A)
\t	Horizontal tab (U+0009)
\v	Vertical tab (U+000B)
\b	Backspace (U+0008)
\r	Carriage return (U+000D)
\f	Form feed (U+000A)
\\	Backslash (\)
\'	Single quote (')
\"	Double quote (")
\0	Null character (U+0000)
\0ooo	A character represented by octal code *ooo*, where *o* is an octal digit (0-7).
\u*nnnn*	A Unicode character represented by the hexadecimal code *nnnn*, where n is a hexadecimal digit (0-F).
\x*nn*	A character represented by hexadecimal code *nn*, where *n* is a hexadecimal digit (0-F).

Let's see a few examples:

```
// I'm here.
var str1 = 'I\'m here.';
// Greek alpha: α
var str2 = "Greek alpha: \u03b1";
// 42
var str3 = "4\0102";
// C:\Program Files\
var str4 = "C:\\Program Files\\";
```

If the string is very long, you can break it into multiple lines with a backslash character directly followed by a line terminator character:

```
// This is a long text broken into short lines
  var str5 = "This is \
a long text \
broken into \
short lines";
```

Strings are immutable, so once they are created, their value cannot be changed.

Converting to Strings

Almost all values (including reference values and primitive values) have a **toString()** method that can be used to convert the value to a string. If the value is a **Number**, you can pass an integer argument to **toString()**, which represents the base of the conversion. Its value must be between 2 and 36:

```
var num = 73;
console.log(num.toString(2));   // 1001001
console.log(num.toString(8));   // 111
console.log(num.toString(16));  // 49
var num1 = 17.25;
console.log(num1.toString(2));  // 10001.01
```

As you can see from this short code snippet, you can invoke **toString()** with a specific radix to convert floating-point numbers, too.

Another way to convert values to strings is to leverage the **String()** casting function. It works similarly to the other casting functions you have already met, such as **Boolean()**, and **Number()**. **String()** uses these rules:

If the value is **null**, "null" is returned. If the value is **undefined**, the casting results "undefined". Otherwise, if the value has a **toString()** method, it is called with no arguments, and its result is returned.

String Properties and Functions

The **String** type has several specific instance methods and properties, as summarized in Table 7-3

Table 7-3: String instance methods and properties

Method/Property	Description
length	Gets the length of the string
charAt()	Returns the character at the specified index from a string. Indexes start with 0.
charCodeAt()	Returns the numeric Unicode value of the character at the specified index.
concat()	Combines the text of two or more strings passed as arguments, and returns a new string.
indexOf()	Returns the index within the calling **String** object of the first occurrence of the specified search value (first argument), starting the search at an optionally specified index (second argument). If the search value is not found, -1 is returned.
lastIndexOf()	Returns the index within the calling **String** object of the last occurrence of the specified search value (first argument), or -1 if not found. The calling string is searched backward. You can specify an optional index

Method/Property	Description
	(second argument) to start the search from.
`localeCompare()`	Returns a number indicating whether a reference string comes before or after or is the same as the given string in sort order. For more details, see the `localeCompare()` reference on MDN.
`match()`	Retrieves an object describing the matches when matching a string against a regular expression passed as the argument of the method.
`replace()`	Returns a new string with some or all matches of a pattern (first argument) replaced by a replacement (second argument). The pattern can be a string or a `RegExp`, and the replacement can be a string or a function to be called for each match.
`search()`	Executes the search for a match between a regular expression (first argument) and this `String` object.
`slice()`	Extracts a section of a string and returns a new string. The first argument is an integer value at which to begin the extraction. The second (optional) argument is an index at which to end the extraction. If the second index is negative, this index value should be added to the length of the string to calculate the end index of extraction.
`split()`	Splits a `String` object into an array of strings by separating the string into substrings. The method accepts a separator (first argument) that can be a string or regular expression. This separator specifies the character(s) to use for separating the string. An optional second argument, an integer, also can be passed to the method, which specifies a limit on the number of splits to be found.
`substr()`	Returns the characters in a string beginning at the specified location (first argument) through the specified number of characters (second argument). For more details, see the `substr()` reference on MDN.
`substring()`	Returns a subset of a string between one index (first argument) and another (second argument), or through the end of the string. For more details, see `substring()` reference on MDN.
`toLocalLowerCase()`	Returns the calling string value converted to lower case, according to any locale-specific case mappings.
`toLocalUpperCase()`	Returns the calling string value converted to upper case, according to any locale-specific case mappings.
`toLowerCase()`	Returns the calling string value converted to lowercase.
`toUpperCase()`	Returns the calling string value converted to uppercase.

The Date Type

JavaScript specifies **Boolean**, **Number**, and **String** as primitive value types. Interestingly, it does not use a primitive value type for handling date and time values. Instead, the standard defines the **Date** type (reference type) that stores dates as the number of milliseconds that have passed since midnight on January 1, 1970 UTC (Universal Time Code). Leveraging this data storage format, the **Date** type can accurately represent dates almost 300,000 years before or after January 1, 1970.

To create a date, use the **Date()** constructor function, and pass the number representation as an argument. When the argument is omitted, the new object is assigned the current date and time:

```
var now = new Date();
var y2001 = new Date(978303600000);
console.log(now.toLocaleString());
console.log(y2001.toLocaleString());
```

The console output shows this:

```
28/10/2013 16:02:19
1/1/2001 00:00:00
```

The first line tells you when this script was run before inserting the output into the manuscript of the book. The second line shows that the strange **978303600000** number means the first moment, of January 1, 2001.

Well, using magic numbers to create a **Date** instance is not the easiest manner. The **Date.parse()** and **Date.UTC()** methods provide a better way; both return a number that represents the date value. **Date.parse()** accepts a string and supports these formats:

ISO 8601 extended format: **YYYY-MM-DDTHH:mm:ss.sssZ** (e.g. 2008-06-12T23:34:02).

month/date/year (e.g. 12/24/2008)

month-name date, year (e.g. October 22, 1996)

day-of-week month-name date year hours:minutes:seconds time-zone (e.g. Sun November 24 2013 12:38:17 GMT+0100)

With **Date.parse()**, you can forget about **978303600000**, and write this more naturally:

```
var y2001 = new Date(
  Date.parse("01/01/2001"));
```

The **Date.UTC()** function accepts many number parameters: year, zero-based month (January is 0, February is 1, etc.), day of the month (1-31), hour (0-23), minutes, seconds, and last, milliseconds. The year and month parameters are required, all others are optional. The default day of the month value is 1, all other parameters default to 0. Let's see a few examples:

```
var num = Date.UTC(2013, 2, 18, 6, 44);
console.log(new Date(num));
num = Date.UTC(2001, 1, 31);
console.log(new Date(num));
```

When you examine the console output, you can observe a few surprising things (lines are broken intentionally):

```
Mon Mar 18 2013 07:44:00 GMT+0100
  (Central Europe Standard Time)
Sat Mar 03 2001 01:00:00 GMT+0100
  (Central Europe Standard Time)
```

The first `Date` construction specified 6:44 as the time part. Because `Date.UTC()` constructs number value for UTC time, it has been modified to 07:44:00 GMT+0001. This code was run in Hungary, which is located in the GMT+1 time zone.

The sample tried to use an invalid date in the second `Date` value: "February 31, 2001". Instead of declaring this date invalid, the `Date.UTC()` method calculated March 3 by correcting February 31 as the third day after February 28.

To make using the `Date` construction easier, you can invoke the `Date` constructor to mimic the `Date.parse()` and `Date.UTC()` functions:

```
var y2001 = new Date("01/01/2001");
var date = new Date(2013, 2, 18, 6, 44);
console.log(y2001);
console.log(date);
```

However, the console output shows that that the second way of `Date` construction uses locale time—in contrast to `Date.UTC()`, which calculates UTC time–, because 6:44 is calculated as 6:44 GMT+1—instead of 7:44 GMT+1, as with `Date.UTC()`:

```
Mon Jan 01 2001 00:00:00 GMT+0100
  (Central Europe Standard Time)
Mon Mar 18 2013 06:44:00 GMT+0100
  (Central Europe Standard Time)
```

You can use dozens of methods with the `Date` type. You can access the date and time parts with methods such as `getDate()`, `getTime()`, `getYear()`, `getMonth()`, `getDay()`, `getFullYear()`, `getUTCMonth()`, and many more. Similarly, you can use a number of methods to set different parts of the `Date` instance, such as `setDate()`, `setTime()`, `setFullyear()`, `setMonth()` among the others. You can use date formatting methods, such as `toDateString()`, `toTimeString()`, `toLocalDateString()`, `toLocalTimeString()`, `toUTCString()`, too.

NOTE: For a complete list of available `Date` methods, see the `Date` type reference on MDN. When you navigate to the reference page, you'll see the methods' reference links as `Date.prototype.methodname()`, for example, `Date.prototype.getDate()`. In the next section you will get a short overview about object prototypes, and you'll understand this notation.

The Object Type

You have already learned that objects are the cornerstones of the JavaScript language. Objects in JavaScript—just like in most programming languages with object-oriented features—keeps data and functionality together. Nonetheless, JavaScript object are very different in their implementation and behavior from traditional objects in Java, C++, or C#. In this section you will learn only the very basics of the Object type. You'll get acquainted with nitty-gritty details in *Chapter 8*.

All objects in JavaScript set out their life as nonspecific groups of data and related functionality. You create instances by utilizing `new` operator that is followed by the name of the object type (constructor function). The easiest way to instantiate objects is the `Object()` constructor that accepts an optional value as its argument. This value is stored as the wrapped value of the object, and it can be accessed through the `valueOf()` function. If you do not use the constructor argument, or specify either null or undefined, an empty object will be used as the wrapped object value:

```
var obj1 = new Object();
var obj2 = new Object(null);
var obj3 = new Object(undefined);
var obj4 = new Object(12.3);
var obj5 = new Object(true);
var obj6 = new Object("Hi");
console.log(obj1.valueOf()); // Object {}
console.log(obj2.valueOf()); // Object {}
console.log(obj3.valueOf()); // Object {}
console.log(obj4.valueOf()); // 12.3
console.log(obj5.valueOf()); // true
console.log(obj6.valueOf()); // Hi
```

If you do not pass any argument to the `Object` constructor, you may omit parentheses:

```
var obj = new Object;
```

Nonetheless, it is a practice to avoid.

In many object-oriented languages, `Object` is a root class of a hierarchy, and all other types inherit its properties, methods, and other members. Well, in JavaScript `Object` properties and methods are present on all object instances, including other, more specific objects.

A Quick Overview of Function Prototypes

Functions in JavaScript—including constructor functions—are created with a `prototype` property, which is an object containing properties and methods that should be available to instances of a particular object type. This object is utilized when creating a new object instances, and all of its properties and methods are shared among object instances. Take a look at Listing 7-14.

Listing 7-14: Exercise-07-14/index.html

```
...
function Car(manuf, type) {
  this.manufacturer = manuf;
  this.type = type;
```

```
}

Car.prototype.wheels = 4;
Car.prototype.getWheels =
    function () {
        return this.wheels;
    }
Car.prototype.name = "Car";

var car1 = new Car("Honda", "CR-V");
var car2 = new Car("BMW", "X5");

console.log("--- Car 1:")
console.log(car1.getWheels());
console.log(car1.name);
console.log(car1.manufacturer);
console.log(car1.type);
console.log("--- Car 2:")
console.log(car2.getWheels());
console.log(car2.name);
console.log(car2.manufacturer);
console.log(car2.type);
...
```

This code adds two properties (`wheels` and `name`) and a function (`getWheels`) to the prototype property of `Car`. When resolving property names, the JavaScript engine examines not only the object instance, but also the constructor function's prototype. As a result of this behavior, the `car1` and `car2` objects will have all properties added to the prototype. So the output of Listing 7-14 is this:

```
--- Car 1:
4
Car
Honda
CR-V
--- Car 2:
4
Car
BMW
X5
```

NOTE: The `prototype` property provides great opportunities that many JavaScript design patterns benefit from. You'll learn about them in *Chapter 8*.

Instance Properties and Methods

Each object instance has a `constructor` property that gets the function that was used to create the object instance. This property plays an important role in object-oriented programming, because it can be used to access the constructor function's `prototype` property.

Each object instance has a set of methods, as summarized in Table 7-4.

294

Table 7-4: Object instance methods

Method	Description
hasOwnProperty()	Indicates if the given property specified in the function argument exists on the object instance (and not on the prototype).
isPrototypeOf()	Checks whether the object specified in the argument is a prototype of another object.
propertyIsEnumerable()	Indicates if the given property (specified in the argument) can be enumerated using the for-in statement.
toLocaleString()	Returns a string representation of the object that is appropriate for the locale of execution environment.
toString()	Returns a string representation of the object.
valueOf()	Returns a string, number, or Boolean equivalent of the object. It often returns the same value as toString().

The Array Type

If JavaScript has a jolly joker type beside Object, that is the Array type—without any doubt. Just like in most programming languages, Array holds an ordered list of data, a collection of items that can be indexed with an integer. However, JavaScript arrays are much more flexible than arrays in other languages. First, an Array instance can hold any type of data in its items; the same array can hold numbers, objects, strings, or even arrays in its elements at the same time. Second, JavaScript arrays are dynamically sized, and automatically grow as data is added to them.

Creating Arrays

You can easily create new Array instances with its constructor function, as this code snippet shows:

```
var emptyArr = new Array();
var arr6 = new Array(6);
var numbers = new Array("1", "two", 3);

console.log(emptyArr);
console.log(emptyArr.length);
console.log(arr6);
console.log(arr6.length);
console.log(numbers);
console.log(numbers.length);
```

This sample demonstrates that you can use the constructor function in three different ways. With passing no parameters, an empty array with zero length is created. Using the constructor function with a number as the single argument creates an empty array and sets its length to the specified value. The third form of construction, where you pass more than one arguments, creates an array initialized with the given elements. The output of the script indicates this fact:

```
[]
0
[]
6
["1", "two", 3]
3
```

It shows that the first two arrays are empty, however, the second array's length is six.

Arrays are so fundamental types in JavaScript that the language provides literals to construct a new `Array` instance. The next sample shows how to construct the same arrays as earlier—but this time using the array literal notation:

```
var emptyArr = [];
var arr6 = [,,,,,,];
var numbers = ["1", "two", 3];

console.log(emptyArr);
console.log(emptyArr.length);
console.log(arr6);
console.log(arr6.length);
console.log(numbers);
console.log(numbers.length);
```

This code snippet produces the same output as the previous one. If you take a closer look at `arr6` initialization, you can count six commas that means seven elements. However, if the last comma is followed by directly a closing square bracket, JavaScript ignores the last comma. You can try to change the declaration of `numbers` by adding a comma after 3:

```
var numbers = ["1", "two", 3,];
```

This results an arrays with three items, and this is the reason why `arr6` represents an array with six items.

NOTE: Due to a bug, Internet Explorer 8 does not handle the last comma properly. It would create an array with seven items for `arr6`.

Array Conversions

Because `Array` instances are objects, they have `toString()`, and `toLocaleString()` methods that can be used to return the string representation of arrays. Both methods iterate through array elements, and call the `toString()`, and `toLocaleString()` methods of elements, respectively. By overriding the `toString()` and `toLocaleString()` methods you can influence how these methods represent the array contents. Listing 7-15 shows an example.

Listing 7-15: Exercise-07-15/index.html

```
...
var MappedNumber = function (name, locName) {
  this.toString = function () {
    return name;
  }
  this.toLocaleString = function () {
    return locName;
  }
}

var num1 = new MappedNumber("one", "egy");
var num2 = new MappedNumber("two", "kettő");
var num3 = new MappedNumber("three", "három");
var arr = [num1, num2, num3];

console.log(arr.toString());
console.log(arr.toLocaleString());
...
```

The `MappedNumber` constructor function accepts two arguments, `name` and `locName`, and defines the `toString()` and `toLocaleString()` methods to retrieve the appropriate argument's value. The `arr` variable represents an array of three `MappedNumber` variables, each containing an English and a Hungarian name for a number. The console logs the following output:

```
one,two,three
egy,kettő,három
```

Array Operations

`Array` is a versatile type. It provides powerful operations that make it possible to use arrays not only as single lists, but also as queues or stacks. The `Array` type is also a great example to demonstrate the strength of JavaScript.

An `Array` instance dynamically resizes itself:

```
var arr = [1, 2, 3];
arr[5] = 6;
console.log(arr.length);     // 6
console.log(arr.toString()); // 1,2,3,,,6
```

In this sample the original array contains only three elements. Setting the sixth element's value—with index 5—automatically augments the array to store six elements, as the log output indicates.

You can easily create a queue from an array, as Listing 7-16 demonstrates.

Listing 7-16: Exercise-07-16/index.html

```
. . .
// --- Queue
var arr = [1, 2, 3];
arr.push(4);
arr.push(5);
console.log(arr.shift());    // 1
console.log(arr.shift());    // 2
console.log(arr.toString()); // 3,4,5

// --- Reverse queue
var arr = [1, 2, 3];
arr.unshift(0);
arr.unshift(-1);
console.log(arr.pop());      // 3
console.log(arr.pop());      // 2
console.log(arr.toString()); // -1,0,1
. . .
```

This code demonstrates two queues. The first implementation appends new elements to the end of the array (after the element with the highest index), and reads the first element; the second does it vice versa. The first way leverages the push() method that appends a new element to the end of the array, and returns its new length. To read from the queue, the shift() method is used that removes the element at the first position and returns it back.

The original content of the array is [1, 2, 3]. As you see, the code puts 4, and then 5 into the queue, that reads two elements that happen to be 1, and 2. At the end, the array contains [3, 4, 5].

The second way uses the unshift() method to add an element to the front of an array, and reads the array with pop() that removes the last element from the array and returns this removed element. The comments in the code show how this second queue implementation changes the array content.

HINT: You can pass not only one, but more elements as arguments to push() and unshift().

Using the push() and pop() methods, it is very simple to create a stack, as Listing 7-17 shows.

Listing 7-17: Exercise-07-17/index.html

```
. . .
var arr = [1, 2, 3];
arr.push(4);
arr.push(5);
console.log(arr.pop());      // 5
console.log(arr.pop());      // 4
console.log(arr.toString()); // 1,2,3
. . .
```

Arrays have a number of methods that can be used to manipulate existing arrays. Listing 7-18 demonstrates two of them, concat(), and slice().

Listing 7-18: Exercise-07-18/index.html

```
. . .
var fruits = ["apple", "banana"];
var fruit2 = fruits.concat(["orange", "lemon"],
  "pear");
console.log(fruit2.toString());

var fruit3 = fruit2.slice(2, 4);
console.log(fruit3.toString());
. . .
```

This code snippet produces this output:

```
apple,banana,orange,lemon,pear
orange,lemon
```

The concat() method returns a new array comprised of this array joined with other arrays and values. In this listing fruits2 is assembled from the original contents of fruits, and from the items in the ["orange", "lemon"] array, plus "pear"—as shown in the first line of the output. It's important to know that concat() does not change the array it is invoked on, instead, it retrieves a new, comprised array.

The slice() method returns an extracted a section of an array—without altering the original array. It accepts two arguments, an index to start extraction (first argument), and an index to end extraction (second argument). The extraction does not include the element at the end index. The slice(2, 4) call in the code extracts the second and third element from the array (second line of the output), but not the fourth one.

There is a more powerful method, splice(), which can be used to delete items from the array, to replace existing items, or even to insert new items, depending on the arguments passed to the method. Listing 7-19 demonstrates these operations.

Listing 7-19: Exercise-07-19/index.html

```
. . .
var nums = ["one", "two", "three"];

// Insert a new element
var removed = nums.splice(2, 0, "hey!");
console.log(nums.toString());

// Remove elements
removed = nums.splice(2, 2);
console.log(nums.toString());

// Replace elements
removed = nums.splice(1, 1, 2, 3, 4);
console.log(nums.toString());
. . .
```

This code creates this output:

```
one,two,hey!,three
one,two
2,3,4,two
```

The **splice()** methods combines two operations. It removes a section of the array, and insert a sequence of new elements. The removed section is returned by the method. The first argument marks the index at which to start changing the array. The second integer argument indicates the number of old array elements to remove. All other arguments are taken into account as elements to add to the array at the starting index specified in the first argument.

The first invocation of **splice()** did not remove any elements because its second argument was set to zero. However, it added "hey!" after the second item, as shown in the first line of the output. Because the second **splice()** call did not passed any elements to insert, is simply removed two elements starting from index 2 (see the second line of the output).

The third call replaced the first element with three new elements (2, 3, and 4), because it removed one element at index 0, and then inserted 2, 3, and 3 to the array—as shown by the last output line.

You can change the order of elements in an array with the **reverse()** and **sort()** methods. Use **reverse()** to reverse the order of the elements. Invoking this method, the first item becomes the last, and the last item becomes the first. The **sort()** method—as its name indicates—sorts the elements of an array in place and returns the array. Listing 7-20 demonstrates using these methods.

Listing 7-20: Exercise-07-20/index.html

```
. . .
var word = ["h", "e", "l", "l", "o"];
word.reverse();
console.log(word.toString());
var nums = [13, 4, 2, 21, 8, 31, 17];
nums.sort();
console.log(nums.toString());
nums.sort(compare);
console.log(nums.toString());
nums.sort(compareDesc);
console.log(nums.toString());

function compare(v1, v2) {
  return v1 - v2;
}

function compareDesc(v1, v2) {
  return v2 - v1;
}
. . .
```

The output of the code is this:

```
o,l,l,e,h
```

```
13,17,2,21,31,4,8
2,4,8,13,17,21,31
31,21,17,13,8,4,2
```

The first line shows that reverse() works exactly as expected. You can use the sort() method in two ways. If you do not specify an argument, the elements in the array are sorted lexicographically according to the string conversion of each element. Alternatively, you can pass a compare function as the argument, and in this case this function is used to establish the sort order. This compare function takes two arguments, let's say v1 and v2, and it should return a value less than zero if v1 should come first, a value greater than zero if v2 should come first, and zero, if v1 equals v2.

The second line of the output shows that array elements are in dictionary order, because sort() was used without an argument. The third and fourth lines show the elements in ascending, and descending order, respectively. The order of the elements in the last two invocation of sort() were defined by the compare(), and compareDesc() functions.

You can search for element positions in the array with the indexOf() and lastIndexOf() methods. Both methods accept an element to search (first argument), and an optional start index. While indexOf() advances from the start index toward the higher indexes, lastIndexOf() advances toward lower indexes. Both methods return the index of the element if found, or a value less than zero, if the specified element is not in the array. Listing 7-21 demonstrates using these methods.

Listing 7-21: Exercise-07-21/index.html

```
. . .
var nums = [13, 4, 2, 21, 8, 2, 17];
console.log(nums.indexOf(2));       // 2
console.log(nums.indexOf(2, 3));    // 5
console.log(nums.lastIndexOf(2));   // 5
console.log(nums.lastIndexOf(11));  // -1
. . .
```

Advanced Array Operations

Arrays are often used to iterate through their elements and carry out some kind of operation on each item. Earlier in this book, you have already seen JavaScript examples where a for loop was utilized to traverse all elements in a collection. Although it was not explicitly mentioned, but in most cases an Array instance was used to represent a collection.

The Array type provides a number of operations to help iterative element processing. The methods representing these operations accept two arguments, a function processing a single element (first argument), and an optional scope object (second argument) in which to run the function. In the processing function, this second argument can be accessed through this.

The processing function must have this form:

```
function processor(element, index, array)
```

Evidently, **element** is the array element to be processed, **index** is this element's index, and **array** is the array instance being traversed.

Table 7-5 summarizes the array iteration methods.

Table 7-5: Array iteration methods

Method	Description
every()	This method tests whether all elements in the array pass the test implemented by the provided function. The provided function should return a Boolean value indicating the result of the test.
filter()	This method creates a new array with all elements that pass the test implemented by the provided function. The provided function should return a Boolean value indicating the result of the test.
forEach()	Executes a provided function once per array element.
map()	Creates a new array with the results of calling the provided function on every element in this array.
some()	Tests whether some element in the array passes the test implemented by the provided function. The provided function should return a Boolean value indicating the result of the test.

The code in Listing 7-22 provides simple examples of using **every()** and **some()**.

Listing 7-22: Exercise-07-22/index.html

```
...
var test = [12, 5, 3, 41, 23].every(isPositive);
console.log(test); // true;
test = [12, 0, 3, -41, 23].every(isPositive);
console.log(test); // false;
var test = [12, 5, 3, 41, 23].some(greaterThan10);
console.log(test); // true;

function isPositive(e, i, a) {
  return e > 0;
}

function greaterThan10(e, i, a) {
  return e > 10;
}
...
```

Using **forEach()**, **filter()**, and **map()** is just as easy as the other iterator methods, as shown in Listing 7-23.

Listing 7-23: Exercise-07-23/index.html

```
...
var nums = [1, 2, 3, 4, 5];
nums.forEach(display);
console.log(nums.filter(even).toString());
console.log(nums.map(square).toString());

function display(e, i, a) {
   console.log("a[" + i + "] = " + e);
}

function even(e, i, a) {
   return e % 2 == 0;
}

function square(e, i, a) {
   return e * e;
}
...
```

This code snippet produces this output:

```
a[0] = 1
a[1] = 2
a[2] = 3
a[3] = 4
a[4] = 5
2,4
1,4,9,16,25
```

Quite often you iterate through an array of elements in order to calculate an aggregate value, such as the sum of elements. The `Array` type provides two methods, `reduce()`, and `reduceRight()`, that let you simplify these kinds of aggregate operations. Both methods accept two arguments, a reduction function to invoke on all item (first argument), and an optional initial value (second argument) upon which the reduction is based.

The reduction function must have this form:

```
function reductor(prev, curr, index, array)
```

Evidently, `index` is this element's index, and `array` is the array instance being traversed. The `prev` argument is the value previously returned in the last invocation of the reduction function, while `curr` is the current element being processed in the array. Both methods work similarly, but while `reduce()` processes array elements from the first index to the last, `reduceRight()` starts from the end of the array and advances backward the first element. Listing 7-24 demonstrates using these methods.

Listing 7-24: Exercise-07-24/index.html

```
...
var nums = [1, 2, 3, 4, 5];
```

```
console.log(nums.reduce(sum));        // 15
console.log(nums.reduce(sum, 20));    // 35
console.log(nums.reduce(calc));       // 9
console.log(nums.reduceRight(calc));  // 13

function sum(prev, curr, i, a) {
  return prev + curr;
}

function calc(prev, curr, i, a) {
  return prev + (curr - i) * 2;
}
...
```

By now, you learned a lot about the fundamental types of JavaScript. It is time to look after how you can create expressions.

Operators

Every programming language needs expressions to describe calculations, algorithms, or even more complex concepts. Most languages use unary, binary, and sometimes ternary operators as basic building blocks of expressions. It is the same for JavaScript, it uses operators to manipulate data values, too. If you have already used curly-brace languages such as C, C++, Java, or C#, you will find the JavaScript operators familiar. However, you must be more considerate with JavaScript operators, for the loosely-typed nature of the language delivers a few surprising things.

Unary Operators

JavaScript supports the unary plus (+), unary minus (-), increment (++), and decrement (--) operators. The last two can be used either as prefix or postfix operators. In most programming languages, you can apply these operators only on numeric types, but JavaScript is more flexible.

It is trivial that you can apply unary plus and unary minus on numbers:

```
var num = 43;
var num2 = +num;
var num3 = -num;
console.log(num2); // 42
console.log(num3); // -42
```

However, you can use these operators in conjunction with non-numeric types as well. In this case, the value is converted with the Number() casting function, and the unary operators are applied on this converted value, as shown in this code snippet:

```
var bool1 = false;
var undef;
var str1 = "12.5";
var str2 = "8";
var str3 = "dummy";
```

```
var obj1 = null;
var obj2 = new Object();
obj2.valueOf = function () {
  return -4.5;
}
var float = 15.6;

console.log(+bool1); // 0;
console.log(-undef); // NaN
console.log(+str2);  // 8
console.log(-str1);  // -12.5
console.log(-str3);  // NaN
console.log(+obj1);  // 0
console.log(-obj2);  // 4.5
console.log(-float); // -15.6
```

The increment and decrement operators have the same semantics as in C, C++, Java, and C#. The increment operator increments its operand by one. If you use it as prefix operator—the **++** is written in front of its operand—, the result of the operation is the value of the operand after it has been incremented. The postfix operator—the **++** is written after its operand—results the value of the operand before it has been incremented. The decrement operator uses exactly the same semantics, except that it decrements the operand by one. Here are a few examples:

```
var num = 23;
var num1 = ++num;
console.log(num);   // 24
console.log(num1);  // 24
var num2 = num++;
console.log(num);   // 25
console.log(num2);  // 24
var num3 = --num;
console.log(num);   // 24
console.log(num3);  // 24
var num4 = num--;
console.log(num);   // 23
console.log(num4);  // 24
```

In contrast to other programming languages, in JavaScript the increment and decrement operators work on any values, including integers, strings, Booleans, floating-point values, and objects. The operators follow these rules regarding values:

When used on a floating-point value, the variable's value is changed by adding or subtracting 1. When used on another type, the variable's type is changed to a `Number`—according to the `Number()` casting function—and this value gets incremented or decremented. This short code snippet shows a couple of examples:

```
var bool1 = false;
var undef;
var str1 = "12.5";
var str2 = "8";
var str3 = "dummy";
```

```
var obj1 = null;
var obj2 = new Object();
obj2.valueOf = function () {
  return -4.5;
}
var float = 15.6;
console.log(++bool1);        // 1
console.log(typeof bool1);   // number
console.log(++undef);        // NaN
console.log(typeof undef);   // number
console.log(++str1);         // 13.5
console.log(typeof str1);    // number
console.log(--str2);         // 7
console.log(typeof str2);    // number
console.log(--str3);         // NaN
console.log(typeof str3);    // number
console.log(obj1++);         // 0
console.log(typeof obj1);    // number
console.log(obj2--);         // -4.5
console.log(typeof obj2);    // number
console.log(++float);        // 16.6
console.log(typeof float);   // number
```

Arithmetic Operators

JavaScript supports the following binary arithmetic operators: add (+), subtract (-), multiply (*), divide (/), and modulus (%). With numeric values, all operators work just as you expect them. Except the add operator, all the others work with non-numeric values by casting the operands to a Number value. The add operator is a bit different:

If one of the operands is a string, the result of the operation is a string, according to these rules: if both operands are strings, the second string is concatenated to the first; if only one operand is a string, the other operand is converted to a string and the result is the concatenation of the two strings.

This behavior of add is a source of common mistakes, as this code snippet shows:

```
var num1 = 12;
var num2 = 23;
console.log("12 + 23 = " + num1 + num2);    // 12 + 23 = 1223
console.log("12 + 23 = " + (num1 + num2)); // 12 + 23 = 35
```

The expression in the first console.log() method converts num1 to a string, because the left operand of add is another string. The result is a string, and so num2 is converted to a string, too. In the second expression the parentheses change the operator precedence, and so first the num1 + num2 expression is evaluated to 35, and then this value is converted to string.

Arithmetic operators can handle special values, such as NaN, Infinity and -Infinity. If any of the operands is NaN, the operation result will be NaN, too. If an operation provides a result that is higher than the maximum value that can be represented by Number, the result is Infinity.

Similarly, if the result is lower the lowest negative value that can be represented by `Number`, the result is `-Infinity`.

There are a number of other rules:

1. `Infinity` added to `-Infinity` results `NaN`.

2. `Infinity` subtracted from `Infinity` results `NaN`.

3. `Infinity` multiplied by 0 results `NaN`.

4. `Infinity` multiplied by `Infinity` results `Infinity`.

5. If `Infinity` is multiplied by any finite number other than 0, the result is either `Infinity` or `-Infinity`, depending on the sign of the second operand.

6. `Infinity` divided by `Infinity` results `NaN`.

7. Zero divided by zero results `NaN`.

8. If a nonzero finite number is divided by zero, the result is either `Infinity` or `-Infinity`, depending on the sign of the first operand.

9. If `Infinity` is divided by any number, the result is either `Infinity` or `-Infinity`, depending on the sign of the second operand.

10. If the dividend is an infinite number and the divisor is a finite number, modulus results `NaN`.

11. If the dividend is zero and the divisor is nonzero, modulus results zero.

These rules are not easy to remember by heart. If you are uncertain, just try to apply them, and see the results.

Equality Operators

Testing equality is an important operation in every programming language, just like in JavaScript. Due to the loosely-typed nature of JavaScript, it defines two kinds of equality: *identically equal* (`===`), and *equal* (`==`). Implicitly, there are two kinds of non-equality: *not identically equal* (`!==`), and *not equal* (`!=`).

The equal and not equal operators use conversion to determine the equality of their operands. During the conversion they follow these rules:

1. If an operand is a Boolean value, it is converted into a `Number` before checking for equality. A value of `false` is converted to 0, whereas a value of `true` is converted to 1.

2. If one operand is a string and the other is numeric, before testing, the string value is attempted to be converted into a `Number`.

3. If one of the operands is an object and the other is not, the `valueOf()` method is called on the object to retrieve a primitive value to compare according to the previous rules.

When making the comparisons, operators follow these rules, too:

1. Values of `null` and `undefined` are equal.

2. Values of `null` and `undefined` cannot be converted into any other values for equality checking.

3. If either operand is `NaN`, the equal operator returns `false` and the not-equal operator returns `true`.

4. If both operands are objects, then they are compared to see if they are the same object. If both operands point to the same object, then the equal operator returns `true`; otherwise, `false`, because they are not equal.

Let's see a few examples:

```
console.log(null == undefined);  // true
console.log(23 == "23");         // true
console.log(1 / 0 == 2 / 0);     // true
console.log(false == 0);         // true
console.log(true == 1);          // true
console.log(true == 2);          // false
console.log(NaN == NaN);         // false
```

NOTE: As it was already treated earlier, `NaN` is a special value that is not equal to itself.

The identically equal and not identically equal operators do not convert the operands before testing for equality. The two operands are identically equal if and only if their types and their values are equal. These short examples demonstrate how they work:

```
console.log(23 == "23");         // true
console.log(23 === "23");        // false
console.log(23 === (12 + 11));   // true
console.log(23 != "23");         // false
console.log(23 !== "23");        // true
```

Relational Operators

Besides the equality operators, JavaScript defines four relational operators—similarly to other programming languages. These are: less than (`<`), greater than (`>`), less than or equal (`<=`), and greater than or equal (`>=`), and each return a Boolean value representing the result of comparison. These operands work according to these rules:

1. If both operands are numbers, a numeric comparison is carried out.

2. If both operands are strings, the character codes of each corresponding character in the string are compared.

3. If one operand is a number, the other operand is converted to a number, and a numeric comparison is performed.

4. If an operand is an object, `valueOf()` is called, and its result is used to perform the comparison according to the previous rules. If `valueOf()` is not available, `toString()` is invoked, and the returned value is used according to the previous rules.

5. If an operand is a Boolean, it is converted to a number and the comparison is performed.

Here are several examples that demonstrate these rules:

```
console.log(3 < 4);        // true
console.log(3 > 4);        // false
console.log(3 <= "4");     // true
console.log(13 <= "4");    // false
console.log("13" <= 4);    // false
console.log("13" <= "4");  // true
console.log("x" < 3);      // false
console.log("x" >= 3);     // false
```

The last two expressions both result `false`, because `"x"` is converted to `NaN`, and as you know, `NaN` is not equal to anything, including itself.

Boolean Operators

JavaScript supports three Boolean operators, logical NOT (!), logical AND (&&), and logical OR (||). While in other programming languages Boolean operators work on only Boolean values, JavaScript allows using them on values of any types.

The logical NOT operator is a unary operator, and it always returns a Boolean value, regardless of the data type it is used on. First, it converts the operand to a Boolean value and then negates it. Logical NOT works according these rules:

1. If the operand is `undefined`, or `NaN` `true` is returned.

2. An object results `false`.

3. A `null` value results `true`.

4. An empty string results `true`, while a nonempty string returns `false`.

5. If the operand is the number 0, `true` is returned.

7. If the operand is any number other than 0 (including `Infinity`), `false` is returned.

Let's see a few examples:

```
console.log(!true);        // false
console.log(!"hello");     // false
console.log(!null);        // true
console.log(!undefined);   // true
console.log(!"");          // true
console.log(!23.2);        // false
console.log(!NaN);         // true
```

Provided its operands are Boolean values, logical AND returns `true` if and only if both of its operands are `true`. This operator is a short-circuited operation, meaning that if the first operand determines the result, the second operand is never evaluated. In the case of logical AND, if the first operand results `false`, it immediately return `false`, because no matter what the value of the second operand is, the result can't be `true`.

You are already got used to the fact that the loosely-typed nature of JavaScript often allows using any type of values. Accordingly, logical AND can be used with any type of operand, not just Boolean values. When either operand is not a primitive Boolean, logical AND does not always return a Boolean value; instead, it applies these rules:

1. If either operand is `NaN`, `undefined`, or `null`, then `NaN`, `undefined`, or `null` is returned, respectively.

2. If the first operand is an object, then the second operand is always returned.

3. If the second operand is an object, then the object is returned only if the first operand evaluates to `true`.

4. If both operands are objects, then the second operand is returned.

Here are a few examples that demonstrate these rules:

```
var obj1 = new Object(1);
var obj2 = new Object(2);
console.log(true && false); // false
console.log(false && obj1); // false
console.log(obj1 && obj2);  // Number {}
console.log(true & undef);  // Never executes
```

Provided its operands are Boolean values, logical OR returns `true` if at least one of its operands is `true`. Just like logical AND, it is short-circuited, and if the first operand is `true`, it immediately returns `true`, leaving the second operand unevaluated. When either operand is not a primitive Boolean—just like logical AND—, logical OR does not always return a Boolean value; instead, it applies these rules:

1. If either operand is `NaN`, `undefined`, or `null`, then `NaN`, `undefined`, or `null` is returned, respectively.

2. If the first operand is an object, then the first operand is returned.

3. If the first operand evaluates to `false`, then the second operand is returned.

4. If both operands are objects, then the first operand is returned.

This short code snippet demonstrates the logical OR rules:

```
var obj1 = new Object(1);
var obj2 = new Object("x");
console.log(true || false);  // true
console.log(false || obj2);  // String
console.log(obj1 || obj2);   // Number
console.log(null || NaN);    // NaN
console.log(false || undef); // Never executes
```

Bitwise Operators

Most programming languages define bitwise operators to allow expressions play with bits. These operators generally use signed and unsigned integer numbers. JavaScript is a bit different. If any operands of the bitwise operators are not integer numbers, first they are converted into 32 bit integers, and after the operation the result is converted back into a 64-bit value, conforming with the IEEE-754 specification (that is used to store Number values). During these conversions, the Number() casting rules are applied. Infinite and NaN values are taken into account as zero values.

JavaScript supports the following bitwise operators: bitwise NOT (~), bitwise AND (&), bitwise OR (|), bitwise XOR (^), left shift (<<), signed right shift (>>), and unsigned right shift (>>>).

NOTE: The IEEE-754 representation uses the two's complement format to represent negative numbers.

Bitwise NOT simply inverts all bits of its operand, 0 bits gets 1, and vice versa. Bitwise AND, OR, and XOR combine the appropriate bits of their two operands to calculate the result. For a single bit, bitwise AND results 1 if and only if both bits are 1. Bitwise OR produces 1 if any of the bits is 1. Bitwise XOR produces 1 if and only if one of the bits is 0, while the other is 1.

Here are a few examples:

```
// 1111 1111 1111 1111 1111 1111 1110 1110 (-18)
// 0000 0000 0000 0000 0000 0000 0000 0010 (2)
// -------------------------------------------
// 0000 0000 0000 0000 0000 0000 0000 0010 (2)
console.log(-18 & 2); // 2

// 0000 0000 0000 0000 0000 0000 0000 1011 (11)
// 0000 0000 0000 0000 0000 0000 0001 0111 (23)
// -------------------------------------------
// 0000 0000 0000 0000 0000 0000 0001 1111 (31)
console.log(11 | 23.5); // 31

// 0000 0000 0000 0000 0000 0000 0000 1000 (8)
// 0000 0000 0000 0000 0000 0000 0000 0000 (0)
// -------------------------------------------
// 0000 0000 0000 0000 0000 0000 0000 0000 (0)
console.log(8 & null);

// 0000 0000 0000 0000 0000 0000 0001 0000 (16)
// 0000 0000 0000 0000 0000 0000 0000 1110 (14)
// -------------------------------------------
// 0000 0000 0000 0000 0000 0000 0001 1110 (30)
console.log(16 ^ 14);

// 0000 0000 0000 0000 0000 0000 0010 1010 (42)
// -------------------------------------------
// 1111 1111 1111 1111 1111 1111 1101 0101 (-43)
console.log(~"42");
```

The left shift operator shifts all bits in a number (first operand) to the left by the number of positions given (second operand). When the bits are shifted, the empty bits to the right of the number are filled with 0s to make the result a complete 32-bit number.

The signed right shift operator shifts all bits in a 32-bit number to the right while preserving the sign (positive or negative). A signed right shift is the exactly opposite of a left shift.

The unsigned right shift operator shifts all bits in a 32-bit number to the right. For numbers that are positive, the effect is the same as a signed right shift. When the bits are shifted, the empty bits to the left of the number are filled with 0s to make the result a complete 32-bit number.

Let's see a few examples:

```
// 0000 0000 0000 0000 0000 0000 0000 1100 (12)
// -----------------------------------------
// 0000 0000 0000 0000 0000 0000 0011 0000 (48)
console.log(12 << 2); // 48

// 0000 0000 0000 0000 0000 0000 0001 1101 (29)
// -----------------------------------------
// 0000 0000 0000 0000 0000 0000 0000 0111 (7)
console.log(29 >> 2); // 7

// 0000 0000 0000 0000 0000 0000 0001 1101 (29)
// -----------------------------------------
// 0000 0000 0000 0000 0000 0000 0000 0111 (7)
console.log(29 >>> 2); // 7

// 1111 1111 1111 1111 1111 1111 1100 1100 (-52)
// -----------------------------------------
// 1111 1111 1111 1111 1111 1111 1111 1001 (-7)
console.log(-52 >> 3); // -7

// 1111 1111 1111 1111 1111 1111 1100 1100 (-52)
// -----------------------------------------
// 0001 1111 1111 1111 1111 1111 1111 1001 (536870905)
console.log(-52 >>> 3); // 536870905
```

Assignment Operators

You can set the value of variables or object instance properties with the assignment operator:

```
var value = 8;
var message = "str" + value;
var obj = new Object();
obj.prop = 42;
```

There are common situations, such as this:

```
var myNum = 12;
myNum = myNum + 23;
```

You can change the second line to use a compound assignment:

```
var myNum = 12;
myNum += 23;
```

Compound assignment is a shorthand notation for these common situations, you can use them for arithmetic and bitwise shift operators, as summarized in Table 7-6.

Table 7-6: Compound assignment operators

Operator	Assignment	Meaning
+	+=	v += a goes to v = v + a
-	-=	v -= a goes to v = v - a
*	*=	v *= a goes to v = v*a
/	/=	v /= a goes to v = v/a
%	%=	v %= a goes to v = v%a
<<	<<=	v <<= a goes to v = v << a
>>	>>=	v >>= a goes to v = v >> a
>>>	>>>=	v >>>= a goes to v = v >>> a

NOTE: These operators do not necessarily provide any performance improvement.

Conditional Operator

Just like in other curly-brace programming languages, in JavaScript you can use the conditional operator that allows a conditional expression that retrieves a value depending on the evaluation of a Boolean expression:

```
expr = conditional_expression ? true_value : false_value
```

If the `conditional_expression` is `true`, then `true_value` is the value of the expression; otherwise, the expression results `false_value`. For example:

```
var sign = value > 0 ? "positive" : "non-positive";
```

You can nest the conditional operator, like in this function definition:

```
function sign(v) {
  return v > 0
    ? 1
    : v == 0 ? 0 : -1;
}
```

Comma Operator

JavaScript uses the comma operator to allow the execution of more than one operation in a single statement, as in this example:

```
var val1 = 1, val2 = 2, val23 = 23;
```

You can use this operator in expressions, too, and in this way the comma operator returns the value of the rightmost (last) expression, such as in this short example:

```
var myValue = (2, 3, 4, 5);
console.log(myValue);              // 5
console.log( 1 + ("a", "b", "c")); // 1c
```

The typeof and instanceof Operators

You already learned that the **typeof** operator can be used to determine the type of a value:

```
console.log(typeof "hey!"); // string
```

Although **typeof** works very well for primitive values, it's of little use for reference values, because is retrieves "object" or "function" for all reference types. Typically, you want to know more than a value is an object—what you really want to know is the type of an object. For example, if you created an instance with the **Car** constructor function, you want to know that the object is an instance of **Car**. To benefit in this identification, ECMAScript provides the **instanceof** operator, which is used with this syntax:

```
result = variable instanceof constructor
```

The **instanceof** operator returns **true** if the variable is an instance of the given reference type. Take a look at this example:

```
// Is the variable car a Car?
console.log(car instanceof Car);
// Is the variable peter a Person?
console.log(peter instanceof Person);
// Is the variable list an Array?
conselo.log(list instanceof Array);
```

NOTE: All reference values, by definition, are instances of **Object**, so the **instanceof** operator always returns **true** when used with a reference value and the **Object** constructor. Similarly, if **instanceof** is used with a primitive value, it will always return **false**.

Operator Precedence

When you use compound expressions, it is very rare that operators are evaluated from left to right. For example, the following expression results 7, and not 9:

```
var expr = 1 + 2 * 3;
```

The precedence of the multiply operator is higher than the precedence of the add operator, so first 2*3 will be evaluated to 6, and then 1 + 6 is calculated. You can change the precedence of operators with parentheses. For example, this expression will result 9:

```
var expr = (1 + 2) * 3;
```

Just as in every programming language, operator precedence is declared in JavaScript, too. Table 7-7 summarizes the operators with their precedence, ordered from highest to lowest precedence. Operators with the same precedence are evaluated from left to right.

Table 7-7: Operator precedence

Operator	Description
. [] ()	Field access, array indexing, function calls, and expression grouping
+ - ++ -- ~ ! delete new typeof	Unary operators, delete operator, object creation, typeof operator
* / %	Multiplicative operators
+ -	Addition (string concatenation), subtraction
<< >> >>>	Bitwise shift operators
< <= > >= instanceof	Relational operators, instanceof operator
== != === !==	Equality operators
&	Bitwise AND
^	Bitwise XOR
|	Bitwise OR
&&	Logical AND
||	Logical OR
?:	Conditional operator
= += -= *= /= %= <<= >>= >>>=	Assignment and compound assignment operators
,	Comma operator

Flow-Control Statements

Imperative programming languages cannot exist without flow-control statements—nor can JavaScript. In this section you will have an overview about all flow-control statements provided by the JavaScript language.

NOTE: Control-flow statements have very similar syntax and semantics to their pairs in C, C++, Java, and C#. This section gives you a very concise description of these statements, and explains more details only upon uncommon constructs.

The if Statement

Probably the most commonly used flow-control statement is—in almost every programming language—the if statement. It has the following syntax:

```
if (condition) true_statement [ else false_statement ]
```

The **condition** can be any expression; it will be automatically converted to a Boolean value with the **Boolean()** casting function. When this expression is true, **true_statement** is executed; otherwise **false_statement**. As shown by the syntax description, the **else** branch with the **false_statement** if optional. Here are a few examples:

```
if (wheel > 4) {
    console.log("This must be a big car!");
}

// ...
if (horsepower < 200) {
    console.log("It's an ordinary car...");
} else {
    console.log("This car must be powerful!");
}
```

HINT: Although you do not need to wrap single statements into braces, only statement blocks, it is a good practice to always use braces.

The while Statement

The **while** statement provides a loop that can be executed zero, one, or more times depending on the loop condition:

```
while (condition) loop_statement
```

The **condition** is evaluated before the **loop_statement** is executed. If the condition results **true**, the **loop_statement** is executed, and the execution goes back to checking the condition in a loop. This goes on while the condition results **false** (the condition fails), and then the loop is aborted. Here is an example that displays numbers between 0 and 9:

```
var index = 0;
while (index < 10) {
    console.log(index++);
}
```

The do-while Statement

In contrast to the **while** statement that is a pretest loop—so it is possible that the loop body is never executed, the **do-while** statement is a post-test loop, so the loop body executes at least once:

```
do {
  loop_statement
} while (condition)
```

If the condition evaluates to **true**, the loop continues; otherwise, it is aborted. Take a look at this example that displays numbers between 0 and 9:

```
var index = 0;
do {
    console.log(index++);
}
while (index < 10)
```

The for Loop

Just as in many programming languages, the for loop provides a pretest with optional variable initialization—before entering the loop—and optional post-loop code to be executed:

```
for (initialization ; condition ; post_loop_expression) statement
```

This example shows the usage of a for loop:

```
for (var i = 0; i < 10; i++) {
    console.log(i);
}
```

The initialization, condition, and post_loop_expression are all optional, so you can create an infinite loop by omitting all of them:

```
for (;;) {
  console.log("Nothing gonna stop me");
}
```

The for-in Loop

There is another for loop in JavaScript, which can be used only to enumerate the properties of an object, the for-in loop:

```
for (property in expression) statement
```

The expression should retrieve on object. The loop iterates through all object properties, and retrieves the current property name in property. Here is an example that retrieves all properties of the document object:

```
for (var propName in document) {
    console.log(propName);
}
```

NOTE: The for-in statement will throw an error if the variable representing the object to iterate over is null or undefined. The ECMAScript standard does not specify the order of the properties retrieved, so it may be different depending on the browser that runs the script.

The break and continue Statements

You have seen that JavaScript implements a number of loops, such as while, do-while, for, and for-in. Two statements, break, and continue provide more control upon loops. The break statement immediately aborts the loop, and passes the execution to the next statement following the loop. On the other hand, the `continue` statement exits the current loop immediately, but execution continues from the top of the loop.

Let's see an example for `break`:

```
var nums = [12, 42, 23, 2, 6, 17, 21]
var index = -1;
for (var i = 0; i < nums.length; i++) {
  if (nums[i] == 6) {
    index = i;
    break;
  }
}
console.log(index);
```

The `for` loop in this code snippet traverses the `nums` array, and searches for the element that contains 6. As soon as this element is found, its index is saved and the `for` loop is terminated by `break`.

This example demonstrates the usage of `continue`:

```
var nums = [12, 42, 23, 2, 6, 17, 21]
for (var i = 0; i < nums.length; i++) {
  if (nums[i] % 2 == 0) continue;
  nums[i] *= 2.5;
  console.log("nums[" + i + "] = " + nums[i]);
}
```

The code iterates through the elements of the `nums` array, and multiplies all elements with 2.5, which represent odd numbers. Here the `continue` statement is used to terminate the current loop when an even number is found. This technique is often used to decrease the nesting of a code block, though, `if` and `continue` can be replaced by an `if` statement with inverted condition.

Both statements have a form when a label is specified. In this case break and continue return a particular location in the code. Any statement can be labeled with the following syntax:

label_name: *statement*

Take a look at this example:

```
var counter = 0;
outer_loop:
  for (var i = 0; i < 10; i++) {
    for (var j = 0; j < 10; j++) {
      if (i == 7 && j == 7) {
        continue outer_loop;
      }
      if (i == 8 && j == 4) {
        break outer_loop;
      }
      counter++;
    }
  }
```

```
console.log(counter); // 81
```

This code contains two nested `for` loops, each executing its body ten times, and the internal loop increments `counter`. Without interrupting the loops, the counter should be 100 at the end. However, the inner loop is interrupted twice. First, when `i` equals to 7 and `j` equals to 7, `continue outer_loop` is used, so the execution goes on with the outer `for` loop. It means that three internal loops are omitted. Second time, when `i` equals to 8 and `j` equals to 4, `break outer_loop` aborts not only the internal, but the outer loop, too. It means that six internal loops (it would increment `counter` by six) and an outer loop (it would increment `counter` by ten) is omitted. So, 19 increments are omitted in total, and that is why counter is set to 81 (100–19).

The switch Statement

As an alternative to compound `if` statements, JavaScript—similarly to other programming languages—defines the `switch` statement which has the following syntax:

```
switch (expression) {
  case value1: statement
    break;
  case value2: statement
    break;
  // "case" can be repeated
  case valueN: statement
    break;
default: statement
}
```

The `expression` is evaluated, and its value is checked again values in `case` branches. If the value equals with the expression, the statement belonging to the `case` branch is executed. The `break` statement automatically terminates the switch statement. Here is a short example:

```
switch (i) {
  case 1:
    console.log(1);
    break;
  case 2:
    console.log(2);
    break;
  case 3:
    console.log(3);
    break;
  default:
    console.log("Other than 1, 2, or 3.");
}
```

You can omit the `break` statement, but in this case the execution falls through to the next case branches, unless a `break` is found. The following sample demonstrates this situation:

```
var num = 1;
switch (num) {
  case 1:
```

```
    case 2:
      console.log(2);
    case 3:
      console.log(3);
      break;
    default:
      console.log("Other than 1, 2, or 3.");
} // logs 2 and 3
```

This example will create two log entries, "2", and "3", although variable num is set to 1. When entering the switch statement, num equals to 1, so case 1 is executed. It does not contain any statement (and no break), and execution flows to case 2 that logs „2". Because there is no break statement, the execution flows to case 3, and here "3" is logged. The next break terminates the switch statement.

When the values in case branches are evaluated, you may use any kind of expressions, and it lets you to use switch in such a way that is generally not allowed in other programming languages:

```
var num = 6;
switch (true) {
  case num >= 1 && num < 6:
    console.log("1-5");
    break;
  case num >= 6 && num < 10:
    console.log("6-10");
    break;
  default:
    console.log(">10");
} // logs 6-10
```

Here, the switch expression is true, and this is matched with the values of case branches. It means, the first case branch is executed in which the branch value is evaluated to true. In this code snippet this is the second branch, so "6-10" will be logged.

The with Statement

Beside flow-control statements, JavaScript provides the with statement that sets the scope of the code within a particular object. This statement was created as shortcut when a single object was being coded to over and over again, such as in this example:

```
console.log(document.title);
console.log(document.anchors.length);
console.log(document.links.length);
console.log(document.images.length);
console.log(document.forms.length);
```

The syntax of the with statement is the following:

```
with (expression) statement;
```

In this case, the statement is executed within the scope of the expression. So, you can rewrite the code above using the `with` statement:

```
with (document) {
  console.log(title);
  console.log(anchors.length);
  console.log(links.length);
  console.log(images.length);
  console.log(forms.length);
}
```

HINT: Avoid using the `with` statement. It is error-prone, and it has negative performance impact. It may be very annoying to debug code that contains `with` statements.

Summary

JavaScript is an unusual, and at the same time a very powerful language, especially in the context of web pages. It is standardized by ECMA with the name of ECMAScript. Right now the up-to-date versions of major browsers support the fifth and sixth (partially) edition of the standard.

JavaScript is a dynamically typed language, and it treats objects in a very special way. It provides great flexibility due to its dynamism and the flexibility as it manages object properties and methods. The programming language supports the usage of regular expressions.

You can add JavaScript code to your HTML pages with the `<script>` tag. Unless you instruct the browser otherwise, scripts are immediately processed as they are loaded with the page.

JavaScript has three primitive value types, Boolean, number, and string. These are immutable, and are always passed to method arguments. JavaScript has a primitive reference type, `Object`, which may contain an arbitrary number of properties and operations. With constructor functions, you can create your own object types. JavaScript offers a number of predefined object types. Some of them wrap value types into objects, such as `Boolean`, `Number`, and `String`; others—such as `Date` and `Array`—provide useful functionality.

The syntax of JavaScript resembles to other curly-brace languages (C, C++, Java, and C#). Its constructs, operators, and flow-control statements are similar to these programing languages, too.

Chapter 8:
Advanced JavaScript Programming

WHAT YOU WILL LEARN IN THIS CHAPTER

Getting to know the JavaScript Object Notation
Understanding the flexibility of functions
Programming with objects, understanding object instantiation, inheritance and module patterns
Using the Browser Object Model
Understanding the error handling constructs of JavaScript

The JavaScript Object Notation

In several code snippets, you already met with an interesting notation when displaying an object value. For example, take a look at this short code:

```
var car = new Object();
car.manufacturer = "BMW";
car.type = "X5";
console.log(car);
```

When you run this code snippet, Chrome displays this console output:

```
Object {manufacturer: "BMW", type: "X5"}
```

The notation you find between the braces—including the braces themselves—are a perfect description of the object. You can understand that this object contains two properties—manufacturer, and type—, and you also know the values of these properties that are "BMW", and "X5", respectively.

This kind of notation is not just an arbitrary one used by Chrome. It is called JavaScript Object Notation (JSON). It is used not only for displaying JavaScript objects, the notation is much more versatile. JSON is a data format, which is widely used for data exchange among components of web applications, as an alternative of XML, and other presentation formats for transmitting structured data over the Internet.

As you will learn, JavaScript uses the JSON syntax, however, JSON is not a part of the ECMAScript specification.

NOTE: The JSON notation format is described in RFC 4627.

JSON Syntax

JSON provides a very simple syntax to describe structured information with a combination of simple values, objects, and arrays. Compared to XML, it contains less noise, and uses less characters to describe the same data.

Numbers, strings, Boolean values, and the `null` value are represented in JSON with the same syntax, as in JavaScript—with the only exception that strings must be written between double quotes. So these are all valid examples of single values in JSON:

```
123
0x35fa
"Hummingbird"
null
true
42.5
```

NOTE: The `undefined` value is not supported in JSON.

Objects are represented with name and value pairs, where names are written between double quotes. The name and value is separated by a colon; properties are delimited by comma characters. The list of properties is wrapped in curly braces. Here is a very simple example:

```
{
  "manufacturer": "BMW",
  "type": "X5"
}
```

Compound objects can be described so that object values are represented with a nested JSON notation, just like in this sample:

```
{
  "id": 4234,
  "name": {
    "first": "John",
    "last": "Doe",
  },
  "enables": true
}
```

Collections of values and objects also can be represented by JSON, similarly to JavaScript arrays. The elements of a collection are wrapped between square brackets, individual elements are written with their native JSON representation, and elements are delimited with comma characters. Here is a simple example:

```
[23, { "type": "S", "name": "Small" }, true]
```

Obviously you can combine the value, object, and array notations to represent compound objects (arrays in object, objects in arrays, and so on), which describe large and complex structures.

JavaScript understands JSON natively. So you can create an order in JavaScript, as shown in Listing 8-1.

Listing 8-1: Exercise-08-01/index.html

```
...
var order = {
  "date": "11/20/2013",
  "customerId": 116,
  "items": [
    {
      "product": "Surface 4 Pro",
      "unitprice": "799",
      "amount": 1
    },
    {
      "product": "Type Cover 4",
      "unitprice": "129",
      "amount": 1
    },
    {
      "product": "Docking station",
      "unitprice": "199",
      "amount": 1
    }
    ]
}
    console.log("Date: " + order.date);
    for (var i = 0; i < order.items.length; i++) {
      console.log("Product: "
        + order.items[i].product);
      console.log("Unit price: "
        + order.items[i].unitprice);
      console.log("Amount: "
        + order.items[i].amount);
}
...
```

NOTE: When using JSON in JavaScript to initialize objects, you can omit the double quotes from property names.

Here, the **order** object is defined with JSON. After initializing the **order** variable, you can access its properties just as if it were created with a constructor setting up its properties with imperative code. Not surprisingly, the output of this code looks like this:

```
Date: 11/20/2013
Product: Surface 4 Pro
Unit price: 799
Amount: 1
Product: Type Cover 4
Unit price: 129
Amount: 1
Product: Docking station
Unit price: 199
Amount: 1
```

Serializing and Parsing JSON

When transferring data from one component to another in a distributed system, JSON is a perfect format, and fits to JavaScript as well. The fifth edition of the ECMAScript specification formalized the serialization (converting an object to a string) and parsing of JSON into a native global object—not surprisingly—named JSON. This object is very simple, for it has only two methods, stringify() and parse().

The stringify() method converts the specified value (first argument) into its JSON representation. The method accepts two other optional arguments, a replacer object (second argument), and a spacing value (third argument). If you append the following code line to Listing 8-1, it will display the JSON representation indented similarly, as it is written in the code:

```
var orderJson = JSON.stringify(order, null, "  ");
console.log(orderJson);
```

NOTE: For more details, see the stringify() method reference on MDN. You can also customize how a concrete object is serialized by defining a toJSON() method for the object instance, which returns the string representation of the object to be used for JSON serialization.

The parse() method converts a JSON string into an object. The first argument of this method is the JSON string to be converted into an object, and it has a second, optional argument, which prescribes how the value originally produced by parsing is transformed, before being returned.

Listing 8-2 shows an example of using parse(). It uses the same order object as Listing 8-1, however, it emulates that the order has been received through a network connection as a JSON string.

Listing 8-2: Exercise-08-02/index.html

```
...
var remoteOrder = {
  "date": "11/20/2013",
  "customerId": 116,
  // Items omitted for brevity
}
var orderString = JSON.stringify(remoteOrder);

// Assume the order is pushed through the network
var order = JSON.parse(orderString);
console.log("Date: " + order.date);
for (var i = 0; i < order.items.length; i++) {
  console.log("Product: "
    + order.items[i].product);
  console.log("Unit price: "
    + order.items[i].unitprice);
  console.log("Amount: "
    + order.items[i].amount);
}
...
```

NOTE: For more details, see the `parse()` method reference on MDN.

Functions

As you learned in the previous chapter, functions are very important concepts in JavaScript. In this section you'll dive deeper into the implementation of functions, and get acquainted with many exciting features that make JavaScript functions powerful.

Function Return Values

Functions may retrieve results. You can use the return statement to pass back a result. If you specify return with no value, the function will immediately return without a value. If you utilize the result of a function that does not return a value, be prepared that you could get `undefined`. Listing 8-3 demonstrates this behavior:

Listing 8-3: Exercise-08-03/index.html

```
...
function hasReturnValue() {
  return "Hey!";
}

function noReturnValue1() {
}

function noReturnValue2() {
  return;
}

console.log(hasReturnValue()); // "Hey!"
console.log(noReturnValue1()); // undefined
console.log(noReturnValue2()); // undefined
...
```

Function Arguments

Evidently, functions may have arguments. In many languages, functions are identified by their signature that covers the name of the function, and the type of their arguments (in the order of their occurrence). In JavaScript, a function is identified only by its name. It does not matter how many arguments you defined when declaring the function, and how many parameters you pass when invoking the very same function. If you pass more arguments than defined, the extra ones will be passed to the function, but—of course—the function will ignore them (unless it is prepared to handle them, as you'll see soon). If you pass fewer arguments, the missing ones will have a value of `undefined` within the function body. So this code is totally legal in JavaScript:

```
function twoArgs(arg1, arg2) {
  return arg1 + arg2;
}

console.log(twoArgs());              // NaN
console.log(twoArgs(12));            // NaN
console.log(twoArgs(12, 23));        // 35
console.log(twoArgs(12, 23, 34));    // 35
```

Only the third call uses the function as intended, but all the other calls are valid. The first two call results NaN, because either arg1 or both arguments are undefined. The last invocation simply ignores the third argument.

This behavior implies that there is no function overload in JavaScript. So, you cannot define two different functions with the same name, but different number of parameters, and use both of them. The following code snippet demonstrates this:

```
function add(arg1, arg2) {
  return arg1 + arg2;
}

console.log(add(12, 23)); // NaN

function add(arg1, arg2, arg3) {
  return arg1 + arg2 + arg3;
}

console.log(add(12, 23, 34)); // 69;
```

In JavaScript, it is totally legal to define a function twice (or even more times). It looks like as if there were two add functions, and the first console.log() uses the first one, the second console.log() the second one. Well, it does not work this way. Because of function hoisting, both log operations invokes the second function definition—this is the only one in this context, and it overrides the first one.

NOTE: Just for a short recap: when a script is processed, the JavaScript engine recognizes named function declarations, and it automatically adds them to the context. This mechanism is called *function hoisting*. It means that a statement can refer to a function that is defined in the context only later.

Function arguments are internally represented by an array. This array is a real object, it is named arguments, and it can be accessed inside a function. The JavaScript engine takes care to assembly this array when a function is invoked. The first element of this array (argument[0]) represents the first argument; the second element (argument[1]) holds the second argument, and so on. Named arguments are totally interchangeable with their representation in the argument array. So, the following four functions are equivalent:

```
// Explicit arguments
function add(arg1, arg2) {
  return arg1 + arg2;
}
```

```
// Mixing explicit and implicit args
function add(arg1, arg2) {
  return arg1 + arguments[1];
}

function add(arg1, arg2) {
  return arguments[0] + arguments[1];
}

// Implicit arguments only
function add() {
  return arguments[0] + arguments[1];
}
```

You can also leverage the fact that `arguments` is an `Array` instance. The example in Listing 8-4 shows that you can easily write a function that sums up all passed arguments.

Listing 8-4: Exercise-08-04/index.html

```
...
function sum() {
  var result = 0;
  for (var i = 0; i < arguments.length; i++) {
    result += arguments[i];
  }
  return result;
}

console.log(sum(12));         // 12
console.log(sum(12, 23));     // 35
console.log(sum(12, 23, 34)); // 69
...
```

Specifying a Function Expression

JavaScript has a number of great things that all are built on *function expressions*. Just like other objects, functions can be assigned to variables:

```
var add = function (a, b) {
  return a + b;
}
```

This assignment ensures that you can invoke the function through the variable, just like if it were a statically declared function:

```
console.log(add(12, 23));
```

Function expressions provide great flexibility. For example, you can define different functions for a certain operation depending on the run time context:

```
var kind = "subtract";
```

329

```
// ...
var op;
if (kind == "add") {
  op = function (a, b) {
    return a + b;
  };
}
else {
  op = function (a, b) {
    return a - b;
  };
}
console.log(op(35, 23)); // 12
```

Here, depending on the value of the kind variable, the op variable holds a function that adds or subtracts two numbers. When the operation is called through the op variable, the function set up previously is invoked. As you can see, functions defined with function expressions do not need a name.

Because functions are objects, function expressions provide you a way to return a function from a function. You can wrap the previous logic into a function:

```
var kind = "subtract";
var op = createOperation(kind);
console.log(op(35, 23)); // 12

function createOperation(kind) {
  if (kind == "add") {
    return function (a, b) {
      return a + b;
    };
  }
  else {
    return function (a, b) {
      return a - b;
    };
  }
}
```

Returning function from another function sounds odd only the first time. If you think it over, all other imperative programming languages provide a way to do that. C and C++ can return function pointers; C# has delegates that can be returned from functions, too.

This mechanism in JavaScript is very powerful, as you will learn soon.

Recursive Functions

A number of algorithmic problems can be solved with recursion, when a function calls itself by name. For example, Fibonacci sequence is defined in a recursive way. By definition, the first two numbers in the Fibonacci sequence are 0 and 1, and each subsequent number is the sum of the previous two. You can create a recursive function that produces the specified number of this sequence by its index, as shown in Listing 8-5.

Listing 8-5: Exercise-08-05/index.html

```
...
function fibonacci(index) {
  if (index == 0) return 0;
  if (index == 1) return 1;
  return fibonacci(index - 1) +
    fibonacci(index - 2);
}

for (var i = 0; i < 10; i++) {
  console.log(fibonacci(i));
}
...
```

This short code creates the 10 numbers in the Fibonacci sequence, as the output indicates (I removed line breaks, and used comma to separate the numbers):

```
0, 1, 1, 2, 3, 5, 8, 13, 21, 34
```

To describe this recursive function with a function expression, you need to provide a name for the function, otherwise you cannot invoke it. Listing 8-6 shows Fibonacci sequence defined with a function expression.

Listing 8-6: Exercise-08-06/index.html

```
...
var fiboSeq =
function fibo(index) {
  if (index == 0) return 0;
  if (index == 1) return 1;
  return fibo(index - 1) +
    fibo(index - 2);
}
...
```

There is another way to use recursion with function expressions. The `arguments` object has a `callee` property, which is a pointer to the function itself. Using `arguments.callee`, you can define the Fibonacci sequence like this:

```
var fiboSeq =
function (index) {
  if (index == 0) return 0;
  if (index == 1) return 1;
  return arguments.callee(index - 1) +
    arguments.callee(index - 2);
}
```

The value of `arguments.callee` is not accessible to a script running in strict mode and will cause an error.

Closures

You already learned that functions can return functions. This feature requires that functions have access to variables defined in another functions' scope. Take a look at Listing 8-7. The code defines a `createOp` function that returns another function, and that uses the `kind` variable within its body. Although `kind` is declared in `createOp`, it is available later in the context of the returned function.

Listing 8-7: Exercise-08-07/index.html

```
...
var addOp = createOp("add");
var subtractOp = createOp("subtract");

console.log(addOp(23, 12));      // 35
console.log(subtractOp(23, 12)); // 11

function createOp(kind) {
  return function (a, b) {
    if (kind == "add") {
      return a + b;
    }
    else if (kind == "subtract") {
      return a - b;
    }
  }
}
...
```

In programming terminology, functions that do not have names are called *anonymous functions*. Functions that have access to variables from other functions' scope are called *closures*. In Listing 8-7, the function returned from `createOp` is an anonymous function, and a closure, too.

To understand how this mechanism works, let's focus on these code lines:

```
var addOp = createOp("add");
// ...
console.log(addOp(23, 12));      // 35
```

When the `createOp` function is called, its execution context looks like as shown in Figure 8-1. The context contains two items in its scope chain, the activation object of `createOp`, and the global activation object.

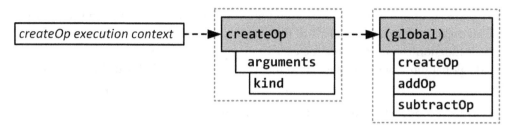

Figure 8-1: The execution context of createOp

Earlier you learned that whenever a variable is accessed inside a function, the specified name is searched for in the scope chain. Once the function has completed, the local activation object is destroyed, leaving only the global scope in memory. Closures, on the other hand, behave differently.

A function that is defined inside another function adds the containing function's activation object into its scope chain. This ensures that the internal function has access to the variables of the containing function. So, in createOp, the returned function's scope chain includes the activation object for createOp. When the console.log() operation invokes the anonymous function through addOp, the execution context of addOp looks like as shown in Figure 8-2.

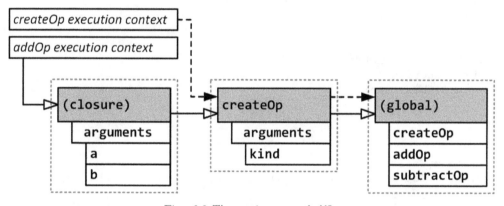

Figure 8-2: The execution context of addOp

Using the this Object

Earlier you used the this object within constructor functions, such as in this example:

```
var Car = function (manuf, type, regno) {
  this.manufacturer = manuf;
  this.type = type;
  this.regno = regno;
}

// Create a Car
var car = new Car("Honda",
  "FR-V", "ABC-123");
```

The `this` object is bound at run time based on the context in which a function is executed. When called in an object method, `this` equals to the object you invoke the method on. In the constructor function `this` represents the execution context of the object just being created. When used inside global functions, this is equal to the `window` object (you'll learn about it soon, in this chapter).

NOTE: In strict mode, `this` equals `undefined` when used inside a global function.

There's a little issue with anonymous functions. They are not bound to an object when you invoke them, so the `this` objects point to `window` (or contains undefined in strict mode). When you compose a closure, this fact is not really clear. Listing 8-8 shows an example unraveling this issue.

Listing 8-8: Exercise-08-08/index.html

```
. . .
var type = "Mercedes";

var myCar = {
  type: "BMW",

  getType: function () {
    return this.type;
  },

  getTypeFuncion: function () {
    return function () {
      return this.type;
    }
  }
};

console.log(myCar.getType());
console.log(myCar.getTypeFuncion()());
. . .
```

The `myCar` object has two functions, the first retrieves the object's `type` property (`getType`), and the second returns a function that obtains the value of the `type` property. The type property is passed back using the `this.type` expression in both methods. You expect this code to write "BMW" twice to the console output. However, when running this code, you see this:

```
BMW
Mercedes
```

The issue is caused by the `this.type` expression within `getTypeFunction`, which retrieves an anonymous function, and `this.type` is used by the anonymous function, which is a closure, too. When the `console.log()` operation invokes `getTypeFunction()`, it is bound to the context of the `myCar` object. However, the anonymous function returned be `getTypeFunction()` is bound to the global context, and so `this.type` is actually the `type` variable defined and initialized in the first line of Listing 8-8, and that is why it returns "Mercedes".

There is an easy remedy for this issue. Before `getTypeFunction()` defines the closure, it saves the context, and uses the stored context to access the `type` property of the object, as this code snippet shows:

```
getTypeFuncion: function () {
  var thisInContext = this;
  return function () {
    return thisInContext.type;
  }
}
```

Using variables in Anonymous Functions and Closures

Sometimes it is not obvious, but variables work in closures unexpectedly. Listing 8-9 demonstrates this issue.

Listing 8-9: Exercise-08-09/index.html

```
...
function giveMeFunctions() {
  var functions = [];
  for (var i = 0; i < 3; i++) {
    functions[i] = function () {
      return i * i;
    }
  }
  return functions;
}

var myFunctions = giveMeFunctions();
for (var i = 0; i < myFunctions.length; i++) {
  console.log(i + ": " + myFunctions[i]());
}
...
```

In this listing, `giveMeFunctions()` returns an array of functions. The code invokes each function in this array, and you expect them to return 0, 1, and 4. However, you see this output:

```
0: 9
1: 9
2: 9
```

What's wrong? Each anonymous function retrieves `i*i`, and `i` goes from 0 to 2, so something strange must happen! The code snippet suggests that `i` is evaluated every time when the anonymous function is defined, but it does not work this way. The anonymous function is evaluated when it is invoked, and using the execution context it resolves the value of `i`—using the context's scope chain. When you call `giveMeFunctions()`, the `i` variable is set to 3 at the time it returns. As you iterate through the elements in the returned function array, the `i*i` expression is evaluated using the value of `i`, which happens to be 3 each time, so that is why you see only nines in the output. There is a quick fix for this issue. Change the definition of `giveMeFunctions`:

```
function giveMeFunctions() {
  var functions = [];
  for (var i = 0; i < 3; i++) {
    functions[i] = function (arg) {
      return function () {
        return arg * arg;
      }
    }(i);
  }
  return functions;
}
```

This definition defines a function with a simple **arg** that retrieves another function. This internal function captures the **arg** variable and returns **arg**'s square value. The outer function is immediately called with **i** passed as its argument—due to the **(i)** appended to the end of the definition. As a result, the three internal anonymous function is bound with three different execution context—where **arg** is 0, 1, and 2, respectively—and they provide the result you expect:

```
0: 0
1: 1
2: 4
```

As you see, JavaScript functions provide a number of great features. Combining them with the versatility of JavaScript objects makes the language very powerful.

Programming with Objects

Objects are fundamental concepts in JavaScript. You can create and setup objects in several ways, as this code snippet illustrates:

```
// "Manual" setup
var car = new Object();
car.manufacturer = "Honda";
car.type = "FR-V";

// Setup with constructor function
var Car = function (manuf, type) {
  this.manufacturer = manuf;
  this.type = type;
}
var car1 = new Car("Honda", "FR-V");

// Setup with JSON
var car2 = {
  manufacturer: "Honda",
  type: "FR-V"
};
```

Each mode of setup results semantically the same object, a **car** that has a **manufacturer** and a **type** property. It is time to look after what properties are, and how JavaScript represents them.

Accessing Properties

By now, you perceived an object as a bag that may hold properties, and each property is a name associated with a value. You also learned the dot notation that allows accessing property values such as `car2.type` in this code snippet:

```
var car2 = {
  manufacturer: "Honda",
  type: "FR-V"
};
console.log(car2.type); // FR-V
```

To access a property, you can use the indexed notation, as shown in this code snippet:

```
var car2 = {
  manufacturer: "Honda",
  type: "FR-V"
};
console.log(car2["type"]); // FR-V
```

This notation allows using property names that otherwise were not allowed with the dot notation, for example, properties starting with numbers or containing spaces, and other punctuation characters or symbols. Listing 8-10 shows an example that cannot be written with the dot notation.

Listing 8-10: Exercise-08-10/index.html

```
...
var license = {
  "1 unit": 122,
  "2 units": 238,
  "3 units": 350
}
license["over 3"] = 400;

var unit2 = "2 units";
console.log(license["1 unit"]);  // 122
console.log(license[unit2]);     // 238
console.log(license["3 units"]); // 350
console.log(license["over 3"]);  // 400
...
```

Object Properties

Object properties may hold any kind of values, including primitive values and object instances. The ECMAScript specification defines two kinds of properties: data properties and accessor properties. Data properties store a data value at a single location. You can directly read or write the location where the data value is stored. In contrast, accessor properties do not contain a data value, but they are a combination of two methods. The *getter method* is responsible to obtain the value of the property; the *setter method* takes care to write the property value.

Internally, JavaScript assigns attributes to properties, and those attributes determine the behavior of the property, including the type of operations available on that specific property.

Both data and accessor properties have two common attributes, `Configurable` and `Enumerable`. `Configurable` indicates whether the property may be redefined by removing the property, changing the property's attributes, or changing the property into an accessor property. `Enumerable` designates whether the property will be returned in a `for-in` loop.

NOTE: By default, `Configurable` and `Enumerable` are `true` for all properties that are defined directly on an object.

Data properties have two other specific attributes, `Value` and `Writeable`. While `Value` holds the actual data value for the property (this is `undefined` by default), `Writeable` indicates whether the property's value can be changed (and it is `true` by default).

Accessor properties have a `Get` and a `Set` attribute, the function to invoke when the property is read from, and the function to call when the property is written to, respectively. Both attributes have `undefined` as their default values.

To query property attributes, you can use the `Object.getOwnPropertyDescriptor()` method. You can create new properties, or change existing ones with the `Object.defineProperty()` method, or set up multiple properties with `Object.defineProperties()`. Listing 8-11 demonstrates setting up a new read-only data property.

Listing 8-11: Exercise-08-11/index.html

```
...
var car = new Object();
Object.defineProperty(car, "type",
  {
    writeable: false,
    value: "FR-V"
  });

console.log(car.type); // FR-V
// This has no effect
car.type = "Other";
console.log(car.type); // FR-V

var descr = Object.getOwnPropertyDescriptor(
  car, "type");
console.log(descr.configurable); // false
console.log(descr.enumerable);   // false
console.log(descr.writable);     // false
console.log(descr.value);        // FR-V
...
```

The `Object.defineProperty()` method accepts three arguments. The first is the object instance, the second one names the property, and the third one provides an object that describes the property attributes to set. This listing defines a read-only attribute, and so the third argument specifies the `writeable` and `value` attributes. When you try to set a read-only attribute, the JavaScript engine does not raise an error; it simply ignores the modification request.

The `Object.getOwnPropertyDescriptor()` method accepts two arguments, the object instance, and the property name, respectively. It retrieves a descriptor object with property names according to the attributes. As you can see from the output of the example, the unset `configurable` and `enumerable` properties are initialized to `false`.

Accessor properties can be great to set up calculated properties and for values that need checking before setting them. Listing 8-12 demonstrates how to define and use them.

Listing 8-12: Exercise-08-12/index.html

```
...
var person = {
  firstName: "John",
  _lastName: "Doe"
};
Object.defineProperty(person, "fullName",
  {
    writeable: false,
    get: function () {
      return this.lastName + ", "
        + this.firstName;
    }
  });
Object.defineProperty(person, "lastName",
  {
    writeable: true,
    get: function () {
      return this._lastName;
    },
    set: function (value) {
      if (value != "") {
        this._lastName = value.toString();
      }
    }
  });

console.log(person.fullName); // Doe, John
person.lastName = "";
console.log(person.fullName); // Doe, John
person.lastName = "Smith";
console.log(person.fullName); // Smith, John
...
```

This code adds two properties to the `person` object—using `Object.defineProperty()` as earlier—, `fullName`, which is a calculated property, and `lastName`, which accepts only non-empty strings. As you see, the last name of the person is stored in the `_lastName` property, and it is set through the setter function of `lastName`. The console output—indicated in comments appended to the `console.log()` calls—indicates that `fullName` works as expected, and `lastName` checks for non-empty strings.

With `Object.defineProperties()` you can set up one or more properties in a single step, as Listing 8-13 shows. This listing sets up the person object just as Listing 8-12 does.

Listing 8-13: Exercise-08-13/index.html

```
...
var person = {
  firstName: "John",
  _lastName: "Doe"
};
Object.defineProperties(person,
  {
    fullName :
    {
      writeable: false,
      get: function () {
        return this.lastName + ", "
          + this.firstName;
      }
    },
    lastName:
    {
      writeable: true,
      get: function () {
        return this._lastName;
      },
      set: function (value) {
        if (value != "") {
          this._lastName = value.toString();
        }
      }
    }
  });
  // console.log() calls omitted for brevity
...
```

The first argument of `Object.defineProperties()` is the object to define the multiple properties for. The second argument is an object that specifies a set of properties (`fullName` and `lastName` in the example above), and sets each property to a descriptor object similarly to the `Object.defineProperty()` call.

Removing object properties

JavaScript provides the `delete` construct to remove properties from objects. This code demonstrates the usage:

```
var myObject = new Object();
myObject.intProp = 23;
```

```
myObject.strProp = "Hi!";

console.log(myObject.intProp); // 23
console.log(myObject.strProp); // Hi!

delete myObject.intProp;

console.log(myObject.intProp); // undefined
console.log(myObject.strProp); // Hi!
```

The code sets up the myObject instance with two properties, intProp and strProp. The delete statement removes intProp from myObject, so the second time it is written to the console, it contains undefined.

Instantiating Objects

In most programming languages constructors are the only way to instantiate new objects. As you already saw in the introduction of this section—and learned earlier—, JavaScript allows you to use manual setup, and you can create objects using the object literal (JSON), too. The most concise way is definitely the object literal; it is easy to read, and also saves you characters when typing. However, it has a significant issue. You can instantiate your objects only one by one, and you must repeat the literal—often including dozens of lines. This way is very error-prone, and pretty laborious to maintain.

JavaScript provides many ways to instantiate objects, and several construction patterns have been applied by JavaScript experts. Most patterns mix generic creation patterns with the peculiarities of JavaScript object management. In this section you will learn a few of the most frequently used patterns with their pros and cons.

First, let's see the standard constructor pattern. You already know this pattern, so Listing 8-14 will look familiar to you:

Listing 8-14: Exercise-08-14/index.html

```
...
var Employee = function (id, firstName,
  lastName, title) {
  this.id = id;
  this.firstName = firstName;
  this.lastName = lastName;
  this.title = title;
  this.getFullName = function () {
    return this.lastName + ", " + this.firstName;
  }
}

var philip = new Employee(1, "Philip", "Moore",
  "CEO");
var jane = new Employee(2, "Jane", "Mortimer",
```

341

```
  "CFO");

console.log(philip.getFullName());
console.log(jane.getFullName());
...
```

At first sight this constructor function seems perfect. It assigns the initial values of properties, and creates the `getFullName()` method. You can easily instantiate an `Employee` object by using the new operator with the `Employee()` constructor function.

Although it looks perfect, it conceals an important issue. Every time you create a new Employee instance it creates a new `getFullName()` method that is an exact copy of the one in the constructor function. When you create 10.000 instances, you'll get 10.000 copies of `getFullName()`, and it is definitely a waste of resources.

Extracting the `getFullName()` method from the object's scope solves this issue, as shown in Listing 8-15.

Listing 8-15: Exercise-08-15/index.html

```
...
var Employee = function (id, firstName,
  lastName, title) {
  this.id = id;
  this.firstName = firstName;
  this.lastName = lastName;
  this.title = title;
  this.getFullName = getEmployeeFullName;
}

function getEmployeeFullName() {
  return this.lastName + ", " + this.firstName;
}

var philip = new Employee(1, "Philip", "Moore",
  "CEO");
var jane = new Employee(2, "Jane", "Mortimer",
  "CFO");

console.log(philip.getFullName());
console.log(jane.getFullName());
...
```

Well, this solution eliminates the issue with multiple method instances. Here, setting the instance's `getFullName` property to `getEmployeeFullName` simply assigns a function pointer to the property, but does not create an individual method instance. Nonetheless, it creates a new problem. If you create many constructor functions for objects having a large number of methods, the global scope will be scattered with a number of functions that really belong to certain object types. This hurts the principle of encapsulation (an object should encapsulate its data and operations), and makes your code less maintainable.

Using Object Prototypes

Prototypes may provide a great solution for both the resource wasting and poor maintainability issue. As you learned in *Chapter 7 (A Quick Overview of Function Prototypes)*, functions in JavaScript are created with a `prototype` property, which is an object containing properties and methods that should be available to instances of a particular object type. Modifying the `Employee` construction as shown in Listing 8-16 offers a remedy for the issues mentioned earlier.

Listing 8-16: Exercise-08-16/index.html

```
...
var Employee = function (id, firstName,
  lastName, title) {
  this.id = id;
  this.firstName = firstName;
  this.lastName = lastName;
  this.title = title;
}

Employee.prototype.getFullName =
  function () {
    return this.lastName + ", " + this.firstName;
  }

var philip = new Employee(1, "Philip", "Moore",
  "CEO");
var jane = new Employee(2, "Jane", "Mortimer",
  "CFO");

console.log(philip.getFullName()); // Moore, Philip
console.log(jane.getFullName());   // Mortimer, Jane
...
```

To understand how prototypes work, here is a short explanation. Each function has a `prototype` property, and whenever a function is created, its `prototype` property is also set. By default, all prototypes get a property called `constructor` that points to the function used to create the object instance. As shown at the right side of Figure 8-3, the `Employee.prototype` has a `constructor` property that points to the `Employee` function.

Each time the constructor function is called to create a new instance, that instance has an internal pointer to the constructor's prototype (see «Prototype» in Figure 8-3). So, there is a direct link between the instance and the constructor function's prototype.

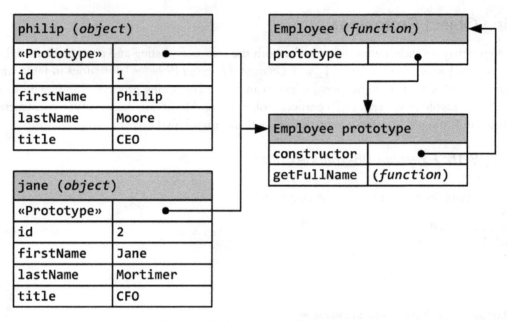

Figure 8-3: Employee instances and the prototype

The figure also shows the relationship between the Employee constructor's prototype, and the two instances of Employee, `philip` and `jane`. Observe that `Employee.prototype` points to the prototype object but `Employee.prototype.constructor` points back to `Employee`. The prototype contains only the constructor property and the `getFullName` method that was added by the highlighted code in Listing 8-16. The `philip` and `jane` instances have a number of internal properties assigned in the constructor function, and the internal «Prototype» property that points back to `Employee.prototype` only; but they have no direct relationship with the constructor function. When property names are resolved, not only the instances, but also the constructor's prototype (through the «Prototype» property) is looked up.

You can check the link between object instances and prototypes. The `Object.getPrototypeOf()` function retrieves the «Prototype» property of the object instance passed as an argument. You can invoke the `isPrototypeOf()` method on a certain constructor's prototype to check whether it is the prototype linked to a specified object instance. You can check these functions by adding these code lines to Listing 8-16:

```
console.log(Employee.prototype
  .isPrototypeOf(philip));
console.log(Employee.prototype
  .isPrototypeOf(jane));
console.log(Object.getPrototypeOf(jane)
  .getFullName === philip.getFullName);
```

All the three `console.log()` calls return `true`. The most interesting is the third one, which proves that the `getFullName` property of `philip` and `jane` point exactly to the same function.

You can easily override properties and functions assigned to the prototype, as Listing 8-17 demonstrates.

Listing 8-17: Exercise-08-17/index.html

```
...
var Employee = function (id, firstName,
  lastName, title) {
  this.id = id;
  this.firstName = firstName;
  this.lastName = lastName;
  this.title = title;
}

Employee.prototype.getFullName =
  function () {
    return this.lastName + ", " + this.firstName;
  }

var philip = new Employee(1, "Philip", "Moore",
  "CEO");
var jane = new Employee(2, "Jane", "Mortimer",
  "CFO");
jane.getFullName = function () {
  return "Jane";
}

console.log(philip.getFullName()); // Moore, Philip
console.log(jane.getFullName());   // Jane
...
```

When the JavaScript engine searches for property names, first it looks up the property in the object instance, then if not found, it goes to look up the properties in the prototype. In Listing 8-17, the jane instance defines its own getFullName property, and this property is found before the same property specified in the prototype.

There are situations when you need to know whether a property has been defined on the object, or in the prototype. The hasOwnProperty() function of an object instance returns true if the property with the specified name exists on the object instance. If you'd like a list of all instance properties, you can use Object.getOwnPropertyNames() function. You can examine the application of these methods when you append the following lines to the end of Listing 8-17:

```
console.log(philip
  .hasOwnProperty("getFullName")); // false;
console.log(jane
  .hasOwnProperty("getFullName")); // true;
console.log(Object
  .getOwnPropertyNames(philip).length); // 4
console.log(Object
  .getOwnPropertyNames(jane).length);   // 5
```

Because prototypes are objects, you can add properties and methods to the underlying objects any time. This allows you to extend object types. Listing 8-18 contains a self-explaining code snippet that extends the `Number` and `String` types with two new functions.

Listing 8-18: Exercise-08-18/index.html

```
...
Number.prototype.square =
  function () {
    return this.valueOf() * this.valueOf();
}

String.prototype.wrap =
  function (begin, end) {
    return begin + this.valueOf() + end;
}

console.log((13).square());        // 169
console.log("Hi!".wrap("[", "]")); // [Hi!]
...
```

NOTE: It is not recommended to modify native object prototypes in a production environment, because this can often cause confusion by creating potential name collisions.

Object Inheritance

Object-oriented programming is unimaginable without inheritance. While most languages support several types in inheritance—implementing interfaces, deriving new types from existing ones, overriding methods, etc.—JavaScript supports only implementation inheritance, where actual methods are inherited. Due to the flexibility and dynamism of JavaScript there are number of ways you can implement inheritance. In this section you'll learn about the two most commonly used patterns, *prototype chaining* and *pseudoclassical inheritance*.

Prototype chaining uses a simple trick: you can change the default prototype of a function to an object of your own. Listing 8-19 demonstrates this technique. It defines three object types (via three constructor functions), `Vehicle`, as the base type, `Car` and `Boat` as derived types. Observe that derived types set their prototypes to an instance of `Vehicle`.

Listing 8-19: Exercise-08-19/index.html

```
...
// --- Base type
var Vehicle = function () {
  this.vendor = "Toyota";
};

// --- Base type behavior
Vehicle.prototype.getVendor = function () {
  return this.vendor;
```

```
};
Vehicle.prototype.getType = function () {
  return "vehicle";
};

// --- Derived type
var Car = function () {
  this.wheel = 4;
};

// --- Chain to base type
Car.prototype = new Vehicle();

// --- Override behavior
Car.prototype.getType = function () {
  return "car";
};

// --- Derived type
var Boat = function () {
  this.propeller = 1;
}

// --- Chain to base type
Boat.prototype = new Vehicle();

// --- Override behavior
Boat.prototype.getType = function () {
  return "boat";
};

// --- Test
var car = new Car();
var boat = new Boat();
console.log("It's a " + car.getType());
console.log(car.getVendor());
console.log("wheels: " + car.wheel);
console.log("It's a " + boat.getType());
console.log(boat.getVendor());
console.log("props: " + boat.propeller);
...
```

When you run this code, the output suggest it really does something that we can achieve in other languages with inheritance:

```
It's a car
Toyota
wheels: 4
It's a boat
Toyota
props: 1
```

The trick behind this pattern is the following. `Car` and `Boat` inherit from `Vehicle` by assigning a newly created instance of `Vehicle` and assigning it to `Car.prototype` and `Boat.prototype`. This action overwrites the original prototype of these types. Having a `Vehicle` instance as the prototype means that all properties and methods that typically exist on an instance of `Vehicle` now also exist on `Car.prototype` and `Boat.prototype`. As you already know, object properties and methods are resolved in in iterative search that starts with the object instance, and provided the property or method has not been found, it goes and searches the prototype. However, the search does not stop here, it traverses to the prototype of the prototype, and along the chain until the property or method is found, or the chain ends. Figure 8-4 depicts the prototype chain, and it helps you to understand how inheritance is implemented.

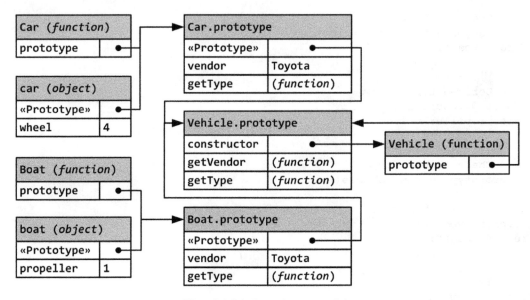

Figure 8.4: Inheritance via prototype chain

For example, when the `boat.propeller` or `car.wheel` properties are passed to `console.log()`, those are found right in the object instances. When the JavaScript engine looks for the `boat.getType` function, it does not find it within the object instance. The search goes on with the `Boat.prototype`, (which happens to be a `Vehicle` instance extended with the `getType` function) where the functions is found. When the `car.getVendor` function is looked up, it cannot be found either in the object instance, or along the next link in the chain, `Car.prototype`. Just like `Boat.prototype`, `Car.prototype` is another `Vehicle` instance extended with the `Car`-specific `getType` function. The search traverses to `Vehicle.prototype`, and there it founds the `getVendor` method.

NOTE: You can extend prototype chaining to create longer inheritance chains. You can use the same technique to create derived types from `Car` and `Boat`.

Figure 8-4 contains a simplification. In reality, `Vehicle.prototype` also contains a «Prototype» property that point to `Object.prototype`. The methods of `Object`—such as `hasOwnProperty()`, `toString()` and the others—are defined in that prototype.

Prototype chaining supports the `instanceof` operator. You can add the following lines to Listing 8-19 to test whether `car` and `boat` are instances of the specified types:

```
console.log(car instanceof Car);       // true
console.log(car instanceof Boat);      // false
console.log(car instanceof Vehicle);   // true
console.log(car instanceof Object);    // true

console.log(boat instanceof Car);      // false
console.log(boat instanceof Boat);     // true
console.log(boat instanceof Vehicle);  // true
console.log(boat instanceof Object);   // true
```

The `instanceof` operator tests whether an object has in its prototype chain the prototype property of the specified constructor. Because car has the `Car`, `Vehicle`, and `Object` constructor functions on its prototype chain, all related `instanceof` expressions return `true`. However, the `Boat` constructor is not in the prototype chain of `car`, so `car instanceof Boat` results `false`.

Although prototype chaining is simple, it has an annoying issue. You cannot pass arguments to the ancestor types when a derived type is created. In Listing 8-19, the `Vehicle` constructor does not accept arguments, and it sets the `vendor` property to a default value (Toyota). This is an ugly solution, just as the implementation of `Car` and `Boat` constructors that set the `wheel` and `propeller` properties with the same method.

Another pattern, *pseudoclassical inheritance* combines prototype chain with a technique, *constructor stealing*, to solve this issue. Listing 8-20 utilizes this method to improve the code.

Listing 8-20: Exercise-08-20/index.html

```
...
// --- Base type
var Vehicle = function (vendor) {
  this.vendor = vendor;
};

// --- Base type behavior
Vehicle.prototype.getVendor = function () {
  return this.vendor;
};
Vehicle.prototype.getType = function () {
  return "vehicle";
};

// --- Derived type
var Car = function (vendor, wheel) {
  Vehicle.call(this, vendor);
  this.wheel = wheel;
```

```
};

// --- Chain to base type
Car.prototype = new Vehicle();

// --- Override behavior
Car.prototype.getType = function () {
  return "car";
};

// --- Derived type
var Boat = function (vendor, propeller) {
  Vehicle.call(this, vendor);
  this.propeller = propeller;
};

// --- Chain to base type
Boat.prototype = new Vehicle();

// --- Override behavior
Boat.prototype.getType = function () {
  return "boat";
};

// --- Test
var car = new Car("BMW", 4);
var boat = new Boat("Yamaha", 2);

console.log("It's a " + car.getType());
console.log(car.getVendor());
console.log("wheels: " + car.wheel);
console.log("It's a " + boat.getType());
console.log(boat.getVendor());
console.log("props: " + boat.propeller);
...
```

In this listing all constructor functions have arguments. `Vehicle` accepts a vendor name, while `Car` and `Boat` accept an additional wheel and propeller argument, too. The `Car` and `Boat` constructors explicitly invoke the `Vehicle` constructor with the `Vehicle.call()` method. The first argument of `call()` is the object instance to invoke the method on, subsequent arguments represent the parameters of the method to pass. So the `Vehicle.call(this, vendor)` expression in the `Car` and `Boat` constructors invokes the `Vehicle` function on the newly created object instance with the specified vendor argument. As a result, the `vendor` property of the new object instance is set to the passed argument value.

NOTE: There are several other patterns to implement object inheritance in JavaScript. You can easily find them when you search the web for "JavaScript inheritance patterns" with your preferred search engine.

Modularity

Most curly-brace programming languages provide some kind of modularity. Besides the fact that you can encapsulate data and operations together in objects, you can also use concepts like namespaces to group objects together and use modules. Modules have a well-defined public interface—a set of properties and operations that can be accessed from outside—, and they may have private members that are intentionally concealed, for they are used internally, and otherwise they would expose implementation details.

The JavaScript language does not have a concept of modules—as of this writing—but most developers use the *module pattern* that mimics the behavior of modules in other programming languages. Listing 8-21 demonstrates this concept.

Listing 8-21: Exercise-08-21/index.html

```
. . .
var CircleOps = (function () {
  // --- Private stuff
  var pi = 3.1415926;
  var radSquare = function (rad) {
    return rad * rad;
  }

  // --- Public stuff
  return {
    PI: pi,
    calcArea: function(rad) {
      return pi * radSquare(rad);
    },
    calcPerimeter: function (rad) {
      return pi * 2 * rad;
    }
  };
})();

var x = 1.5;
var area = CircleOps.calcArea(x);
var perim = CircleOps.calcPerimeter(x);
var pi = CircleOps.PI;
console.log("value of PI: " + pi);
console.log("area: " + area);
console.log("perimeter: " + perim);
. . .
```

In this listing, `CircleOps` is an object with members such as `PI`, `calcArea`, `calcPerimeter`. The key of this pattern that makes `CircleOps` look and behave like a module is the form as the object is created:

```
var CircleOps = (function () {
  // --- Private stuff
  return {
```

```
    // --- Public stuff
  };
})();
```

This code defines a function expression and immediately executes the function. Every variable you define in the body of the function is scoped to the function, and so cannot be directly accessed. However, the object retrieved by the function contains properties and functions that are available by the external world.

The great thing this pattern uses is that all properties and functions retrieved in the returned object are *privileged members*, which may access the variables within this function. This way ensures that internally you can define the `pi` variable and the `calcSquare` function, you can use them through the returned object, but cannot access them directly through `CircleOps`.

The Browser Object Model

In Chapter 6, you learned that the ECMAScript specification defines the Document Object Model (DOM) to provide access to the model of the HTML page. Beside DOM, the specification defines another model, Browser Object Model (BOM) to expose the web browser functionality that is totally independent of web page content. In this section you'll get a brief overview of BOM.

NOTE: This section will contain only a few code snippets to demonstrate the most important aspects and functionality of BOM objects. For more detailed samples search the internet with the name of the BOM object, for example "JavaScript window object".

The Window Object

The pivotal object of the Browser Object Model is `window`. It represents not only a browser object, but also the global scope: every variable and function you define in your script globally, becomes a property of `window`, as the following code snippet demonstrates:

```
var name = "Joe";
function sayHello() {
  console.log("Hello " + name);
}

console.log(window.name);  // Joe
window.sayHello();         // Hello Joe
```

NOTE: Although global variables become the properties of `window`, you cannot remove them with the `delete` operator.

The `window` object has a few dozen properties and methods. Table 8-1 summarizes `window` properties.

Table 8-1: The properties of the window object

Property	Description
closed	Indicates whether a window has been closed (**true**) or not (**false**)
defaultStatus	Gets or sets the default text in the status bar of a window
document	Gets the **document** object of the window
frames	Returns an array of all the frames (including the ones defined with `<iframe>` tags) in the current window
history	Gets the **history** object for the window
innerHeight	Gets or sets the inner height of a window's content area
innerWidth	Gets or sets the inner width of a window's content area
length	Returns the number of frames (including the ones defined with `<iframe>` tags) in a window
location	Gets the **location** object for the window
name	Gets or sets the name of the window
navigator	Gets the **navigator** object for the window
opener	Retrieves a reference to the window that created the window
outerHeight	Gets or sets the outer height of a window, including toolbars/scrollbars
outerWidth	Gets or sets the outer width of a window, including toolbars/scrollbars
pageXOffset	Gets the number of pixels the current document has been scrolled (horizontally) from the upper left corner of the window
pageYOffset	Retrieves the number of pixels the current document has been scrolled (vertically) from the upper left corner of the window
parent	Retrieves the parent window of the current window
screen	Returns the **screen** object for the window
screenLeft, screenX	Gets the x coordinate of the window relative to the screen
screenTop, screenY	Gets the y coordinate of the window relative to the screen
self	Retrieves the current window
status	Gets or sets the text in the status bar of a window
top	Returns the topmost browser window

As you see, you can access a number of important objects such as document, navigator, location, history, and screen. You already know document from Chapter 6, and you will learn about the other objects in this section. Table 8-2 summarizes the methods of window.

Table 8-2: The methods of the windows object

Method	Description
alert()	This method displays an alert box with a specified message (first argument) and an OK button. An alert box is often used if you want to make sure information comes through to the user.
atob()	Decodes a base-64 encoded string passed in the method argument
blur()	Removes the focus from the current window
btoa()	Encodes the string specified in the argument to its base-64 representation
clearInterval()	Clears a timer set with setInterval()
clearTimeout()	Clears a timer set with setTimeout()
close()	Closes the current window
confirm()	Displays a dialog box with a message and an OK and a Cancel button. The method returns true if the user clicked "OK", and false otherwise.
focus()	Sets the focus to the current window. This method makes a request to bring the current window to the foreground. It may now work as you expect in all browsers, due to different user settings.
moveBy()	Moves a window relative to its current position. It requires two number parameters that specify the number of pixels to move the window horizontally, and vertically, respectively.
moveTo()	Moves a window to the specified position. It requires two number parameters that specify the horizontal and vertical coordinates to move the window to.
open()	Opens a new browser window. It accepts a number of optional parameters that specify the URL of the page to open, the name of the target window, a specification of options to use, and a flag that specifies whether the URL creates a new entry or replaces the current entry in the history list, respectively.
print()	Prints the content of the current windows
prompt()	Displays a dialog box that prompts the visitor for input. The method returns the input value if the user clicks "OK". If the user clicks "Cancel" the method returns null.
resizeBy()	Resizes the window by the specified number of pixels. It requires two number parameters that specify how many pixels to resize the width and height by.
resizeTo()	Resizes the window to the specified width and height. It requires two number parameters that specify the width and height of the window.
scrollBy()	Scrolls the content by the specified number of pixels. It requires two number parameters that specify how many pixels to scroll by, along the

Method	Description
	x-axis (horizontal), and y-axis (vertical). Positive values will scroll to the right or up, while negative values will scroll to the left or down.
scrollTo()	Scrolls the content to the specified coordinates. It requires two number parameters that set the coordinates to scroll to horizontally or vertically.
setInterval()	This method calls a function or evaluates an expression at specified intervals given in milliseconds. The method will continue calling the function until clearInterval() is called, or the window is closed. The handle identifier value returned by setInterval() is used as the parameter for the clearInterval() method.
setTimeout()	This method calls a function or evaluates an expression after a specified number of milliseconds. The function is only executed once. Use the clearTimeout() method to prevent the function to run. The handle identifier value returned by setTimeout() is used as the parameter for the clearTimeout() method.

In the source code download folder of this chapter you find a sample project in the Exercise-08-22 folder. In your code editor, open the project folder, and examine the index.html and smallwindow.html files that demonstrate most of the properties and methods of the window object.

The History Object

You can access the user's navigation history through the history object. The history is a property of window, and so each tab, browser window—and frame—has its own history, since the specific window was first used. Using the length property—which indicates the number of history items—, you can check whether the user started from your page:

```
if (history.length == 1) {
  console.log("The user started from this page");
}
```

For security reasons, the URLs of the navigation history are not available. You can use the go(), back(), and forward() methods to navigate within the history. While back() loads the previously visited page in the history, and forward() loads the next URL in the history list, go() is a bit more flexible, as shown in this code snippet:

```
<!DOCTYPE html>
<html>
<head>
  <title>History go()</title>
</head>
  <body>
    <button onclick="window.history.go(-2)">
      Go back two pages
    </button>
```

```
    <button onclick="window.history.go(1)">
      Go forward one page
    </button>
  </body>
</html>
```

The Location Object

The location object provides a set of useful information about the document that is currently loaded in the browser windows, and it also provides basic navigation functionality. You can access the location object through either `window` or `document`—as `window.location` and `document.location`—, and both points to the same object. Table 8-3 summarizes the properties of `location`.

Table 8-3: The properties of the location object

Property	Description
hash	This property sets or returns the hash (anchor) portion of a URL, including the hash sign—or an empty string, if the URL does not have a hash. You can also use this property to set the anchor value, but in this case, do not include the hash sign (#).
host	Gets or sets the hostname and port of a URL. If the port number is the default (80), the port is not returned.
hostname	Gets or sets the hostname part of the URL
href	Gets or sets the entire URL
pathname	Gets or sets the path name part of the URL
port	Gets or sets the port of a URL. If the port number is the default (80), the port is not returned.
protocol	Gets or sets the protocol name part of the URL, including the first colon
search	Gets or sets the query portion of the URL, including the question mark

Although you can navigate within the current documents or to another document by settings these properties, you can also use the methods of location, as summarized in Table 8-4.

Table 8-4: The methods of the location object

Method	Description
assign()	This method loads a new document, the URL of which is passed in the method argument.
reload()	This method is used to reload the current document; it does the same as the reload button in your browser. By default, it reloads the document from the cache, but you can force the reload to get the page from server by passing true as the argument.

Method	Description
replace()	This method replaces the current document with a new one, as specified in the method argument. It differs from assign(), which adds the new navigation target to the page history, while replace() removes the URL of the current document from the document history, meaning that it is not possible to navigate back to the original document.

The Navigator Object

You often need information about the browser your webpage is displayed in—either to allow the web page provide the same user experience in all browser, or to leverage some great browser-specific features. The navigator object is a standard solution for this task in all JavaScript-enabled browsers. This object provides a number of properties and several methods, as summarized in Table 8-5.

Table 8-5: Properties and methods of the navigator object

Property/Method	Description
appCodeName	This property returns the code name of the browser. For compatibility reasons, all modern browsers returns "Mozilla".
appName	Gets the name of the browser. For compatibility reasons, most browsers return "Netscape".
appVersion	Returns the version information of the browser
cookieEnabled	Gets a Boolean value that specifies whether cookies are enabled in the browser
javaEnabled()	This method returns a Boolean value that specifies whether the browser has Java enabled
language	Returns the browser's primary language
mimeTypes	Retrieves an array of MIME types registered with the browser
onLine	This property returns a Boolean value that specifies whether the browser is in online (true) or offline (false) mode
plugins	Retrieves an array of plug-ins installed on the browser
platform	This property returns the platform for which the browser is compiled
product	Returns the engine name of the browser
registerContentHandler()	This method registers a web site as a handler for a specific MIME type. It accepts three arguments: the MIME type to handle, the URL of the page that can handle that MIME type, and the name of the application, respectively.

Property/Method	Description
`registerProtocolHandler()`	This method registers a web site as a handler for a particular protocol. It accepts three arguments: the protocol to handle (such as "mailto" or "ftp"), the URL of the page that handles the protocol, and the name of the application, respectively.
`userAgent`	This property returns the value of the user-agent header sent by the browser to the server.

Listing 8-22 contains a sample web page using the navigator properties. As of this writing, it provided the information about Chrome, as shown in Figure 8-5.

Listing 8-22: Exercise-08-23/index.html

```
<!DOCTYPE html>
<html>
<head>
  <title>Using the navigator object</title>
  <style>
    body {
      font-family: "Verdana", "Arial", sans-serif;
    }
  </style>
  <script>
    function queryNavigator() {
      var label = document.getElementById("props");
      var out = "";

      function addText(text, value) {
        out += text + ": " + value + "<br/>";
      }

      addText("appCodeName", navigator.appCodeName);
      addText("appName", navigator.appName);
      addText("appVersion", navigator.appVersion);
      addText("cookieEnabled", navigator.cookieEnabled);
      addText("javaEnabled()", navigator.javaEnabled());
      addText("language", navigator.language);
      addText("platform", navigator.platform);
      addText("product", navigator.product);
      addText("userAgent", navigator.userAgent);
      label.innerHTML = out;
    }
  </script>
</head>
<body onload="queryNavigator()">
  <h3>Navigator properties</h3>
  <p id="props"></p>
</body>
</html>
```

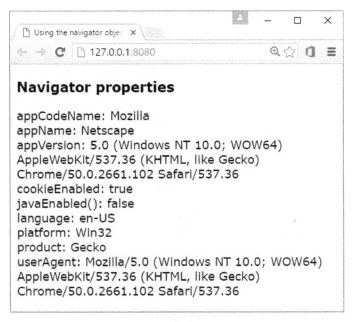

Figure 8-5: Navigator properties in Chrome

NOTE: Most browsers extend the `navigator` object with their own browser-specific properties. Table 8-5 contains only those that can be accessed in all major browsers.

The Screen Object

From `window`, you can access the `screen` object (`windows.screen`) that provides a handful of read-only properties to access the display capabilities of the browser. Table 8-6 summarizes the properties of `screen`.

Table 8-6: The properties of the screen object

Property	Description
`availHeight`	The pixel height of the screen minus system elements such as Windows Taskbar
`availWidth`	The pixel width of the screen minus system elements such as Windows Taskbar
`colorDepth`	Retrieves the number of bits used to represent colors on images
`height`	Gets the pixel height of the screen
`pixelDepth`	Returns the color resolution (in bits per pixel) of the screen
`width`	Gets the pixel width of the screen

NOTE: Most browsers extend the `screen` object with their own browser-specific properties. Table 8-6 contains only those that can be accessed in all major browsers.

Error Handling

To write robust programs that resist common user errors and other issues in the usage context, you must endeavor to find and handle all potential errors. In most cases, validating input arguments takes the lion's share of this work, but this is not always enough. There might be issues that cannot be checked in advance, and you'll observe the error only after an operation has been invoked. Most modern programing languages contain exception handling mechanism to cope with this situation.

The try-catch Construct

JavaScript provides this machinery, too, it uses the `try-catch` exception handling block, just like the other curly-brace languages. The syntax of the statement block is this:

```
try {
  // --- Code that may cause an error
} catch (error) {
  // --- Activity to do when an error occurs
} finally {
  // --- Cleanup code
}
```

You enclose the code that may cause an error into the block between `try` and `catch`. When the error occurs, the execution is immediately transferred to the `catch` branch, where `error` is an object that carries information about the error. The code in the `finally` block is always executed, independently whether the `try` block was completed or interrupted by an error. There is no way to prevent the `finally` block from running.

You can omit either the `catch` or the `finally` block, but not both. If you omit the `finally` block, you do not have chance for cleanup activity (you often do not need this). If you omit the `catch` block, you cannot specify code to handle the error, but you can be sure that your cleanup code runs.

Error Types

There are several types of errors that may occur during code execution. The ECMAScript standard defines a set of object types to represent these errors, as summarized in Table 8-7.

Table 8-7: JavaScript error types

Type	Description
Error	This is the base type from which all other error types inherit. An error of type Error is rarely, if ever, thrown by a browser; it is provided mainly for developers to throw custom errors.
EvalError	This type was originally defined to be thrown when an exception occurs

Type	Description
	while using the `eval()` function. The fifth edition of the ECMAScript specification does not use it within the specification (no constructs in the standard raise this exception), but it was kept for compatibility with the previous specifications.
RangeError	This type indicates that a numeric value has exceeded the allowable range.
ReferenceError	This error type indicates that an invalid reference value has been detected.
SyntaxError	When the JavaScript parser catches an error (it means there is a syntax error in the JavaScript code), this type of error is provided.
TypeError	This type indicates that the actual type of an operand is different than the expected type.
URIError	When one of the global URI handling functions was used in a way that is incompatible with its definition, this error type is provided.

In many cases, a block of code may raise more types of exceptions. In order to handle an exception, you must know its type and traits. The `error` variable of the `catch` clause points to the object describing the exception, and you can use it to branch the handler code, as shown in this code snippet:

```
try {
  myFunctionThatMayRaiseErrors();
} catch (error){
  if (error instanceof TypeError){
    // An unexpected type provided,
    // handle here
  } else if (error instanceof ReferenceError){
    // An invalid reference value
    // was used, handle here
  } else {
    // Other kind of error found,
    // handle here
  }
}
```

Throwing Exceptions

An exception handling mechanism must allow not only catching, but also throwing exceptions. With the **throw** operator you can indicate an error that can be caught with **try-catch**, as shown here:

```
throw new EvalError("Can't evaluate this.");
throw new RangeError("Posotive value expected.");
throw new ReferenceError("Can't handle this reference");
throw new SyntaxError("What's this: 'oumaer'?");
```

```
throw new TypeError("A RegExp instance expected");
throw new URIError("Can't find this resource");
```

Although the JavaScript core throws only the exceptions defined by the ECMAScript specification, you can throw any kind of object, as show in this sample code:

```
throw "Hey! This is an error!"
throw 42;
throw {code: 42, message: "Disk access failure"};
```

With *prototype chaining* you can easily define your own error objects, as demonstrated by this short example:

```
function NegativeNumberUsed() {
  this.name = "NegativeNumberFound";
  this.message = "A negative number found";
}

NegativeNumberUsed.prototype = new Error();

// ...
throw new NegativeNumberUsed();
```

The onerror Event

Depending on how your browser is configured, unhandled errors (exceptions that have not been handled by the code) are displayed. For example, Internet Explorer displays the `NegativeNumberUsed` exception specified in the previous code snippet as shown in Figure 8-6.

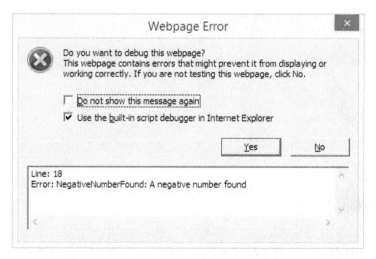

Figure 8-6: Internet Explorer displays an unhandled exception

The `window` object provides an `onerror` event (beside many other events, as described in Table 6-5). You can provide an event handler to define a way to handle exceptions that are otherwise not treated by the page.

The onerror event expects an event handler function with three arguments, such as the exception message, the document URL that causes the unhandled exception, and a line number referring the code line where the exception originates from. Listing 8-23 demonstrates the usage of the onerror event handler method.

Listing 8-23: Exercise-08-24/index.html

```html
<!DOCTYPE html>
<html>
<head>
  <title>The onerror event</title>
  <script>
    function sometimesWorks(arg) {
      if (arg == 1) return;
      throw "You're unlucky";
    }

    function bet(arg, catchHere) {
      if (catchHere) {
        try {
          sometimesWorks(arg);
        } catch (error) {
          // --- Caught
        }
      } else {
        sometimesWorks(arg);
      }
    }

    function tryThis() {
      onerror =
        function (message, url, line) {
          alert("URL '" + url
            + " caused this message '"
            + message + "' in line "
            + line);
          return false;
        };

      // These work
      bet(1, true);
      bet(1, false);

      // This raises an error
      bet(3, false);
    }
  </script>
</head>
<body onload="tryThis()">
</body>
</html>
```

The `sometimesWorks()` method raises an exception when invoked with any argument except 1. The `bet()` method accepts a parameter that specifies whether any exception should be caught within the method body or not.

When the page is loaded, `tryThis()` is invoked, and it configures the `onerror` event to display a message when an unhandled exception is caught. In this method, `bet()` is called three times, and the last call raises an exception that is caught by `onerror`.

Managing Errors

Preventing and handling errors is definitely a topic that deserves a full book dedicated to this subject. Here, I give you only a brief overview and some useful advice.

You must have an error-handling strategy for the JavaScript layer of a web application, because any JavaScript error can cause a web page to become unusable. The basis of this strategy should be the understanding when and why errors occur. Most users are not technical and can easily get confused when something doesn't work as expected. In most cases when they face an error, they reload the page or try to navigate away and then back. If the problem does not get fixed after their attempts, they get frustrated and stop using your app for a long time.

As the developer, you should create robust applications that prevent users making errors, and whenever possible, they catch potential issues before they become errors. You should design and implement the UI so that it immediately indicates potential errors (such as specifying invalid values or options). If users provide invalid data, you must respond with helpful—and non-technical—messages that lead the user to the right way to correct what they misused. For example, users get frustrated with an error message "Use the '\[A-Z]{3}-\d{3}' format to specify registration number", because they do not understand it. Instead, use the "Registration number must be three letters, followed by a dash, and closed by three decimal digits" message to really help them.

If possible, check any data before sending it to a web server. Although a robust application must check all input data at server side, and omitting validation at the client side must not hurt the business logic, checking data in the browser will save resources at the server side—provided invalid data is not sent to the server.

Since JavaScript is loosely typed, and its function arguments are not verified by the engine, many errors will come to light only when the code is executed. There are a number of errors that might be caused by these peculiarities of JavaScript.

Due to the loosely-typed nature of JavaScript, variables and function arguments aren't compared to ensure that the correct type of data is being used. *Data type errors* most often occur as a result of unexpected values being passed into a function. For example, this code snippet causes an error in the highlighted line:

```
function splitName(str) {
  var posComma = str.indexOf('=');
  if (posComma > 1) {
    return str.substring(0, posComma);
  }
  return "";
}

var name1 = splitName("key=value");
console.log(name1);

var name2 = splitName(123);
console.log(name2);
```

The `splitName()` function implicitly expects a string. When you pass a number—as the code does in the highlighted line—the execution fails, because a number does not have an `indexOf()` function.

It is up to you, as the developer, to do an appropriate amount of data type checking to ensure that an error will not occur.

The JavaScript language has a number of constructs that automatically change the type of a value or an expression. This behavior leads to *coercion errors*, which are not easy to catch. For example, the `getKeyValuePair()` function in this example has an `if` statement that may lead to coercion error:

```
function getKeyValuePair(key, value) {
  var result = key + "=";
  if (value) {
    result += value;
  }
  return result;
}

var pair1 = getKeyValuePair("key");
var pair2 = getKeyValuePair("key", 13);
var pair3 = getKeyValuePair("key", 0);

console.log(pair1); // key=
console.log(pair2); // key=13
console.log(pair3); // key
```

The aim of the `if` statement is to check whether the value argument is provided. If it is not, `value` evaluates to `undefined`, and it is coerced by the JavaScript engine to `false` in the condition of the `if` statement. The issue is that there are other values that are also coerced to `false`—such as the number 0—, and so the method provides faulty operation.

Communication with the server side also provide an opportunity for errors to occur, including malformed URLs, network issues, timeouts, etc.

NOTE: Most web applications log user activities and other system events at the server side into files or databases. For diagnostic purposes you may use the same services to log JavaScript errors. There are many logging patterns, search the web for "JavaScript error logging" with your favorite search engine.

Summary

JavaScript has a number of great features that allow you to implement advanced scenarios. In this chapter you learned the most powerful of them.

You can use the JSON syntax within your code to create objects, serialize them to strings, and parse JSON strings back to objects.

JavaScript functions are the cornerstones of useful programming patterns. Functions can have an arbitrary number of arguments, and you have the opportunity to check their value and type during runtime. You can be very flexible with how you take the parameters provided by a function call into account. JavaScript allows you to provide function expressions, accept functions as arguments, and can retrieve functions as return values. Anonymous functions and closures let you work with JavaScript in a manner that resembles to functional programming.

Object are really first class citizens in JavaScript. You can create properties programmatically and implicitly, and you can also influence their behavior. With the help of constructor functions and function prototypes, you can implement object inheritance with multiple techniques, including prototype chaining and pseudoclassical inheritance, among the others.

The ECMAScript specification defines the Browser Object Model (BOM), which allows you to interact with the browser your document is displayed in. The `window`, `history`, `location`, `navigator`, and `screen` objects all provide you properties and methods to query browser values—such as the current window's position, the parts of the documents URL, etc.—and initiate actions—such as displaying dialogs, opening or closing browser windows, and many more.

Just as other curly-brace programming languages, JavaScript has its own error handling mechanism based on the `try-catch` construct.

Chapter 9:
Getting to Know Cascading Style Sheets

WHAT YOU WILL LEARN IN THIS CHAPTER

Understanding the fundamental concepts behind Cascading Style Sheets

Getting to know the various selectors to specify style rules

Describing style rules with property declarations

Understanding the idea of cascading order and the resolution of competing properties

Using media types and media queries to accommodate to device features

In the previous chapters you already learned establishing the structure of your web pages with HTML, and using the JavaScript programming language to manipulate the page structure and create interactive pages that respond to user events. In many sample programs you already used Cascading Style Sheets to set up the appearance of pages—including typography, colors, layout, and so on.

In the early days of HTML styling was the part of the markup language. A number of HTML tags existed only for the sole purpose of providing style—such as font type, color, alignment, margins, paddings, etc.—for parts of the web page. This structural approach resulted in verbose web pages where structural elements were mingled with styling elements. Where a certain set of style attributes were used in many different parts of a page, it meant redundancy: the HTML markup snippets that specified a particular style had to be repeated for every structural part where the style should have been applied. This approach not only increased the size of web pages, but also made them more laborious to maintain.

The idea of Cascading Style Sheets (CSS) is more than 20 years old, and the first specification (CSS level 1) became an official W3C recommendation in December, 1996. As the specification evolved, CSS level 2 and CSS level 2.1 were published. The newest available specification, CSS3—which is used mostly with HTML5—is divided into several separate specs, called modules. Today, there are more than sixty modules and each has its own status, as different groups work on them.

Similarly to CSS3, the specification of CSS4 is divided into modules. A few of them extends CSS3 modules, but there are ones that define entirely new features and functionality.

In this chapters you will learn the fundamentals of using CSS with your web pages. This chapter covers only the most important things and does not treat every nitty-gritty details, but definitely provides the basics you can begin styling your web pages with.

Styles and Style Sheets

The HTML5 markup does not contain any elements for the sole purpose of setting up the visual style of a certain part of the page. Instead, you can use either the `style` or the `class` attributes of any HTLM element to describe its appearance, as shown in Listing 9-1.

Listing 9-1: Exercise-09-01/index.html

```
<!DOCTYPE html>
<html>
<head>
  <title>The style and class attributes</title>
  <style>
    body {
      font-family: Verdana, Arial, sans-serif;
    }

    .blue {
      color: blue;
    }
  </style>
</head>
<body>
  <h1 class="blue">
    Set to blue by its class attribute
  </h1>
  <p style="font-family: monospace">
    This paragraph is displayed with monospace
    characters due to its <strong>style</strong>
    attribute.
  </p>
</body>
</html>
```

The `<h1>` tag uses the `class` attribute to set up its style. The attribute's value is `blue`, and so the `.blue` style defined in the `<style>` node under `<head>` is applied, and thus the heading's color is set to blue. The subsequent `<p>` tag sets the `style` attribute to display the tag with monospace font. The `<body>` tag's style is set implicitly: although neither the class nor the style attribute is set, the `body` rule that is specified within `<style>` is automatically applied by the rendering engine—this is the way CSS works by its specification. The font family of the page is set to Verdana, or Arial (if there's no Verdana), or a browser-chosen san-serif font, if neither Verdana nor Arial is found. The result of the markup in Listing 9-1 is shown in Figure 9-1.

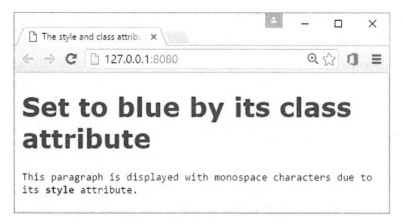

Figure 9-1: Styles applied by the class *and* style *attributes*

Actually, both `<h1>` and `<p>` apply two styles for their contents: the first is the font family setting coming from the `body` rule; and the second is the blue color for `<h1>` (set by the `.blue` rule), and the monospace font for `<p>` (as specified by the `style` attribute).

Styling Page Elements

You can apply styles to a webpage—in several ways, as you'll see soon. A *style* (or often referred as *rule*), is a compound expression that is built from a *selector* and a *declaration block* that contains zero, one, or more *declaration*. Each declaration is a pair of a *property* and a *value*. The syntax of a rule is the following:

```
selector {
  property1: value1;
  property2: value2;
  propertyN: valueN;
}
```

Let's take a look at this example:

```
h1 {
  color: white;
  background-color: blue;
}
```

Here, `h1` is a selector, and braces wrap the declaration block. The first declaration sets the `color` property to `white`. The second one specifies that the `background-color` property's value should be `blue`. Each declaration is closed with a semicolon.

Internal and External Styles

In Listing 9-1 the styles are placed directly into the web page (nested into the `<style>` tag), and this is called an *internal* style sheet. You already met with several examples in this book where

369

styles were put into a separate text file with `.css` extension, and this file was linked to the page with the `<link>` tag. This separate file is called an *external* style sheet.

Assuming that you copy the styles in Listing 9-1 to a separate file, `mystyle.css`, which is located in the `Theme` folder, the `<head>` section refers to this file with the highlighted `<link>` tag:

```
<head>
  <title>The style and class attributes</title>
  <link href="Theme/mystyle.css" rel="stylesheet" />
</head>
```

Internal style sheets are applied only for the web pages they are nested in. External style sheets can be referenced from any page, and styles defined in them are applied for each page that links to them. You can mix internal and external style sheets, there is no limit how many of them can be used for a single web page.

CSS At-Rules

Just like most of the programming languages allows using pragmas to instruct the parser to handle special language elements, CSS defines directives for the same purpose. You can easily recognize them, because they start with an at character (@), and thus they are often mentioned as "at-rules". Table 9-1 lists them.

Table 9-1: CSS at-rules

At-Rule	Description

@charset	With this CSS directive you can specify the character encoding used in the style sheet. It can be used only within a style sheet file, but not within the `<style>` elements or in the style attribute. To define the encoding, you must use one of the web-safe encoding that is declared in the IANA-registry (see `http://www.iana.org/assignments/character-sets` for details). Here are a few examples:
	`@charset UTF-8;`
	`@charset "ISO-8859-2"`
	There are a few restrictions to use the `@charset` at-rule: this directive must be the first element in the style sheet, and not be preceded by any character. If several `@charset` at-rules are defined, only the first one is used.

@import	This at-rule allows you to import style rules from other style sheets. To define the style sheets to be imported, add a string or URL after the `@import` keyword, such as in these samples:
	`@import url("content/mystyle.css");`
	`@import 'custom.css';`
	You can additionally include media queries (you'll learn about them later). For example, to import a style sheet that should be used only when printing a web page, use this at-rule:

At-Rule	Description
	`@import 'styleForPrint.css' print;`
`@font-face`	This at-rule allows designers to specify online fonts to display text on their web pages. By allowing them to provide their own fonts, `@font-face` eliminates the need to depend on the limited number of fonts users have installed on their computers. You will learn more details about this at-rule in *Chapter 10*.
`@namespace`	This at-rule defines the XML namespaces that will be used in the style sheet. See more details in the MDN documentation.
`@page`	You can use this at-rule to modify some CSS properties when printing a document. You can only change the margins, orphans, widows, and page breaks of the document; attempts to change any other CSS properties will be ignored. See more details in the MDN documentation.
`@media`	This CSS at-rule associates a set of nested statements, in a CSS block, with a condition defined by a media query. You can use this directive to define styles that should be used only with the media types that satisfy the specified condition. You will learn more details about this at-rule later in this chapter.

The Concept of Cascading

Each rule has a selector that defines the part of the web page—more precisely, the set of HTML tags—the rule is applied to. Frequently, more than one selector is applied for most HTML tags, and in this case selectors are applied in a specific order—according to the CSS specification. Soon, after understanding selectors, you'll learn this order.

NOTE: If there are more applicable selectors that specify the same property with different values, the most specific selector wins. However, it is not always easy to guess out which selector is the most specific, as you will see.

Rules declare a number of properties. When a rule—as specified by its selector—is applied to an HTML tag, certain properties are inherited by all child elements of the tag. For example, the `font-family` property is inherited, so when you apply it to the `<body>` tag, the whole page will use the specified font, unless an HTML tag nested into `<body>` overrides it by its own `font-family` definition.

This mechanism, which governs how styles interact and which styles get precedence when there's a conflict, is known as the *cascade*. This is how *Cascading* Style Sheets got its name.

Selectors

You can easily define what a rule in a style sheet does: it declares one or more of property and value pairs to apply on a set of HTML nodes within the current document. In this approach, selectors identify the part of the document that should be styled. Here, you'll learn them through simple examples.

Tag, Class, and ID selectors

The three most frequently used selector types are the *tag selector*—it is applied to every occurrence of an HTML tag—, the *class selector* —applied to every occurrence of an HTML tag that has a specific value in its `class` attribute—, and the ID selector that is applied to the HTML tag with a specific identifier (the value of the `id` attribute). The tag selector uses the same name as the corresponding HTML tag, the class selector prefixes the `class` attribute value name with a dot (.), while the ID selector uses a number sign (#) prefix before the identifier value. Listing 9-2 demonstrates these concepts.

Listing 9-2: Exercise-09-02/index.html

```
<!DOCTYPE html>
<html>
<head>
  <title>Tag, class, and ID selectors</title>
  <style>
    /* Tag selector*/
    h1 { color: red; }

    /* Class selector */
    .blue { color: blue; }

    /* ID selector */
    #greenLabel { color: green; }
  </style>
</head>
<body>
  <h1>This should be RED</h1>
  <h2 class="blue">This should be BLUE</h2>
  <h3 id="greenLabel">This is set to GREEN</h3>
  <h1>This is also RED</h1> </body>
</html>
```

The `h1` style is applied to both `<h1>` tags, so both first level heading is displayed in red. The `.blue` style (observe the dot prefix) is taken into account only for the single `<h2>` tag, because only this tag has a `class` attribute set to `blue`. The `<h3>` tag has an identifier of `greenLabel` so the `#greenLabel` rule (observe the number sign prefix) is applied. The page is displayed as shown in Figure 9-2.

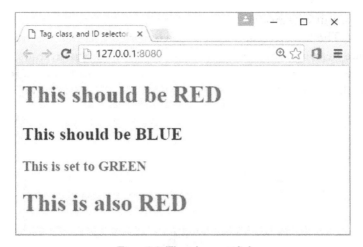

Figure 9-2: The styles are applied

You can apply more selectors for a single HTML element. Listing 9-3 contains three `<h1>` tags, in which one, two, and three rules are applied, respectively. The `h1` selector is bound to all headings, the `.blue` selector applies to the last two of them, while `#greenlabel` is taken into account only for the third heading.

Listing 9-3: Exercise-09-03/index.html

```
<!DOCTYPE html>
<html>
<head>
  <title>Multiple selectors applied</title>
  <style>
    /* Tag selector*/
    h1 { color: red; }

    /* Class selector */
    .blue {
      color: blue;
      background-color: yellow;
    }

    /* ID selector */
    #greenLabel { color: green; }
  </style>
</head>
<body>
  <h1>This should be RED</h1>
  <h1 class="blue">Now this should be BLUE</h1>
  <h1 class="blue" id="greenLabel">GREEN!</h1>
</body>
</html>
```

The `.blue` selector specifies that the background color should be set to yellow, and as you can see in Figure 9-3, it is applied to the last two headings just as expected. It is obvious that the first heading has a transparent background while the last two are yellow. The more interesting thing is the color of the text. The first heading's color is taken from the `h1` rule, but there is a conflict for the second and third heading, where multiple rules define the text color. In the second heading the `h1` rule defines red, the `.blue` rule sets blue color. The third heading has another candidate: green specified by the `#greenLabel` rule.

Figure 9-3: Multiple selectors applied for the second and third heading

By the CSS specification, if multiple selectors set the same property, the most specific is applied. Comparing the tag, class, and ID selectors, the ID selector is the most specific, followed by the class selector, and the tag selector is the least specific. This results that the first heading is red (tag selector), the second is blue (class selector is more specific than the tag selector), and the third heading is green (ID selector is more specific than either the class or the tag selector).

Attribute selectors

CSS provides selectors to format a tag based on any HTML attributes it has. Maybe, you want to style links according to the pages they point to, or set border around highlighted images. This extra information used to set up the appropriate styles can be based on attribute values. Attribute selectors can be specified with one of the following expressions:

```
selector[attr]
selector[attr operator "value"]
```

In this notation, *selector* identifies any selector (tag, class, ID, or other), *attr* names the attribute that should be compared to the specified *value*. If only the *attr* tag is specified, the selector matches with all tags within the *selector* that have an attribute named *attr*. If an *operator* is specified the attribute is checked against the *value*, as described in Table 9-2.

Table 9-2: Attribute selector checks

Operator	Test
=	The attribute's value is exactly the one specified in the expression
^=	The attribute's value begins with the one specified in the expression
$=	The attribute's value ends with the one specified in the expression
*=	The attribute's value contains the one specified in the expression
~=	The attribute's value contains the word in the specified expression

Listing 9-4 demonstrates all attribute selectors. It defines a page with five links and four paragraphs, and a number of style rules with various attribute selectors. The page is displayed as shown in Figure 9-4.

Listing 9-4: Exercise-09-04/index.html

```
<!DOCTYPE html>
<html>
<head>
  <title>Attribute selectors</title>
  <style>
    body {
       font-family: Verdana, Helvetica, sans-serif;
    }

    a {
      display: block;
      margin: 4px 8px;
      padding: 4px 8px;
    }
    a[href="http://msdn.com"] {
      background-color: orange;
    }
    a[href^="http://v"] {
      background-color: orangered;
    }
    a[href$=".com"] { border: 2px solid blue; }
    a[href*="iki"] { border: 4px dotted green; }
    p[title] { font-style: italic; }
    p[title*="HTML"] { background-color: green; }
    .par[title~="HTML"] { background-color: orange; }
  </style>
</head>
<body>
  <h1>My favorite links</h1>
  <a href="http://msdn.com">MSDN</a>
  <a href="http://visualstudio.com">
    Visual Studio Services Home
  </a>
```

```
<a href="http://visualstudiogallery.com">
   Visual Studio Extensions
</a>
<a href="http://wikipedia.org">
   Wikipedia
</a>
<a href="http://facebook.com">
   Facebook
</a>
<p title="This is HTML" class="par">
   This paragraph contains the HTML word
</p>
<p title="SomewhereHTMLIsHere" class="par">
   This paragraph contains the HTML pattern
</p>
</body>
</html>
```

Figure 9-4: Attribute selectors in action

The "a" rule is applied for all `<a>` tags. The `a[href="http://msdn.com"]` selector matches with all `<a>` tags that have an `href` attribute with the exact value of "http://msdn.com". There is only one, the first link, so its background is set to orange. The `a[href^="http://v"]` selector applies to those `<a>` tags, which have an `href` that begins with "http://v". As a result, the two Visual Studio links get an orange-red shading. In contrast to this, `a[href$=".com"]` marks those links that end with ".com", and this is why all `<a>` tags except Wikipedia have a solid blue border. The Wikipedia link does not remain without a border, because it matches the `a[href*="iki"]` selector—its `href` contains "iki".

The p[title] rule applies to all <p> tags that have a title attribute, so both paragraphs are displayed with italicized text. The p[title*="HTML"] rule matches with both paragraph, as they contain the "HTML" string in their title, so this rule sets their background to green. However, the first paragraph has an orange background. How could it be?

The first paragraph matches with the .par[title~="HTML"] selector, because it has a class attribute with value "par", and contains the "HTML" word. The second paragraph contains HTML, but not as a separate word, and it does not have a class attribute. So, there are two matching selector for the first paragraph (p[title*="HTML"] and .par[title~="HTML"]), and both intend to set the background color. The second selector wins, because it extends a class selector (.par), while the first extends a tag selector (p), and the class selector is more specific. The cascading results the orange shading.

You can apply multiple attribute selectors to a tag to extend an existing attribute selector with a new one, such as this:

```
a[href$=".com"][href^="https://"]
```

This rule applies to all HTTPS links that point to an URL ending with ".com".

Group Selectors

When you have the same declaration block for several selectors, you can construct a group from them separating the selectors with comma. For example, Listing 9-4 contains the following selectors:

```
a[href="http://msdn.com"] { background-color: orange; }
.par[title~="HTML"]       { background-color: orange; }
```

You can declare them with the group selector construct:

```
a[href="http://msdn.com"], .par[title~="HTML"]
  { background-color: orange; }
```

The Universal Selector

In a few situations, you need to apply a style for all HTML tags in your page. Instead of combining all HTML tags with the group selector, you can simply use the asterisk, like in this sample:

```
* { font-style: italic }
```

This style applies the italic font style to every single HTML tag in your document. Of course, you can combine the universal selector with others. For example, this example sets all tags to use boldfaced font, which have a title attribute.

```
*[title] { font-weight: bold; }
```

Pseudo-Element Selectors

CSS3 defines a pair of pseudo-element selectors, `:first-letter` and `:first-line`, respectively. They are called pseudo-elements, because they refer to parts of existing HTML tags, such as the first line of a paragraph, and not to entire HTML nodes in the document tree. Listing 9-5 shows an example that makes it easy to understand how they work.

Listing 9-5: Exercise-09-05/index.html

```
<!DOCTYPE html>
<html>
<head>
  <title>Pseudo-element selectors</title>
  <style>
    body {
        font-family: Verdana, Helvetica, sans-serif;
    }

    p:first-line { font-weight: bold; }
    p:first-letter { font-size: 2em; }
  </style>
</head>
<body>
  <p>
    Lorem ipsum dolor sit amet,
    consectetur adipiscing elit fusce vel sapien
    elit in malesuada semper mi, id sollicitudin
    urna fermentum ut fusce varius nisl ac ipsum
    gravida vel pretium tellus tincidunt integer.
  </p>
</body>
</html>
```

This example demonstrates both pseudo-element selectors. They are used in the context of p, such as `p:first-line`, and `p:first-letter`, so they provide formatting for the first line, and the first letter of every single `<p>` tag in the sample. In seems obvious, but it is still worth to confirm it `:first-line` is applied to the first line of the paragraph by means of rendering, and not the first line of the markup as written in the source. Figure 9-5 shows how the example page is displayed.

NOTE: You can apply the pseudo-element selectors only for terminal block elements (block elements that render real information, such as `<p>`, `<h1>`, etc.), and cannot be used for inline elements (such as `<span>`, `<strong>`, etc.). They also do not work with structural block elements, such as `<div>`, `<dl>`, `<article>`, and the others.

You can also use a third pseudo-element, `::selection` that represents a part of the document that has been highlighted by the user, including text in editable text fields. Only a small subset of CSS properties can be used in rules that apply to this pseudo-element.

Figure 9-5: Using the pseudo-element selectors

Pseudo-Class Selectors

There are a few selectors that allow you to specify style settings for HTML elements in a particular state. For example, you may apply a different style to links when the mouse hovers above them, or input text boxes with invalid data. These selectors are called pseudo-class selectors.

Two of them, namely `:link` and `:visited` are applied only to links. You can set the style of a link element that is determined to be unvisited or visited with `:link`, and `:visited`, respectively.

Another pseudo-class, `:active`, matches any element that's in the process of being activated. It would apply, for instance, for the duration of a mouse-click on a link, from the point at which the mouse button's pressed down until the point at which it's released again. The `:hover` pseudo-class matches any element that's being hovered by a pointing device (the cursor is hovered over the box generated by the element).

When an element in the page is ready to receive user input, its style can be marked with the `:focus` pseudo element. Evidently, `:focus` can apply to a form control, for instance, or to a link if the user navigates using the keyboard.

It is a common web design task to set up the style for user interface elements that are disabled (or sometimes, enabled). You can use the `:disabled` and `:enabled` pseudo-classes for this purpose. You can also style checkboxes or radio buttons that are checked or toggled to the "on" state with the `:checked` selector.

Listing 9-6 demonstrates using the `:hover` selector.

Listing 9-6: Exercise-09-06/index.html

```
<!DOCTYPE html>
<html>
<head>
  <title>Pseudo-element selectors</title>
  <style>
```

```
   body {
      font-family: Verdana, Helvetica, sans-serif;
   }

   a:hover {
      border: 2px solid blue;
      background-color: aliceblue;
      padding: 2px 4px;
   }
 </style>
</head>
<body>
 <h1>My favorite links</h1>
 <a href="http://msdn.com">MSDN</a>
 <br/>
 <a href="http://visualstudio.com">
   Visual Studio Services Home
 </a>
 <br/>
 <a href="http://visualstudiogallery.com">
   Visual Studio Extensions
 </a>
 <br/>
</body>
</html>
```

As shown in Figure 9-6, the `a:hover` rule is applied when you move the mouse over any link.

Figure 9.6: The :hover selector in action

The HTML page represents a hierarchy, and you often need to select elements using the ideas in regard to this hierarchy, such as descendent elements, children, and siblings. CSS provides simple syntax to allow building selectors that work with these concepts.

Descendent Selectors

Descendent selectors let you take advantage of the page hierarchy by styling tags differently when they appear inside certain other tags or styles. For example, let's say you have an `<h1>` tag on your web page, and you want to emphasize a word within that heading with the `<strong>` tag. However, most browsers display both `<h1>` and `<strong>` in bold, so you'd like to change the `<strong>` tag within `<h1>` to use red color. Creating a tag selector to change the `<strong>` tag's color does not help, because you end up changing the color of every `<strong>` tag on the page.

A descendent selector allows you to do what you really want, as shown in Listing 9-7.

Listing 9-7: Exercise-09-07/index.html

```
<!DOCTYPE html>
<html>
<head>
  <title>Descendant selectors</title>
  <style>
    body {
      font-family: Verdana, Helvetica, sans-serif;
    }

    h1 strong {
      color: red;
    }

    div.important strong {
      color: white;
      background-color: #404040;
    }
  </style>
</head>
<body>
  <h1>This is <strong>Important</strong></h1>
  <div class="important">
    <p>
      Lorem ipsum dolor <strong>sit</strong>
      amet, consectetur <strong>adipiscing</strong>
      elit fusce vel sapien elit in malesuada semper mi,
      <strong>id</strong> sollicitudin urna fermentum.
    </p>
  </div>
  <div>
    <p>
      Lorem <strong>ipsum</strong> dolor sit amet, consectetur
      adipiscing elit fusce vel.
    </p>
  </div>
</body>
</html>
```

This listing uses two rules with descendant selectors the first is `h1 strong`, the second is `div.important strong`. Both use the `strong` name separated by a space from the preceding part of the selector. The descendant selector is used with the meaning of any direct or indirect descendant of the parent selector. With this meaning `div.important` means any `<div>` tag with its `class` attribute set to "important", so `div.important strong` means any strong tag as a descendant of a `<div>` tag that has its `class` attribute set to "important".

Figure 9-7 shows how the page in Listing 9-7 is displayed.

Figure 9-7: Using descendant selectors

You can observe that the two paragraphs use different styles for `<strong>`. The reason is that the second paragraph is within a `<div>` tag, but without a `class` attribute, so the `div.important strong` selector is not applied on any descendant `<strong>` tags.

Child Selectors

Similar to the descendent selector, CSS lets you style the children of another tag with a child selector. The child selector uses an angle bracket (>) to indicate the relationship between the two elements. While the descendent selector applies to all descendants of a tag (children, grandchildren, and so on), the child selector lets you specify which child of which parent you want to deal with.

For example, if you want to select the `<h2>` tags within an `<article>` tag, use the `article > h2` child selector, as demonstrated in Listing 9-8.

Listing 9-8: Exercise-09-08/index.html

```
<!DOCTYPE html>
<html>
<head>
```

```
<title>Child selectors</title>
<style>
  article > h2 {
    font-style: italic;
  }
</style>
</head>
<body>
  <h2>Outside of article</h2>
  <article>
    <h2>Within article</h2>
    <div>
      <h2>Not directly within article</h2>
    </div>
  </article>
</body>
</html>
```

When you display this page (Figure 9-8), only the second <h2> will be shown in italic, because only that <h2> tag matches the article > h2 rule. The first <h2> is outside of <article>, and the third <h2> is nested in <article>, but it is not a direct child.

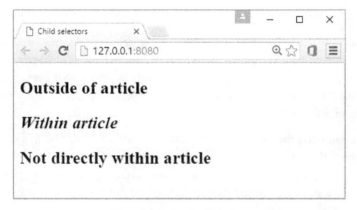

Figure 9-8: Using the child selector

Very often, you need to select children of a certain HTML node by their position and type. You have already learned about pseudo-class selectors, but those were only a part of them. CSS3 includes a few very specific pseudo-class selectors for selecting child elements, as summarized in Table 9-3.

Table 9-3: Pseudo-class selectors for child elements

Selector	Description
:first-child	Matches only with the first child of the parent element
:last-child	Matches only with the last child of the parent element
:only-child	Matches an element if it's the only child element of its parent

Selector	Description
`:nth-child(N)`	Matches elements that are preceded by `N-1` siblings in the document tree
`:nth-last-child(N)`	Matches elements that are followed by `N-1` siblings in the document tree.
`:first-of-type`	Matches the first child element of the specified element type, and is equivalent to `:nth-of-type(1)`.
`:last-of-type`	Matches the last child element of the specified element type, and is equivalent to `:nth-last-of-type(1)`
`:only-of-type`	Matches an element that's the only child element of its type.
`:nth-of-type(N)`	Matches elements that are preceded by `N-1` siblings with the same element name in the document tree
`:nth-last-of-type(N)`	Matches elements that are followed by `N-1` siblings with the same element name in the document tree

As you see, a number of pseudo-class selectors use an argument, `N`, which can be a keyword, a number, or can be given as *an+b*, where *a* and *b* are integers, for example (`2n+1`). Use the odd keyword for selecting odd-numbered elements, and even for selecting even-numbered elements.

If `N` is a number, it represents the ordinal position of the selected element. For example, 3 represents the third element. If `N` is given as *an+b*, *b* represents the ordinal position of the first element that we want to match, and *a* represents the ordinal number of every element we want to match after that. So, the expression `3n+2` will match the second element, and every third element after that: the fifth, eighth, eleventh, and so on.

There is difference between the `nth-` and `nth-last-` pseudo-classes. The `nth-` pseudo-classes count from the top of the document tree down—they select elements that have `N-1` siblings before them; meanwhile, the `nth-last-` pseudo-classes count from the bottom up—they select elements that have `N-1` siblings after them.

Listing 9-9 demonstrates these concepts. Instead of providing a static web page, it is dynamic: there's a text box where you can type in the child selector to apply. It uses JavaScript to dynamically add a style rule to the internal style sheet to mark the selected children with red color and italicized font.

The items, on which the demonstration is carried out, are nested into a `<div>` tag, and are one of these types: `<p>`, `<span>`, and `<strong>`. The items within `<p>` tags are marked with a "(p)" suffix to help you identify how the selectors work.

384

Listing 9-9: Exercise-09-09/index.html

```html
<!DOCTYPE html>
<html>
<head>
  <title>Pseudo-class child selectors</title>
  <style>
    body {
      font-family: Verdana, Helvetica, sans-serif;
      margin-left: 16px;
    }

    #selector { width: 200px;}
    div p { margin: 0; }
    div span, div strong { display: block; }
  </style>
  <style id ="childStyle">
  </style>
  <script>
    function applyStyle() {
      var child = document.getElementById('selector')
        .value;
      var rule = 'div ' + child +
        '{ color: red; font-style: italic }';
      var styleTag = document.getElementById('childStyle');
      styleTag.innerText = rule;
    }
  </script>
</head>
<body>
  <h1>Pesudo-class selectors</h1>
  <p>
    Type the name of a pseudo-selector in the
    following textbox, such as <code>:first-child</code>
    or <code>:nth-child(3n+1)</code>, etc., and
    then click the Apply button.
  </p>
  Selector:
  <input id="selector" type="text" autofocus />
  <button onclick="applyStyle()">Apply</button>
  <hr/>
  <p>This is a sample list:</p>
  <div>
    <p>Item #01 (p)</p>
    <span>Item #02</span>
    <p>Item #03 (p)</p>
    <span>Item #04</span>
    <span>Item #05</span>
    <p>Item #06 (p)</p>
    <p>Item #07 (p)</p>
    <p>Item #08 (p)</p>
    <span>Item #09</span>
```

```
    <p>Item #10 (p)</p>
    <strong>Item #11</strong>
    <span>Item #12</span>
    <p>Item #13 (p)</p>
    <p>Item #14 (p)</p>
    <span>Item #15</span>
  </div>
</body>
</html>
```

Figure 9-9 shows what you see when you use the `:nth-child(3n+2)` selector.

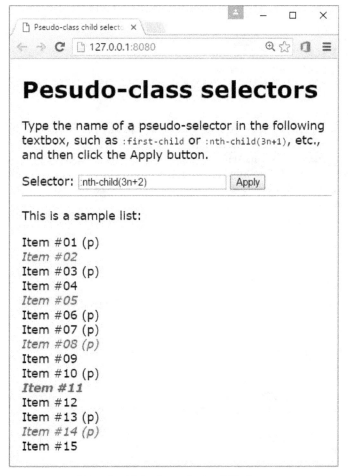

Figure 9-9: Using the pseudo-class child selectors

HINT: Try applying the following selectors as well, and check how they work: `:nth-child(odd)`, `:nth-child(even)`, `strong:only-of-type`, `:nth-last-of-type(2)`, `span:nth-last-of-type(2)`, `p:nth-last-of-type(2)`, and `span:first-of-type`.

Sibling Selectors

Often you need to select HTML tags that are based on their surrounding siblings. To carry out this task, CSS3 offers you two sibling selectors, the *adjacent sibling*, and the *general sibling* selectors. The adjacent sibling selector selects all elements that are the adjacent siblings of a specified element, meanwhile the general sibling selector matches all elements of a specific type that are siblings of a given element.

You can use the plus sign (+) for the adjacent sibling selector. So, h1 + p (you can omit spaces and write this expression as h1+p) means the <p> sibling of <h1> tag that is adjacent with <h1>. The general sibling is marked with the tilde (~) character. So, h1 ~ p (or written as h1~p) covers all <p> tags that are siblings of <h1>.

To understand these selectors better, take a look at Listing 9-10.

Listing 9-10: Exercise-09-10/index.html

```
<!DOCTYPE html>
<html>
<head>
  <title>Sibling selectors</title>
  <style>
    body {
      font-family: Verdana, Helvetica, sans-serif;
      margin-left: 16px;
    }
    p { margin: 0; }
    h1 + p { background-color: yellow; }
    h1 + span { background-color: orangered; }
    h1 ~ p { font-style: italic; }
    h1 ~ span {
      display: block;
      font-weight: bold;
    }
    h1 ~ * { margin-left: 24px; }
  </style>
</head>
<body>
  <h1>I'm looking for my siblings...</h1>
  <p>I'm a direct sibling (p)</p>
  <span>I'm a (span) sibling of (h1)</span>
  <p>I'm another sibling of type (p)</p>
  <p>Let me tell you, I'm (p), too</p>
  <span>I'm another span of (h1) :-)</span>
</body>
</html>
```

The markup uses five sibling selectors in its <style> section, which specify the appearance of the <h1> tag's siblings. This <h1> tag has two types of siblings, <p> and <span> tags. The page is displayed as shown in Figure 9-10.

387

Figure 9-10: Using sibling selectors

The `h1 + p` selector is applied to the paragraph directly following `<h1>`, and it is marked with yellow background. Since `<h1>` does not have an adjacent `<span>` sibling, `h1 + span` is not applied to any tag. All `<p>` siblings of `<h1>` are italicized, because `h1 ~ p` matches them. The `<span>` siblings of `<h1>` are set to be displayed in bold, according to the `h1 ~ span` rule. With the `h1 ~ *` (here * is the universal selector) all `<h1>` siblings are indented to right with 24 pixels.

Other Selectors

Now, your head must be full with the types of selectors offered by CSS. There are a few others, here you will learn about them.

There are two additional pseudo-element selectors, `:before` and `:after` that do something no other selector can: they let you add content preceding or succeeding a given element, respectively. When you remove the `h1 ~ *` style rule from Listing 9-10, and replace with these, you can change the content of the web page, as shown in Figure 9-11:

```
h1 ~ *:before { content: "*** "; }
h1 ~ *:after { content: " ***"; }
```

You can use the `:not()`, selector, also called negation pseudo-class, to match something that is not something else. Listing 9-11 shows how using the `:not()` selector modifies the appearance of the page in Listing 9-10.

Figure 9-11: Using the :before and :after pseudo-element selectors

Listing 9-11: Exercise-09-11/index.html

```html
<!DOCTYPE html>
<html>
<head>
  <title>Sibling selectors</title>
  <style>
    /* Unchanged rules omitted */
    span:not(.ex) { background-color: red; }
  </style>
</head>
<body>
  <h1>I'm looking for my siblings...</h1>
  <p>I'm a direct sibling (p)</p>
  <span class="ex">I'm a (span) sibling of (h1)</span>
  <p>I'm another sibling of type (p)</p>
  <p>Let me tell you, I'm (p), too</p>
  <span>I'm another span of (h1) :-)</span>
</body>
</html>
```

The highlighted rule sets the appearance of the last `<span>` tag's background to red, as shown in Figure 9-12.

In this section you have had an overview of all important selectors defined by CSS. Now, it is time to learn about properties.

Figure 9-12: The :not() selector in action

Style Properties

Style rules contain zero, one, or more property declarations. Rules with no property declarations do not have great value, because even if they are applied to any HTML tag, they do not cause any change it the particular tag's visual properties. Nonetheless, empty rules may be used as placeholders for future enhancements. To make it clear that an empty rule has such a role, put a comment that explicitly declares this intention.

Property Names and Values

Property names are composed from one or more words with lowercase letters, and words are separated by a dash, such as in these names: `background-color`, `text-size`. Although by default all properties have a value, when you declare a property, you must set a value. So you cannot declare a rule like this:

```
h1 { color: } /* This is invalid */
```

If you want to set the initial value of a property, use the `initial` keyword:

```
h1 { color: initial; }
```

Most properties are inherited along the HTML hierarchy, so a child HTML element inherits the property from its parent. As a general rule, properties that affect the placement of elements on the page or the margins, background colors, and borders of elements aren't inherited. If you want to use the property of a parent element explicitly, use the inherit keyword to state your intention:

```
p { white-space: inherit; }
```

Some properties can be combined into *shorthand notation*—a notation that allows us to specify values for related properties in a single declaration. For example, you can set the margins of a paragraph like this:

```
p {
  margin-top: 2px;
  margin-right: 4px;
  margin-bottom: 6px;
  margin-left: 8px;
}
```

Instead of writing these four separate property values, you can write a shorthand notation with `margin`:

```
p { margin: 2px 4px 6px 8px; }
```

Colors

CSS provides several different ways to specify a color that you can assign to many different properties—including those for fonts, backgrounds, and borders. The most readable way of declaring a color value is using a keyword such as `red`, `green`, `blue`, `gray`, `black`, `white`, `orange`, `cyan`, `magenta`, and so on. Here you can find the full list of color keywords defined by the CSS3 specification: `http://www.w3.org/TR/css3-color/#svg-color`. This list is limited only a very few percentages of all colors available with other notations:

You can use hexadecimal values with the *#hhhhhh* notation where *h* represents a hexadecimal digit. The six digits represent three values (each with two digits), the RGB (red, green, and blue) components of the color. For example:

```
p {
  color: #ff0000; /* red */
  background-color: #00ff00; /* green */
}
```

If all three two-digit values are repeated pairs of digits, you can shorten the hex value by using just the first number of each pair. For example, `#0f8` means the same thing as `#00ff88`.

You can use the RGB notation using either percentages or integer values between 0 and 255, as you can see in this example:

```
p {
  color: rgb(100%, 0%, 0%); /* red */
  background-color: rgb(0, 255, 0); /* green */
}
```

With the RGBA notation you can add a fourth value for transparency. This float value must be between 0 and 1. For example, the following rule adds a half-transparent background to the p rule:

```
p {
  background-color: rgba(255, 255, 0, 0.5); /* yellow */
}
```

As an alternative, you can use the HSL (hue, saturation, and luminance) notation, where the hue value is a degree value between 0 and 360, saturation and luminance are percentage values. You can also use HSLA that add a transparency value to HSL:

```
p {
  color: hsl(0, 100%, 50%); /* red */
  background-color: hsla(60, 100%, 50%, 0.5); /* yellow */
}
```

Length and Size Types

When designing the layout of a page, you often need to specify sizes, such as the width or height of a box, top and bottom margins of paragraphs, and so on. To indicate size, CSS offers a number of type size options including pixels, points, picas, inches, centimeters, millimeters, em-heights, ex heights, and even percentages. When you define a style property that specifies a size or length value, you always need to specify the unit of measure as well, as show in this example:

```
p {
    margin-top: 4px;
    margin-right: 1in;
    margin-bottom: 0.5em;
    margin-left: 0;
}
```

The only value that does not need a unit of measure is zero, for it is exactly the same independent of the unit used to calculate it. Table 9-4 summarizes the size type options.

Table 9-4: Size type options

Unit	Description
px	px stands for *pixels*. Pixels are most often used when you want to precisely align elements to images because images are measured in pixels.
in	in stands for *logical inches*. The epithet "logical" refers to the fact that the actual physical size depends on the monitor and settings chosen by the operating system or the user. The size of dots of a monitor determines the physical size of its pixels, and thus the physical size of the logical inch. Be careful when using logical inches—and all other fixed units of measure—, because they do not scale well on systems with different dot-per-inch settings.
pt	This unit specifies *points*. A point is 1/72 of a logical inch.
pc	This unit stands for *picas*. A pica is 12 points or 1/6 of a logical inch.
cm	It stands for *centimeters*. One logical inch is 2.54 centimeters.
mm	This unit specifies *millimeters*. One logical inch is 25.4 millimeters.

Unit	Description
em	While all entries above are fixed units of measure, em is a flexible unit; it is the font-size value assigned to an element. The only exception is the font-size property itself, when you assign a value to it, em represents the font-size value of the parent element. For example, 3em is three times the font-size. Use ems when you want to size an element relative to the size of its text. This allows the layout of your documents to flex with the size of the text.
ex	ex is also a flexible unit, is the height of the letter "x" of an element's current font. This measurement is rarely used.

Logical units (in, pt, pc, cm, mm) do not scale well on systems with different dot-per-inch settings. What may seem just right on Windows 8 at 96 dpi, may be too large or too small on other systems. Instead of these size types, use percentages or ems if you want to provide the best cross-platform compatibility.

To understand better how ems work, take a look at this sample:

```
<!DOCTYPE html>
<html>
<head>
  <title>Using ems</title>
  <style>
    body { font-size: 30px; }
    p {
        margin-top: 0.5em;
        margin-bottom: 0.5em;
        font-size: 0.8em;
    }
    h1 { font-size: 2em; }
  </style>
</head>
<body>
  <h1>I'm a heading</h1>
  <p>I'm paragraph</p>
</body>
</html>
```

Here, body defines that the font size should be 30 pixels. The <p> tag within <body> uses the p style rule, which specifies all sizes in ems. The font-size value is specified as 0.8em, and it is calculated by the font-size of the parent element (<body>), so the paragraph will use a 30px*0.8=24px font.

The margin-top and margin-bottom values are also specified with ems, but they use the <p> font size (24px) as the base of height calculation. So margin-top and margin-bottom is set to 24px*0.5=12px. Using the same logic, the font-size of the <h1> tag is to 60 pixels.

There is another flexible unit of measure you can use: percentages. CSS uses this unit for many different purposes, like determining the width or height of an element, sizing text, specifying the placement of an image in the background of a style, and so on. What is taken into account as a

393

percentage of varies from property to property. For example, for font sizes, the percentage is calculated based on the text's inherited value. When applied to width, however, percentages are calculated based on the width of the page or on the width of the nearest parent element.

URL Values

A few properties in CSS use URL values. For example, the `background-image` property accepts a URL that points to a file on the web. This file is used to assign an image as a background for a related page element. The syntax of specifying URLs is simple:

```
body {
  background-image: url(Images/pageBkg.png)
}
```

As you expect, this property value gets the `pageBkg.png` file from the `Images` folder.

You can use optional single quotes or double quotes to wrap URLs, such as in these examples:

```
url('Images/pageBkg.png')
url("Images/pageBkg.png")
```

Baseline Style Sheet

As you already learned, browsers apply their own styles to tags. The HTML standard does not specify any of this formatting. It is up to web browser vendors to add this formatting to make basic HTML more readable. Even though browsers treat all tags almost the same, they don't treat them identically, and they assign different default style settings to them.

The style sheet you apply to your web pages define the properties to set on various HTML elements. These style rules generally set visual properties *additionally* to default style settings. But, provided that the default settings are different, the styled web page may be different as well.

To cope with this potential issue, you may want to build rules into your style sheets to define baseline settings for each element. For example, different browsers assign the `<h1>`, `<h2>`, ..., and `<h6>` elements to different sizes and margins. By assigning your own size and margins to headings, you can standardize their appearance in all browsers.

The simplest approach (and the easiest to maintain) is to create a baseline set of rules for all elements and to load those rules in the first style sheet you attach to a document. Although you can find standard sets of baseline rules on the Internet, often it is enough to use the concept CSS reset—an approach that erases browser styling to remove the differences in built-in browser formatting.

Here is a simple CSS reset style sheet:

```
html, body, div, dl, dt, dd, ul, ol,
li, h1, h2, h3, h4, h5, h6, pre,
form, fieldset, input, p, blockquote,
th,td {
```

```
  margin: 0;
  padding: 0;
}
table {
  border-collapse: collapse;
  border-spacing: 0;
}
fieldset, img { border: 0; }
address,caption,cite,code,dfn,em,
strong,th,var {
  font-style: normal;
   font-weight: normal;
}
ol,ul {
  margin: 1em 0;
  margin-left: 40px;
  padding-left:0;
}
ul { list-style-type: disc; }
ol { list-style-type: decimal; }
caption,th { text-align: left; }
h1, h2, h3, h4, h5, h6 { font-size:100%; }
```

There are more sophisticated solutions to set up a baseline style sheet, but in most cases using this simple CSS reset is enough.

The Cascading Order

Now, you have a basic understanding of the syntax and semantics of style sheets. When your page is displayed, all style rules that match an HTML tag are utilized to determine the visual properties of that specific tag. While these rules set separate properties, it's easy to define the result: all property settings are applied to the HTML tag—of course the ones that are not applicable, are simply omitted.

Nonetheless, it may happen that multiple rules define values for the same property. While these rules define exactly the same property value, it does not matter which rule wins, because all set the same value. However, most often these are different values, and you must know which value is used.

CSS was designed with the intention to allow assigning multiple rules to the same element. As you already know, each browser has its own default style sheet that sets a number of properties for each type of HTML tags. If you add a style sheet to the page—it does not matter if it's an internal or external style sheet—, it is very likely that there are competing styles, because your style assignment may compete with the browser's default one. Browsers use the *cascading order* to determine which rule in a set of competing rules gets applied. In this section you will learn the details of the cascading order.

The Three Steps of Cascading

If there are competing rules, there are three main steps to determine which rule wins. These are the following ones:

1. *The more specific selector (the selector with the highest priority) wins.* The fundamental principle behind the cascade order is that there are general selectors (these set overall styles for a document), and more specific selectors that override the general selectors to apply more specific styles. If the same property is set by two or more selectors, the more specific selector wins. If two or more selectors are equally specific, the competition goes on with the next step.

Earlier, Listing 9-2 demonstrated this situation with the following rules:

```
h1 { color: red; }
.blue { color: blue; }
#greenLabel { color: green; }
```

Let's assume you have an **<h1>** tag in your page like this:

```
<h1 class="blue" id="greenLabel">
  This should be GREEN
</h1>
```

Here, the most specific selector is the **#greenLabel** ID selector, so the heading's color is set to green.

2. *The selector with a higher specificity wins.* A specificity value can be calculated for each selector. If the same property is set by two or more selectors with the same specificity, the competition goes on with the last (third) step.

Take a look at these rules:

```
h1.spec { color: yellow; }
.spec { color: blue; }
```

Let's assume, you have this **<h1>** tag in your page:

```
<h1 class="spec">Heading</h1>
```

Here, the first selector is applied, and the heading is displayed with yellow color. Both selector are equally specific (both are class selectors), so the second step is used to determine the one with highest selectivity. By this calculation—as you will learn soon—, **.spec** has lower specificity value than **h1.spec**, and so **h1.spec** is the winner.

3. *The selector with a higher priority location wins.* If the first two steps does not announce a winner, the final decision is made by the location of the rule. According to the location where the selector was defined, the one with the highest priority can be found (there is exactly one of them), and the rule at this location wins the right to set up the particular property.

Now, let's look behind these steps in more details.

Selector Group Priorities

To determine which selector has the higher priority, CSS divides the rules into six priority group from the highest to the lowest:

1. The first priority group contains rules with the `!important` modifier added to them. They override all rules that do not contain this modifier.

Let's assume, you have an HTML tag that is affected by this selector:

```
p { color: blue !important; }
```

It does not matter how many other selectors specify the `color` property, because the `!important` tag signs that the `p` rule should win over them.

NOTE: You should always place `!important` at the end of the property declaration, right before the closing semicolon.

2. The second priority group contains rules embedded in the `style` attribute of an HTML tag.

Even if you use the `h1 { color: red; }` rule, the following `style` attribute overrides it, and the heading will be shown in green:

```
<h1 style="color: green;">Heading</h1>
```

3. The third priority group contains rules that have one or more ID selectors.

4. The fourth priority group contains rules that have one or more class, attribute, or pseudo selectors.

5. The fifth priority group contains rules that have one or more element selectors.

6. And last, the sixth (and lowest) priority group contains rules that have only a universal selector.

Calculating Selectivity

If the winner rule cannot be selected by the highest priority (there are more rules with the same priority), the selectivity of the competing rules are calculated. This calculation is pretty simple:

The rule is assigned a selectivity value based on three source values within the selector: the count of ID selectors (A); the count of class selectors, attributes selectors, and pseudo-classes (B); and the count of type selectors and pseudo-elements (C). Then, these three numbers are concatenated into a single number, and taken into account as the selectivity value.

The universal selector is ignored, and the selectors inside the `:not()` pseudo-class are counted like any other, but the negation itself does not count as a pseudo-class.

Let's see an example (the property declarations are omitted):

```
/* A=0, B=0, C=0 -> specificity = 0 */
*

/* A=0, B=0, C=1 -> specificity = 1 */
```

```
li

/* A=0, B=0, C=2 -> specificity = 2 */
ul li

/* A=0, B=0, C=3 -> specificity = 3 */
ul ol+li

/* A=0, B=1, C=1 -> specificity = 11 */
h1 + *[href$='http:']

/* A=0, B=1, C=3 -> specificity = 13 */
ul ol li.spec

/* A=0, B=2, C=1 -> specificity = 21 */
li.spec.next

/* A=1, B=0, C=0 -> specificity = 100 */
#myTag

/* A=1, B=0, C=1 -> specificity = 101 */
#yourTag:not(foo)
```

Location Priorities

If the winner rule cannot be selected by the highest priority, and even the selectivity of the competing rules does not lead to a decision, the last step uses the priority of the rule's location to get the winner. The decision is made by the six location priorities, as listed here from the highest to the lowest:

1. The first priority location is the `<style>` element in the head of the HTML document.

2. The second priority location is a style sheet imported by an `@import` at-rule embedded within the `<style>` element

3. The third priority location is a style sheet attached by a `<link>` element.

4. The fourth priority location is a style sheet imported by an `@import` at-rule embedded within a style sheet attached by a `<link>` element.

5. The fifth priority location is a style sheet attached by an end user. An exception is made for `!important` rules in an end-user style sheet. These rules are given the highest priority.

6. And last, the sixth (lowest) priority location is the default style sheet supplied by a browser.

It may happen that multiple style sheets are attached or imported at the same location level. In this case, the order in which they are attached determines the priority. Style sheets attached later override style sheets attached previously.

NOTE: As you can see from the algorithm that determines the cascading order, only one winner remains at the end, so there is no indeterminism in applying a CSS rule. Sometimes it's not easy to trace which rule brings the winner property declaration into the picture, but it is always unambiguous.

Media-Dependent Style Sheets

Most of the time you see web pages in front of your PC or notebook, and the page is displayed in a browser. Sometimes—for example after check-in with your airline—, you print a web page. You very likely have at least one mobile device, such a smartphone or tablet, and—just like other people—you use it to browse web pages.

Media types

The creators of CSS designed the recommendation with different ways and devices people might view websites. To accommodate these different methods of surfing, they enabled CSS to create your own styles and style sheets that specifically target a particular media type. Table 9-5 summarizes the media types supported by CSS3.

Table 9-5: CSS media types

Type	Description
all	Suitable for all devices.
screen	Intended primarily for color computer screens.
print	Intended for paged material and for documents viewed on screen in print preview mode.
projection	Intended for projected presentations, for example projectors.
tv	Intended for television-type devices (low resolution, color, limited-scrollability screens, and sound available).
handheld	Intended for handheld devices (typically small screen, limited bandwidth).
braille	Intended for Braille tactile feedback devices.
embossed	Intended for paged Braille printers.
tty	Intended for media using a fixed-pitch character grid (such as teletypes, terminals, or portable devices with limited display capabilities).
speech	Intended for speech synthesizers.

When you do not specify the media type your style sheet is intended for, all is assumed. It is always your decision whether you want to support different media types or not. However, if you create pages that need printer-friendly font sizes, colors, images, and other visual properties when printed, specify styles for the print media type.

Adding Media Style Sheets

Media-dependent style sheets use exactly the same syntax as any other CSS declarations. When attaching an external style sheet to your page, the media attribute of the `<link>` tag lets you specify the media type. This sample shows how you can add three style sheets to your web page:

```
<link rel="stylesheet" href="allStyle.css" />
<link rel="stylesheet" media="screen, projection, handheld, tv"
  href="screenStyle.css" />
<link rel="stylesheet" media="print"
  href="printStyle.css" />
```

The first `<link>` tag loads a CSS file that contains all style rules that are suitable for every media type. The second and third `<link>` tags target specific media types, the second devices with screens, the third only printing devices, respectively.

Using the `media` attribute you can attach the same style sheet file to different media types. This method cannot work with internal style sheets, because there is no `media` attribute to set up. With the `@media` at-rule, you can define sections within the style sheet, and put style rules into them, as demonstrated in Listing 9-12.

Listing 9-12: Exercise-09-12/index.html

```
<!DOCTYPE html>
<html>
<head>
  <title>Using @media</title>
  <style>
    @media all {
      h1 {
        background-color: blue;
        color: white;
      }
    }

    @media print {
      h1 {
        background-color: white;
        color: blue;
      }
    }
  </style>
</head>
<body>
  <h1>Introduction</h1>
  <p>
    Lorem ipsum dolor sit amet, consectetur
    adipiscing elit fusce vel sapien elit
    in malesuada semper mi, id sollicitudin
    urna fermentum.
  </p>
```

```
</body>
</html>
```

Here, the `all` and `print` media type identifiers define the target type of the section. As you can see, the `<h1>` tag is defined to use a blue background with a white text color when the page is displayed with screen-like devices, but it is instructed to use blue color with white background on printers.

NOTE: Technically, it doesn't matter whether you put all styles in a single file and use the `@media` method or put media-specific styles in their own external style sheets.

Media Queries

CSS3 added an extension to media types that allows you more sophisticated control over defining styles for different devices. This extension is called *media queries*, and it allows building logical expressions in conjunction to media types. You can test the features of the output device you intend to render the output for, and so you can create styles that accommodate to your "screens" better than with simple media types.

Media queries are composed from simple test expressions that are combined with logical AND and logical OR operators. Here is a sample:

```
@media handheld and (min-width: 640px) {
    /* Add rules here */
}
```

This media query is pretty easy to read and understand. The section defines style rules that should be applied for handheld type devices with a horizontal resolution of 640 pixels or above.

Media queries can be added to the `@media` and `@import` at-rules, and they also can be used in the media attribute of `<link>` tags. You can use multiple comma separated media queries in a single rule—in the case the comma acts as logical OR. For example, this media query imports the `myStyle.css` file for screens with at least 8 bit color per component, and for projectors that support colors:

```
@import url(myStyle.css)
  screen and (min-color: 8),
  projection and (color);
```

The media queries extension defines a number of features that can be tested, as listed in Table 9-6. Most features can be used with the `min-` and `max-` prefix to test for minimum and maximum values.

Table 9-6: Media features

Feature	Description
color	This feature represents the number of bits per color component with an integer value.
color-index	Represents the number of entries in the color lookup table (integer value)
device-aspect-ratio	This feature describes the aspect ratio of a device with a w/h value, where w and h are integer numbers, such as 16/9.
device-height	Represents the height of the output device with a length value (such as 8in or 12em).
device-width	Represents the width of the output device with a length value.
grid	Retrieves true for a grid-based device. Does not support the min- or max- prefixes.
height	Represents the height of the rendering surface with a length value.
monochrome	This feature represents number of bits per pixel in a monochrome frame buffer (integer value)
resolution	Represents the resolution of the output device specified in dpi or dpcm, such as 300dpi or 118dpcm.
scan	Used to describe the scanning process of a tv media type. Values can be progressive or interlaced. Does not support the min- or max- prefixes.
width	Represents the width of the rendering surface with a length value.

Summary

Cascading Style Sheets (CSS) is a fundamental technology to separate the structure of web pages (markup) from the visual styles the page is rendered with. The basic idea behind this technology is simple: you define a selector that specifies a set of HTML nodes in the document tree of the page, and assign values to a number of predefined visual properties. A selector with the properties to apply builds up a single style rule, and a set of rules composes a style sheet.

You can declare style sheets as external files with .css extension, and add them to your page with the <link> HTML element. Alternatively, you can embed style rules directly to your page with the <style> tag. You can link more than one CSS file to the page, add more <style> sections, and you can combine internal and external style sheets as you wish.

There are a number of selectors to define the set of HTML nodes to apply a style rule for. These include the universal selector, the class, ID, attribute selectors; the descendant, child, sibling selectors; a number of pseudo-element and pseudo-class selectors. If more rules select an HTML node, all of them are applied. If there are competing properties (properties specified by more than one rule), the winner (the one that is applied) is selected by the cascading order mechanism.

CSS supports several media types, such as devices with screens, printers, handhelds, etc. You can define styles that apply only for one or more specific media types. With the media queries extension of CSS3, you can test device features, so you can take a far greater control over rendering across different devices than with media types alone.

In Chapter 10, you will learn basic CSS patterns that allow you to establish the visual style of your web pages.

Chapter 10:
Basic Style Patterns

WHAT YOU WILL LEARN IN THIS CHAPTER

Formatting text elements on your web pages
Getting to know the box model
Adding background images to the page and its components
Getting acquainted with a few styling tricks for tables and forms

In the previous chapter you learned all fundamental concepts about using Cascading Style Sheets. Creating web pages with the proper usage of HTML and CSS is a combination of art, craftsmanship, and science. I cannot promise that you will learn anything about CSS that that immediately makes you a web designer. Nonetheless, I'm sure that after reading this chapter you'll be able to understand the basic CSS patterns, and analyze ready web pages to peek how they work and what tricks they utilize to achieve a particular design effect.

This chapter introduces the majority of CSS properties and demonstrates their usage with short examples.

Text Formatting

At the beginning of this book you started learning HTML at the very basics, by using text. It is worth to do the same thing with CSS.

CSS offers a number of text-formatting options, which let you assign font types, color, sizes, line spacing, and many other properties to display text in your web pages. Table 10-1 summarizes the CSS properties that allow you customize the rendering of text elements—ranging from simple text snippets to paragraphs and lists.

Table 10-1: Text properties

Property	Description
color	Sets the color of text. This property is inherited, thus if you set the color of an HTML tag—let's say `<body>`—to blue, all text and all other tags inside that tag—`<body>`—is set to blue, too. In *Chapter 9*, you already learned how you can specify colors.

Property	Description
font	This is a shorthand notation for packing the following text properties into a single style declaration: font-style, font-variant, font-weight, font-size, line-height, and font-family.
font-family	Specifies the font the browser should use to display text. When you specify font names, provide a comma-separated list of names (should the font name have spaces, surround the name with quotes).
	The browser attempts to use the font names from left to right, it uses the font it finds installed on the web page visitor's device. The last font in the list is usually set to one of the following generic font types: serif, sans-serif, monotype, fantasy, or cursive. This setting instructs browsers to choose a suitable font if the other listed fonts aren't installed.
font-size	Sets the size of the text. Do not forget, this property is inherited, so if you use one of the flexible size types (em or ex) the size is relative to the font size of the parent HTML element (see the example after Table 9-4 and the related explanation).
font-style	Allows transforming the text to italic (with the values of italic or oblique), or back to normal.
font-variant	Allows transforming the text to use small caps (small-caps), or remove small caps from text (normal).
font-weight	Makes text bold or removes bolding from text. Although about a dozen keywords and values from 100 to 900 can be used as the value of this property, most browsers and devices work only with bold and normal.
letter-spacing	Adjusts the space between letters to spread out them (adding extra space between each) or pack letters together (removing space). Use any valid CSS size type unit—a positive value to increase, and a negative value to condense space. The value normal resets letter-spacing to 0.
line-height	Sets the space between lines of text in a paragraph. The normal line height is 120 percent of the size of the text. Use any valid size type units.
text-align	Positions a block of text to the left, right, or center of the page or container element. The value justify aligns the left and right edges of the text to the edges of the container.
text-decoration	Adds decorations to text elements, such as lines above, under, and/or through text. The color of the decoration is the same as the font color of the tag being styled. You can use any combination of the following keywords (separated by whitespaces): underline, overline, line-through, blink (makes the text flash, however most browsers ignore this option). The none value turns off all decorations.

Property	Description
text-indent	Sets the indent size of the first line of a block of text. You can use any valid size types. With a negative value, you can make the first line off the left edge. Percentage values are based on the width of the box containing the text.
text-shadow	Adds a drop shadow to any text. You can apply four values (each separated by a whitespace): two size type values (ems or pixels) for horizontal and vertical offset, a value for the amount of blur to the text, and a color value, respectively. For the horizontal and vertical offset, a negative number places the shadow to the left or above of the text, a positive value to the right or below.
text-transform	Sets the capitalization of text, to make it appear in all uppercase or lowercase. The value capitalize makes only the first letter of each word capitalized. The none option lets the text remain in the case as it is specified in the HTML markup.
vertical-align	Sets the baseline of an inline element relative to the baseline of the surrounding contents. You can use the baseline, sub, super, top, text-top, middle, bottom, text-bottom keywords, or size values (even negative ones). Percentages are calculated based on the element's line-height value. *This value is used for inline elements only, and it is not inherited.*
white-space	Use this property to control how the browser displays space characters in the HTML code. The value normal uses the standard behavior of browsers, and removes the extra spaced between words. The nowrap value prevents the text from splitting a line of text at a space, if the line will not fit within the browser's window. The pre value instructs to preserve the spaces in the text, just like the <pre> HTML tag does. *This value is not inherited.*
word-spacing	This property works similarly to letter-spacing, but it adjusts the space between words, and not between letters.

Let's see a few examples.

Font Type, Size, and Color

You have already seen many examples that set font properties. Listing 10-1 shows another sample that demonstrates the color, font-family, font-size, and font properties.

Listing 10-1: Exercise-10-01/index.html

```
<!DOCTYPE html>
<html>
<head>
  <title>Font type, style, and color</title>
```

```
<style>
  body {
    font-family: Britannic, "Times New Roman", serif;
    color: dimgray;
  }

  .highlighted {
    font-size: 1.25em;
    color: blue;
  }

  .main {
    font: small-caps bold 1em Verdana, Helvetica, sans-serif;
    color: black;
  }
</style>
</head>
<body>
  <h1>This is the page font</h1>
  <p class="highlighted">
    This is a highlighted paragraph
  </p>
  <p class="main">
    Lorem ipsum dolor sit amet, consectetur adipiscing
    elit fusce vel sapien elit in malesuada semper mi,
    id sollicitudin urna fermentum.
  </p>
</body>
</html>
```

It's pretty easy to follow how the rules in this style sheet work. The body rule sets up the default font family to this page to one of the available serif fonts. The .highlighted rule changes the size of the first paragraph to a 25% taller font than the original (1.25em), and sets its color to blue. The .main rule uses the font shorthand notation to set the font-variant, font-weight, and font-family properties. The CSS parser is intelligent enough to infer the appropriate properties from the values provided. This page is displayed in the browser as shown in Figure 10-1.

This figure clearly indicates that the size of the font is not measured with an absolute size. You can see that the first paragraph after the heading—which is set to 25% taller than the normal font size—is almost equal with the font size of the second paragraph, which is set to the normal size. The reason behind this fact is that the Britannic font (used in the heading and in the first paragraph) is smaller than the Verdana font (used to display the second paragraph)

Play a little bit with Listing 10-1, and try to modify a few properties. For example, when you change the Britannic font to a not available font name (such as Britannicasdfg), you can see that the browser will apply Times New Roman (or the default serif font), as shown in Figure 10-2.

Figure 10-1: Using font type, size, and color

Figure 10-2: The Britannicasdfg (non-available) font falls back to Times New Roman

Text Styles

Listing 10-2 demonstrates using the `letter-spacing`, `text-shadow`, and `word-spacing` properties.

Listing 10-2: Exercise-10-02/index.html

```
<!DOCTYPE html>
<html>
<head>
  <title>Text styling</title>
  <style>
```

```
    body {
      font-family: Verdana, Arial, sans-serif;
      font-size: 1.25em;
    }
    #obliqued {
        font-style: oblique;
     }
    #normal-styled {
      font-style: normal;
    }
    .spread-out {
      letter-spacing: 2px;
    }
    .condensed {
      letter-spacing: -1px;
      font-weight: bold;
    }
    .shadowed {
      font-size: 1.5em;
      font-weight: bold;
      text-shadow: 4px 4px 2px dimgray;
    }
    #stretched-words {
      word-spacing: 3ex;
    }
  </style>
</head>
<body>
  <p id="obliqued">
    This paragraph is displayed in italic except
    <span id="normal-styled">this</span> word.
  </p>
  <p class="spread-out">
    This text uses spread-out letter spacing,
    while
    <span class="condensed">this fragment</span>
    is condensed.
  </p>
  <p class="shadowed">
    Look at this shadowed text!
  </p>
  <p id="stretched-words">
    Lorem ipsum dolor sit amet, consectetur
    adipiscing elit fusce vel sapien elit in malesuada.
  </p>
</body>
</html>
```

This page is displayed in the browser as shown in Figure 10-3.

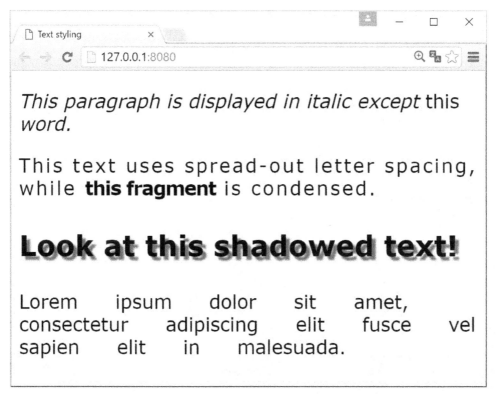

Figure 10-3: Using text styles

NOTE: The style sheet in Listing 10-2 intentionally mixes class and ID selectors, just for the sake of getting used to different selectors. Normally I would use class selectors for all styles in this sheet.

Paragraphs

You can style the outlook of paragraphs with the `line-height`, `text-align`, and `text-indent` properties, as shown in Listing 10-3.

Listing 10-3: Exercise-10-03/index.html

```
<!DOCTYPE html>
<html>
<head>
  <title>Styling paragraphs</title>
  <style>
    body {
      font-family: Verdana, Arial, sans-serif;
      margin-left: 48px;
    }
    .stretched-line {
      line-height: 200%;
```

411

```
      text-align: right;
    }
    .condensed-line {
      line-height: 90%;
      text-align: center;
    }
    .indented-line {
      text-indent: 32px;
      text-align: justify;
    }
    .outdented-line {
      text-indent: -32px;
      text-align: justify;
    }
  </style>
</head>
<body>
  <p>
    Normal line height: Lorem ipsum dolor sit
    amet, consectetur adipiscing elit fusce vel
    sapien elit in malesuada.
  </p><hr />
  <p class="stretched-line">
    Stretched line height: Lorem ipsum dolor sit
    amet, consectetur adipiscing elit fusce vel
    sapien elit in malesuada.
  </p><hr />
  <p class="condensed-line">
    Condensed line height: Lorem ipsum dolor sit
    amet, consectetur adipiscing elit fusce vel
    sapien elit in malesuada.
  </p><hr />
  <p class="indented-line">
    Indented line: Lorem ipsum dolor sit
    amet, consectetur adipiscing elit fusce vel
    sapien elit in malesuada.
  </p><hr />
  <p class="outdented-line">
    Outdented line: Lorem ipsum dolor sit
    amet, consectetur adipiscing elit fusce vel
    sapien elit in malesuada.
  </p>
</body>
</html>
```

Figure 10-4 demonstrates the effect of styles in this listing. The body style uses a 48-pixel margin at the left so that you can recognize the positive and negative indents in the last two paragraphs.

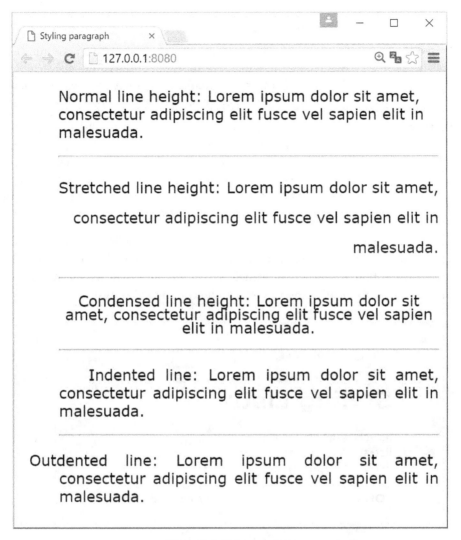

Figure 10-4: Styling paragraphs

Styling Lists

When you create lists, you can apply additional style properties, as summarized in Table 10-2.

Table 10-2: List properties

Property	Description
`list-style`	This is a shorthand notation for specifying the `list-style-type`, `list-style-image`, and `list-style-position` property values.
`list-style-image`	Specifies an image to use for a bullet in a bulleted list. Use a URL value, as you learned in *Chapter 9*.

413

Property	Description
`list-style-position`	Set this property to specify the position of bullets or numbers in a list. By default, these markers appear `outside` of the text, hanging off to the left. You can move them `inside` the text—exactly where the first letter of the first line normally begins.
`list-style-type`	With this property you can set the type of bullet for a list. Use the `disc`, `circle`, or `square` values for unordered lists, and `decimal`, `decimal-leading-zero`, `upper-alpha`, `lower-alpha`, `upper-roman`, `lower-roman`, or `lower-greek` for ordered lists. You can even turn an unordered list into an ordered list, and vice versa, by changing this property.

Instead of displaying a short code listing, I created a simple web application that you can find in the `Exercise-10-04` folder within this chapter's source code download. This app uses the same approach that you can find in Listing 9-9, namely, it dynamically builds up a style that is applied on `<ul>` and `<ol>` tags. Figure 10-5 shows the default style applied for lists.

Figure 10-5: Default style applied for lists

This app uses a shaded background to mark an ordered list (with a style rule for ol). The reason is that it clearly shows that changing the list-style-type property to a bullet type used by an unordered list visually changes an ordered list as if it were unordered, as shown in Figure 10-6. You can also see the effect of setting the list-style-position value to inside.

Figure 10-6: Changing an ordered list visually mimic an unordered list

HINT: You can also try other effects with this sample application. For example, you can set the list-style-image property to in invalid URL. In this case the bullet defined by the list-style-type is used. If you set the list-style-image property to a valid URL, it overrides the bullet set by list-style-type.

Using Web Fonts

As you learned earlier, the font-family property can be used to set the font type to be used by an HTML tag. However, there's an issue with this property: you are limited to fonts likely to have installed on the devices of your visitors. In many cases, especially if you need a unique design for a brand, it is a real and annoying limitation. With using the CSS web fonts feature, you can instruct the browser to download the font from a web server, and immediately (without installation) use it to display text on the web page.

The web font technology is designed to support a number of font formats, but as of this writing, only the WOFF (Web Open Font Format)—a kind of compressed versions of Open Type and True Type font formats—is a W3C recommendation. Nonetheless, major browsers support the OTF and TTF font types as well.

There are number of web sites that allow you to download WOFF (and other types of web fonts), such as Google Web Fonts, Fontex.org, Font Squirrel, The Open Font Library, and many others.

NOTE: Be sure to check the license of the selected font to avoid any legal issues.

To add a web font to your style sheet, use the `@font-face` at rule, as shown in Listing 10-4. This project utilizes web font files that can be found in the `Exercise-10-05/fonts` folder.

Listing 10-4: Exercise-10-05/index.html

```
<!DOCTYPE html>
<html>
<head>
  <title>Using web fonts</title>
  <style>
    @font-face {
      font-family: BPDots;
      src: url(Fonts/BPdots-webfont.woff) ;
      font-weight: normal;
    }
    @font-face {
      font-family: BPDots;
      src: url(Fonts/BPdotsBold-webfont.woff) ;
      font-weight: bold;
    }
    @font-face {
      font-family: "Cowboy Hippie Pro";
      src: url(Fonts/Cowboy_Hippie_Pro-webfont.woff) ;
    }
  </style>
  <style>
    h1 {
      font-family: "Cowboy Hippie Pro", sans-serif;
      font-size: 3em;
    }

    p {
      font-family: BPDots, sans-serif;
      font-size: 1.5em;
    }

    p.bold {
```

```
      font-weight: bold;
    }
  </style>
</head>
<body>
  <h1>This is awesome!</h1>
  <p>
    Sollicitudin urna fermentum ut fusce
    varius nisl ac ipsum gravida vel pretium
    tellus tincidunt integer eu augue augue.
  </p>
  <p class="bold">
    Sollicitudin urna fermentum ut fusce
    varius nisl ac ipsum gravida vel pretium
    tellus tincidunt integer eu augue augue.
  </p>
</body>
</html>
```

This listing contains three @font-face at-rules, each defines exactly one web font. You can use the font-family property inside @font-face to define a name for the font, and you should use this name in the font-family properties of style rules. Use the src property to specify the URL that provides access to the font file.

You can also specify other properties of the font, such as font-weight, font-style, and font-variant. The reason is that you can have a separately designed web font version for rendering the bold or italic representation.

In the listing, the first two fonts represent the regular and bold version of BPDots. They use the same font-family value, but the second definition specifies the font-weight as bold. The result is that the first paragraph will use the first web font, the second will be displayed with the second @font-face definition, as its style instructs the browser to render a boldfaced font. Figure 10-7 clearly shows how this works.

Now, you have a good understanding of styling texts. It is time to learn about an important concept, the *box model*.

The Box Model

Every content—every HTML tag—displayed in the web browser is treated as a box, independently whether you display text, image, video or whatever other content. There is a model—the *box model*— that determines how these boxes are rendered—how their size is calculated, how their content is placed, and so on. It is very important to get acquainted with this model, because it provides many fundamental details to understand how and why HTML elements are displayed in a particular web page as they are.

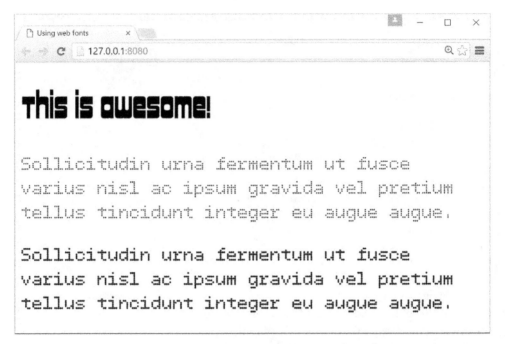

Figure 10-7: Using web fonts

The box model starts from the content, and allows you to surround it with other things. An HTML tag may have a *border*, a line that is drawn around the edges of the box. There is an optional *padding*—space—between the content and the border, for example, a frame around a photo that separates it from its border. The box may have a *background* that is displayed in the background of the content, and fills the padding area, too. You can also define a *margin* that separates the HTML tag from other tags. In most web pages you see some space between headings and paragraphs, this is generally the margin.

Figure 10-8 shows the elements of the box model. As you can see, all adornments, the margin, the border, and the padding can be defined separately for the top, right, bottom, and left edges of the box.

You can use a number of CSS properties to specify the visual properties of the box model. You can apply the `margin`, `border`, and `padding` shorthand notations to set values for the corresponding properties. If you want to deal with a specific edge of the box, you can add the `top`, `right`, `bottom`, and `left` tags to any property names (separated by a dash). For example, if you want to set the properties of the left edge of the border, use the `border-left` property. Similarly, you can specify the value of the top margin with `margin-top`.

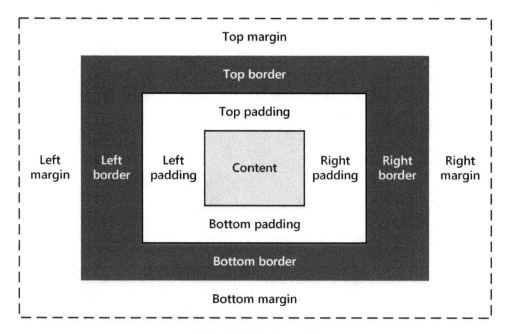

Figure 10-8: The box model

Margins and Paddings

There are several ways to specify spacing with the `margin` and `padding` properties. You can use any size type units to set these values. To demonstrate how you can set them, let's start with the page defined in Listing 10-5.

Listing 10-5: Exercise-10-06/index.html

```
<!DOCTYPE html>
<html>
<head>
  <title>Margins and paddings</title>
  <style>
    .box {
      border: 4px solid blue;
      background-color: #a0a0a0;
    }

    .spacing {
      margin: 12px;
      padding: 24px;
    }

    .content {
      width: 100px;
      height: 80px;
      background-color: red;
```

```
      }

    table {
      border-collapse: collapse;
    }

    td {
      border: 1px dashed black;
    }
  </style>
</head>
<body>
  <table>
    <tr>
      <td>
        <div class="box spacing">
          <div class="content" />
        </div>
      </td>
    </tr>
  </table>
</body>
</html>
```

The <body> of this page contains a single-cell table that marks the table cell borders with a dashed line to designate the outer edge of the box. There are two nested <div> tags in the table cell, the internal one representing the content with a red rectangle that is 100 pixels wide and 80 pixels tall (set by the .content rule). The outer <div> tag represents the box. It uses two classes, box and spacing, where the box class—through the .box rule—styles the border and background color of the tag, the .spacing rule sets up margins and paddings:

```
.spacing {
  margin: 12px;
  padding: 24px;
}
```

This specification sets all margins to 12 pixels and paddings to 24 pixels, as you can see in Figure 10-9.

Figure 10-9: Paddings and margins (1)

420

The red rectangle in the middle is the actual content, the dark blue border is the border of the box. The space between the dashed line and the border is the margin, the light grey area between the border and the content is the padding.

Change the `.spacing` rule to this:

```
.spacing {
  margin: 8px 16px;
  padding: 8px 16px 24px 32px;
}
```

Now, the page is displayed as you can see in Figure 10-10.

Figure 10-10: Paddings and margins (2)

In the `margin` property, you have used the two values that represent the vertical (top and bottom), and the horizontal (left and right) margins, respectively. The four values in `padding` specify the top, right, bottom, and left padding values, respectively. Now, change the `.spacing` rule to this:

```
.spacing {
  margin: 16px;
  margin-bottom: 32px;
  padding: 8px;
  padding-left: 32px;
}
```

The `margin` property sets all margins to 16 pixels. The `margin-bottom` property changes the bottom margin to 32px. Both properties set the bottom margin, but according to the cascade order, as you learned in *Chapter 9*, the last declaration wins, thus the bottom margin is set to 32 pixels. Should you exchange these two lines, all margins would be set to 16 pixels. With similar logic, all paddings are set to 8 pixels, except the left one which uses 32 pixels. Figure 10-11 shows the result:

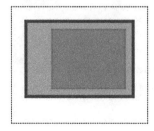

Figure 10-11: Paddings and margins (3)

Listing 10-5 uses a trick, it sets the width and height of the `<div>` element that represents the content, and utilizes the default behavior of the `<td>` tag that accommodates its size to the size of the content.

Generally, when rendering content, the width of a block element—unless specified differently—is set according to the width of the containing element. When using percentages for any of the `margin` or `padding` properties, the base of the calculation is the width of the containing element, as shown in Listing 10-6. This listing is very similar to Listing 10-5, except, that it does not use a table cell, and spacing is declared with percentage values.

Listing 10-6: Exercise-10-07/index.html

```
<!DOCTYPE html>
<html>
<head>
  <title>Spacing with percentages</title>
  <style>
    .box {
      border: 4px solid blue;
      background-color: #a0a0a0;
    }

    .spacing {
      margin: 20%;
      padding: 10%;
    }

    .content {
      height: 80px;
      background-color: red;
    }

    body {
      margin: 0;
      border: 2px dashed black;
    }
  </style>
</head>
  <body>
    <div class="box spacing">
      <div class="content"/>
    </div>
  </body>
</html>
```

As you resize the browser window, the width of the containing element (`<body>`) changes, so the margins and paddings change together with the browser window's width, as shown in Figure 10-12 and Figure 10-13.

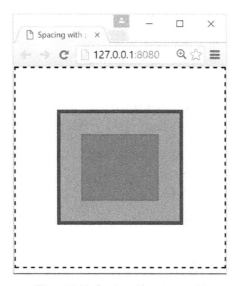

Figure 10-12: Spacing with percentages (1)

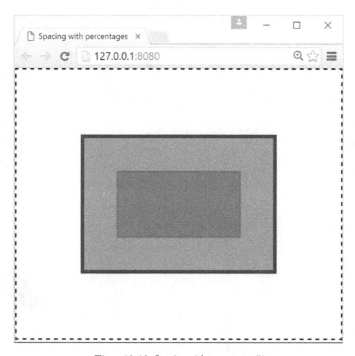

Figure 10-13: Spacing with percentages (2)

Listing 10-6 sets all margins to 20%, and all paddings to 10%. So, provided the browser window's width is 400 pixels, margins are set to 80 pixels, paddings to 40 pixels.

NOTE: Even if you specify vertical margins and paddings with percentage values, the base of their calculation is the width of the containing element, and not the height of it, as you very likely expect.

Special Behavior of Margins

CSS has a feature, called *collapsing margins*, which means that two separate margins became a single margin. Listing 10-7 shows two situations when this phenomenon occurs.

Listing 10-7: Exercise-10-08/index.html

```html
<!DOCTYPE html>
<html>
<head>
  <title>Spacing with percentages</title>
  <style>
    body {
        font-family: Verdana, Arial, sans-serif;
    }

    h1 { margin-bottom: 25px; }
    p { margin-top: 20px; }

    #warning {
      border: 2px dotted dimgray;
      padding: 8px;
    }
    h2 { margin: 16px; }
    #head {
      background-color: navy;
      color: white;
    }
    #head p { margin: 16px; }
  </style>
</head>
<body>
  <h1>Heading with margin-bottom: 25</h1>
  <p>Paragraph with margin-top: 20</p>
  <div id="warning">
    <h2>Did you know...</h2>
    <div id="head">
      <p>It is special!</p>
    </div>
    <p>
      Lorem ipsum dolor sit amet, consectetur
      adipiscing elit fusce vel sapien elit
      in malesuada semper mi, id sollicitudin.
    </p>
  </div>
</body>
</html>
```

According to the style sheet, the `<h1>` tag has a 25 pixels bottom margin, and the adjacent `<p>` tag has a 20 pixels top margin. These two are 45 pixels altogether. However, as shown in Figure 10-14, there is only a 25 pixels space between these two tags. This behavior is defined by CSS intentionally: the two margin areas are collapsed to one, keeping the bigger space—in this case 25 pixels.

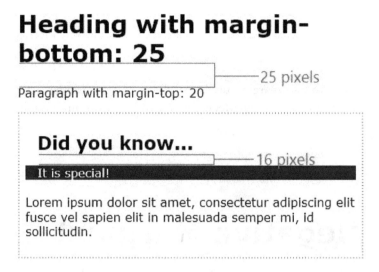

Figure 10-14: Collapsing margins

Collapsing margins may occur with non-adjacent HTML tags as well. The `<h2>` tag (with text "Did you know...") is followed by a `<div>` tag that nests a `<p>`. According to the style settings, `<h2>` has a margin of 16 pixels in all direction, the subsequent `<div>` has no margin, but the `<p>` within the `<div>` has a 16 pixels margin as well. According to the CSS specification, the rendering engine collapses the two margins (`<h2>` and `<p>`) to a single 16 pixels margin, as Figure 10-14 indicates.

Originally the designer wanted to create a thick blue margin for the "It's special" text, as shown in Figure 10-15.

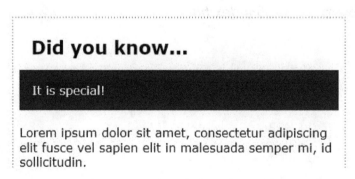

Figure 10-15: The original intention of the designer

This rendering can be achieved if the rendering engine can be prevented from collapsing the margins. It's pretty easy: You must add a 1 pixel padding between the margins to prevent collapsing them. To fix Listing 10-7, simply change the definition of the **#head** rule by adding this **padding**:

```
#head {
  background-color: navy;
  color: white;
  padding: 1px;
}
```

There is another great feature of margins: unlike paddings, margins can have negative values, and with this trick you can create nice visual effects. Figure 10-16 shows an example.

Figure 10-16: Using negative margins

The thick bluish line under the heading is actually the top border of the paragraph below. The heading has a negative margin, and this setting moves the paragraph up. Listing 10-8 shows the source of this simple page.

Listing 10-8: Exercise-10-09/index.html

```
<!DOCTYPE html>
<html>
<head>
  <title>Negative margins</title>
  <style>
    body {
      font-family: Verdana, Arial, sans-serif;
      margin-left: 16px;
    }

    h1 { margin-bottom: -28px; }

    p {
      border-top: 14px solid lightseagreen;
      padding-top: 16px;
    }
```

```
    </style>
  </head>
  <body>
    <h1>Negative Margins!</h1>
    <p>
      With negative margins, you can create great
      effects... Lorem ipsum dolor sit amet,
      consectetur adipiscing elit fusce vel sapien
    </p>
  </body>
</html>
```

Setting Up Borders

A border is simply a line that runs around an element, and it optionally can be rounded at the corners. As you already learned, you can use the `border` shorthand notation to set all edges of the box, or using `border-top`, `border-right`, `border-bottom`, or `border-left` to specify the properties of a particular edge. When setting up the edges of the border, you can specify three individual properties: `color`, `width`, and `style`. To make the setup a bit more complicated, you can specify these attributes with other notations. For example, you can specify the border width of all edges with `border-width`:

```
h1 { border-width: 4px; }
```

Similarly, you can use the `border-color`, and `border-style` properties:

```
h2 {
  border-style: dotted;
  border-color: fuchsia;
  }
```

If you want, you can specify any of these attributes for a specific edge. For example, you can set the color of the left border to red:

```
h3 { border-left-color: red; }
```

When using any shorthand notation, you can specify the `color`, `width` and `style` properties in any order. Moreover, you can optionally leave any of them: the CSS parser is smart enough to infer your intention from the values you specified.

You can use any valid color values for the `color`, and any valid size value for the `width` property. The `style` property determines the line style used to draw the border, and it can be any of the following values: `solid`, `dashed`, `dotted`, `double`, `groove`, `inset`, `outset`, `ridge`, and `none`. The `none` value removes the border.

When setting up border properties, do not forget about the cascade order: if a certain property is specified by multiple declarations in the same rule, the last will win. Take a look at this rule:

```
p {
  border: 3px solid blue;
  border-width: 4px;
```

```
    border-color: red;
    border-top: 2px solid green;
}
```

It will result a four pixels wide solid red border around the paragraph, except the top edge, which is a two pixels wide solid green border. Why? Although the `border` declaration set a 3-pixel solid blue border, the `border-width` declaration set it to four pixels wide, and `border-color` changes all edges to red. At this point, all border edges are four pixels wide solid red ones. The `border-top` declaration keeps all edge properties, except the top edge that becomes two pixels wide and green.

Listing 10-9 shows a simple code that displays four border styles. This example is really simple, and thus you do not need any further explanation. You can also try to modify it in order to display the remaining border styles (`groove`, `inset`, `outset`, and `ridge`).

Listing 10-9: Exercise-10-10/index.html

```html
<!DOCTYPE html>
<html>
<head>
  <title>Using borders</title>
  <style>
    body {
        font-family: Verdana, Arial, sans-serif;
    }

    .box {
      margin: 16px;
      padding: 16px;
      border: 8px solid blue;
      display: inline-block;
    }

    .content {
      width: 100px;
      height: 80px;
      text-align: center;
    }
  </style>
</head>
<body>
  <div class="box" style="border-style: solid">
    <div class="content">solid</div>
  </div>
  <div class="box" style="border-style: dashed">
    <div class="content">dashed</div>
  </div>
  <div class="box" style="border-style: dotted">
    <div class="content">dotted</div>
  </div>
  <div class="box" style="border-style: double">
    <div class="content">double</div>
```

```
    </div>
  </body>
</html>
```

NOTE: The `display` property set in the `.box` rule may seem unfamiliar to you. Soon, you'll learn more about it.

This code displays the page shown in Figure 10-17.

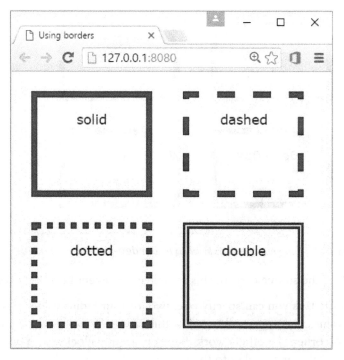

Figure 10-17: A few border styles

By default, all borders have angular (square) corners, but you can change them to rounded corners with the `border-radius` property. This property is a shorthand that can be used to set up the rounding style for all corners. You can set up the rounding with a single corner using one of the following properties: `border-top-left-radius`, `border-top-right-radius`, `border-bottom-right-radius`, and `border-bottom-left-radius`. Each corner can be circular or elliptical.

Figure 10-18 demonstrates a few settings of `border-top-left-radius`. The two borders in the first row are circular, because they use `20px`, and `40px` settings, so the radius of the corner is set to 20 pixels and 40 pixels, respectively. In the second row, the borders are elliptical. The first border specifies two radii, 80 pixels and 40 pixels, so an arch of a 160 pixels wide and 80 pixels tall ellipse is used to round the corner. The second border in the second row uses 50% for radius, and because the box is rectangular (not square), it will use different horizontal and vertical radius values.

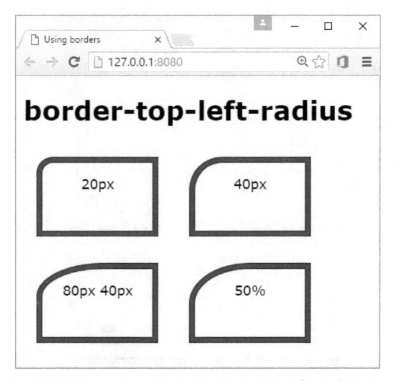

Figure 10-18: Using rounded corners by setting the **border-top-left-radius** *property*

NOTE: You can find the source code of this sample in the **Exercise-10-11** folder.

When using **border-radius** you can specify one, two, or four radius value. If you set up this property with one value, all corners will be set to this radius. If you specify four values, the first specifies the top-left corner, the others work their way around clockwise. You can also supply two values, and in this case the first applies to the top-left and bottom-right corners, the second applies to the remaining two corners. If you want to use elliptical corner with fixed size units (pixel, inches, ems, etc.) you can specify two of them separated with a slash, such as **40px/80px**. Figure 10-19 shows a few examples of setting up the **border-radius** property.

NOTE: You can find the source code of this sample in the **Exercise-10-12** folder.

Height and Width of the Box

Normally, the browser calculates the width of a box from the width of its container. From the width of the box, the content width is calculated by subtracting the sizes of these six elements: the left margin, the left border, the left padding, the right padding, the right border, and finally the right margin. For all direct children of the **<body>** tag, the width of the container is the browser window's width.

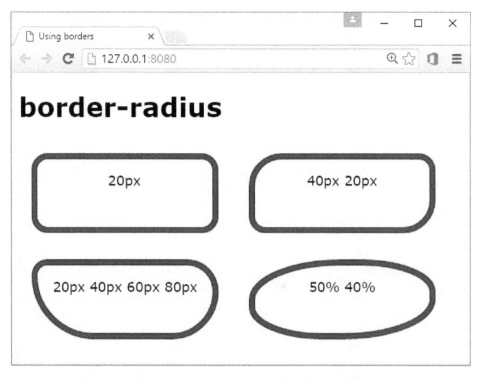

Figure 10-19: Using rounded corners by setting the **border-radius** *property*

Let's make an example calculation. Assume, we have an <h1> tag nested directly into <body>, and the style sheet defines this rule:

```
h1 {
  margin: 20px;
  border-left: 8px;
  border-right: 16px;
  padding: 12px;
}
```

If the browser window's width is 1000 pixels, the width of the <h1> tag is **1000-20-8-12-12-16-20 = 912** pixels.

The height of the box is calculated from the height of the content by adding to it the sizes of the following six elements: the top margin, the top border, the top padding, the bottom padding, the bottom border, and finally, the bottom margin. Now, let's make a calculation for the same <h1> tag we used before, provided, the browser window's width is 1000 pixels, the height of the <h1> tag's content is 80 pixels, and the style sheet defines this rule:

```
h1 {
  margin: 5%;
  border: 8px;
  padding: 12px;
}
```

Because the margin is defined in percentages, the real size is the 5% of the browser window's width, namely 50 pixels. The height of the `<h1>` box is `80+50+8+12+12+8+50` = `220` pixels.

If you need, you can specify the size of the box explicitly with the `height` and `width` properties, such as shown in Listing 10-10.

NOTE: You cannot control the size of inline elements.

Listing 10-10: Exercise-10-13/index.html

```
<!DOCTYPE html>
<html>
<head>
  <title>Explicit box size</title>
  <style>
    .sizedbox {
      width: 200px;
      height: 100px;
      background-color: yellow;
      border: 2px solid black;
      padding: 12px;
      margin: 4px;
      font-size: 2em;
    }
  </style>
</head>
<body>
  <div class="sizedbox">
    This content does not really
    fit into the box, it overflows...
  </div>
  <div class="sizedbox"></div>
</body>
</html>
```

This simple markup uses two `<div>` tags and set their contents to 200 pixels wide 100 pixels tall. According to the margin, border, and padding settings, each box around its content is 236 pixels wide and 136 pixels tall. Figure 10-20 uncovers an issue related to the explicit size: the content of the first box is too big, so it overflows the box.

This is a common issue. Normally, the browser adjusts the size (generally the height) of the box so that the content can fit within the box. However, when you set the box size explicitly, you lose this convenient feature.

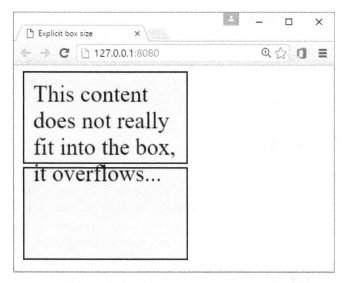

Figure 10-20: Explicit box sizing: the content overflows

Fortunately, with the `overflow` property, you can control what a browser should do in this situation. Specify the `visible` value (this is the default) to let the browser do its normal rendering. Set the property value to `hidden` to hide any content outside of the box. Using the `scroll` value, the box gets a scrollbar and you'll be able to scroll the content within the box. The `auto` value checks if the content fits into the box, and automatically uses the `scroll` value, if it overflows. Figure 10-21 demonstrates these settings.

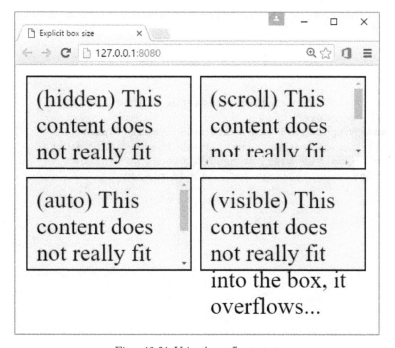

Figure 10-21: Using the overflow property

NOTE: You can find the source code listing in the `Exercise-10-14` folder.

In many cases, you need a bit more flexibility between letting the browser size the box, or set the box dimensions explicitly. You can add this flexibility by setting minimum and maximum heights and widths with the `min-height`, `max-height`, `min-width`, and `max-width` properties. These settings let the browser size the box between the size limits you specify.

Boxing Inline Elements

Inline elements are handled another way than block elements, and this is why you cannot set their size explicitly—or if you set, those size properties are ignored. However, you can still apply the box model properties (`margin`, `border`, and `padding`), but they generally provide a different result than you expect. Take a look at Listing 10-11, which defines box model properties for an inline `<span>` tag, and then, in Figure 10-22, check how this markup is rendered.

Listing 10-11: Exercise-10-15/index.html

```
<!DOCTYPE html>
<html>
<head>
  <title>Explicit box size</title>
  <style>
    .highligted {
      margin: 24px;
      border: 2px solid darkgray;
      background-color: yellow;
      padding: 24px;
    }
  </style>
</head>
<body>
  <p>
    Lorem ipsum dolor sit amet, consectetur adipiscing
    elit fusce vel sapien elit
    <span class="highligted">in malesuada semper</span>
    mi, id sollicitudin urna fermentum ut fusce varius nisl
    ac ipsum gravida vel pretium tellus tincidunt integer
    eu augue augue nunc elit dolor, luctus placerat
  </p>
</body>
</html>
```

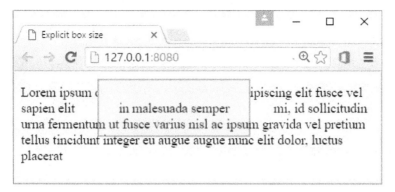

Figure 10-22: Boxes with inline elements

This unexpected behavior is a direct result of the rendering algorithm used by the browser. Inline elements are rendered line by line, and lines are calculated according to the width of the browser window. When calculating the height of an inline element, the `margin`, `border`, and `spacing` properties are ignored, so the browser does not take into account the box properties of the "in malesuada semper" `<span>` tag. Nonetheless, the calculation of width takes these properties into account, and also, the box with the border and padding area is drawn when the `<span>` is displayed.

The first line is rendered before the `<span>` tag, so it is covered by the box that is drawn together with the second line. However, the third line is drawn after the second line, so it is stacked upon the box already drawn.

Using Floating Elements

The browser renders the elements of a HTML page with flowing layout. It means, that it places the inline elements from left to right, and when it is necessary (for example the next word of a paragraph does not fit in the line), it starts a new line. Block elements are rendered from the top of the window down to the bottom.

You can change this behavior with the `float` property. Setting its value to `left` or `right` moves the related block element to the left or to the right, and the subsequent content wraps around the floating element. Listing 10-12 shows a simple web page that does not contain floating elements, it is displayed in Figure 10-23.

Listing 10-12: Exercise-10-16/index.html

```
<!DOCTYPE html>
<html>
<head>
  <title>Using floating elements</title>
  <style>
    body {
      font-family: Verdana, Arial, sans-serif;
      margin: 16px;
```

```
      }

      .image {
        width: 120px;
        height: 90px;
        margin-left: 8px;
        margin-bottom: 8px;
        border: 2px solid dimgray;
        background-color: lightgreen;
        /*float: right;*/
      }

      .sidebar {
        width: 240px;
        margin-right: 8px;
        margin-bottom: 8px;
        border: 2px solid dimgray;
        background-color: lightskyblue;
        padding: 0 8px;
        /*float: left;*/
      }

      .sidebar h2 { margin: 8px; }
    </style>
  </head>
  <body>
    <div class="image"></div>
    <aside class="sidebar">
      <h2>Did you know?</h2>
      <p>
        HTML block elements can be set to float
        at the left or at the right edge of
        the page
      </p>
    </aside>
    <p>
      Lorem ipsum dolor sit amet, consectetur
      <!-- lorem ipsum text omitted -->
    </p>
  </body>
</html>
```

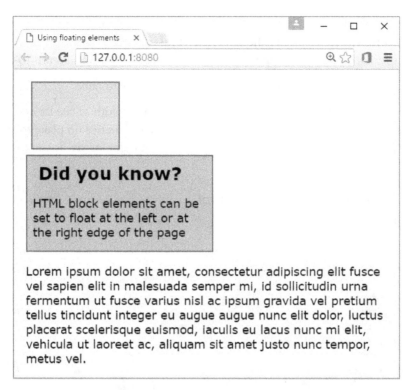

Figure 10-23: Page with three block elements

This page contains three block elements (`<div>`, `<aside>`, and `<p>`), and by the standard rendering algorithm they are placed from top to bottom, each block element starting from the left.

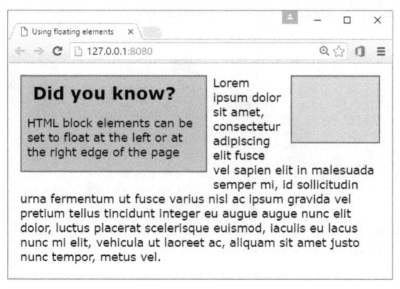

Figure 10-24: Page with floating elements

Now, if you uncomment the **float** properties in the code listing, the layout of the page changes. The first empty box (**<div>**) moves to the right, the "Did you know" sidebar (**<aside>**) moves to left, and the "Lorem ipsum" paragraph wraps around them, as shown in Figure 10-24.

NOTE: You can turn off floating by setting the **float** property to none.

When multiple elements float, the rendering engine fills up the width of the browser window as it places the HTML elements in their order in the markup. When there's no place for the next element, a new line is started. Take a look at Listing 10-13, it contains six floating elements, three moved to the left, and three moved to the right.

Listing 10-13: Exercise-10-17/index.html

```
<!DOCTYPE html>
<html>
<head>
  <title>Explicit box size</title>
  <style>
    .left, .right {
      margin: 4px;
      background-color: lightgray;
      border: 2px solid blue;
      width: 80px;
      height: 60px;
    }

    .left { float: left; }

    .right {
      float: right;
      border-radius: 10px;
      height: 70px;
    }
  </style>
</head>
<body>
  <div class="left"></div>
  <div class="left"></div>
  <div class="right"></div>
  <div class="right"></div>
  <div class="left"></div>
  <div class="right"></div>
</body>
</html>
```

Figure 10-25 shows three different snapshots of the page while the user resizes the browser window. Try to trace, how the rendering engine displays each of these snapshots!

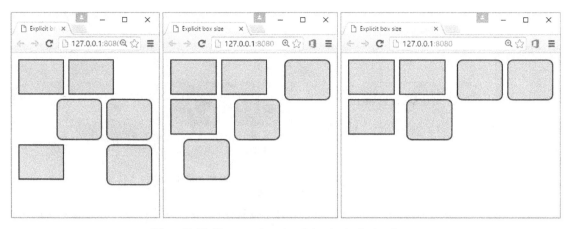

Figure 10-25: Three snapshots of rendering the six floating elements

NOTE: Inline elements cannot float.

Sometimes, you need more control on how the floating elements are wrapped around with other content. Although the non-floating elements' content wrap around the floating elements, borders and background colors do not, they use the full width of the containing element. For example, if you add an <h1> element to Listing 10-12, right before the <p> tag, it may be displayed as shown in Figure 10-26.

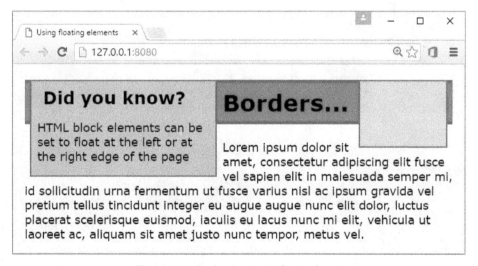

Figure 10-26: Borders do not wrap floating elements

This is not the behavior you expect, since you do not need the border behind the floating elements. The **overflow** property is to help you: set it to **hidden** for the heading tag that represents "Borders…", and you'll get exactly what you want, as shown in Figure 10-27.

Figure 10-27: The effect of the `overflow: hidden;` *property declaration*

NOTE: You can find the source code for Figure 10-26 and Figure 10-27 in the `Exercise-10-18` and `Exercise-10-19` folders, respectively.

Although wrapping around floating elements is a very useful feature of the browser, there are situations when you want to get rid of it for specific elements. Listing 10-14 demonstrates such a situation.

Listing 10-14: Exercise-10-20/index.html

```
<!DOCTYPE html>
<html>
<head>
  <title>Floating mess</title>
  <style>
    body {
      font-family: Verdana, Arial, sans-serif;
      margin: 16px;
    }

    .image {
      width: 120px;
      height: 90px;
      margin-left: 8px;
      margin-bottom: 8px;
      border: 2px solid dimgray;
      background-color: lightgreen;
      float: left;
    }

  </style>
</head>
<body>
```

```
<div class="image"></div>
<p>
  Lorem ipsum dolor sit amet, consectetur
  adipiscing elit fusce vel sapien elit
</p>
<div class="image"></div>
<p>
  Gravida vel pretium tellus tincidunt integer
  eu augue augue nunc elit dolor, luctus
  placerat scelerisque euismod, iaculis eu.
</p>
</body>
</html>
```

The `<body>` section contains two content parts, each composed from a `<div>` with a subsequent paragraph. The `<div>` tag represents a thumbnail image, the `<p>` tag is intended to contain some text related to the thumbnail. The `<div>` tags are set to float to left so that the explaining text appears to the right of the thumbnail. However, what this page displays, is not really what you expect, as shown in Figure 10-28. Because the text wrapping around the first thumbnail is short, the second thumbnail also wraps the first thumbnail.

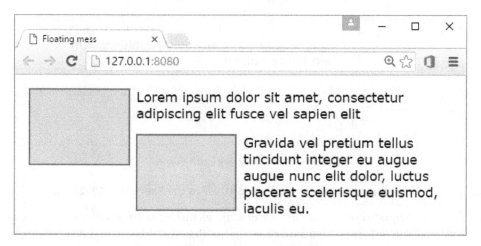

Figure 10-28: Floating elements make this page messy

You can use the `clear` property to instruct the browser to not wrap around any floated element. It can set one of the `left`, `right`, `both`, or `none` values. Use `left` to drop below elements that are floated left but you intend still wrap around right-floated objects. When you set this value to `right`, the rendering engine drops below right-floated objects but still wraps around left-floated objects. As you expect, the `both` value forces a drop below both left-floated and right-floated elements. You can turn off clearing with `none`; this is the default value of this property.

To fix the issue with Listing 10-14, add the `clear` property with `left` value to the `.image` rule:

```
.image {
  width: 120px;
  height: 90px;
  margin-right: 8px;
  margin-bottom: 8px;
  border: 2px solid dimgray;
  background-color: lightgreen;
  float: left;
  clear: left;
}
```

The result is shown in Figure 10-29. As you see, it aligned the thumbnails to the left, and let the text wrap around them.

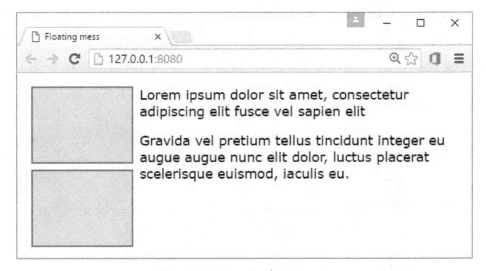

Figure 10-29: Using the `clear` *property*

NOTE: You can find the source code for Figure 10-29 in the `Exercise-10-21` folder.

You can use percentages to set up the size of floating elements, but sometimes you may be surprised. Take a look at Listing 10-15 that sets up the floating boxes with a 33% width, so three of them can fit in the browser window's width.

Listing 10-15: Exercise-10-22/index.html

```
<!DOCTYPE html>
<html>
<head>
  <title>Floating boxes</title>
  <style>
    body {
      font-family: Verdana, Arial, sans-serif;
      margin: 16px;
    }
    .box {
```

```
      width: 33%;
      height: 80px;
      float: left;
   }
   .red { background-color: red; }
   .green { background-color: green; }
   .blue { background-color: blue; }
  </style>
</head>
<body>
  <div class="red box"></div>
  <div class="green box"></div>
  <div class="blue box"></div>
</body>
</html>
```

When you display this page, you will see the three boxes in a single row, as shown in the left pane of Figure 10-30. However, when you add a border to the .box rule (for example, border: 2px solid lightgray), only two boxes fit in the first row, the third one drops below to the second row, as the right pane shows.

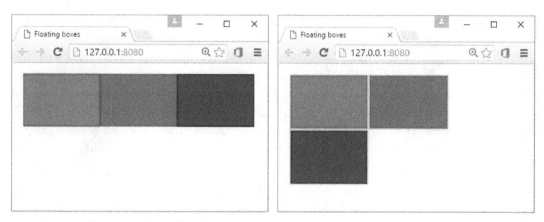

Figure 10-30: Left—Three boxes fit in a single row. Right—Borders drop the third box below

This phenomenon is not a bug. This is how the browser works by default. As you remember, when you specify percentages, the width of the content is calculated from the width of the containing element (in this case, the browser window's width). While there is no border, three boxes fit in a single row (each has a width of 33%). However, with the borders that add extra width to the boxes, only two fits in the first line.

You can instruct the browser to use a different sizing mode. With the box-sizing property, you can change the default content-box option (the browser calculates the content's width, and then adds border and padding widths) to border-box (the borders and paddings are also taken into account when calculating the width).

So, if you add the box-sizing: border-box property declaration to the .box rule in Listing 10-15, It will fix the sizing issue, and the three boxes with borders will fit in a single row.

To make sure the `box-sizing` setting works in all of those browsers as well, you should write three declarations like this:

```
-moz-box-sizing: border-box;
-webkit-box-sizing: border-box;
box-sizing: border-box;
```

Now, you have learned all important details about the box model, it is time to get acquainted with adding graphics to your web pages.

Using Background Images

At the very beginning of this book, in *Chapter 2*, you learned about the `<img>` tag that can be used to add graphics to you web pages. Since that, you already met many simple tricks to use images, you even created small interactions using JavaScript. CSS also helps you add powerful visual elements and effect with images—and goes far beyond the features of the `<img>` tag. In this section you will get to know a number of CSS features based on graphics and images.

The samples can be found within the `Exercise-10-23` folder, these are in the `Sample1.html`, `Sample2.html`, ..., `Sample14.html` files. The `index.html` file contains a list of links to access them.

Specifying Background Images

You know that the `background-color` property sets the color of an HTML element's background. You have many other properties with the `background-` prefix—`background` can be used as a shorthand notation to set a number of other background properties—, the `background-image` can be set to specify an image to be displayed in the background of an HTML element.

Figure 10-31 shows a sample that uses the following style rule to define the background of the page:

```
body {
  background-image: url(Backgrounds/spaceneedle.jpg)
}
```

This image contains only one instance of the Space Needle; it is tiled on the screen by the browser—this is the default appearance of background images.

You can turn off tiling by setting the `background-repeat` property (Figure 10-32):

```
body {
  background-image: url(Backgrounds/sandwaves.jpg);
  background-repeat: no-repeat;
}
```

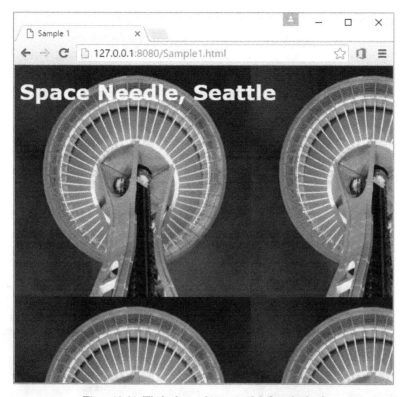

Figure 10-31: The background image is tiled (Sample1.html)

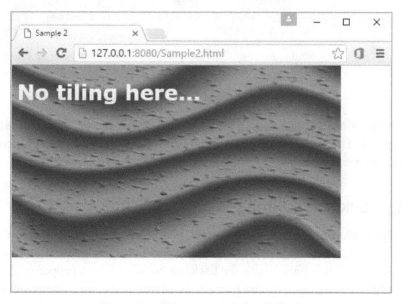

Figure 10-32: Tiling is turned off (Sample2.html)

The background-repeat property can have the repeat (tile vertically and horizontally), repeat-x (tile only horizontally), repeat-y (tile only vertically), and no-repeat (stop tiling) values. You can create nice effects by using `repeat-x`, or `repeat-y`. The left pane in Figure 10-33 uses `repeat-x`, while the right pane applies `repeat-y`:

```
/* Left pane */
body {
  background-image: url(Backgrounds/yellowrice-horizontal.gif);
  background-repeat: repeat-x;
  background-color: lightgreen;
}
/* ... */

/* Right pane */
body {
  background-image: url(Backgrounds/yellowrice-vertical.gif);
  background-repeat: repeat-y;
  background-color: lightgreen;
}
```

Figure 10-33: Left—Using repeat-x (Sample3.html). Right—Using repeat-y (Sampl4.html)

As you can see from the `body` style rules, the `background-image` and `background-color` properties can be used together. The `background-color` is applied for the whole `<body>` element, and then it is overlaid with `background-image`.

Positioning Background Images

By default, background images scroll together with their parent elements. So, if you have a page that can be vertically scrolled, the background image moves with the page while you scroll up and down. You can change this behavior with the `background-attachment` property. This property can have one of these values: `scroll` (the background scrolls along with the element, this is default), `fixed` (the background is fixed with regard to the current browser window), and `local` (the background scrolls along with the element's contents). Figure 10-34 shows the difference between the `scroll` and `fixed` values.

Figure 10-34: Left–The normal position (Sample5.html). Middle–The page is scrolled (Sample5.html). Right–The page is scrolled with background-attachment set to fixed (Sample6.html)

In most webpages, you need more control on positioning background images. The `background-position` property provides you three ways to place these images. First, you can specify horizontal and vertical alignment values. Second, you can define exact positions, and last, you can use percentage vales. Let's see how these methods work.

You can use the horizontal alignment values (`left`, `center`, and `right`) in pair with vertical alignment values (`top`, `center`, `bottom`) to place the background image to the specified screen position. When you want to position the background image to the top right corner, set background-position like this:

```
background-position: top right;
```

You can see the result of this positioning in Figure 10-35.

Figure 10-35: The background image is put to the top right position (Sample7.html)

If you intend to put the image into the browser window's center, use this setting:

```
background-position: center center;
```

However, to be able to position the image vertically, you must set the `background-attachment` property to fixed; otherwise the vertical position is set to `top`, even if you specify `center` or `bottom`. Figure 10-36 demonstrates this situation. Both panes set `background-position` to `center center`, but the right pane uses `fixed` for `background-attachment`.

447

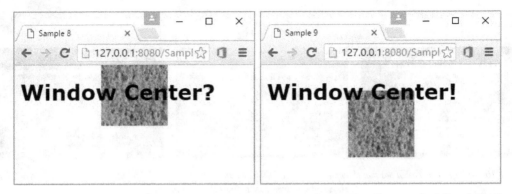

Figure 10-36: Left—The vertical centering does not work (Sample8.html). Right—Now, the issue is fixed (Sample9.html)

You can apply exact sizes (pixels, inches, ems, etc.) to set the left and top position of the background image's top-left pixel. For example, the `Sample10.html` file uses this position setting to produce the result shown in Figure 10-37:

```
background-position: 36px 56px;
```

Figure 10-37: Using precise background image positions (Sample10.html)

Instead of precise positions, you can apply percentage values, for example, you can put the background image into the center of the browser window with these property settings:

```
background-position: 50% 50%;
background-attachment: fixed;
```

If you check how the "50% 50%" setting puts the background image into the center of the screen (Figure 10-38), you must recognize something strange. If the "50% 50%" setting positions the top-left pixel of the screen to the center of the window, the background image is not centered. It would be only if the center pixel of the image would be positioned to the window's center. Well, this is exactly what "50% 50%" does!

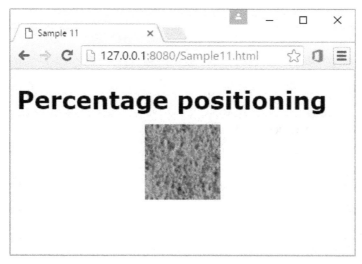

Figure 10-38: Using percentage positioning, "50% 50% (Sample11.html)

When you use percentage values, the specified values are used to calculate two positions. First, these values are used to calculate the image's pin position; second, the pin position of the background is calculated. Then the browser moves the background image so that the image's pin position will be right above the background pin position. If you're a bit confused, the following example will help:

Let's assume that you have a background image with a size of 100*80 pixels (width * height). You position this image to the "20% 40%" position in the browser window, which is 800*600 pixels. The pin position of the image is (100, 80) * "20% 40%" = (100*20%, 80*40%) = (20, 32). The pin position of the background is (800, 600) * "20% 40%" = (800*20%, 600*40%) = (160, 240). When you move the image's pin position to the background's pin position, it means that the image's top-left corner is (160, 240) – (20, 32) = (160-20, 240-32) = (140, 208). Figure 10-39 demonstrates this calculation for better understanding.

Aligning Background Images with Borders and Paddings

When you use background images with elements that have paddings and borders, there are a few issues that should be taken into account. Sometimes you need a pixel-precise design, and it does matter how your background image is aligned to its context. With the `background-origin` property, you can specify whether image is aligned with the full box containing the border and paddings around the context (`border-box`), or with the padding (`padding-box`, this is the default). If you need, you may align the image with the content (`content-box`). An example of each setting is shown in Figure 10-40. The background image (that is repeated vertically and horizontally) is the bordered square with a filled circle within. In the figure, you can observe, how the top-left corner of the square is aligned with the boxes, depending on the value of `background-origin`.

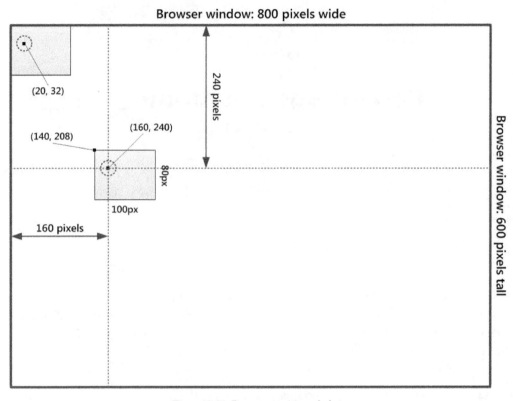

Figure 10-39: Percentage position calculation

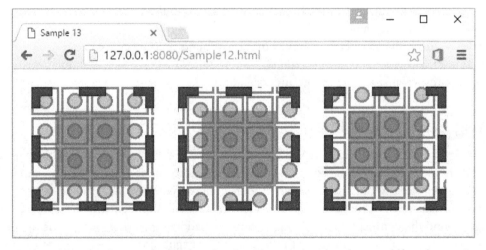

Figure 10-40: Using different **background-origin** *values, from left to right:* **border-box**, **padding-box**, *and* **content-box** *(Sample12.html)*

With the **background-clip** property you can limit the area where the background image appears. You can use the same values as with **background-origin** to specify where the image appears.

Figure 10-41 shows each `background-clip` settings while using the default `background-origin` setting, `padding-box`.

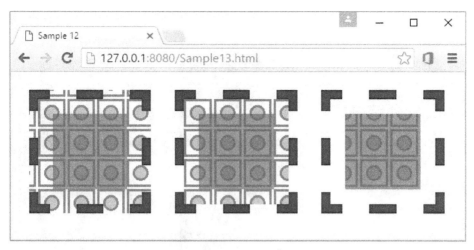

Figure 10-41: Using different `background-clip` values, from left to right: `border-box`, `padding-box`, and `content-box` (Sample13.html)

Sizing Background Images

All background images are displayed at the size you created them. This kind of sizing does not fit for every situation, and you need more control to handle the displayed size of the image. The `background-size` property is the tool you can use in such situations. You can use the `cover` or `contain` keyword, specify exact pixel sizes, or use percentage values, such as in these samples:

```
background-size: cover;
background-size: contain;
background-size: 80px 120px;
background-size: 100% 100%;
background-size: 66% auto;
```

The `cover` value scales the background image to be as large as possible so that the background area is completely covered by the background image. With this method, some parts of the background image may be hidden. The `contain` value scales the image to the largest size such that both its width and its height can fit inside the content area. Both values keep the aspect ratio of the image. The first two elements in Figure 10-42 use `cover` and `contain`. When you specify exact pixel values (width and height)—or other fixed size units, such as ems or inches—, the image is resized to the specified size. For example, the third picture in the first row in Figure 10-42 uses exact pixel values ("80px 120px").

You can specify percentage values, too. In this case, the width and height of the background image is set in percent of the parent element's width or height. The first value sets the width, while the second value sets the height. You can set any of the values to `auto`, to size the picture with keeping the aspect ratio. The second row of Figure 10-42 shows percentage value examples.

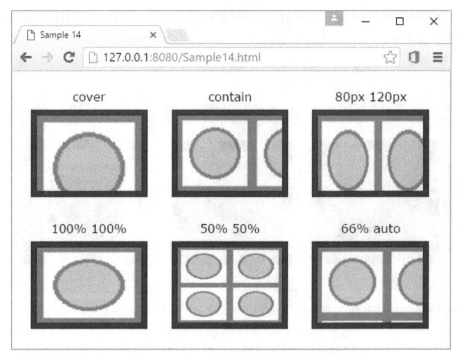

Figure 10-42: Using the background-size property (Sample14.html)

The Background Shorthand Notation

In this section you have learned a number of background image related properties. With the background shorthand notation, you can combine multiple properties—background-image, background-color, background-position, background-repeat, background-size, background-attachment, background-origin, and background-clip—into a single declaration. Let's assume you have the following declaration:

```
.box {
  background-color: red;
  background-image: url(Backgrounds/spaceneedle.jpg);
  background-position: top center;
  background-repeat: no-repeat;
  background-origin: content-box;
  background-clip: border-box;
  float: left;
  padding: 20px;
  border: 8px solid orangered;
  margin: 16px;
}
```

You can collapse the highlighted properties into one declaration using background:

```
.box {
  background: red url(Backgrounds/spaceneedle.jpg)
    top center no-repeat content-box border-box;
```

452

```
  float: left;
  padding: 20px;
  border: 8px solid orangered;
  margin: 16px;
}
```

You do not need to specify all the property values; you can use one or any combination of them.

Styling Tables

In *Chapter 3*, you learned that HTML tables were used for a long time to establish table layout. You also learned that in HTML5 tables should be used for what they were created: to display tabular data. In this section, you are going to learn a few basic things to style your tables with CSS.

In order to demonstrate the fundamentals, you are about to get to know, you will start from a simple, unformatted table that can be found in the `Exercise-10-24` folder. This project displays a three-column table, as shown in Figure 10-43.

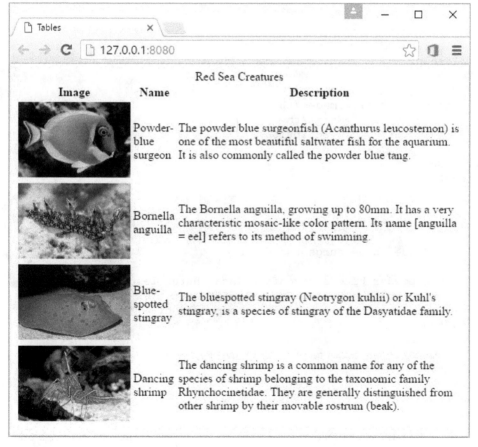

Figure 10-43: A simple table to start from

NOTE: In this section, you will learn only a few new CSS properties. The emphasis of this section is on the easiness of combining separate CSS features into a nice design by only modifying the style sheet, as you will experience soon.

The only thing that saves this table from being boring is the set of pictures in the first column, and frankly, it needs a few steps to give it a neat design. Just for a short recap, Listing 10-16 shows the HTML markup for this table.

Listing 10-16: Exercise-10-24/index.html

```html
<!DOCTYPE html>
<html>
<head>
  <title>Tables</title>
  <link href="style.css" rel="stylesheet" />
</head>
<body>
  <table>
    <caption >Red Sea Creatures</caption>
    <colgroup>
      <col class="name" />
      <col class="image" />
      <col class="desrc" />
    </colgroup>
    <thead>
      <tr>
        <th scope="col">Image</th>
        <th scope="col">Name</th>
        <th scope="col">Description</th>
      </tr>
    </thead>
    <tbody>
      <tr>
        <td>
          <img src="Images/fish_001.jpg" width="150" height="100" />
        </td>
        <td>Powder-blue surgeon</td>
        <td>
          The powder blue surgeonfish (Acanthurus leucosternon)
          is one of the most beautiful saltwater fish for the aquarium.
          It is also commonly called the powder blue tang.
        </td>
      </tr>
      <!-- Other rows are omitted for brevity -->
    </tbody>
  </table>
</body>
</html>
```

The content of the table is wrapped into the `<table>` tag, where `<caption>` defines a title for the table, `<colgroup>` lists column definitions. The header section of the table is wrapped into the

`<thead>` element, while the real data behind the table is nested into `<tbody>`. As you see from Listing 10-16, the `index.html` file links the `style.css` style sheet, so during the styling you have to add all rules to the `style.css` file.

Basic Font and Colors

Let's assume that a designer created a basic typography for your table, and she suggested to use the "Segoe UI Light" font for standard text elements, and "Segoe UI Semibold" for strong text. The designer also collected a number of colors, the shades of blue, which is a perfect accompanying set for the ocean theme. None of these colors have standard name in the CSS palette, so the designer listed them by their fantasy name and the six-digit hexadecimal code: "Sky Blue Midnight" (`#07093D`, for dark backgrounds), "High Sky Blue" (`#107FC9`, for highlighted backgrounds), and for the alternating table rows "Threadless light" (`#9CC4E4`), and "Threadless box" (`#E9F2F9`).

Let's start applying the font settings! Basically you have two options. Because the page you are about to style contains only the table, it seems to be a good choice to set the font through the body rule, like this:

```
body {
  font-family: "Segoe UI", Arial, sans-serif;
}
```

However, if later you will add some other information to the page, such as headings and text, then those will use this font setting by default. It seems a better idea to add the `font-family` style to the table rule:

```
table {
  font-family: "Segoe UI", Arial, sans-serif;
}
```

Because this table is special (it contains fish pictures), the best thing is to define a class for the table in the `index.html` file, like this:

```
<body>
  <table class="fish-table">
  <!-- ... -->
  </table>
</body>
```

Now, you can add the font-family setting to the right style rule, to `.fish-table`:

```
.fish-table {
  font-family: "Segoe UI", Arial, sans-serif;
}
```

Specifying Borders and Paddings

To emphasize the content of the table, you need to create borders. Generally, when you are about to define border style, you must specify borders for the entire table, and for individual cells, which might be declared with `<td>` and `<th>` tags. Now, let's forget about `<th>` cells, and define the table and cell border using the "Sky Blue Midnight" color, by adding the highlighted rule and property declarations to the style sheet:

```
.fish-table {
  border: 2px solid #07093D;
  font-family: "Segoe UI", Arial, sans-serif;
}
.fish-table td {
  border: 1px solid #07093D;
  border-left: 0;
  border-right: 0;
}
```

You expect a table that has an outer border, and borders for each row, but no lines separating the cells in the same row. Nonetheless, the table displayed in the browser looks a bit weird, as shown in Figure 10-44.

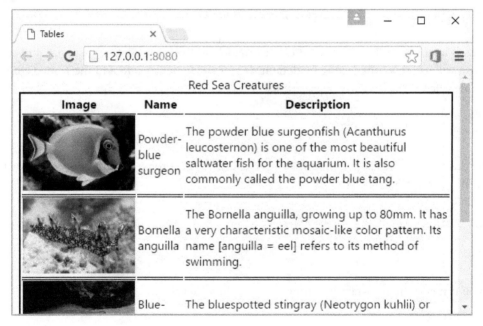

Figure 10-44: Borders between rows seems a bit weird

NOTE: See the source code in the `Exercise-10-25` folder.

The reason of this phenomenon is that by default there is spacing among the cell borders. You can set this through the `border-spacing` property. If you want to remove this spacing, set `border-spacing` to zero, like this:

```
.fish-table {
  border: 2px solid #07093D;
  border-spacing: 0;
  font-family: "Segoe UI", Arial, sans-serif;
}
```

If you look at the table borders, you can observe that the spacing between the row borders have been moved away. However, each cell has its own top and bottom border separately, and instead of displaying a single line, you may see double lines separating rows. To fix this issue, use the `border-collapse` property. The default value is `separated` (adjacent borders are drawn separately with the border spacing specified), but you can use `collapse` to draw adjacent borders as a single border. So change the definition of `.fish-table` like this:

```
.fish-table {
  border: 2px solid #07093D;
  border-collapse: collapse;
  font-family: "Segoe UI", Arial, sans-serif;
}
```

This will fix the issues with cell borders, as shown in Figure 10-45.

NOTE: See the source code in the `Exercise-10-26` folder.

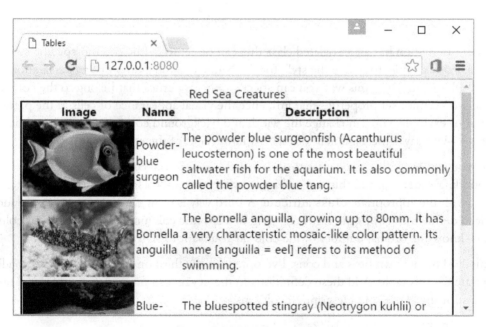

Figure 10-45: Border issues fixed

NOTE: There is an `empty-cells` property that can be set to `hide` or `show`. When set to `hide`, no background or borders are shown around empty cells.

When you look at Figure 10-45, you see that images are very close to borders and texts in adjacent cells. As you already learned, you can add paddings to cells. Apply these settings to table cells (`td` style):

```
.fish-table td {
  border: 1px solid #07093D;
  border-left: 0;
  border-right: 0;
  padding: 0.25em 0.5em;
}
```

Adjusting Text

To emphasize textual information in the fish catalog table, the `Name` columns should be stronger than the `Description` column. To style columns, you have a few ways. First, you can assign a class to columns defined for the table. If you open the `index.html` file, you can see that the table definition contains a `<colgroup>` definition:

```
<table class="fish-table">
  <!-- … -->
  <colgroup>
    <col class="image" />
    <col class="name" />
    <col class="desrc" />
  </colgroup>
  <!-- … -->
</table>
```

Each `<col>` definition has an associated class that can be set to define column-specific style attributes. For example, to define the style for the Name column, add property declarations to the `.name` rule. Unfortunately, this way you can specify only properties that belong to the column itself, but you cannot set properties that influence the visual appearance of cells in the particular column. For example, you can change the width and background color of the column, but you cannot set—let's say—the alignment of the text in the cells of the column.

Second, you can assign the same class to all cells belonging to the column as assigned to the corresponding `<col>` tag, and this way cell-level styling will work. However, it requires every cells being set with the appropriate `class` attribute. A third way is using the `:nth-child()` pseudo-class selector to define the set of `<td>` tags belonging to a specific column. To define a set of columns, you must know the ordinal number of the column you want to style.

Each method has its own pros and cons. I've opted for the third one, because it seems totally appropriate for this table. Add these definitions to the `style.css` file to define additional text properties for the Name and Description columns:

```
.fish-table tr td:nth-child(2) {
  font-family: "Segoe UI Semibold", Arial, sans-serif;;
}

.fish-table tr td:nth-child(3) {
  font-size: 0.9em;
  padding-top: 12px;
}
```

The first selector specifies the set of second `<td>` tags within the table rows, and by definition these cells compose the second column. The second selector works similarly, but it defines the cells of the third table column. Figure 10-46 shows how these changes are applied to the table cells.

Bornella anguilla — The Bornella anguilla, growing up to 80mm. It has a very characteristic mosaic-like color pattern. Its name [anguilla = eel] refers to its method of swimming.

Figure 10-46: Font changes are applied to cells

It would be great, if the Name column would be a bit wider. You can set either a precise width, or set the minimum width of this column, and let the column be wider as the browser window is enlarged. The easiest way would be to extend the style definition of the second column with the `min-width` property:

```
.fish-table tr td:nth-child(2) {
  font-family: "Segoe UI Semibold", Arial, sans-serif;;
  min-width: 160px;
}
```

Instead doing this, try adding this style definition:

```
.name {
  min-width: 140px;
}
```

Here the .name selector applies to the "name" class that is assigned to the second column's definition within `<colgroup>`, and demonstrates a column property.

The Name and Description columns should both be aligned to the top. Add the following property declarations to the selectors defining the cells of these columns:

```
.fish-table tr td:nth-child(2) {
  font-family: "Segoe UI Semibold", Arial, sans-serif;;
  min-width: 160px;
  vertical-align: top;
  padding-top: 12px;
}

.fish-table tr td:nth-child(3) {
  font-size: 0.9em;
  vertical-align: top;
  padding-top: 12px;
}
```

These settings align the texts in the cell to the top, and provide space between the top border and the text. When you display the table with these settings, you can see that the text in the Name and Description columns are not aligned properly, as shown in Figure 10-47.

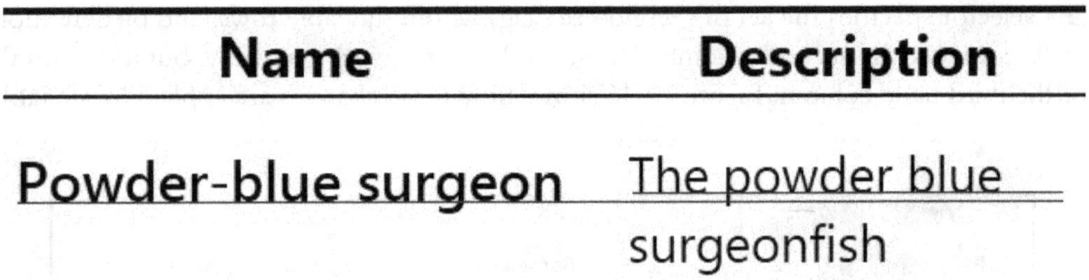

Name	Description
Powder-blue surgeon	The powder blue surgeonfish

Figure 10-47: Text alignment is not proper

The cause of this issue is that these columns use different fonts and font sizes. The text would look nice if the baselines were aligned. Fortunately, CSS provides a `baseline` value for the `vertical-align` property. So change the top values to baseline, and remove the padding-top property from the third column:

```
.fish-table tr td:nth-child(2) {
  font-family: "Segoe UI Semibold", Arial, sans-serif;;
  min-width: 160px;
  vertical-align: baseline;
  padding-top: 12px;
}

.fish-table tr td:nth-child(3) {
  font-size: 0.9em;
  vertical-align: baseline;
}
```

Now, as you can see, the text in the columns is displayed exactly as you expect (Figure 10-48).

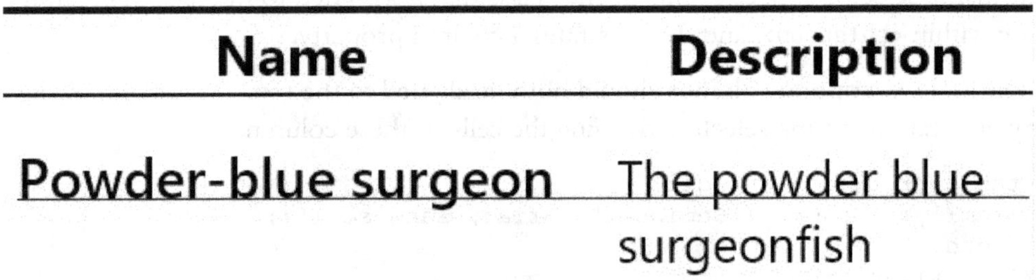

Name	Description
Powder-blue surgeon	The powder blue surgeonfish

Figure 10-48: The alignment is fixed

Setting Up Table-Specific Properties

The table is almost entirely styled. Changing the boring default row colors can add a nicer emphasis to the table. First, change the header rows' color with the following definition:

```
.fish-table th {
  font-size: 1.1em;
  text-align: left;
  background-color: #07093D;
```

```
  color: white;
  padding: 4px 0 8px 8px;
}
```

These settings will give a nice "Sky Blue Midnight" color to the header row—using the same color as the table's border. With two lighter shades of blue— "Threadless light" and "Threadless box"—you can add alternating row colors:

```
.fish-table tr:nth-child(even) {
  background-color: #9CC4E4;
}

.fish-table tr:nth-child(odd) {
  background-color: #E9F2F9;
}
```

As the mouse moves over the table rows, a hover color can add a nice effect, too:

```
.fish-table tr:hover {
  background-color: #107FC9;
}
```

NOTE: Be sure to add the `.fish-table tr:hover` rule *after* the rules setting up the alternating row colors; otherwise—due to the cascade order—the hover effect won't work. In that case, the alternating color rules would override the `background-color` property set by the hover rule.

And last, you can change the table caption's style:

```
.fish-table caption {
  font-size: 1.25em;
  font-style: italic;
  text-align: right;
  margin-bottom: 8px;
}
```

Now, the originally boring (and ugly) table has a nice look, as shown in Figure 10-49. This styling required only a few style definitions, most of them used the same properties you learned before, but applied them in the context of table-related HTML elements.

NOTE: You can find the solution file for the newly-styled fish catalog table in the `Exercise-10-27` folder.

After learning a few details about table styling, let's get acquainted a few tricks in regard to HTML forms.

Styling Tips for Forms

This book dedicated *Chapter 4* entirely for forms and controls. Now, you are familiar with almost all great CSS properties that can be used to style form elements. In this section you will learn a number of simple techniques to make your forms more attractive.

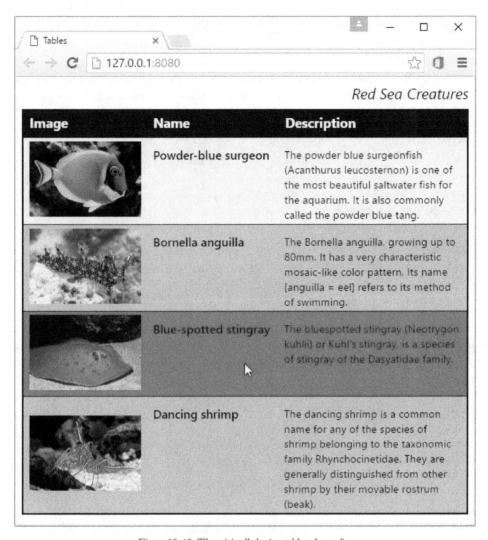

Figure 10-49: The originally boring table–after styling

Chapter 4 demonstrated a simple conference registration form that would look very ugly without styling, as shown in Figure 10-50.

NOTE: You can find the HTML markup of this simple registration form in the `Exercise-10-28` folder, which is not listed here for the sake of brevity.

Setting up the page and font style would make only a tiny change in typography, but would not remove the fragmentation of the web page (Figure 10-51):

```
body {
  width: 540px;
  margin-left: 24px;
  font-family: Tahoma, Arial, sans-serif;
}
```

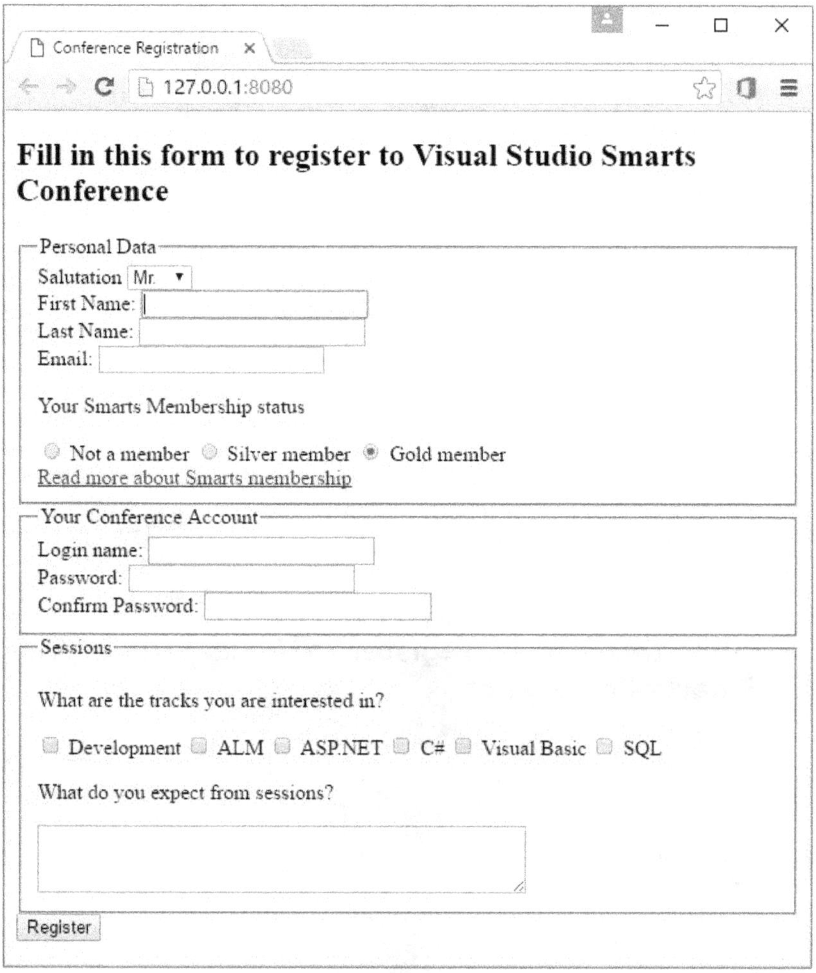

Figure 10-50: The plain form without styling

Aligning fields and their labels into columns would remove the fragmented look. As you already learned, you could use tables for this task, but this would be an old-school solution. Instead, you can set the width of labels to provide a column-like look, as shown in Figure 10-52:

```
fieldset label {
  display: inline-block;
  width: 140px;
  margin-top: 4px;
  margin-bottom: 4px;
}
```

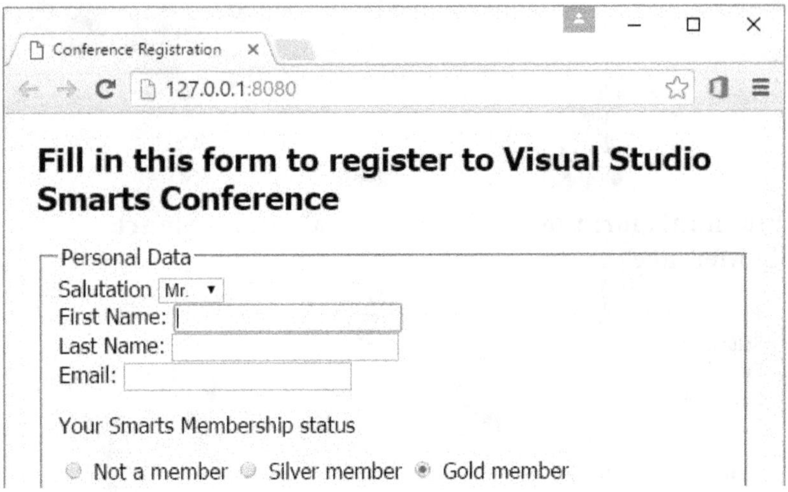

Figure 10-51: Applying a few typography element

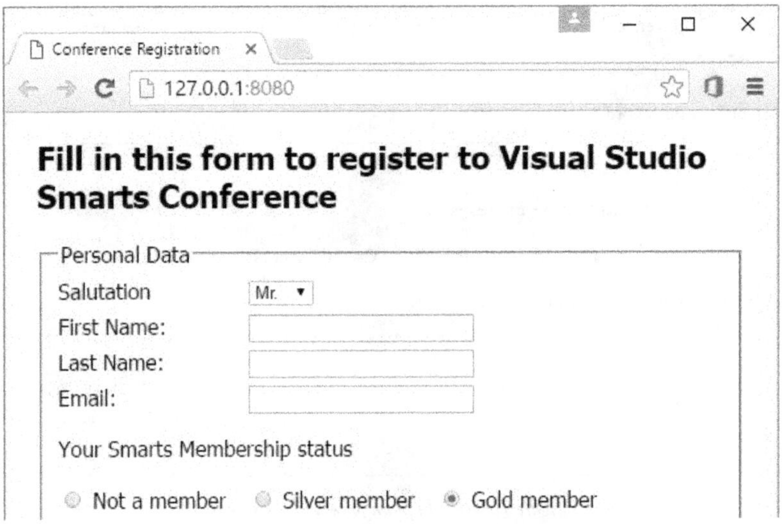

Figure 10-52: Column-like look by setting label widths

The key attribute of this style is the `display: inline-block` setting. It declares that the label is taken into account as an inline element with a settable width. Otherwise, even if you set the width of labels, the rendering engine would ignore it, because inline elements' width is calculated automatically by the screen estate they need. The `inline-block` value allows setting the width of such an element explicitly.

With a few settings, you can emphasize the regions of the registration form (Figure 10-53):

```
fieldset {
  padding: 8px 12px;
  background-color: skyblue;
  border: 1px solid blue;
  margin-top: 18px;
```

```
    margin-bottom: 8px;
}

fieldset legend {
  background-color: navy;
  color: white;
}
```

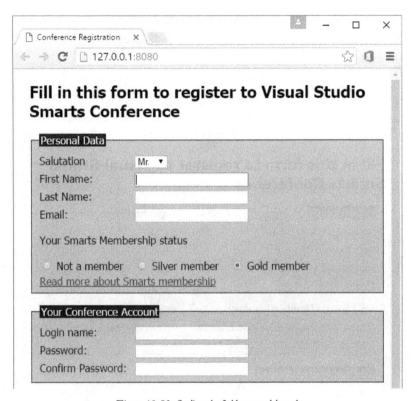

Figure 10-53: Styling the field sets and legends

And, finally, you can add a few simple styles to set up field widths, informative text parts, and the Register button (Figure 10-54):

```
#salutation {
  width: 100px;
}

#fname, #lname, #login, #pwd, #pwd2 {
  width: 160px;
}

#email {
  width: 240px;
}

p {
```

```
  margin-top: 10px;
  margin-bottom: 8px;
  font-weight: bold;
  font-size: 0.9em;
}

input[type='submit'] {
  padding: 8px 16px;
  border: 1px solid blue;
  background-color: navy;
  color: white;
}
```

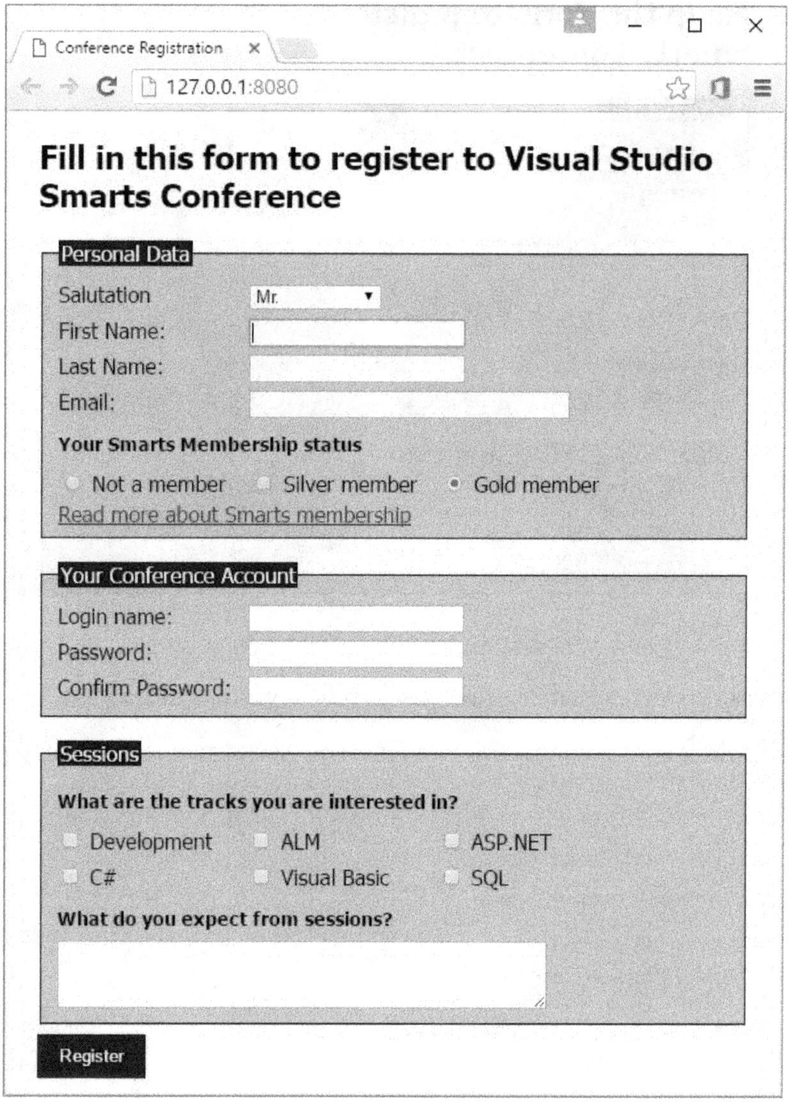

Figure 10-54: The final design of the registration form

NOTE: You can find the complete page in the `Exercise-10-29` folder.

Summary

CSS provides you more than a dozen attributes to set up the style of text elements, such as font and color setting, text alignment, spacing, indentation, and much more. You can apply background images to your entire web page or a number of selected elements to highlight certain parts.

To display block elements (such as paragraphs, headings, images, list, etc.), CSS uses the *box model*, which provides margins, borders, and paddings around the content. Understanding this model is a key to styling page elements.

Boring tabular data can be turned into beautiful illustrations by applying simple styles—such as borders, background colors, paddings, text and image alignments, etc.—on tables and table cells. In the same way, gray and uninteresting forms can be turned into exciting ones with a few simple touches.

www.ingramcontent.com/pod-product-compliance
Lightning Source LLC
Chambersburg PA
CBHW060644060326
40690CB00020B/4513